This volume of essays is about something which (for many) does not exist and yet which remains central to our understanding of English politics, history and national identity – the constitution. As European integration and demands for constitutional reform have once again moved the constitution to the centre of contemporary politics, an impressive team of contributors re-examines aspects of the debates over the meaning of the constitution and 'public opinion' in the long nineteenth century, from a sedition trial in the 1790s to the enfranchisement of certain women in 1918.

With essays engaging with the histories of law, medicine and even with History as a discipline, the book takes stock of the current state of the new cultural history of English politics after the so-called 'linguistic turn', consolidating upon much of the most innovative work in recent years – particularly by younger scholars – as well as suggesting new ways of re-reading the traditional narratives of English political history.

Re-reading the constitution

Re-reading the constitution

New narratives in the political history of
England's long nineteenth century

Edited by

JAMES VERNON

University of Manchester

CAMBRIDGE
UNIVERSITY PRESS

Published by the Press Syndicate of the University of Cambridge
The Pitt Building, Trumpington Street, Cambridge CB2 1RP
40 West 20th Street, New York, NY 10011–4211, USA
10 Stamford Road, Oakleigh, Melbourne 3166, Australia

© Cambridge University Press 1996

First published 1996

Printed in Great Britain at the University Press, Cambridge

A catalogue record for this book is available from the British Library

Library of Congress cataloguing in publication data

Re-reading the constitution: new narratives in the political history of
England's long nineteenth century / edited by James Vernon.
p. cm.
ISBN 0 521 46474 9
1. Great Britain – Constitutional history.
2. Great Britain – Politics and government – 19th century.
1. Vernon, James.
JN216.R47 1996 95–51800
320.941'09'034–dc20 CIP

ISBN 0 521 46474 9 hardback
ISBN 0 521 58941 X paperback

To Jack

CONTENTS

ᗡ

FIGURES

∾

NOTES ON THE CONTRIBUTORS

∾

IAN BURNEY's Ph.D 'Decoding Death: Medicine, Public Inquiry and the Reform of the English Inquest, 1839–1926' was completed at the University of California, Berkeley in 1993. He is currently a member of the Michigan Society of Fellows.

ANNA CLARK is Associate Professor of History at the University of North Carolina, Charlotte. Her most recent book is *The Struggle for the Breeches: Gender and the Making of the British Working Class* (London, 1995).

JAMES EPSTEIN is Professor of History at Vanderbilt University. He has written extensively on the nature of radical politics in the late eighteenth and early nineteenth centuries, most recently in his *Radical Expression: Political Language, Ritual and Symbol in England, 1790–1850* (New York, 1994).

JONATHAN FULCHER was awarded his Ph.D at Cambridge University in 1993. He has interrupted a Postdoctoral Fellowship at the Australian National University at Canberra to work for the state of Queensland on issues of aboriginal land rights.

PATRICK JOYCE is Professor of Modern History at the University of Manchester. His most recent books include *Visions of the People: Industrial England and the Question of Class, 1840–1914* (Cambridge, 1991); *Democratic Subjects: The Self and the Social in Nineteenth Century England* (Cambridge, 1994); *Class: A Reader* (Oxford, 1995).

ANTONY TAYLOR is Lecturer in History at the Institute of Education at Warwick University. His Ph.D, 'Modes of Political Expression: Working

Class Politics, the Manchester and London Examples, 1850–1880', was awarded at Manchester University in 1993. He is co-editor of *The Era of the Reform League: English Labour and Radical Politics 1857–1872: Documents Selected by Gustav Mayer* (Mannheim, 1995).

JAMES VERNON is Lecturer in Modern History at the University of Manchester. He is author of *Politics and the People: A Study in English Political Culture, c.1815–1867* (Cambridge, 1993).

DROR WAHRMAN is Research Fellow at the Centre for Social History at Warwick University. He is author of *Imagining the Middle Class: The Political Representation of Class in Britain, c.1780–1840* (Cambridge, 1995).

ACKNOWLEDGEMENTS

My thanks to all the contributors for their help in putting together this book, I hope it was not too onerous a task and that we are still friends. I am grateful to William Davies for his patience and support and to all who have helped with the production of the book at Cambridge University Press, especially Pauline Leng and Cherrill Richardson. To Ros and Jack fell the burden of keeping me (almost) sane. Without them I would have given up years ago, which is hardly what they want to hear.

1

∾

Notes towards an introduction

JAMES VERNON

This is a book about something which (for many) does not exist and yet which dominates English politics, history and national identity. Without recognisable shape or form, absent and yet always present, the unwritten constitution has assumed a mystical, almost transcendental, position within English culture. In occupying this sacred place it inherits the symbolic capital previously invested upon the monarch, who as God's representative on earth was perceived to have two bodies, one mortal, the other divine.[1] It is impossible to precisely date this transition from the monarch to the constitution as the sacred centre of English political culture; although some might suggest that Cromwell's Commonwealth and the execution of Charles I in 1649 fatally undermined the mystic fiction of the king's divine authority,[2] others could rightly point to the continued centrality of the monarchy as proof that such a transfer of sacral authority was never anything but a very long, tortuous and uneven affair.[3] Nonetheless, unlike the monarch the constitution could not desecrate itself; if it fell from grace it was as a consequence of

My thanks to Anna Clark, James Epstein, Rohan McWilliam, David Sugarman, Antony Taylor and Dror Wahrman for their comments on earlier drafts.

[1] On the king's two bodies see Ernst H. Kantorowicz's classic work *The King's Two Bodies: A Study in Medieval Political Theology* (Princeton, 1957). However, this paragraph owes much to the suggestive comments in the Epilogue of Lynn Hunt's, *The Family Romance of the French Revolution* (London, 1992), pp. 197–200.

[2] See J. G. A. Pocock, *The Ancient Constitution and the Feudal Law: A Study of English Historical Thought in the Seventeenth Century* (Cambridge, 1987); Glenn Burgess, *The Politics of the Ancient Constitution: An Introduction to English Political Thought 1603–1642* (Basingstoke, 1992).

[3] Linda Colley, 'The Apotheosis of George III: Loyalty, Royalty and the British Nation, 1760–1820', *Past and Present*, 102 (1984); David Cannadine, 'The Context, Performance and meaning of Ritual: The British Monarchy and the "Invention of Tradition", 1820–1977', in E. Hobsbawm and T. Ranger (eds.), *The Invention of Tradition* (Cambridge, 1983); Tom Nairn, *The Enchanted Glass: Britain and its Monarchy* (London, 1988).

human frailty and original sin. There was never any shortage of martyrs happy to sacrifice themselves in the struggle to protect the constitution's ancient purity. This struggle was not just a war of words: it was a war in which people were prepared to lose their livelihoods, their homes, their freedom, and even their lives, in the name of the religion of the constitution.

The essays in this collection will, I hope, powerfully evoke how deeply the constitution was embedded within English culture during the long nineteenth century; it was central to the way people imagined themselves as both individuals and members of a sex, a class, a political movement as well as, perhaps most forcefully of all, a nation. And yet, being unwritten, lacking a definitive text whose interpretation could be fixed and secured as definitive, its meaning, and the identities it gave voice to, were always unstable and endlessly contested. The very word constitution itself conveys something of this fluidity and lack of fixity, suggesting that meanings and identities were never assumed as essential but were rather continually in the process of construction and (re-)constitution.

It was this very ambiguity which made it such a potent symbol of Englishness: although few could agree on the nature and meaning of constitutional liberty all recognised that it was uniquely and quintessentially English. Invariably, historians and politicians, whether from the 1790s or the 1990s, have read these discourses of the constitution at face-value, accepting their emphases on the ancient continuity and stability of English liberty as self-evident, rather than as a symptom of their absence, an anxious attempt to invent the very stability and continuity they evoked. In contrast, the emphasis in this book is precisely on this sense of instability and insecurity. It tells the story of a perpetual crisis in the categories of political identification throughout the long nineteenth century and the consequent attempts to categorise and secure English constitutional liberty.

In doing so, it serves as a pertinent reminder to those 'postmodern' theorists who caricature a classical age of nineteenth-century 'modernity' where power, knowledge and identity were always centred and stable, in order to contrast it with a 'postmodern' era in which all is decentred, insecure and fluid. Ironically, this 'postmodern' parody of 'modernity' is based upon a sense of history culled from historians still working unproblematically within the categories and narratives of 'modernity'.[4] This is a pity, because the promise of 'postmodernism' is

[4]   In fairness this is easy to do as few historians of Britain have engaged with 'postmodern'

precisely the historicity of its radical scepticism. Its interrogation of those very discourses, categories and identities that, as creatures of 'modernity', we have taken to be naturalised, the essential foundations of our knowledge and power relations, is by its very nature a historical project.[5]

It is a project given renewed urgency by the propensity of current debates about the constitution to accept the existing categories of constitutional discourse as natural and universal. Whether conceived in terms of the post-colonial nature of national identity and sovereignty by protagonists on either side of the arguments about immigration and European integration, or as a discussion about the nature of citizenship and the need for constitutional reform generated by Charter 88, the debate has been remarkable for its failure to historicise the categories in which it has been conducted. So, for example, Charter 88, priding itself on an intellectual radicalism and self-consciously founded in the tercentenary of 1688, endlessly reinforces the distinction between a written and unwritten constitution classically formulated by those children of 'modernity' Edmund Burke and Thomas Paine. It is a distinction which rests upon a series of discursive strategies and oppositions such as real–ideal, fact–fiction, reason–emotion, theory–practice, English–French, which, far from being universal, were products of particular historical moments.[6]

critical theory. See, for example, the debate on 'History and Postmodernism' in *Past and Present*, 131 (May 1991); 133 (November 1991); 135 (May 1992); as well as the debate on 'Social History and its Discontents' in *Social History*, 17, 2 (May 1992); 18, 1 (January 1993); 19, 1 (January 1994); 19, 2 (May 1994); 20, 1 (1995); Derek Attridge, Geoff Bennington and Robert Young (eds.), *Post-Structuralism and the Question of History* (Cambridge, 1987); Bryan D. Palmer, *Descent into Discourse: The Reification of Language and the Writing of Social History* (Philadelphia, 1990); Raphael Samuel, 'Reading the Signs' *History Workshop Journal*, 32 (1991), pp. 88–109 and 33 (1992), pp. 220–51; Gertrude Himmelfarb, 'Telling It As You Like It: Post-Modernist History and the Flight from Fact', *Times Literary Supplement*, 16 October 1992, pp. 12–15; G. R. Elton, *Return to Essentials: Some Reflections on the Present State of Historical Study* (Cambridge, 1992); Anthony Easthope, 'Post-Modernism and the Historians: Romancing the Stone', *Social History*, 18, 2 (May 1993), pp. 235–49. The latest contribution to the debate is J. Appleby, L. Hunt and M. Jacob's *Telling the Truth About History* (London, 1994).

5   One of the constructive features of the debate about history and 'postmodernism' has been the call to the sympathetic to define what is meant by 'postmodernism' (significantly the meaning of the term history is assumed to be unproblematic). I am using the term to describe a condition of knowledge which critically reflects upon and problematises modernity's meta-narratives of progress and their conceptions of power, knowledge and identity. Cast so widely, such a definition usefully incorporates many different theoretical strands, but it does not seem to me necessary to create too monolithic a definition. For helpful emphases upon the plurality of postmodern positions see Judith Butler, 'Contingent Foundations: Feminism and the Question of "postmodernism"', in J. Butler and J. Scott (eds.), *Feminists Theorize the Political* (London, 1992), pp. 3–21; Thomas Docherty (ed.), *Postmodernism: A Reader* (London, 1993).

6   There were different logics and knowledge claims at work here. Burke's *Reflections on the*

Re-reading the Constitution is then, in part, a product of these broader theoretical and political concerns. It is an attempt to excavate and explore the changing meanings and uses of appeals to the constitution at the very moment when the standards of English constitutional liberty are once more being invoked. Inextricably connected to this project are a set of wider historiographical issues about the state of political history after the so-called 'linguistic turn', for it has been an emphasis on the creative role of the cultural forms of representation that has led many of the contributors to re-examine the historical meanings of the constitution.[7] However, it needs to be emphasised that in no sense does this collection represent a unitary theoretical, political or historiographical position. Each of the contributors is differently situated within (or without) these debates, and although the intention of this introduction is to bring together common themes and concerns, they are those which most interest the editor alone.

As I have argued elsewhere, in Britain the shift of attention by social and political historians to the language of politics, and constitutionalist discourse specifically, has often had much less to do with 'the linguistic turn' than with a series of other quite disconnected historiographical revisions.[8] Not least of these has been the questioning of Edward Thompson's chronology of 'the making of the English working class' in the light of the current emphasis on the long and uneven nature of the 'industrial revolution'.[9] In his portrayal of the formation of a 'working

---

Revolution in France, to which Paine was responding in his *Rights of Man*, used a set of oppositions between theory and practice and English and French to contest the French Revolution's refusal of the past. Paine, in contrast, inspired by Enlightenment ideals upheld this distinction between the past and present to reinforce his rationalist dichotomies between real and ideal and fact and fiction, in the much quoted phrase 'A Constitution is not a thing in name only, but in fact. It has not an ideal, but a real existence; and wherever it cannot be produced in visible form, there is none'; Thomas Paine, *Rights of Man* (1791–2; London, 1915), pp. 48–9. It should be noted that in claiming Burke was no less a product of modernity than Paine, I am not equating 'modernity' simply with the Enlightenment – its genealogy was far more complex.

[7] I do not mean to conflate 'postmodernism' with what historians have characterised as the 'linguistic turn'. For an excellent attempt to historicise the many different 'linguistic turns' see Samuel's 'Reading the signs'.

[8] James Vernon, '"Who's Afraid of 'the Linguistic Turn'?" Social History and its Discontents', *Social History*, 19, 1 (1994), pp. 81–97.

[9] John Belchem, 'Radical Language and Ideology in Early Nineteenth Century England: The Challenge of the Platform', *Albion*, 20 (1988), pp. 247–59. For useful summaries of the problems raised for Thompson's model by the historiographical dismantling of the industrial revolution, see Patrick Joyce (ed.), *The Historical Meanings of Work* (Cambridge, 1987); Harvey Kaye and Keith McClelland (eds.), *E. P. Thompson: Critical Perspectives* (Cambridge, 1990). For a recent attempt to reverse this revision see Maxine Berg and Pat Hudson, 'Rehabilitating the Industrial Revolution', *Economic History Review*, 65 (1992), pp. 24–50.

class' Thompson privileged what he perceived as the proto-socialist influence of Thomas Paine upon the radical politics of the late eighteenth and early nineteenth centuries. It was therefore necessary to deride constitutionalist discourse, which he did to dazzling effect:

it was necessary that this [constitutionalist] rhetoric should be broken through, because ... it implied the absolute sanctity of certain conventions: respect for the institution of monarchy, for the hereditary principle, for the traditional rights of the great landowners and the Established Church, and for the representation not of human rights, but of property rights. Once enmeshed in constitutionalist arguments ... reformers became caught up in the trivia of piecemeal constitutional renovation. For a plebeian movement to arise it was essential to escape from these categories altogether and set forward far wider democratic claims.[10]

There are here some typically large and romantic assumptions about what revolutionary plebeian movements and democracy should look like, or even that the latter necessarily follows the former. As ever with Thompson, where his argument relied much upon its utopian politics it was fortified by a passionate turn of phrase which, in large measure, convinced a generation of historians that during the 1790s Paine provided a revolutionary vocabulary which displaced the reformist language of the ancient constitution in radical politics.

Although he denied his project was a revisionist one, John Belchem's work was crucial in reassessing Thompson's neglect and dismissal of radical uses of the constitutional idiom.[11] Yet, despite his rightful indignation at attempts to dismiss constitutionalist discourses as 'an anachronistic impediment to the development of a proper revolutionary perspective' and his insistence of its centrality to radical politics up to 1848, there is still a wistful air of regret that the true path to socialism had been lost in an imperfect world where the language of the constitution 'offered the best means of attracting the normally apathetic, if not those beer-swilling, male chauvinist, xenophobic, flag-waving workers whom historians are no longer allowed to forget'.[12] Published

---

[10] Edward Thompson, *The Making of the English Working Class* (London, 1968), p. 96. Thompson inherited this distinction between a revolutionary Paineite language which replaced a reformist constitutionalist one during the 1790s from Christopher Hill's 'The Norman Yoke', in his *Puritanism and Revolution* (London, 1955), pp. 50–122, esp. p. 108.

[11] See, especially, his seminal article 'Republicanism, Popular Constitutionalism and the Radical Platform in Early Nineteenth Century England', *Social History*, 6 (1981), pp. 1–35. For the denial of the revisionary nature of his work see John Belchem, *'Orator' Hunt: Henry Hunt and English Working Class Radicalism* (Oxford, 1985), p. 2.

[12] Belchem, *'Orator' Hunt*, pp. 4 and 5. There is in this passage much that is familiar from Thompson's dismissal of constitutionalism as bound up in bad history and the instinctive emotionalism of 'the crowd' as opposed to the reasoned and sensible tone of Paine. For the

in 1985 in the wake of the Falklands War, this passage was typical of the anguish felt by many historians on the 'Left' in their attempt to make historical sense of Thatcherism's electoral hegemony and the 'Right's' apparent monopoly of the languages of patriotism.[13] Given these discontents, many either shifted their attention to the reactionary rather than the revolutionary moments of English political history or, like Belchem, to a more nuanced analysis of how seemingly traditional and conservative languages were capable of being appropriated to more radical ends.[14]

These concerns had already been evident in Gareth Stedman Jones' 'Rethinking Chartism', an essay which many have subsequently taken to mark the beginning of 'the linguistic turn' in British political history.[15] Like Belchem, Stedman Jones sought to revise the Thompsonian chronology of radical politics and class formation by reassessing the significance of Chartism's use of the constitutionalist discourse of 'Old Corruption' in articulating a sense of political exclusion. Yet, unlike Belchem, he argued that this language of political exclusion was not a reflection of the 'working classes' now deferred 'experience' of indus-

---

continuity of constitutionalism up to 1848 see his '1848: Feargus O'Connor and the Collapse of the Mass Platform', in James Epstein and Dorothy Thompson (eds.), *The Chartist Experience: Studies in Working Class Radicalism and Culture, 1830–1860* (London, 1982), pp. 269–310. A similar air of regret is also present in Ross McKibbin's seminal essay 'Why Was There No Marxism in Great Britain', first published in 1984 and reprinted in his *Ideologies of Class: Social Relations in Britain, 1880–1950* (Oxford, 1990), pp. 1–41.

[13] See the struggle of History Workshop to historicise the popular appeal of the Falklands War. Raphael Samuel (ed.), *Patriotism: The Making and Unmaking of British National Identity*, 3 vols. (London, 1989). Also the useful analysis of Miles Taylor, 'Patriotism, History and the Left in Twentieth Century Britain' *Historical Journal*, 33, 4 (1990), pp. 971–87.

[14] The growing concern with 'populism', and indeed loyalist, Tory and Conservative politics, was also part of this history. On 'populism' see Patrick Joyce, *Visions of the People: Industrial England and the Question of Class, c.1848–1914* (Cambridge, 1991); W. D. Rubinstein, 'British Radicalism and the 'Dark Side' of Populism' in his *Elites and the Wealthy in Modern British History* (Brighton, 1988); Rohan McWilliam, 'Radicalism and Popular Culture: The Tichborne Case and the Politics of "Fair Play" 1867–1886' in E. Biagini and A. Reid (eds.), *Currents of Radicalism: Popular Radicalism, Organised Labour and Party Politics in Britain, 1850–1914* (Cambridge, 1991). On 'conservative' politics see R. R. Dozier, *For King, Constitution and Country: The English Loyalists and the French Revolution* (Lexington, 1983); Linda Colley, *Britons: Forging the Nation, 1707–1837* (London, 1992); Patrick Joyce, *Work, Society and Politics: The Culture of the Factory in Later Victorian England* (London, 1980); Martin Pugh, *The Tories and the People: 1880–1935* (Oxford, 1985); Ross McKibbin, 'Class and Conventional Wisdom: The Conservative Party and the "Public" in Inter-War Britain', in his *Ideologies of Class: Social Relations in Britain, 1880–1950* (Oxford, 1990), pp. 259–94; Bill Schwarz, 'The Language of Constitutionalism: Baldwinite Conservatism' *Formations* (1984), pp. 1–18. Ewen Green, *The Crisis of Conservatism: The Politics, Economics and Ideology of the British Conservative Party* (London, 1994); Alison Light, *Forever England: Femininity, Literature and Conservatism Between the Wars* (London, 1991).

[15] Gareth Stedman Jones, 'Rethinking Chartism', in his *Languages of Class: Studies in English Working Class History, 1832–1982* (Cambridge, 1983), pp. 90–178.

trialisation, but was crucial to the construction of that 'experience' and their self-identity as a class.[16] Although this rethinking of the categories of 'experience' and 'class' were important theoretical developments, it has been the emphasis on the continuity of radical discourse between the 1760s and 1840s and the state's use of liberal reforms to defuse the critique of 'Old Corruption', that have proved more influential among political historians.[17]

No doubt this is partly because many have found these strands of Stedman Jones' work useful sticks with which to beat Jonathan Clark. Although Jonathan Clark's *English Society 1688–1832* has received much less serious attention than 'Rethinking Chartism', it is arguably more radical in its attempt to replace liberal and marxist teleologies of a constitutional bourgeois revolution with a portrayal of an aristocratic and confessional ancien régime that persisted up to, and possibly beyond, 1832.[18] In the rush to reinstate at least some qualified certainties of the old orthodoxies, the historiographies of the long eighteenth and nineteenth centuries have found common ground in tracing the genealogies of the language of 'Old Corruption' in civic humanist traditions and their connection to changes in state formation and policy.[19] This has tended to reproduce the old chronology of an emergent eighteenth-

[16] For subsequent attempts to refer this language back to the belated process of industrialisation see Belchem, 'Radical Language and Ideology in Early Nineteenth Century England: The Challenge of the Platform', *Albion*, 20 (1988), pp. 247–59; Jon Lawrence and Miles Taylor, 'The Poverty of Protest: Gareth Stedman Jones and the Politics of Language – A Reply', *Social History*, 18 (1993), pp. 1–16.

[17] For useful criticisms of Stedman Jones' theoretical move see Robert Gray, 'The Deconstruction of the English Working Class', *Social History*, 11 (1986), pp. 363–73; Joan Scott, 'On Language, Gender, and Working Class History', in her *Gender and the Politics of History* (New York, 1988), pp. 53–67.

[18] The most perceptive theoretical engagement with Clark can be found in Patrick Curry's, 'Towards a Post-Marxist Social History: Thompson, Clark and Beyond', in Adrian Wilson (ed.), *Rethinking Social History: English Society, 1570–1920 and its Interpretation* (Manchester, 1993). For a more grudging assessment see Joanna Innes, 'Jonathan Clark, social history and England's "Ancien Régime"', *Past and Present*, 115 (1987), pp. 165–200.

[19] The work of J. G. A. Pocock has been absolutely crucial here, see especially his *Virtue, Commerce and History: Essays on Political Thought and History, Chiefly in the Eighteenth Century* (Cambridge, 1985); I. Hont and M. Ignatieff (eds.), *Wealth and Virtue: The Shaping of the Political Economy in the Scottish Enlightenment* (Cambridge, 1983); S. Collini, D. Winch and J. Burrow, *That Noble Science of Politics: A Study in Nineteenth Century Intellectual History* (Cambridge, 1983); B. Fontana, *Rethinking the Politics of Commercial Society: The Edinburgh Review, 1802–1832* (Cambridge, 1985); Gregory Claeys, *Citizens and Saints: Politics and Anti-Politics in Early British Socialism* (Cambridge, 1989). Significantly, many of these works emerged from the Political Economy and Society research project at King's College, Cambridge, of which Stedman Jones was an important member. On the state see John Brewer, *The Sinews of Power: War, Money and the English State, 1688–1793* (London, 1989); Lawrence Stone (ed.), *An Imperial State at War: Britain from 1689–1815* (London, 1994); Philip Harling and Peter Mandler, 'From "Fiscal–Military" State to Laissez-Faire State, 1760–1850', *Journal of British Studies*, 32, 1 (1993), pp. 44–70.

century 'middle class' being supplemented by a 'working class' during
the early nineteenth century, albeit this time at the level of a history of
political ideas rather than a social history of industrialisation.[20]

This stress on the continuity of political ideas drawn from civic
humanism has also been extended further within the political history of
the long nineteenth century. Most obviously this has manifested itself in
a renewed interest in the history of nineteenth-century Whiggism as a
set of ideas that helped revitalise the ancien régime with interventionist
reforms during the 1830s and, in the latest versions, persisted not only
through the mid Victorian Liberal party (until it was hijacked by
Gladstone over Home Rule in 1886), but also after the Victorians, in the
spirit of public service.[21] This, in turn, has been complemented by a
series of studies tracing the continuities between early-nineteenth-
century radicalism, mid Victorian popular Liberalism and the labourism
of the late nineteenth and early twentieth centuries, with the emphasis
placed on shared conceptions of the state and citizenship drawn very
often, once again, from civic humanism.[22]

Re-reading the Constitution draws on this revisionist historiography but

[20] Paul Langford, *A Polite and Commercial People: England, 1727–1783* (Oxford, 1989); idem, *Public Life and the Propertied Englishman, 1689–1798* (Oxford, 1991); Nicholas Rogers, *Whigs and Cities: Popular Politics in the Age of Walpole and Pitt* (Oxford, 1989); Eckhart Hellmuth (ed.), *The Transformation of Political Culture: England and Germany in the Late Eighteenth Century* (Oxford, 1990); Catherine Hall and Leonore Davidoff, *Family Fortunes: Men and Women of the English Middle Class, 1780–1850* (London, 1987); Belchem, *'Orator' Hunt*; Malcolm Chase, *The People's Farm: English Radical Agrarianism, 1775–1840* (Oxford, 1988); Iain McCalman, *Radical Underworld: Prophets, Revolutionaries and Pornographers in London, 1795–1840* (Cambridge, 1988); James Epstein, *Radical Expression: Political Language, Ritual and Symbol in England, 1790–1850* (Oxford, 1994).

[21] Peter Mandler, *Aristocratic Government in the Age of Reform: Whigs and Liberals, 1830–1852* (Oxford, 1990); Ian Newbould, *Whiggery and Reform, 1830–1841: The Politics of Government* (Stanford, 1990); Jonathan Parry, *The Rise and Fall of Liberal Government in Victorian Britain* (London, 1993); Peter Mandler and Susan Pedersen, *After the Victorians: Private Conscience and Public Duty in Modern Britain* (London, 1994).

[22] These themes are most apparent in E. Biagini and A. Reid (eds.), *Currents of Radicalism: Popular Radicalism, Organized Labour and Party Politics in Britain 1850–1914* (Cambridge, 1991). See also Margot C. Finn, *After Chartism: Class and Nation in English Radical Politics 1848–1874* (Cambridge, 1993); Eugenio Biagini, *Liberty, Retrenchment and Reform: Popular Liberalism in the Age of Gladstone, 1860–1880* (Cambridge, 1992); E. D. Steele, *Palmerston and Liberalism, 1855–1865* (Cambridge, 1991); Patrick Joyce, *Visions of the People: Industrial England and the Question of Class, c.1848–1914* (Cambridge, 1991); Jon Lawrence, 'Popular Radicalism and the Socialist Revival in Britain', *Journal of British Studies*, 31, 2 (1992), pp. 163–86; Duncan Tanner, *Political Change and the Labour Party* (Cambridge, 1990); David Blazaar, *The Popular Front and the Progressive Tradition: Socialists, Liberals and the Quest for Unity, 1884–1939* (Cambridge, 1992); Steven Fielding, 'What Did "The People" Want? The Meaning of the 1945 General Election', *Historical Journal*, 35, 3 (1992), pp. 623–40; Fielding, 'Labourism in the 1940s', *Twentieth Century British History*, 3, 3 (1992), pp. 138–53; Bill Schwarz, '"The People" in History: The Communist Party Historians Group, 1945–56', in R. Johnson et al. (eds.), *Making Histories: Studies in History Writing and Politics* (London, 1982).

also aims to critically extend it in a number of ways. By concentrating on just one set of discourses, those centring on the constitution, it expands an often rather limited conception of language as political ideas, with all the attendant concerns for the continuity and coherence of static and passive ideological systems. The essays that follow show little interest in preserving the traditional dichotomy between constitutionalist and Paineite idioms as based respectively on notions of historical or natural rights.[23] Freeborn Englishmen had little regard for the niceties of intellectual historians, for them the constitution was theirs by right of history, nature and scripture, irrespective of the apparently contradictory logics at work. Antony Taylor, for instance, forcefully demonstrates the continual slippage between these forms of argument, the language of republicanism owing less to its traditional association with Paine than to a reworking of Cromwell's Commonwealth and the critique of 'Old Corruption'.

The point is that because constitutionalist rhetoric was used strategically as a language of legitimation, it was continually reproduced in different and contrasting ways. Read in this way it becomes difficult to conceive of the language of the constitution as a unitary discursive system, for it always intersected with other discourses, its boundaries continually shifting as it was used for different strategic purposes. This recognition enables us to avoid the teleology at work in studies that take as their object a subject such as 'the working class' or 'radicalism', for there is always a tendency in such an approach to exaggerate the coherence and development of those discourses which helped construct or activate that object. In contrast, by working outwards from the uses of the constitutional discourses, *Re-reading the Constitution* has no object whose unity and continuous development has to be realised, it allows the emphasis to be placed on the fluidity, fragility and discordances of constitutional discourses and the subjects they imagined.

Although this approach necessarily leaves many stones unturned – those searching for a comprehensive survey of the politics of the constitution should look elsewhere – it does suggest one way to problematise the now well-established portrayal of seamless continuity in the political discourses of a nineteenth century that is stretched ever longer. Indeed,

---

[23] A dichotomy which several of the contributors have already been critical of in previous work, see James Epstein, 'The Constitutionalist Idiom: Radical Reasoning, Rhetoric and Action in Early Nineteenth Century England' *Journal of Social History*, 23, 2 (1990), pp. 553–74; Anna Clark, 'The Rhetoric of Chartist Domesticity: Gender, Language and Class in the 1830s and 1840s', *Journal of British Studies*, 31, 1 (1992), pp. 62–88; Vernon, *Politics and the People*, pp. 295–330.

it is worth emphasising that while I have used this idea of a 'long nineteenth century', I have done so in order to show how these essays remain informed and defined by a prevailing orthodoxy they seek to move beyond. For the essays in this collection suggest that, given the fluidity and fragility of constitutional discourse, it would be difficult to subscribe to a historiographical category that conveys a coherence, stability and continuity where there was little or none.

Consequently, many of the essays are concerned with some of those historical moments – such as times of war and constitutional reform – when the discourse of the constitution and its categories of identity were generally perceived to be in flux. Thus James Epstein locates his study in the 1790s when the wars with revolutionary France threatened to upset the social fabric of the precarious constitutional settlement of 1688. In different ways both Dror Wahrman and Jonathan Fulcher reveal how these wars cast a long shadow over the political agenda of peace, transforming the meanings of 'the public' and constitutional politics while enabling reformers to reclaim the language of 'the nation' from loyalists. Developing these themes, Ian Burney maps how, during the age of reform, the redefinition of civil society and 'public opinion' was played out in debates about the purpose of that mythically ancient part of the constitution – the coroner's inquest. Similarly, it is the reform crisis of 1866 which provides the backdrop for Patrick Joyce's analysis of the way in which the narrative of the constitution empowered the powerless and politically excluded by creating a sense of the moral right of a people, 'the public', in movement.

In contrast, Anna Clark and Antony Taylor show how, following the passing of the Second Reform Act in 1867, the categories of constitutionalist discourse and the force of its narrative forms came under renewed pressure (a point also apparent in Joyce's consideration of the campaign against the 'Bulgarian Horrors' of 1876). Instead of associating this period with stability and consensus, they both emphasise how the categories of political identity were being renegotiated and reconstituted not only by male radicals using republicanism as the foundation upon which to rebuild a mass platform for reform, but also by men and women campaigning for women's suffrage. As Clark suggests, although citizenship had always been confined to specific conceptions of masculinity, under the challenge of the early suffragists these began to dissolve and be thrown into a state of crisis at the very moment at which they appeared to harden as a consequence of the Second Reform Act and the revitalised imperial crusade.

Indeed, Joyce, Clark and Taylor's essays could all be seen as part of a continuing reassessment of 1867 as a critical moment in the construction of a new 'rational and respectable' male political subject.[24] As Clark suggests, this new category of citizenship was a fragile sign of a constitutional settlement whose finality was always undermined by the absence of those it had excluded. Framed in the shadow of the Morant Bay Rebellion, Fenian 'outrages', unruly Reform League demonstrations and growing demands for womens' suffrage, 1867 was a very particular product of a set of debates about the nature of government, the constitution and the rule of law both at home but also, crucially, abroad. It is, as Catherine Hall suggests, 'a metropolitan tale which cannot be told outside of its peripheries, of a colonial encounter which made both colonisers and colonised'.[25] Just as Gladstone and Stead spoke for the Bulgarian subaltern in the name of constitutional liberty, so the colonial subaltern – those deemed to lack the requisite independence, rationality and respectability, such as the parishioners of St Catherine Jamaica and the National Society for Women's Suffrage in Britain – continued to appeal to 'the genius of the British constitution' and its ancient Anglo-Saxon past as the repository of their lost rights.[26]

The attempt to manfully master the 'Other', to govern the dark unknown continent that was variously the empire, women or the residuum, is also evident in my own account of the attempt by constitutional historians in the late nineteenth century to write the unwritten constitution so as to include or exclude these groups. Their desire to permanently enshrine the meaning of the constitution in increasingly restrictive terms reflected their anxiety about the fluidity of the terms of political identification in the closing decades of the nineteenth century. One can not over estimate the significance of the empire in both fuelling and soothing these anxieties; as post-colonial historians have reminded us, politicians, historians and lawyers used the empire as a laboratory within which they could make their constitutional

---

[24] The following paragraph owes much to a session on 1867 organised by Catherine Hall, Keith McClelland and Jane Rendall at the Social History Society conference in York during January 1995. See Catherine Hall, 'Rethinking Imperial Histories: The Reform Act of 1867', *New Left Review* (December 1994), pp. 3–29; Keith McClelland, 'Rational and Respectable Men: Gender, the Working Class and Citizenship in Britain, 1850–1867', in L. Frader and S. Rose (eds.), *Gender and the Reconstruction of Working Class History in Modern Europe* (Ithaca, 1995); Jane Rendall, 'Citizenship, Culture and Civilisation: The Languages of British Suffragists, 1866–1874', in C. Daley and M. Nolan (eds.), *Suffrage and Beyond: International Feminist Perspectives* (Aukland, 1994), pp. 127–150.

[25] Hall, 'Rethinking Imperial Histories', p. 9. See also her 'From Greenland's Icy Mountains to Africa's Golden Sand: Ethnicity, Race and Nation in Mid-Nineteenth Century England', *Gender and History*, 5, 2 (1993), pp. 212–30.

[26] Hall, 'Rethinking Imperial Histories', p. 20; Rendall, 'Citizenship, Culture and Civilisation', pp. 140–3.

experiments – if they could control 'the savages' overseas, they reasoned, they would be able to manage the 'Other' within.[27] In this sense it makes more sense to talk of England importing her constitution from overseas, rather than as the myth of the mother parliament runs, exporting her constitution to its imperial dominions. So even the apparent stability and continuity of constitutional discourse in England during the long nineteenth century was underwritten by the displacement of its anxieties and instabilities abroad.

Clearly, however, a book about the uses of the language of the constitution during the long nineteenth century must also take account of the persistent resonance of this discourse. In earlier work several of the contributors have sought to explain the continuing force of constitutionalist rhetoric in terms of it representing the meta-narrative of nineteenth-century English politics.[28] Drawing upon the work of Fredric Jameson, they have suggested that the discourse of the constitution can be interpreted as a 'shared code', the imaginative expression of a collective 'political unconscious', through which individuals and groups defined themselves differently by using it in contrasting ways.[29] As we shall see later, this has proved an important way of theorising the history of difference, that is how identity was constructed through the ordering of difference; but for the time being I want to stress how it has enabled historians to think about the history of unity. Simply put, it is impossible to understand the politics of difference without having first conceptualised the politics of unity.

At one level it has been suggested that the discourse of the constitution represented the meta-narrative of nineteenth-century politics because it so powerfully fused together stories of English liberty, history and national identity that no one could afford to refuse it – to do so would have represented a retreat, a relinquishing of the very language through which people had habitually imagined themselves as acting

---

[27] Ganajit Guha and Gayatari Chakravorty Spivak (eds.), *Selected Subaltern Studies* (New York, 1988); Dipesh Chakrabarty, 'Postcolonialty and the Artifice of History: Who Speaks for the "Indian" Pasts?', *Representations*, 37 (winter 1992), pp. 1–26; Gyan Prakash, 'Writing Post-Orientalist Histories of the Third World: Perspectives from Indian Historiography', *Comparative Studies in Society and History*, 32, 2 (1990), pp. 383–408; 'Science as a Sign of Modernity in Colonial India' (paper presented to Language and History conference at Warwick University, May 1994).

[28] Epstein, 'The Constitutional Idiom'; Clark, 'The Rhetoric of Chartist Domesticity'; Vernon, *Politics and the People*; Joyce, *Visions of the People*; idem, *Democratic Subjects*. A similar argument, couched in different terms, is evident in Burgess, *The Politics of the Ancient Constitution*.

[29] Fredric Jameson, *The Political Unconscious: Narrative As A Socially Symbolic Act* (Ithaca, 1981) esp. pp. 83–4.

political subjects.[30] Certainly, the essays that follow testify to the reluctance to abandon a narrative whose grip upon the political imagination seemed as secure in the early twentieth century as it had in the late eighteenth century.

Even though the durability of this discourse owed much to its hybridity and elasticity, it is important to remember that its different uses drew their authority from invoking the same foundational texts. As we shall see, there is a sense in which the constitution was partly written, for as one reads *Re-reading the Constitution* one is struck not just by the diversity of these foundational texts – they range from devotional works like Bunyan's *Pilgrim's Progress* and Foxe's *Book of Martyrs*, to legal tracts like Blackstone's *Commentaries* and Dicey's *Law of the Constitution*, political pamphlets like Burke's *Reflections* and Bagehot's *The English Constitution*, and the constitutional histories of Hallam, Macaulay, Stubbs and Maitland – or the frequency with which they are invoked, but by the way they mapped a common historical landscape that included the Anglo-Saxon folkmoot, the Norman Conquest of 1066, the Magna Carta of 1215, the Glorious Revolution of 1688 and the various Reform Acts of 1832, 1867, 1884, 1918 and 1928. Remarkably the 'ancient constitution' evoked by the Conservative Stanley Baldwin in the 1920s was not dissimilar to that evoked by the radical Gerrald in the 1790s.[31]

And yet, as the contributions of Epstein, Joyce and myself make clear, it is impossible to understand the continuing appeal of this story of the English constitution without analysing the way in which it was told. This attention to the rhetorical structures and tropes that frame narratives, what Hayden White has called 'the content of the form', enables historians to place the symbolic and imaginative structures of politics – and therefore the question of agency – at the centre of their concerns.[32] It was precisely through the construction of constitutional narratives that dramatised politics in the form of stories, with their own trajectories and logics, that individuals and collectivities were able to realise a sense of agency and purpose. By emplotting otherwise seemingly chaotic events (past and present, real and imagined) within these constitutional narratives they not only became meaningful, but enabled subjects to

---

[30] See n. 29. For other accounts attentive to the content, not the form, of similar meta-narratives see William H. Sewell, *Work and Revolution in France: The Language of Labour from the Old Regime to 1848* (Cambridge, 1980); Sean Wilentz, *Chants Democratic: New York City and the Rise of the American Working Classs 1780–1850* (New York, 1984).

[31] On Baldwin see Schwarz, 'Baldwin and the Language of Constitutionalism'.

[32] Hayden White, *The Content of the Form: Narrative Discourse and Historical Representation* (Baltimore, 1987).

imagine themselves as actors within these dramas, without whom the story could never reach its rightful end.

As both Joyce and I argue, this understanding of narrative as a form of representation raises a number of difficult epistemological questions about the essentialist practices of historians as they were institutionalised in the late nineteenth century. The polemic of my essay is that we need to blur the essentialist opposition between 'the real' and 'the imaginary' upon which English political history was founded and remains trapped. The concept of narrative enables us to do this, for, as Joyce suggests, it shifts the focus from politics as a reflection of 'the real' to how politics imagined 'the real'; a formulation which denies we can appeal to some anterior 'context' from which to interpret the 'text' of politics, for it insists that that 'context' is itself 'textualised'. It is an approach whose utility in conceptualising the political unconscious in terms of narrative has recently been demonstrated by a number of scholars – one thinks of the work of Homi K. Bhabha on the nation, Judith Walkowitz on the city, Lynn Hunt on the family and Patrick Joyce on class.[33]

In his essay here Joyce identifies melodrama as the key aesthetic form through which the narrative of the constitution and its subjects were mobilised in nineteenth-century England. Echoing Peter Brooks and Judith Walkowitz, he argues that the melodramatic imagination of politics in the mid nineteenth century instilled in its subjects a sense of agency and purpose by moralising the world into a narrative of struggle between the forces of good and evil, one which held out the utopian promise of the restoration of a 'golden age' before the fall of all that was good – innocence, honesty, virtue.[34] In earlier work several of the contributors have also emphasised the way in which this melodramatic imagination of politics informed constitutional narratives and provided their subjects with a particularly potent sense of historical agency.[35] Many of the essays collected here confirm this account, showing how much political discourse was framed in terms of an epic melodramatic struggle to define the constitution in which only one side, their side, could win. It was a struggle which was not only dramatised in terms of individuals, but in terms of restoring the lost golden age of the

---

[33] Homi K. Bhabha, *Nation and Narration* (London, 1990); Judith K. Walkowitz, *City of Dreadful Delight: Narratives of Sexual Danger in Late-Victorian London* (London, 1993); Lynn Hunt, *The Family Romance of the French Revolution* (London, 1993); Patrick Joyce, *Democratic Subjects: The Self and The Social in Nineteenth Century England* (Cambridge, 1994).

[34] Peter Brooks, *The Melodramatic Imagination: Balzac, Henry James and the Mode of Excess* (New Haven, 1976); Walkowitz, *City of Dreadful Delight*.

[35] Joyce, *Visions of the People*; Clark, 'The Rhetoric of Domesticity'; Vernon, *Politics and the People*.

'ancient constitution' variously defined. Thus, the argument runs, it was the imaginative structure of melodrama which enabled the meta-narrative of the constitution to be used and appropriated in different ways; or, to put it in the terms in which I began, melodrama allowed the code of the constitution to be shared.

Although there is much in these essays that confirm this analysis, there is also unease with its totalising ambition. I suspect that part of this unease is a consequence of the increasing promiscuity of the melodramatic imagination. Clearly, given that melodrama now appears everywhere from early-nineteenth-century popular theatre to Hollywood films of the 1950s, we need a much keener historical sense of its changing forms and uses.[36] And yet, just as it makes little sense to talk of the seamless continuity of melodramatic forms, so we also need to avoid equally totalising explanations of how these were displaced by the ironic imaginations of realism or naturalism.[37] Just as Walkowitz has shown how the city was conceived through both realist and melodramatic modes during the 1880s, so the contributions of Joyce and myself emphasise the increasing authority of the discourse of the real in disseminating narratives of the constitution, albeit one which still owed much to the melodramatic forms in which they were expressed.[38] Indeed, although much further research is required, we probably need to be much more discerning about the way in which we categorise aesthetic modes as discrete imaginative structures.

Re-reading the Constitution also suggests an element of caution about conceptualising constitutionalist discourse as the meta-narrative of English politics during the long nineteenth century. Arguably, it is a concept which, although useful in emphasising the importance of constitutionalist discourse as a form of narrative identity, is unable to accommodate the type of narrative instability and ambivalence identified in these essays. The longevity of constitutionalist discourse should not be mistaken for a sign of its cultural hegemony for its endurance throughout the long nineteenth century exemplifies its lack of a totalising narrative closure. As a story without an end, in which paradise was always postponed, it could never realise its totalising ambitions. Indeed, it was

[36] For a useful account of the promiscuity of melodrama see Rohan McWilliam, 'The Melodramatic Turn in Modern Historiography' (paper presented to Historiography Study Group at the Institute of Historical Research, May 1993).

[37] Despite assertions of continuity Joyce basically asserts that the First World War, together with the emergence of scientific and realist discourses from the late nineteenth century, assured the dissolution of melodrama as the organising imaginative structure of the political unconscious; Joyce, *Democratic Subjects*, pp. 156, 222–3.

[38] Walkowitz, *City of Dreadful Delight*, pp. 33–5, 93–4.

precisely this sense of movement, in Homi K. Bhabha's phrase of a narrative 'caught, uncertainly, in the act of composing' itself which, as we have seen, invited such a powerful sense of historical agency, for politics was resolved into an act of composition, a struggle to write the end of the constitutional story.[39] Even when appeals were made to an extra-political, and/or an extra-discursive, scientific and academic authority upon which to close this narrative, as with mine and Burney's accounts of the operations of medical reformers and constitutional historians, it is apparent this in turn dissolved – the contest over the constitution remaining central to English politics, history, medicine and law.

What these essays demonstrate most forcefully is that this perpetual struggle to claim a privileged position at the end of the constitutional story, required a continual shifting of the grounds of knowledge and authority that forever implicated the narrative of the constitution in other discursive systems. Burney's essay is particularly revealing of how, during attempts to reform the coroner's inquest, the discourse of medical science remained entwined with the mythology of ancient constitutional rights. Given this blurring of discursive boundaries it makes little sense to argue that it was only the unity of a shared meta-narrative of the constitution that allowed the expression of difference. For however much one stresses the fluidity and multi-vocality of this meta-narrative, it is disingenuous to assert that the presence of all other discursive systems and categories simply reaffirm the total authority of the constitutional narrative against or through which they were defined as different.[40]

So it is through an analysis of the politics of difference that we can best trace the fragmentation of constitutionalist discourse. All the essays are keen to assert the relational qualities of constitutionalist discourse, the way in which it was used to define difference in oppositional terms. The renewed interest in trials, exemplified here by the contribution of James Epstein, typifies this concern with the antagonistic and dualistic uses of discourse, in which the metaphor of the court's adversarial system helps illustrate the way in which identities were always constructed in opposition to an 'Other'.[41]

This was especially clear in the imagination of national identity. This

[39] Bhabha, Introduction in Aomi K. Bhabha (ed.), *Nation and Narration* (London, 1990), p. 3.
[40] As, for instance, in my *Politics and the People*.
[41] For the resurgence of the trial see Olivia Smith, *The Politics of Language, 1791–1819* (Oxford, 1981); John Barrell, 'Imaginary Law, Imaginary Treason: The State Trials of 1794', in his *The Birth of Pandora and the Division of Knowledge* (London, 1992); Jonathan Fulcher, 'Gender, Politics and Class in the Early Nineteenth Century English Reform Movement', *Historical Research*, 1 (1994), pp. 58–74; Epstein, 'Narrating Liberty's Defense: T. J. Wooler and the

is quite deliberately a book about English, as opposed to British, political history, for the concern is less with how England was defined in relation to its 'Celtic' neighbours or a still more remote colonial subaltern, as with how Englishness was conceived internally upon a series of exclusions of 'the Other' within. So Taylor demonstrates how the republican movement of the 1870s responded to its opponents' claim that it was peddling 'un-English' ideas by claiming to speak for the nation, rooting its critique of the monarchy in the very English language of 'Old Corruption' and demonising the 'Germanic' royal House of Brunswick. Fulcher also unravels the way in which the terms of radical politics were defined against those of their Whig and loyalist adversaries: their definitions of 'the constitution' and 'the people' always conceived in opposition to those of their opponents.

Yet, it has been feminist scholars, especially those influenced by post-structuralism, who have done most to alert historians of the absolute centrality of the politics of difference.[42] Faced with the relative absence of women in nineteenth-century politics, they have shown how the privileging of a male political subject relied upon the exclusion of the apparently silent feminine 'Other'. The contention is that the invention of an enlightened civil society and a discourse of liberal democracy during the Age of Revolution depended not only upon the active exclusion of women as irrational creatures of biology from this public sphere, but also their physical subordination within the private sphere.[43] An awareness of the gendered nature of constitutionalist discourses informs all the essays in a way unimaginable even a decade ago, yet it is brought in to sharpest focus by Clark's account of the late Victorian attempt to confine citizenship to a masculine political subject distinguished by the strength and sexual potency of his body. It is not – as Joyce illustrates in his examination of Gladstone's appeal to the humanity of 'women' against the atrocities of the cruel Turk, or as Wahrman's treatment of the dismissal of the unruly and undisciplined nature of politics during the Queen Caroline affair as feminine and

---

Law', in his *Radical Expression: Political Language, Ritual and Symbol in England, 1790–1850* (Oxford, 1990), pp. 29–69.
[42] See especially the inspirational work of Joan Scott, *Gender and the Politics of History* and Denise Riley, '*Am I That Name?' Feminism and the Category of 'Women' in History* (London, 1988).
[43] Jean Bethke Elshtain, *Public Man, Private Woman: Women in Social and Political Thought* (Princeton, 1981); Carole Pateman, *The Disorder of Women: Democracy, Feminism and Political Theory* (Cambridge, 1991); Joan B. Landes, *Women and the Public Sphere in the Age of the French Revolution* (Ithaca, 1988); Catherine Hall, 'Private Persons Versus Public Someones: Class, Gender and Politics in England, 1780–1850', in C. Steedman *et al.* (eds.), *Language, Gender and Childhood* (London, 1985), pp. 10–33.

trivial shows – that the category of 'woman' was not brought into the discourse of politics but that it was done so as its object not its subject.

One of the consequences of this concern with the political construction of masculinity and femininity is to problematise the idea of the body as the foundation of sexual identity and instead to conceive it as a metaphor of politics, a site of power.[44] The centrality of the metaphor of the body politic to constitutional discourse is reaffirmed in Burney's essay where the proper public scrutiny of dead bodies is seen as critical to the contract of representative government to protect and regulate its citizens' lives. Although the other essays only address this issue obliquely, they do point to an urgent need for further research on the nature of the English body politic – especially on the growing crisis of masculinity, and hence the categories of citizenship, from the 1870s but associated, above all, with the horrors of the First World War.[45]

No doubt because some of the earliest work by British social historians in this anti-essentialist vein were attempts to rethink the politics of class identity, the attempt to retain an essentialist definition of class as ultimately determined by the 'experience' of industrialisation has generated much debate in the new cultural history of politics, as well as some of the less well-informed renunciations of 'the linguistic turn'.[46] *Re-reading the Constitution* offers no tidy resolution of this controversy. Whereas some of the contributors are happy to work with a notion of class as a pre-existing social category which is sometimes undermined or reinforced by the language of politics, others see class as primarily a political construct in which constitutionalist discourses were used to define different class experiences of state power and inclusion or

[44] For a critique of essentialist notions of the body as the source of sexual identity see Michel Foucault, *The History of Sexuality*, Vol. 1, *An Introduction* (London, 1979); Donna Haraway, 'A Manifesto for Cyborgs: Science, Technology and Socialist Feminism in the 1980s', *Socialist Review*, 15, 2 (1985), pp. 65–107; Riley, *'Am I That Name?'*, pp. 96–114; Judith Butler, *Gender Trouble: Feminism and the Subversion of Identity* (London, 1990).

[45] For the best work connecting the history of sexuality and the body to English political history see Judith Walkowitz, *Prostitution and Victorian Society: Women, Class and the State* (Cambridge, 1980); idem, *City of Dreadful Delight*; Frank Mort, *Dangerous Sexualities: Medico-Moral Politics in England Since 1830* (London, 1987); Lucy Bland, *Banishing the Beast: English Feminism and Sexual Morality, 1885–1914* (London, 1995); Mary Poovey, *Making a Social Body: British Cultural Formation, 1830–1864* (London, 1995). On the crisis of the masculine body politic see Susan Kingsley Kent, *Sex and Suffrage in Britain, 1860–1914* (London, 1990); idem, *Making Peace: The Reconstruction of Gender in Inter War Britain* (Princeton, 1994); Light, *Forever England*; Paul Fussell, *The Great War and Modern Memory* (Oxford, 1975).

[46] For the attempt to rethink class see Stedman Jones, 'Rethinking Chartism' and Joyce, *Visions of the People*. For the most recent example of the materialist defence of class see Neville Kirk, 'History, Language, Ideas and Post-Modernism: A Materialist View', *Social History*, 19, 2 (1994), pp. 221–40.

exclusion from the political nation. If there is unanimity it is in the recognition that class was by no means the primary category of identity of constitutionalist discourse as it was frequently undercut by other highly gendered subjectivities such as 'the people', 'the nation' or 'the empire'.

It should already be clear that this book is not an attempt to blithely reassert the autonomy of politics and revive the old 'high political' constitutional history.[47] In a number of ways these essays suggest a much broader definition of politics, one which seeks to move beyond tired reformulations of the relationship between 'politics', 'society' and 'culture'. Instead what is at issue is precisely the way in which 'the political' was constituted and represented as a discrete sphere of operations, either independent from or determined by 'the social'.

Consequently the focus is on the representation of politics and its technologies and metaphors. In common with much of the linguistic turn in modern British history, the predominant concern is with the metaphor of language as the means of representation. Although there are often difficulties with this approach, it has proved a productive way of expanding our conception of 'the political' and its 'publics'. It was not just that the narrative of the constitution intersected with a range of other discursive systems but that it did so through a number of different technologies of communication, few of which were the sole preserve of 'politics'.

The state has, of course, long been the traditional agent of much political history, and several of the essays help develop the renewed interest in its role in shaping the discursive context of politics[48]. Fulcher not only traces the way in which changes in financial policy helped shape radical reworkings of constitutionalist discourse after the Napoleonic Wars, but also shows how the institution of the Suspension of Habeas Corpus and the Seditious Meetings Acts in 1817 effectively foreclosed radical discursive strategies. This concern with how the state's definition of the constitution was always inscribed by the threat of violence and force is also elaborated in Epstein's analysis of how individuals like Gerrald regularly faced the full force of the state with the possibility of execution, deportation and incarceration. Yet, while it is important to recognise that the discourse of politics was always

---

[47] Robert Gray, 'Class, Politics and Historical "Revisionism"', *Social History*, 19, 2 (1994), pp. 209–20.

[48] Stedman Jones, 'Rethinking Chartism'; Ross McKibbin, 'Class and Conventional Wisdom'.

curtailed by such power relations, it is apparent from Epstein's essay that it was almost impossible for the state to prevent its subjects from stretching and subverting the limits of constitutionalist discourse – especially in that unique political site of the courtroom.

This opens up the possibility of a much more decentred notion of the micro-technologies of power and communication – in which power emanated from all those who sought to claim the constitution as their own – than those evident in traditional political history. Something of this should already be apparent from the previous discussion of the agency of the melodramatic imagination of politics, the way in which it empowered 'the helpless and unbefriended' by creating a moral court of appeal in which all were judge and jury regardless of wealth, knowledge or gender.[49] If melodramatic tropes allowed all to write their own narrative of the constitution in which they appeared as heroes, so the technologies of constitutional rule came increasingly to depend less on the state's policing of an undisciplined demos as on the regulation of 'the public' by itself. The emergence of a self-regulating, self-disciplining civil society in which the citizenry became less the object of government than the source and subject of power, able to govern and regulate itself, is evident in the contributions of Wahrman and Burney.[50] While Burney discusses the importance attached by medical reformers of the coroner's inquest to the public knowledge (and even display) of dead bodies as an object-lesson in public health from which the citizenry would learn how to help each other avoid a similar fate, Wahrman charts the appearance during the late 1810s and early 1820s of a self-regulating 'public opinion' which defined the limits of a legitimate constitutional politics – even if he wisely warns us how shallow and vulnerable were the roots of this notion of 'public opinion' as the referent and arbiter of constitutionality.

Clearly then, as Wahrman's essay testifies, the mode of communication in which political discourse was articulated was critical to its meaning and reception – indeed, to its very acceptance as constitutional. The contributions of Epstein, Joyce and Clark all illustrate not only the continued centrality of oratory to nineteenth-century politics – whether it is Gerrald's courtroom defence, Bright's speeches on the platform, or parliamentary debates – but its symbiotic relationship with the press in

[49] M. Booth, *English Melodrama* (London, 1965); Martha Vicinus, 'Helpless and Unbefriended: Nineteenth Century Domestic Melodrama', *New Literary History*, 13, 1 (1981), pp. 127–43; E. Ann Kaplan, 'The Political Unconscious in the Maternal Melodrama: Ellen Wood's *East Lynne*', in Derek Longhurst (ed.), *Gender, Genre and Narrative Pleasure* (Hemel Hempstead, 1988), pp. 31–50; Anna Clark, 'Queen Caroline and the Sexual Politics of Popular Culture in London, 1820', *Representations*, 31 (1990), pp. 47–68.

[50] Tony Bennett, 'The Exhibitionary Complex', *New Formations*, 4 (1988), pp. 73–103.

being disseminated to a much broader reading public. The concern with how the press invents its own publics and then positions itself as a mediator between the elusive category of 'public opinion' and the politicians who claim to represent it, is taken up most forcibly in Fulcher's treatment of the loyalist press and editors like Shadgett and Merle, as well as by Joyce's examination of the relationship between W. T. Stead's *Darlington Echo* and Gladstone's Midlothian campaign. Wahrman and Taylor's essays, in contrast, remind us of the importance of the visual representation of the constitutional narrative, both through the too often neglected world of satirical prints and through the symbolic uses of public spaces and styles of dress as modes of political organisation.

These elaborations of a cultural history of politics enables us to examine the changing ways in which contemporaries themselves conceived 'the political'. All the contributors emphasise, in different ways, that much of constitutionalist discourse revolved around debates about the nature of civil society, whose 'public opinion' should be given weight, and what constituted legitimate political activity. So if the discourse of the constitution tended to reify the category of 'public opinion' as the primary referent of politics it is essential to trace its shifting meanings and their consequences for conceptions of 'the political'. It is by no means clear from these essays that it is possible to write this history in the unilinear grand narrative form so beloved of political historians, as a progressive or regressive sequence towards Democracy, Freedom, Socialism, Liberalism or Conservatism. Instead, as I have tried to suggest, it may be more helpful to conceive this history of 'the political' in terms of a fluctuating series of inclusions and exclusions, openings and closings, which were themselves shaped in relation to the emerging discourses of 'the economy' and 'the social', each with their own 'publics' and objects of concern.

2

∾

'Our real constitution': trial defence and radical memory in the Age of Revolution

JAMES EPSTEIN

Yet, notwithstanding, the present system of government is a libel upon our real constitution; the word 'constitution, constitution!' is rung in our ears with unceasing perseverance. This is the talisman which the enemies of reform wield over the heads of the credulous and the simple; and like old and wicked enchanters, having first bound them in a spell, take advantage of the drowsiness which their arts have created.

The words are those of Joseph Gerrald, defending himself against charges of sedition before the High Court of Justiciary at Edinburgh in March 1794.[1] During the 1790s, in Scottish and English courtrooms, the leading figures of the radical reform movement, many of whom were inspired by the example of revolutionary France, faced charges of sedition, seditious libel and high treason. They confronted accusations that they had transgressed the bounds of the British constitution; that their words and actions were aimed not merely at legitimate efforts to improve but disguised attempts to overthrow the very structure and substance of Britain's government and law.

Yet how were these boundaries defined: what constituted 'our real constitution' and the liberty so precious to Britons? And how were radicals to respond to charges that they had moved outside the constitution; how did they represent themselves and their understanding of constitutional liberty; what stories were available for retelling, for

My thanks to Greg Claeys, Mona Frederick, Cynthia Herrup, Larry Lerner and James Vernon for their helpful comments on an earlier draft of this chapter.

[1] T. B. Howell and T. J. Howell (eds.), *A Complete Collection of State Trials*, 33 vols. (London, 1809–26), vol. XXIII (1793–4), 'Proceedings on the Trial of Joseph Gerrald', (hereafter, 'Trial of Gerrald') col. 965.

remembering the nation's past in the age of revolution? During the 1790s these questions were particularly acute as the language of politics was itself thrown into unprecedented confusion.[2] A new language of rational liberty challenged older constitutionalist notations and shifted the meanings ascribed to key words in the nation's political vocabulary. The world was to be spoken anew. It is against this background that this chapter explores Gerrald's trial and the possibilities for his defence.

I

There was a powerful alternative to counter-constitutionalist language or to any recasting, however radical, of the nation's constitutional past. Radicals might reject the venerated British constitution in favour of a notion of liberty based on the universal principles of Reason and Nature and on an appeal to the present rather than to the past. In this mode democrats identified the constitution and the liberty it was thought to guarantee as an enslaving fiction, 'the talisman' used to delude the credulous and the simple into mistaking oligarchical corruption for real liberty and virtue, binding them in a spell. John Thelwall, the leading orator of the London Corresponding Society who was himself tried for high treason in 1794, thus referred to 'the enchanted castle of the British constitution', lending a Gothic touch to the common image of the constitution as a stately edifice.[3] The constitution represented a kind of haunted house, full of mystery and ruled by figments of the imagination. The British constitution was an imaginary construct that lacked real substance; it was without definition. 'We have long been amused with the lofty sounds of *timetried constitution and happy frame of government*, but we have never been favoured with an explicit definition of them', observed Henry 'Redhead' Yorke, the Sheffield radical.[4]

In *The Rights of Man* Paine provided the most coherent and popular portrayal of the British constitution as 'anti-constitution'. According to Paine, there was quite simply no legitimate British constitution because there was nothing derived from the sovereign will of the people or based on reason and natural rights. Paine's challenge to Burke to produce the constitution could not be met because a constitution did not exist.[5]

---

[2] See John Barrell, 'Imagining the King's Death: The Arrest of Richard Brothers', *History Workshop*, 37 (1994), pp. 1–33.

[3] John Thelwall, *The Natural and Constitutional Right of Britons To Annual Parliaments, Universal Suffrage, and the Freedom of Popular Association* ... (London, 1795), p. 36, reprinted in *The Politics of English Jacobinism: Writings of John Thelwall*, ed. Gregory Claeys (Pennsylvania, PA, 1995).

[4] Henry Yorke, *These are the Times that Try Men's Souls!* (London, 1793), p. 6.

[5] Thomas Paine, *Rights of Man* (1791–2; Harmondsworth, 1984), pp. 71–2.

What passed for government and law was mere imposition, the fraudulent rule of kingcraft and priestcraft. Moreover, no such constitution had ever existed: there was no visible moment of constitutional founding and, therefore, no recovery of lost liberty or rights was possible. There was no story to be re-told, nothing worthy of remembering.

Paine's concept of legitimate constitution-making is inseparable from Enlightenment notions of language derived principally from Locke.[6] Particularly important is the way in which Paine, along with other democratic writers, links transparency of rational expression to democratic politics and to the encoding of democratic principles within a constitution. Democratic government, like democratic language, must be directly accessible to rational understanding. At his trial in 1801, for example, Thomas Spence declared that he had reduced the 'Anarchy' of politics and language to order: 'The one by a New Alphabet, and the other by a New Constitution'. Paine drew a direct analogy between good grammar and good government: 'The American constitutions were to liberty, what grammar is to language; they define its parts of speech, and practically construct them into syntax.'[7] In direct contrast to such order, Burke's use of language (what Paine called his 'incoherent rhapsodies') like his vision of the constitution, is promiscuous; his writing, like monarchical government itself, relies on elaborate techniques of artifice and disguise and on a profligate appeal to the emotions in place of reason. Thus Mary Wollstonecraft, in *A Vindication of the Rights of Men*, takes Burke to task for fostering 'every emotion till the fumes ... dispel sober suggestions of reason'. Burke is guilty of substituting feelings for 'fixed principles'.[8] Language, in this view, is dangerously seductive when it resists determinate meaning and allows free play to the imagination. This anxiety about the emotional and imaginary appeal of language (particularly figurative language) accounts for the need to control meaning through the careful definition of words and concepts and for the preference for language modelled on scientific demonstration rather than imaginative literature. Like language itself, a constitution must be under the control of precise definitions; only in this way can meaning be rendered stable, coherent and visible.

The commitment to linguistic transparency was typically linked to

---

[6] John Turner, 'Burke, Paine, and the Nature of Language', *Yearbook of English Studies*, 19 (1989), pp. 36–53; Olivia Smith, *The Politics of Language, 1791–1819* (Oxford, 1984), chapter 2; David A. Wilson, *Paine and Cobbett: The Transatlantic Connection* (Kingston and Montreal, 1988), pp. 19–33, 76–82.

[7] Thomas Spence, *The Important Trial of Thomas Spence ...*, 2nd edn (London, 1807), p. 59; Paine, *Rights of Man*, p. 95; Turner, 'Burke, Paine', p. 51; Smith, *Politics of Language*, p. 99.

[8] Mary Wollstonecraft, *A Vindication of the Rights of Men*, 2nd edn (London, 1790), pp. 6, 9.

allegiances that were decidedly presentist and cosmopolitan. History and custom were polluting agents: enemies of reason and philosophy. 'Where was the dignity of thinking of the fourteenth century?' asked Wollstonecraft. The appeal to precedent was an invitation to chaos: 'is Magna Charta to rest for its chief support on a former grant, which reverts to another, till chaos becomes the base of the mighty structure?'[9] In 1793 Henry 'Redhead' Yorke, in his work *Reason Urged Against Precedent*, observed: 'Reason and Philosophy are making hasty strides, and precedent and hereditary notions go fast [in]to decline.'[10] Paine demanded that the present generation be released from the 'manuscript assumed authority of the dead'.[11] *The Rights of Man* is, of course, a profoundly anti-historical work. Democratic rights thrive in an imminent, an immaculate present. The belief in the possibility of free action taken in an unencumbered present marks Paine as a quintessential modern theorist.[12]

Moreover, the present world offered shattering examples of such free collective action. Against the illusion of the British constitution stood real constitutions, those of the United States and France. The first great era of modern constitution-making had begun.[13] It would be difficult to exaggerate the impact of revolutionary nations actually designing governments from scratch. In the early 1790s, admiration for France at the expense of Britain was a common sentiment among British reformers. As late as 1795, the *Cabinet*, a Norwich journal of philosophic radicalism, compared the British constitution most unfavourably to that of France.[14] Major John Cartwright, whose politics are often mistakenly reduced merely to an antiquarian extolling of the ancient constitution, regarded the American and French constitutions as models of conciseness and clarity:

In America and in France doubt and obscurity is [*sic*] done away. The whole constitution of France, digested and arranged under proper heads, is contained in a little manual; what is constitutional and what is not, is settled in a moment ... In vain would an Englishman ransack his whole library for the same information; although Blackstone himself were on the shelf.[15]

---

[9] *Ibid.*, pp. 18, 14. Cf. Paine, *Rights of Man*, p. 65.

[10] Henry Yorke, *Reason Urged Against Precedent, in a Letter to the People of Derby* (London, 1793), p. 45.

[11] Paine, *Rights of Man*, p. 42.

[12] Jack P. Greene, 'Paine, America, and the 'Modernization' of Political Consciousness', *Political Science Quarterly*, 93 (1978), pp. 71–92.

[13] Geoff Ely, 'Culture, Britain, and Europe', *Journal of British Studies*, 31 (1992), pp. 390–1.

[14] *Cabinet: By a Society of Gentleman*, 3 vols. (Norwich, 1795), vol. ii, pp. 238–48.

[15] John Cartwright, *A Letter to the Duke of Newcastle ... Together with Some Remarks Touching the French Revolution ...* (London, 1792), pp. 102–3.

The American Revolution, Paine's 'morning of reason', left a deep and lasting impression. The traditionally negative value attached to words such as youth, innocence and simplicity are reversed in the writings of revolutionaries like Paine and Spence, now regarded as the very essence of wisdom and virtue.[16] For Cartwright, America stood like 'naked Eve – "when unadorned, adorned the most" – the Americans, when stripped of the political garb of civil rule, appeared with the greater lustre, enrobed in political wisdom and virtue'.[17]

By 1789 the meaning of the term 'patriot' had already shifted for many radicals; local attachments were displaced by an enlightened cosmopolitanism, by the desire to be a citizen of the republic of humanity.[18] The French revolution intensified this shift in meaning. To be a patriot in the narrow sense of mere love of one's own country possessed no claim to virtue; it was, according to Thelwall, a 'contemptible and illiberal' feeling when compared to universal principles of reason, liberty and human fellowship.[19] In *A Summary of the Duties of Citizenship*, a widely circulated pamphlet associated with Richard 'Citizen' Lee, the author who described himself as 'a perfect cosmopolitan', denounced love of country as 'amongst the confused train of disorderly passions that enter the human disposition', favouring in its stead 'a diffusive spirit of universal affection'.[20] A new age of virtue and human understanding loomed, one based on an openness between citizens; the republic of virtue was founded on 'an apocalyptic vision of restored transparency' in personal relations. Millennarian expectations ran high: human civilisation was in the midst of being reborn.[21]

---

[16] Greene, 'Paine, America', p. 79; Ian Dyck, 'Local Attachments, National Identities and World Citizenship in the Thought of Thomas Paine', *History Workshop*, 35 (1993), pp. 117–35; Thomas Spence, *Marine Republic, or a Description of Spensonia* (London, 1795).

[17] John Cartwright, *The Commonwealth in Danger* ... (London, 1795), p. xci. See more generally Arthur Sheps, 'The American Revolution and the Transformation of English Republicanism', *Historical Reflections*, 2 (1975), pp. 3–28; Colin Bonwick, *English Radicals and the American Revolution* (Chapel Hill, 1977).

[18] Linda Colley, 'Radical Patriotism in Eighteenth-Century England', in Raphael Samuel (ed.), *Patriotism: The Making and Unmaking of British Identity*, 3 vols. (London, 1989), vol. 1, pp. 169–87; J. C. D. Clark, *The Language of Liberty, 1660–1832: Political Discourse and Social Dynamics in the Anglo-American World* (Cambridge, 1994), p. 20; Gordon S. Wood, *The Radicalism of the American Revolution* (New York, 1991), pp. 213–25.

[19] *Tribune*, 18 April 1795, pp. 132–3.

[20] *A Summary of the Duties of Citizenship: Written Expressly for Members of the London Corresponding Societies* (London, 1795), pp. 19, 22, 27–28; Public Record Office (PRO), TS 11/837 (2832), *King* v. *Lee*.

[21] J. W. Burrow, *Whigs and Liberals: Continuity and Change in English Political Thought* (Oxford, 1988), p. 61; Lynn Hunt, *Politics, Culture, and Class in the French Revolution* (Berkeley, 1984), pp. 44–5. See also E. P. Thompson, *The Making of the English Working Class* (London, 1963), pp. 116–20; Jon Mee, *Dangerous Enthusiasm: William Blake and the Culture of Radicalism in the 1790s* (Oxford, 1992), chapter 1; Clarke Garrett, *Respectable Folly: Millenarians and the French*

II

In a long and revealing letter written to Joseph Gerrald little over a month before he stood trial, William Godwin advised his friend on how best to defend himself at trial.[22] His advice was framed predominantly by rationalist assumptions and an extraordinary optimism about the power of reason to foster human understanding and to open the human heart. 'Your trial', he wrote, 'may be a day such as England, and I believe the world, never saw. It may be the means of converting thousands, and, progressively millions, to the cause of reason and public justice.' Gerrald had a great deal at stake; therefore, he must not suffer without using this opportunity 'of telling a tale upon which the happiness of nations depends'. Godwin implores Gerrald not to forget that the jury, although no doubt carefully packed by those in authority, are men, 'and that men are made of penetrable stuff: probe all the recesses of their souls'. Godwin rejects the view that there are men upon whom truth, 'fully and adequately stated', will make no impression as a 'groundless calumny upon the character of the human mind'.

Godwin recommends that Gerrald's actual defence turn on bold principles not legal quibbles. Arrested for his part at the British Convention at Edinburgh in late 1793, Gerrald must establish the legality of this meeting, a point, Godwin maintains, that is fully contained in the Bill of Rights (1688). However, Gerrald must appeal beyond such local authority to an authority 'paramount to all written Law and parchment constitutions; the Law of universal Reason'. Later the same year Godwin was to advise Thelwall in similar terms regarding his up-coming trial: 'To quote authorities is a vulgar business; every soulless hypocrite can do that ... Appeal to that eternal law which the heart of every man of common-sense recognises immediately.'[23] Gerrald must further show that he is actuated by selfless motives, by principles of 'pure philanthropy and benevolence' so that 'The jury, the world will feel your value.' In short, Gerrald is asked to put Godwin's theory of

Revolution in France and England (Baltimore, 1975); J. F. C. Harrison, 'Thomas Paine and Millenarian Radicalism', in Ian Dyck (ed.), *Citizen of the World: Essays on Thomas Paine* (London, 1987), pp. 73–85.

22 William Godwin to Joseph Gerrald, 23 January 1794, Abinger Collection, Bodleian Library, Oxford, microfilm copy, reel 13, Duke University Library. The letter is reprinted nearly in full in C. Kegan Paul, *William Godwin: His Friends and Contemporaries*, 2 vols. (London, 1876), vol. I, pp. 125–8.

23 William Godwin [to John Thelwall], 18 September 1794, Abinger Collection, microfilm copy, reel 13, reprinted in both [Cecil Thelwall], *The Life of John Thelwall, by his Widow* (London, 1837), p. 207 and Charles Cestre, *John Thelwall* (London, 1906) p. 202.

universal benevolence and rational communication to the test of practice.

The terms and sentiments expressed in this letter are what might be expected from the author of *Enquiry Concerning Political Justice*, Godwin's masterwork first published the previous year. An opponent of violent revolution who also disapproved of the proceedings of popular political societies, Godwin looked to the potential of rational persuasion and human benevolence to affect progressive change. He condemned all forms of dissimulation. Sincerity was a paramount virtue; no truth must be left unspoken; progress depended on total openness and freedom of discussion so that truth can emerge. 'Sound reasoning and truth,' Godwin maintains, 'when adequately communicated, must always be victorious over error: Sound reasoning and truth are capable of being so communicated.'[24] Godwin's faith in the possibility of communicating rational truth depends in turn on the demand for accurate language, stripped of rhetorical devices and purified to achieve transparency of expression.

The Law was itself a major offender against the protocols of truthful understanding, a prime example of irrationality, dishonesty and the mechanisms of oppression. In the chapter 'Of Law' in *Political Justice*, Godwin regards law as an impediment to progress, tending 'no less than creeds, catechisms and tests, to fix the human mind in a stagnant condition'. The 'wisdom of our ancestors' is a contradiction in terms. Men and women must be taught

that the mountains of parchment in which they have been hitherto entrenched are fit only to impose upon ages of superstitions and ignorance ... In reality, whatever were the original source of law, it soon became cherished as a cloak for oppression.

Contrary to Truth and Reason, the Law is characterised by uncertainty, obscurity and deception. The field of law invites dishonesty. For Godwin the only principle that can replace the empire of Law 'is that of reason exercising an uncontrolled jurisdiction upon the circumstances of the case'. Law as a system based either on fixed codes or on judicial precedent was to perish along with the need for political force.[25]

In 1793 Godwin's ideas had a profound impact on the younger and more philosophically inclined reformers; his work was much in vogue

---

[24] William Godwin, *Enquiry Concerning Political Justice and Its Influence on Modern Morals and Happiness*, 3rd edn (1798; Harmondsworth, 1985), p. 140; James T. Boulton, *The Language of Politics in the Age of Wilkes and Burke* (London, 1963), particularly pp. 209–26.
[25] *Political Justice*, pp. 688–91, 693, 695, and chapter 8, book 7, *passim*. See more generally Mark Philp, *Godwin's Political Justice* (Ithaca, 1986).

among the literary Left. Unlike Paine, Godwin was a philosopher: the true prophet of universal liberty. He captured that sense of utopian promise in which all authority might be overthrown: nothing was held to be sacred, nothing was beyond the searching gaze of reason.[26] *Political Justice* was not, however, a work that appealed to a wide readership, although a popularised version of Godwin's ideas did gain currency among plebeian radicals principally through Thelwall's writings and lectures.[27] Gerrald was certainly both familiar with and sympathetic to Godwin's philosophy. As reflected in Godwin's letter, there were bonds of mutual esteem between the two men. Together with Thelwall, Gerrald was the principal link between the radical intelligentsia and the plebeian radical movement.[28] Among the most prominent leaders of the London Corresponding Society, Gerrald was himself a gifted intellectual. The son of a wealthy West Indian planter, he was a favourite pupil and close friend of Dr Samuel Parr, 'the Whig Dr Johnson'.[29] Following his father's death, Gerrald had taken over the family's estate in St Kitts which was already declining in profitability and ran through the remains of his family fortune. In the early 1780s, he moved to the United States, where he associated and quarrelled with Paine and practised law in Pennsylvania. Returning to England in 1788, Gerrald soon began taking an active part in radical politics; a confirmed republican he joined both the Society for Constitutional Information and the London Corresponding Society. By 1793 Gerrald moved comfortably within John Horne Tooke and Godwin's overlapping circles of friends. While free on bail in January 1794, he dined with Godwin, Thomas Holcroft, Horne Tooke and other prominent radical intellectuals and discussed the prospects of his impending trial.[30]

Gerrald was brought to trial for his role, along with Maurice

---

[26] See William Hazlitt, *Lectures on the English Poets and The Spirit of the Age* (London, 1910), *The Spirit of the Age* (1835), p. 183.

[27] *Political Justice* ran to 4,000 copies in three editions published in 1793, 1796 and 1798. See Claeys' introduction to *Politics of English Jacobinism*, for Thelwall's role.

[28] Gerrald sponsored Thelwall's membership of the London Corresponding Society (LCS) in October 1793 (*Life of Thelwall*, p. 115).

[29] William Field, *Memoirs of the Life, Writings, and Opinions of the Rev. Samuel Parr, LLD*, 2 vols. (London, 1828), vol. 1, chapter 22; Warren Derry, *Dr Parr: A Portrait of the Whig Dr Johnson* (Oxford, 1966), pp. 24, 27, 152–8. For biographical details see entry for Gerrald in Joseph O. Baylen and Norbert J. Gossman (eds.), *Biographical Dictionary of Modern British Radicals*, (Hassocks, 1979), vol. 1, pp. 186–9; *Gerrald, A Fragment; Containing Some Account of the Life of the Devoted Citizen . . .* (London, 1795); *The Trial of Joseph Gerrald . . . with an Original Memoir, and Notes* (Glasgow, 1835); *The Political Martyrs . . . Who Were Persecuted in the Year 1793–4 . . .* (London, 1837), pp. 17–21, copy in the British Library, Add. ms. 27816.

[30] *Selections from the Papers of the London Corresponding Society, 1792–1799*, ed. Mary Thale (Cambridge, 1983), pp. 86–8, for Gerrald's election as delegate to the Convention; Godwin Diary, Abinger Collection, microfilm copy, reel 1; Paul, *Godwin*, pp. 78, 123–4; William St

Margarot, as delegate from the London Corresponding Society to the British Convention of the Delegates of the Friends of the People, associated to obtain Universal Suffrage and Annual parliaments, which had first convened in October 1793 in Edinburgh.[31] Gerrald took a leading part in the Convention's proceedings upon his arrival in November and was closely identified with schemes for a national convention. Indeed, besides his trial defence, he was best known for his pamphlet *A Convention the Only Means of Saving Us from Ruin*, written around the time of the British Convention. In large part, the pamphlet is a condemnation of Pitt's policy of war with France and a defence of the French Revolution, including the execution of Louis XVI. War is denounced as a product of monarchical rule, for 'Man is not naturally hostile to man.'[32]

A work clearly influenced by Godwinian and Paineite views, it drew on a current vocabulary of universal benevolence and rational liberty. The pamphlet's final section, however, where the author fully details his plan for a convention, would appear to subvert the work's central theoretical premises. In familiar Paineite fashion, Gerrald traces all suffering to a want of adequate political representation. He supports male universal suffrage through an expansive definition of property: 'the manual labour of the peasant, the ingenuity of the artists, the talents of the scholar, are the property of each ... and fit objects of protection'. Gerrald's remedy is also Paineite: the assembling of a convention vested with popular sovereignty that should determine the best mode of promoting public welfare. Acknowledging that there is no written law that invests the people with the right to convene a convention, Gerrald argues that many rights depend not on written law but on custom. Happily the right claimed rests

not upon reasonings of great expediency, or abstract speculations of right. Precedents of conventions, folkmotes, or meetings of the people are to be found

---

Clair, *The Godwins and the Shelleys* (London, 1989), pp. 112–14; Don Locke, *Fantasy of Reason* (London, 1980), p. 64; Philp, *Godwin's Political Justice*, appendix B, p. 243.

[31] Albert Goodwin, *The Friends of Liberty: The English Democratic Movement in the Age of the French Revolution* (London, 1979), pp. 290–305; Henry W. Meikle, *Scotland and the French Revolution* (Glasgow, 1912), pp. 137–44, and more generally for the two earlier Scottish conventions. The minutes of the British Convention are reprinted in *State Trials*, vol. XXIII, cols. 391–471. Extracts from the minutes are reprinted in *The Second Report from the Committee of Secrecy of the House of Commons ... To Which are Added the First and Second Reports of the House of Lords* (London, 1794), pp. 100–11.

[32] Joseph Gerrald, *A Convention the Only Means of Saving Us from Ruin, in a Letter Addressed to the People of England* (London, 1793), pp. 35–42, 53, 76. The pamphlet came out in late December 1793.

in the early periods of our history, and are coeval with the existence of our constitution itself.

Thus rather than making the obvious Paineite move of founding the convention solely on the people's natural right of sovereignty, Gerrald summons the myth of the Norman yoke and the pristine democratic purity of the Anglo-Saxon constitution that the Norman intruders vanquished: 'The plan proposed, therefore, is not a breach, but a renovation of our constitution.' The golden age of Alfred, 'a patriot king', was brought to an end by the Norman Conquest that planted 'the tree of feudal tyranny in England'. Gerrald further observes that in times of crisis the practices of their Saxon forebears are always sought for as precedents 'and examples to be imitated'.[33] Much the same language and reasoning is found in *The Address of the British Convention Assembled at Edinburgh ... to the People of Great Britain*, also written by Gerrald, which seeks to legitimate the existence and proceedings of the Convention: 'anxious to guard against the imputation of *novelty*, among the records of former times, and in the established usages of our ancestors, we sought for precedent, and we found it'.[34] Anglo-Saxon precedent apparently could serve for all Britons, the Scots as well as the English.

The vocabulary of renovation and the desire to restore a golden past, however distant and mythical, seem at odds with modernising notions of rational progress and the universalising philosophy of the age. What we see in Gerrald's writing and the address adopted by the Convention, however, is an ambivalence about history, a hesitation about moving wholly outside the realm of custom and relying solely on the persuasive force of natural reason. During the 1790s, a similar ambivalence thrived at the heart of the popular radical movement's language and actions. Paineite rationalism and natural rights language never simply displaced constitutionalist rhetoric; democratic writers and speakers freely mixed historical and natural concepts of rights, moving with little sense of incompatibility between the twin poles of natural reason and the constitutional past; the language of radicalism was eclectic.[35] Gerrald's

---

[33] Gerrald, *Convention*, pp. 80, 108, 87–90, 105 and 111–19, for his elaborate plan for a convention. See T. M. Parssinen, 'Association, Convention and Anti-Parliament in British Radical Politics, 1771–1848', *English Historical Review*, 88 (1973), pp. 504–33; Christopher Hill, 'The Norman Yoke', in his *Puritanism and Revolution* (London, 1967), pp. 50–122.

[34] *The Address of the British Convention Assembled at Edinburgh ... to the People of Great Britain* (London, 1793), pp. 4–5, reprinted along with Gerrald's *Convention* in *The Political Writings of the 1790s*, ed. Gregory Claeys, 8 vols. (Cambridge, 1995), vol. IV. See also the report of Gerrald's speech to the Convention on 21 November, PRO, HO 102/9, fos. 214–16.

[35] See, in particular, Mark Philp, 'The Fragmented Ideology of Reform', in Mark Philp (ed.),

speech from the dock was steeped in the language of British libertar-
ianism and became one of the most celebrated courtroom performances
of the age. Schooled in the new vocabulary of universal liberty and a
staunch defender of the French Revolution, Gerrald's decision to place
his defence within the boundary of 'our real constitution', not to shout
back at his accusers in the language of the anti-constitution, is particularly noteworthy.

III

But was a Godwinian, or for that matter a Paineite, defence really
possible given the prevailing conditions? As Godwin himself observed:
'Terror was the order of the day.'[36] What could be written, said, or
publicly displayed in 1793–4 was circumscribed by the power of the
government and the law. The broad retreat from the language of
rational liberty and the example of the French Revolution can be
explained, at least in part, by the storm of government repression that
set in. Paine had been declared an outlaw, having been found guilty *in
absentia* of seditious libel for the second part of *The Rights of Man*.
Moreover, by the time Gerrald stood trial at Edinburgh for his role at
the Convention there was already a host of convictions in Scottish courts
and the judges at the High Court of Justiciary had established senten-
cing practices of unremitting savagery. The Scottish sedition trials were
in full swing: Thomas Muir, the Scottish Jacobin tried in part for his
role at the first Convention at Edinburgh (December 1792), and Thomas
Fyshe Palmer, Unitarian minister and reformer, were sentenced to
fourteen and seven years' transportation respectively; William Skirving,
secretary of the British Convention, and Margarot were both sentenced
to fourteen years' transportation in January 1794. Obviously democrats
had to be circumspect about what they said or be prepared to suffer the
consequences.

At trial the pragmatics of the courtroom were crucial to framing what

---

The French Revolution and British Popular Politics (Cambridge, 1991), pp. 50–77; John Dinwiddy,
'Conceptions of Revolution in the English Radicalism of the 1790s', in Eckhart Hellmuth
(ed.), *The Transformation of Political Culture: England and Germany in the Late Eighteenth Century*
(Oxford, 1990), pp. 535–60; H. T. Dickinson, *Liberty and Property: Political Ideology in
Eighteenth-Century Britain* (London, 1977), chapter 7; Gregory Claeys, *Thomas Paine: Social and
Political Thought* (London, 1989), chapter 5.
[36] William Godwin, *Caleb Williams* (1794; Harmondsworth, 1988), preface, p. 4. Cf. Clive
Emsley, 'Repression, "Terror" and the Rule of Law in England During the Decade of the
French Revolution', *English Historical Review*, 100 (1985), pp. 801–25; *idem*, 'An Aspect of
Pitt's "Terror": Prosecutions for Sedition During the 1790s', *Social History*, 6 (1981),
pp. 155–84.

could or could not be said: specific kinds of language and arguments are deemed appropriate to the courtroom and the law. Courtrooms offer anything but an 'ideal-speech situation' (that is, a free zone of egalitarian exchange). A distinct hierarchy of speakers prevails: certain practitioners (i.e. judges and lawyers) are vested with an authority denied other speakers. Authorised speakers and authorised modes of speech hold sway. Democrats were therefore faced with a decision whether to seek legal representation or to defend themselves. Radicals shared a concern that lawyers might not conduct a bold and principled defence. Paine was, for example, less disappointed with the verdict in his trial – indeed, he managed to undermine his own lawyer's case – than he was with Thomas Erskine's failure to defend the actual principles of *The Rights of Man*.[37] Henry Erskine, Thomas' brother and among Scotland's most accomplished advocates, agreed to defend Muir, but only on the condition that the conduct of the defence be left entirely in his control and that Muir not address the court. Muir preferred to take his chances and defend himself.[38]

Reformers looked to the jury to counterbalance the advantages of the legal establishment. Because of the jury, the mysteries of the law had to be rendered into lay language. Indeed, the jury was the one constitutional institution that English Jacobins consistently praised.[39] Radicals inherited a pro-jury tradition of opinion dating from the seventeenth century in which the jury was seen as a representative institution whose origins were coeval with the ancient law itself and whose capacities included that of finding and interpreting law. Juries were vested with the authority to set aside laws and precedents deemed to be unconstitutional. In contrast to such broad claims for the jury's power, the role of the judge was, in this tradition, regarded as severely limited, reduced to explaining the law and maintaining order in the courtroom; judge-made law was condemned.[40]

Yet, as Godwin indicates in his letter to Gerrald, in practice the jury's status as the bulwark of liberty was fragile; vetting and packing juries on behalf of the crown was common practice. Juries were not necessarily

---

[37] A. O. Aldridge, *Man of Reason: The Life of Thomas Paine* (Philadelphia and New York, 1959), p. 185; *The Genuine Trial of Thomas Paine For a Libel Containing in the Second Part of Rights of Man* ... (London, 1792).

[38] 'Trial of Gerrald', cols. 806–7 n. Muir was trained as a lawyer.

[39] E. P. Thompson, 'Subduing the Jury', *London Review of Books*, 4 December 1986, p. 8; for example, Yorke, *These are the Times*, p. 10; *Tribune*, 45, 1795, pp. 225–37; *Cabinet*, 2, 1795, pp. 240–1.

[40] Thomas A. Green, *Verdict According to Conscience: Perspectives on the English Criminal Trial Jury* (Chicago, 1986), chapters 6–8.

favourable to the cause of democracy. Moreover, Gerrald was to be tried in Scotland where the legal system was much more severely rigged against radicals than in England. Juries were 'filtered into the box' in a way that made them creatures of the court. Jurors were essentially appointed by the Lord Justice-Clerk and his agent; the final jury was selected by the presiding judge; no peremptory challenges were allowed and challenges for cause were so narrowly defined as to be almost unheard of.[41] Thus Muir's objection that all the members of the jury selected to try his case were members of a loyal association of gentlemen who had publicly denounced him for his political views was not allowed.[42]

Cases at the High Court of Justiciary at Edinburgh were tried before a panel of judges presided over by the Lord Justice-Clerk Robert McQueen, Lord Braxfield, who was renowned for his coarseness and anti-reform sentiments. There was no grand jury presentment. The judges ruled, however, on the relevancy of the charges as a preliminary matter.[43] At this stage in the proceedings Braxfield and his colleagues consistently over stepped the bounds of proper legal procedure, offering what were, in effect, judgements on the cause. Compliant juries were more or less instructed on the question of guilt before either evidence or arguments were even heard. Yet all proceedings of the court were final; as Scotland's highest court, there was no appeal to any other authority and thus no remedy for judicial error or misconduct. The prejudices of the judges were undisguised. They repeatedly insisted that the reformers' demand for universal (male) suffrage itself constituted sedition or worse.[44] According to Braxfield, the first thing that had always to be acknowledged was that the British constitution was 'the best that ever was since the creation of the world'. As for political representation, the landed interest alone had the right to representation; 'as for the *rabble*, who have nothing but personal property, what hold has the nation of them?'[45]

'Bring me prisoners, and I'll find you law', Braxfield was reported to have told friends.[46] In 1793–4 finding law was a matter of some urgency.

---

[41] Lord [Henry Thomas] Cockburn, *An Examination of the Trials for Sedition Which Have Hitherto Occurred in Scotland*, 2 vols. (Edinburgh, 1888), vol. 1, pp. 80–2.

[42] *An Account of the Trial of Thomas Muir, Esq. . . . for Sedition* (Edinburgh, 1793), pp. 30–3.

[43] Cockburn, *Examination of the Trials for Sedition*, vol. 1, pp. 83–9. The other judges were Lords Eskgrove, Henderland, Swinton, Dunsinnan and Abercromby.

[44] *The Trial of the Rev. Thomas Fyshe Palmer before the Circuit Court of Judiciary . . . for Seditious Practices* (Edinburgh, 1793), p. 64, for Lord Eskgrove's view.

[45] *Trial of Thomas Muir*, pp. 131–2.

[46] Cockburn, *Examination of the Trials for Sedition*, vol. 1, p. 87.

Under the Act of Union (1707) Scottish and English law remained distinct. But in 1709 parliament had brought Scotland's law of treason into conformity with English law. Unlike the crime of high treason, however, the Scottish law of sedition was vague at best; indeed, it was unclear whether there had actually been any trials for sedition as such either before or after 1703, the date of a statute abolishing the death penalty for the crime of leasing-making. Such political cases had been tried either under the ancient law of treason or as leasing-making, a crime broadly defined in terms of uttering sentiments reproaching the king or his government. English common law does not use the term 'sedition', but considers seditiousness only as a quality of some other offence (for example, seditious libel or seditious meeting). It was also unclear what penalties pertained to the crime of sedition; much turned on whether the term 'banishment' encompassed transportation. However, in all the cases of sedition arising from the Edinburgh conventions, the judges treated the words and actions of the accused as falling little short of treason. They further asserted large discretionary power to determine sentences: anything short of death was permitted.[47] As radicals and their lawyers argued, the doctrine of sedition as practised in 1793–4 was really one of constructive sedition. At Margarot's trial Braxfield outlined his elastic concept of sedition:

the crime of sedition consists in poisoning the minds of the lieges, which may naturally in the end have a tendency to promote violence against the state; and endeavouring to create a dissatisfaction in the country, which nobody can tell where it will end, it will very naturally end in overt rebellion; and if it has that tendency, though not in the view of the parties at the time, yet if they have been guilty of poisoning the minds of the lieges, I apprehend that that will constitute the crime of sedition to all intents and purposes.[48]

Here guilt is ascribed to remote and unintended consequences of utterances; the requirement to prove clear intent to promote violence against the state slips away.

Set against the brutal design of Braxfield's court, notions of universal benevolence and truth's power to dispel error came up short. Yet such proceedings lent force to the rationalist critique of the uncertain and oppressive workings of the common law, particularly when judges were

---

[47] *Ibid.*, vol. I, pp. 1–75 and vol. II, pp. 100–32; David Hume, *Commentaries on the Law of Scotland, Respecting the Description and Punishment of Crimes* (Edinburgh, 1797), offers the fullest legal justification for the judges' ruling; *Acts of the Parliaments of Scotland, 1124–1707*, 12 vols. (1814–75), vol. XI, pp. 104–5, 'Act anent Leasing Makers and Slanderers'; *An Introduction to Scottish Legal History, by Various Authors* (Edinburgh, 1958), pp. 283–4.

[48] 'Proceedings on the Trial of Maurice Margarot', *State Trials*, vol. XXIII (1793–4), col. 766.

permitted an unrestricted power to determine judicial precedent and
thus make law. The free play of the law was deadly. Scottish proceedings
also gave ample support to views of the superiority of English law and
English constitutional history. The Scottish sedition trials are often
contrasted to the English trials of late 1794 at which Thomas Hardy,
Horne Tooke and Thelwall won acquittals on charges of high treason;
the Scottish trials are, however, perhaps best seen as the testing ground
for the treason trials. Law based on constructive sedition paved the way
for trials based on constructive treason and 'imaginary law'.[49] Robert
Dundas, Scottish Lord Advocate, who orchestrated the sedition trials
worked closely with his brother Henry Dundas, British Home Secretary.
Pitt firmly supported the Scottish judicial sentences and Henry Dundas
resisted parliamentary attempts to reform Scottish criminal procedure
so as to allow the House of Lords an appellate jurisdiction in certain
Scottish criminal cases.[50]

As for Gerrald's trial, the simple truth was that neither the verdict nor
the sentence was ever in doubt. Gerrald had the option, however, not to
return to stand trial. Allowed out on bail to go to London in order to
put his personal affairs in order, Gerrald was strongly urged by friends
to flee to republican shores. His old teacher Parr offered to find the
means to indemnify his bailsmen. Gerrald refused this generous offer,
explaining that honour compelled him to stand by those whom he had
led to the bar with him.[51] In the event, both Gerrald and his judges
understood that he was on trial for his life; sentenced to fourteen years'
transportation and suffering from tuberculosis, he did not survive the
first year in New South Wales.[52]

However, by returning to stand trial and thereby accepting his fate,
Gerrald reversed the conditions of discursive exchange; he was free to

---

[49] See John Barrell's superb 'Imaginary Treason, Imaginary Law', in his *The Birth of Pandora
and the Division of Knowledge* (Philadelphia, PA 1992), pp. 119–43.

[50] *The Parliamentary History of England* (London, 1817), vol. xxx (1792–4), cols. 1453–4 (24
February, 1794, for Dundas), 1572–6 (10 March, for Pitt); Godwin, *Friends of Liberty*, p. 313.
See *Life of Thelwall*, p. 146, for Gerrald's letter to Henry Dundas, charging that his sentence
had been determined in the English cabinet.

[51] Derry, *Dr Parr*, p. 155; *Life of Thelwall*, p. 124; *Gerrald, A Fragment*, p. 10; *Papers of the London
Corresponding Society*, p. 109, n. 21, for popular concerns that Gerrald would jump bail. John
D. Brims, 'The Scottish Democratic Movement in the Age of the French Revolution'
(Ph.D, 2 vols., Edinburgh University, 1983), vol. II, pp. 525, 542–7, argues against all
contemporary opinion that Gerrald might well have been acquitted had he not addressed
the court.

[52] Robert Hughes, *The Fatal Shore: The Epic of Australia's Founding* (New York, 1986), pp. 177–80;
George Rudé, *Protest and Punishment: The Story of the Social and Political Protesters Transported to
Australia, 1788–1868* (Oxford, 1978), p. 182. Gerrald was imprisoned for a year before being
transported, fostering the hope that he might be pardoned. He died in March 1796.

defend himself in any way that he saw fit. Nothing was to be gained by temporising. Without hope of persuading the judges or jury of his benevolence there remained, as Godwin suggested, an opportunity to convert thousands to 'the cause of reason and public justice'. Beyond the bench and jury box was ranged the audience that mattered. As Margarot had announced at the opening of his own trial: 'What I say this day will not be confined within these walls, but will spread far and wide.'[53] Gerrald understood that he was creating a literary text. The London Corresponding Society assumed the costs of sending a short-hand writer to Edinburgh. Not only was Gerrald's trial like all such political trials published in full, but his concluding defence was published separately as a cheap pamphlet.[54]

IV

Gerrald appeared to stand trial on Monday, 3 March 1794; however, proceedings were delayed for a week by Gerrald's request for legal representation. He based his request on his not being a native of Scotland and being ignorant of its laws; he had been turned down by all those to whom he had applied to take his case. Eventually two prominent Foxite lawyers, Adam Gillies and Malcolm Laing, accepted the case and conducted a well-argued defence.[55] The Solicitor-General, Robert Blair, led the prosecution in Dundas' absence.[56]

Gerrald left the more strictly legal part of his defence to his lawyers who rehearsed what were by then familiar legal arguments. Gillies maintained that sedition as charged was too vague, insisting on a distinction that Henry Erskine had pressed between verbal and 'real' sedition. Even were Gerrald to be found guilty, it must be only of the lesser crime of verbal sedition. Moreover, the objects of the Convention were not seditious; seeking reform based on universal suffrage and annual parliaments was not criminal. Delegates had not met violently or with arms, but only to petition for reform. As Laing argued, unable to

[53] *The Trial of Maurice Margarot, Delegate from London to the British Convention ... for Sedition* (London, 1794), p. 4.
[54] *Papers of the London Corresponding Society*, p. 112; *The Defence of Joseph Gerrald on a Charge of Sedition* ... (Edinburgh, 1794); *Gerrald, A Fragment*, p. 11. Gerrald's full trial sold for 4s and his defence for 1s 6d.
[55] John Clerk was also part of the defence team. The case was originally turned down, Laing explained, due to an aversion to giving the impression of a fair trial where none existed (Cockburn, *Examination of Trials for Sedition*, vol. 11, p. 44).
[56] There are several versions of Gerrald's trial, including *The Trial of Joseph Gerrald* ... (Edinburgh, 1794) which is based on the same comprehensive report as that in *State Trials*. All references are to the account in *State Trials*.

satisfy the exacting requirements to prove treason, the government charged sedition by way of inferences and innuendos capriciously attached to speeches and resolutions. Constructive treason having been abolished, a new crime, 'incapable of proof, and unknown in law', had been created, one of constructive sedition.[57] Gillies and Laing also argued that there was no basis for the criminal punishment of transportation in this case.[58] The defence strategy was really aimed at reducing the severity of judgement rather than seeking an acquittal. Unfortunately arguments that might otherwise have proved compelling, had previously been ruled on by the court: there was a common law sanction for both the crime of sedition and the punishment of transportation.

In fact, little was in doubt at the High Court of Justiciary except for Gerrald's speech. The trial proceedings lasted three days (10, 13 and 14 March); Gerrald addressed the court on the second day. His defence was the object of intense interest both within and outside the courtroom. Gerrald made no attempt to mollify the bench; he addressed the jury and the world. Battle lines between the defendant and the bench had been drawn much earlier. During the trial's preliminary stages Gerrald had pleaded that the judges rule on a personal objection to Lord Braxfield sitting on the bench on the grounds that he could prove that the Lord Justice-Clerk had prejudged the cause of every person who had been a member of the British Convention. Gerrald renewed a charge that Margarot had first made, alleging that at a private dinner Braxfield had declared that all members of the Convention deserved fourteen years' transportation and public whipping and that when it was objected that the people might not quietly endure such sentences, Braxfield replied that 'the mob would be the better for the spilling of a little blood'. The judges repelled Gerrald's plea in a manner that suggested the entire bench had prejudged the case.[59] Although he had also unsuccessfully challenged several jurors for cause, throughout the trial Gerrald maintained the formal expectation that the jury fulfil its duty to judge according to conscience.

Godwin had advised Gerrald to defend himself so that the jury and the world might 'feel your value'. To this end Gerrald drew on the cultural 'value' of the patriot martyr. He opened his defence by making an argument in terms of character; he was a selfless patriot, 'a simple individual' upon whom fell the 'sacred trust' of defending the rights of millions of people. He could easily have escaped trial; his very presence

[57] 'Trial of Gerrald', cols. 828–9, 834, 838, 841, 844–5, 872–3, 881–2.
[58] *Ibid.*, cols. 848–53, 885–89.
[59] *Ibid.*, cols. 808–14; Cockburn, *Examination of Trials for Sedition*, vol. II, pp. 28–32, 45–58.

proclaimed the purity of his principles and motives. By 1794, however, the word patriot had come under intense pressure; the context of war made it increasingly difficult to sustain universalist notions of patriotism. Gerrald turned, therefore, to England's own revolutionary heritage, framing his defence within the politics of the mid seventeenth century, 'a period that must be dear and valuable to every Englishman', and identifying himself with the canonised martyrs John Hampden and Algernon Sidney. The very term patriot had emerged as a fully fledged part of England's political vocabulary during the late seventeenth century and was directly linked to the self-sacrifices of Hampden, Sidney and Russell whose trials constituted defining moments in the Whig-libertarian tradition.[60]

Once again an individual stood poised against the tyranny of the state and law. According to Gerrald, the history of Britain furnished abundant examples of judges who had violated the law, as in 'the great case of ship-money'; he charged that the proceedings of the High Court of Justiciary 'too much resemble the proceedings of the Star-chamber'. The victories of the seventeenth century seemed to have gone unregistered in Scottish courts. In England, he pointed out, an individual's civil and legal rights were more securely protected than in Scotland; the articles of Union, however, provided 'that natives of both countries are entitled to the same privileges'.[61] Gerrald maintained a sustained critique of the Scottish law and its insulation from a British libertarian heritage framed in distinctly English terms.

Having cast himself and his judges in seventeenth-century roles, Gerrald proceeded to answer the specific charges against him. As in previous trials the indictment charged sedition based on the character of the Convention: the style 'The British Convention of the People', delegates addressing each other as 'citizen', dividing into 'sections', receiving reports from sections dated 'Liberty Hall', 'Liberty Stairs', 'First year of the British Convention' and reports prefixed 'vive la convention' and ending with the revolutionary song 'Ça Ira', granting honours of sitting, all this and more marked the Convention as an illegal body modelled on French revolutionary design and seeking to usurp the legitimate role of government. The sedition trials reinforced the

---

[60] Mary G. Dietz, 'Patriotism', in Terrence Ball, James Farr and Russell L. Hanson (eds.), *Political Innovation and Conceptual Change* (Cambridge, 1989), p. 183; Peter Karsten, *Patriot-Heroes in England and America* (Madison, 1978); Blair Worden, 'The Commonwealth Kidney of Algernon Sidney', *Journal of British Studies*, 24 (1985), pp. 1–40; Lois G. Schwoerer, 'William Lord Russell: The Making of a Martyr, 1683–1983', *Journal of British Studies*, 24 (1985), pp. 41–71.

[61] 'Trial of Gerrald', cols. 947–51.

warning of loyalism: the secret aim of popular reformers was violent revolution in imitation of Jacobin France.[62] These trials occasioned endless debate about the inherent seditiousness of French words, English words now inflected with French meaning, and symbols and gestures deemed unquestionably French in character. At Muir's trial evidence was presented of a letter impressed with a seal bearing a cap of liberty mounted on a spear (the symbol of the United Irishmen), of a request for a street organist to play 'Ça Ira', of a reading by Muir of an extract from Volney's *Ruins of Empires*. Margarot's trial featured a ludicrous cross-examination in which the defendant asked a witness whether he could be sure the word 'tocsin' (regarded as highly seditious by Dundas and the judges) was not instead of one French word, two Chinese words.[63]

Gerrald's lawyers maintained that the revolutionary posturing of the Convention delegates was mere foolishness, poor judgment but not sedition. Gerrald in turn dismissed the charge as 'ridiculous' and 'fallacious', a malicious attempt to make it appear as if he favoured cooperating with France. He dissociated himself from the insertion of French terms in the records of the Convention's proceedings. Moreover, there was nothing seditious about the French language; the very language of England's 'old law-proceedings are in that language'. The word citizen, he insisted, was 'a term of peace' denoting 'that relationship in which we stand to each other, as members of the same community, for the performance of our civil duties'.[64]

However, the importance of the realm of symbol and ritual to eighteenth-century politics undercut efforts to present the Convention's symbolic practices as innocuous. Margarot had marched to his trial attended by a procession headed by a twenty-foot tree of liberty in the shape of the letter M and carried on two poles by two former members of the Convention. The tree was demolished by a loyalist mob, the procession was broken up and Margarot was unceremoniously dragged into court. Contemporaries often contrasted Gerrald's dignified conduct to Margarot's reckless provocations. Nonetheless, Gerrald appeared at the bar dressed in contemporary French style, 'with unpowdered hair,

---

[62] See H. T. Dickinson, 'Popular Conservatism and Militant Loyalism, 1789–1814', in his edited volume, *Britain and the French Revolution* (London, 1989), pp. 103–125; *idem*, 'Popular Loyalism in Britain in the 1790s', in *Transformation of Political Culture*, pp. 503–33; Robert Hole, 'British Counter-Revolutionary Propaganda in the 1790s', in Colin Jones (ed.), *Britain and Revolutionary France: Conflict, Subversion and Propaganda* (Exeter, 1993), pp. 53–69.

[63] *Trial of Thomas Muir*, pp. 7, 14–15, 50, 68–70, 72, 119–20, 125; *Trial of Maurice Margarot*, pp. 65–6, and also 99, 105–6, 113–14, 119.

[64] 'Trial of Gerrald', cols. 836, 951–3.

hanging loosely down behind – his neck bare, and his shirt with a large collar, doubled over'. He might not defend the revolution and its symbols, but his costume signalled a refusal to abandon his allegiance to the egalitarianism encoded in the revolution.[65]

As for the Convention, Gerrald argued that its criminality must depend on its principles or its actual conduct. The object of the Convention was to procure by peaceful means universal suffrage and annual parliaments, objects conformable not only to the maxims of sound government 'but congenial to the spirit of the British government itself'. In a speech delivered at the Convention (21 November) that was charged in the indictment, Gerrald rested the right to universal suffrage on a dual claim:

I apprehend that we may justly claim it as our inheritance from nature; but we can with confidence ... appeal to antiquity for our title to this right; and it will be found to have been exercised by our ancestors in its fullest extent.

At the Convention he dwelt almost exclusively on reclaiming the heritage of Anglo-Saxon freedom, an emphasis reflected in the Convention's *Address*.[66]

At his trial, however, before summoning the ancient constitution – before speaking of the Anglo-Saxon assemblies of folkmoot, witena-gemot and myclegemot – Gerrald thought it necessary to review 'the fundamental principles of society itself'; man 'is by his nature social and rational', entering society to improve his faculties through common exercise of his powers of reason. His argument rested largely on the authority of Locke, quoting liberally from the *Two Treatises of Government* (1690). The great and universal object for which men formed themselves into society is 'the safe enjoyment of their lives and property'. Gerrald continued:

Now, as every man claims from nature a right of judging for himself, on the best manner of promoting his own interest, and no individual is born with any distinguishing mark of pre-eminence over his fellow-men ... so every act of authority exercised by one man over another, or by a legislature over the collective body of people, unless it be exercised by the consent of the individual, or of the collective body of the people governed, must be an act of tyranny.

Moreover, after the enactment of positive law, the authority of law depends on the continued consent of the majority of the people.

[65] Cockburn, *Examination of Trials for Sedition*, vol. ii, pp. 23–4, 43–4; idem., *Memorials of His Time* (Edinburgh, 1856), p. 71; Michael Roe, 'Maurice Margarot: A Radical in Two Hemispheres, 1792–1815', *Bulletin of the Institute of Historical Research*, 31 (1958), pp. 68–78.
[66] 'Trial of Gerrald', cols. 953, 816.

Gerrald, like Paine, resisted the notion that when men agree to come under government they surrender certain rights: 'They give up nothing; but by combining their own particular force with the force of others, they adopt a plan, by which they are enabled to possess their rights in greater security.' On the crucial connection between ownership of property and political rights, Gerrald claimed that all men in society were possessed of some form of property 'either inherited or acquired by his daily labour'. He also cited his own experience of American democracy as evidence against the view that universal suffrage was visionary or impractical.[67]

Only after having outlined the general principles on which society and government depended, did Gerrald move to England's history, going over ground familiar to scholars of the ancient constitution and supporting historical claims to universal suffrage and annual parliaments. He cited Montesquieu and translated passages from Tacitus' *Germania* to demonstrate that the 'rudiments of our excellent constitution' were to be found in the liberty of the Teutonic forests. In the earliest stages of society, 'when commerce was scarcely budding', almost every (male) inhabitant owned a portion of land and participated in the institutions of Anglo-Saxon government. All freemen, meaning all those who were not slaves, were entitled to vote. Personal slavery having been abolished in the reign of Charles II, it followed that all British citizens 'being freemen, they are of course entitled to all those privileges which even the express letter of our early constitution conferred upon them'. Gerrald grafted notions of the cyclical recovery of lost political rights onto the Scottish Enlightenment model of society's progress through four stages of property from primitive to commercial.[68]

While acknowledging that he was not as well versed in ancient Scottish history, Gerrald reported that his readings on the public law and early constitution of Scotland uncovered striking similarities between the constitutions of Scotland and England. In Scotland 'the whole community of the kingdom', meaning every freeman, was represented in passing those laws which it swore to maintain. Such coincidences between the early constitutions of England and Scotland could only be explained by the fact that 'they must be congenial to the natural order of all government itself'.[69] History's diversity was thus reconciled with universal law in a typical Enlightenment move.

---

[67] Ibid., cols. 948, 953–7.

[68] Ibid., cols. 958–9. Government is generally regarded as being founded in the third stage dominated by landed property.

[69] 'Trial of Gerrald', cols. 960–1. He drew primarily on Gilbert Stuart, *Observations Concerning*

Moreover, the ancient constitutions of England and Scotland provided a true foundation for political union and liberty. Throughout his defence Gerrald demanded that the laws of Scotland be brought into line with English law: one law, known to all citizens, should prevail throughout Britain. He charged as a violation of the articles of Union that by merely crossing the Tweed a man could be transported for an action that he might commit with impunity in England. The sedition trials touched off a wider debate over the character of the Union and thus the meaning of 'Britishness' itself.[70]

In his speech to the Convention, Gerrald had repeated 'citizen' Alexander Callender's charge that from the time of the Union between England and Scotland the people of both countries had suffered 'the greatest encroachments ... on public liberty, but if that union has operated to rob us of our rights, let it be the object of the present one to regain them'. A new, democratic union was to be formed between the nations of Scotland and England. Gerrald had also given the Glorious Revolution short-shrift as not having produced 'the advantages which might have been expected from such an event' – it reconfirmed the right to alter the line of succession and change the constitution, but failed to recover the people's ancient right to vote; still, he continued, the present government 'no more resembles the revolution, than a dead putrid carcase does a living body'. The Glorious Revolution and the Union of Scotland to England and Wales were sacred moments closely linked in British history; indeed, the invention of Great Britain and its identity as a Protestant nation rested on this twin foundation. Gerrald devalued both. It was in defence of these views that Gerrald uttered the words quoted at the beginning of this essay, condemning the present government as 'a libel upon our real constitution'. He carefully documented the depredations of the settlement of 1688, citing the role of placemen and pensioners in parliament, the Septennial Act and the unrestricted power of ministers. How could the jury, he asked, convict him of attempting to overthrow a system 'of which it has been proved to you not a vestige remains'? Under such conditions the Convention was fully justified in meeting peacefully to discuss the best means of reclaiming the rights of Britons.[71]

---

the *Public Law and the Constitutional History of Scotland with Occasional Remarks Concerning English Antiquity* (Edinburgh, 1779). Gerrald argued that the word '*magnates*' found in the laws of Robert I on further examination would be discovered to be 'strictly applicable to the representation of the people', noting that in England the word appears in the same sense and citing Rymer and Petyt.

[70] 'Trial of Gerrald', cols. 968, 683, 689; *Parliamentary History of England*, vol. xxx (1792–4), cols. 1486–576 (10 March 1794), vol. xxxi (1794–5), cols. 54–83 (25 March).

[71] 'Trial of Gerrald', cols. 963–6. See John D. Brims, 'The Scottish "Jacobins", Scottish

In his opening statement the Solicitor-General had underscored the revolutionary implications of Gerrald's position, countering that all subjects owed allegiance to the constitution established at the revolution which remained firmly in place:

We are not here in a state of nature, we are not savages, and now for the first time to choose a constitution for ourselves ... From our birth we owe allegiance to the Constitution established at the Revolution, and we are not to venture to say that another constitution would do better in its place ... and no body of men have a liberty to say that we will indulge in speculation, and there is no harm in speculation.[72]

In his own reply, Gerrald maintained that 'the excellence of the British constitution', 'the constant theme of the supporters of government', must be open to the exercise of reason and not rest merely on blind faith. By disallowing the free use of reason, loyalists resembled supporters of the Catholic Church at the Reformation:

the very same kind of arguments, which at the dawn of the Reformation were made use of by the Catholic clergy, who were endeavouring to hold the people in the fetters of superstition, are now made use of by those very persons, who for purposes equally selfish, are repressing the progress of political information ... Religion in those days, it seems, like government in the present, was to be believed and confided in without being examined.

In fact, Gerrald noted that Burke's lament that 'learning should be trodden down under the hoof of the [sic] swinish multitude' was borrowed from 'a monkish writer' of the sixteenth century deploring the publication of the scripture for the common people.[73]

Gerrald rejected the doctrine of constitutional immutability on the grounds that every nation had the right to improve its mode of governance. To deny this right is to say 'that our ancestors had a privilege we have not a right to exercise ... no generation can annihilate or curtail the rights of a subsequent one'. Gerrald paraphrased Paine, but turned to the seventeenth-century commonwealthmen for explicit authority, quoting from Sidney's *Discourses on Government* (1698):

Laws and constitutions ought to be weighed, and whilst all due reverence is paid to such as are good, every nation may not only retain in itself a power of changing or abolishing all such as are not so, but ought to exercise that power according to the best of their understanding.

Nationalism and the British Union', in Roger A. Mason (ed.), *Scotland and England, 1286–1815* (Edinburgh, 1987), pp. 247–65; Linda Colley, *Britons: Forging the Nation, 1707–1837* (New Haven and London, 1992), chapter 1.
[72] 'Trial of Gerrald', col. 937.   [73] Ibid., cols. 968–9.

Sidney further observes that some writers (i.e. Machiavelli) have proposed a necessity 'of reducing every state, once in an age or two to the integrity of its first principles' and determining if such principles are good or evil, for if this is not done 'no change would render errors perpetual' and deprive humankind of the possibility of improvement founded on experience and 'the right use of reason'. In a flourish that brought instant rebukes from the bench, Gerrald asserted: 'The revolution was an innovation; the reformation was an innovation; christianity itself was an innovation.'

'All you have been saying is sedition', interrupted Braxfield, 'and now, my lords, he is attacking christianity'. Lord Henderland added that to compare the present situation with that at the revolution, 'when the forms of civil government ... were done away with by the infringement of all law; or with that period, in which the sovereign is said to have forfeited his life' constituted 'a most indecent defence'. Gerrald denied any intention to attack Christianity or to draw a parallel between the present situation and that of 1688.[74] However, his defence constantly brought to view enshrined moments of origination. Gerrald implied that the present was a time for refounding British liberty, for unravelling the skein of precedent back to first principles to be re-examined in the light of reason.

The concept of the convention itself carried distinct connotations of constitution-making, republicanism and political refounding. The Convention's adoption of a motion to make its sittings 'permanent' in the event of certain constitutional transgressions, including the introduction of an English convention act, any attempt to disband the Convention, the suspension of habeas corpus and the introduction of foreign troops into Britain or Ireland, was highlighted in the indictments at all the sedition trials. Much emphasis was placed on the Convention's resolution to resist any action 'subversive of our own acknowledged constitutional liberties' and to continue to assemble 'and consider of the best means by which we can accomplish a real representation of the people, and annual election, until compelled to desist by superior force'. True to the spirit of this resolution, Gerrald and his fellow delegates had refused to disperse on the order of legal authorities who had to forcibly remove the presiding officers, including Gerrald, from their places.[75]

In reply to this count Gerrald expressed his surprise to hear the principle of resistance to which 'we owe our liberties' denied. Sidney, Grotius and Locke all confirmed the right to resist unlawful government.

---

[74] Ibid., cols. 970–2. According to Cockburn, *Memorials*, p. 116, Gerrald added that all great men had been reformers 'even our Saviour himself', to which Braxfield chuckled under his breath, 'Muckle he made o'that, he was hanget'.

[75] 'Trial of Gerrald', cols. 820, 822–3.

It was for his continual struggle against tyranny and faction that 'that sage and hero, the immortal Sidney . . . fell a martyr to the liberties of his country'. The principle of resistance was one 'deeply interwoven in our constitution', supported not only by speculative writers but writers on British law. Gerrald quoted Blackstone on the constitutional right to bear arms. The principle of resistance was confirmed at the Glorious Revolution; it was neither new nor dangerous, although Gerrald again stressed the peaceful intent of the Convention and the conditional character of the Convention's resolution. He insisted, however, on the right to resist oppression, including unconstitutional acts of parliament.[76]

Gerrald's long peroration was styled in high and moving tones, drawing on the rhetorical traditions of libertarian defence and classical republicanism. 'Whatever may become of me, my principles will last forever. Individuals may perish; but truth will last forever.' Dungeons, exile, death itself could not persuade him to abandon the justice of his principles. He quoted a well-known passage from Sidney, a declaration of the patriot-martyr's creed: 'I hope that I shall die in the same principles in which I have lived.' Gerrald's own words invoked the standards of republican virtue and were themselves to become part of the rhetorical memory of democrats.

Surely the experience of all ages should have taught our rulers, that persecutions never can efface principles; and that the thunders of the state will prove impotent, when wielded against patriotism, innocence, and firmness. Whether, therefore, I shall be permitted to glide gently down the current of life, in the bosom of my native country, among those kindred spirits whose approbation constitutes the greatest comfort of my living; whether I be doomed to drag out the remainder of my existence amidst thieves and murderers, a wandering exile on the bleak and melancholy shores of New Holland, my mind equal to either fortune, is prepared to meet the destiny that awaits it:

> . . . 'seu me tranquilla senectus
> Expectat, seu mors atris circumvolat alias;
> Dives, inops, Romae, seu fors ita jusserit, exsul.'

Gerrald placed his cause in the jury's hands: 'You are Britons. You are Freemen.' After listening to the judges' summations and withdrawing for only twenty minutes, the jury returned a guilty verdict. The judges pronounced the sentence of transportation as 'the mildest that can be inflicted'.[77]

---

[76] Ibid., cols. 977–8.

[77] Ibid., cols. 994–6, 1002–12. The Latin quotation, from Horace's *Satires*, book II, i, lines 57–60, translates: 'Whether a serene old age awaits me, or Death hovers round on sable

V

In conclusion, it is worth reflecting briefly on Gerrald's achievement and Godwin's advice – on the gap between practice and theory. First, we should note that trials were occasions of the spoken word and we have no direct access to Gerrald's speech as delivered in court; like most contemporaries, who read rather than heard his speech, we are left with a printed text. However, we know that contemporaries praised Gerrald's skills as an orator; they were particularly struck by his capacity to speak forcefully before a hostile bench and despite poor health. In an age that prided itself on rhetorical eloquence Gerrald's speech was widely judged among the most brilliant of its kind. 'Hitherto I had never known what public eloquence was', observed the poet Thomas Campbell who as a sixteen-year-old was present at court. 'Gerrald's speech annihilated the remembrance of all the eloquence that had ever been heard within the walls of that house. He quieted the judges ... and produced a silence in which you might have heard a pin fall to the ground.'[78]

The formal art of rhetoric had its origins in Greek and Roman courts of law. Gerrald had been schooled in both classical literature and the law, the distinguishing markers of eighteenth-century polite culture. The Scottish jurist Lord Cockburn regarded Gerrald's speech as the only one by a seditious prisoner that was entirely free of 'all impudence and bluster' or of anything 'vulgar'. 'Throughout', he commented, 'it is the sedition of a literary gentleman.'[79] The comment is telling. Polished and formal, Gerrald's mode of expression contrasts with the vernacular style of political address pioneered by Paine and favoured by Godwin; there was nothing plain or 'vulgar' about Gerrald's speech.[80] Replete with rhetorical devices and Latin quotations (which Gerrald usually translated), allusions to Roman history and references to learned authority, Gerrald relied on more than transparent reason to establish meaning and to assert his own competence as a speaker.

Above all, Gerrald showed himself to be motivated by sincerity and benevolence. For the young romantic poets he represented a model of

---

wing, rich or poor, in Rome, or if fortune so bid, in exile.' I am grateful to Professor Thomas McGinn for identifying this quotation.

[78] Cockburn, *Examination of the Trials for Sedition*, vol. II, p. 83 n. See also *Quarterly Review*, 39 (1829), p. 281.

[79] Cockburn, *Examination of the Trials for Sedition*, vol. II, pp. 79–80. See also reviews of his published trial, *Critical Review*, 13, 1795, pp. 104–6; *British Critic*, 4, November 1794, pp. 559–60; *Gerrald, A Fragment*, pp. 12, 20–3.

[80] Cf. Godwin to [Thelwall], 18 September 1794, Abinger Collection, advising Thelwall to 'strip' his defence 'of all superfluous appendages; banish from it all useless complexity'.

republican virtue. Coleridge, who visited Gerrald in prison, ranked him among 'that small but glorious band' composing the highest order of 'thinking and disinterested Patriots'. Southey sought Gerrald's advice on pantisocracy and poetry. The calm fortitude with which he met his fate – his 'unconquerable mind' to quote Southey's poem dedicated to Gerrald – was widely praised.[81] His personal comportment and character were inseparable from his politics – although it is difficult to disentangle the influences of neo-stoicism, rationalism and Puritanism.

But whereas universal benevolence, natural justice and reason are abstract concepts (particularly for Godwin), Gerrald fixed his political persona by identification with the patriot-martyrs of the seventeenth century and their cause, particularly with Sidney's republicanism and stoicism. He modelled parts of his defence on Sidney's trial and writings. Added to his defence when published separately were parallel passages between the speeches of Jeffreys in Sidney's case and Braxfield in his own. Yet this was just what Godwin advised against. In his letter to Thelwall, he warns: 'I understand that you are endeavouring to accumulate material from Sidney and others. I am afraid you are on a wrong scent.'[82] In an important respect, however, Thelwall and Gerrald were on the right scent. For political trials offered irresistible opportunities for retracing the story of the nation's past. By turning to a radicalised and highly selective version of Britain's own 'century of revolution', Gerrald engaged important matters of national memory, constitutional rights and 'true' patriotism.

To be a citizen of the world has always been problematic. By 1794, however, it had become particularly difficult to defend one's allegiance to universal liberty through reference to France. Moreover, it appeared to many British observers, including many radicals, that the revolutionaries had failed to profit from 'the wisdom of experience'; their over-reliance on ideas had led, as Burke charged, to violent anarchy.[83]

---

[81] Samuel Taylor Coleridge, *Lectures 1795 On Politics and Religion*, ed. Lewis Patton and Peter Mann (London, 1971), pp. 40–1; *New Letters of Robert Southey*, ed. Kenneth Curry, 2 vols. (New York and London, 1965), vol. 1, pp. 86, 91; Nicholas Roe, *Wordsworth and Coleridge: The Radical Years* (Oxford, 1988), pp. 8–9; Geoffrey Carnall, *Robert Southey and His Age: The Development of a Conservative Mind* (Oxford, 1960), pp. 49–50.

[82] Godwin to [Thelwall], 18 September 1794, Abinger Collection; *Life of John Thelwall*, p. 207. Both Thelwall and Gerrald maintained that their papers were not sealed when seized. Gerrald also argued that the prosecution must prove matters of handwriting. Sidney made similar arguments pertaining to the confiscated manuscript of his *Discourses* (*State Trials*, vol. IX (1682–4), 'The Trial of Colonel Algernon Sidney', cols. 818–1022). See also the manuscript notes of Thelwall's lecture 'Historical Strictures on the Trials of Hampden, Sidney, and Russell', PRO, TS 11/951/3495.

[83] See, for example, Mary Wollstonecraft, *An Historical and Moral View of the Origin and Progress of the French Revolution* (1795; repr. New York, 1975), pp. 510–11, 467, 252, 300–4.

During the 1790s 'anti-theoretical rhetoric' became a central theme in defining British nationalism: British experience stood opposed to French theory.[84] By returning, however, to the 'experience' of British liberty, and particularly to the terrain of the seventeenth century, Gerrald might mediate tensions between experience and theory, historicism and universalism, nationalism and internationalism, elite and demotic political cultures.

There were distinct parallels between the 1640s–50s and the 1790s; in both periods fundamental questions about the nature and source of political authority were thrown open to popular debate and scrutiny. During the 1640s radicals constructed arguments based on natural reason and the free consent of the people, tracing government back to original principles. Levellers reinterpreted the common lawyers' version of the ancient constitution; where Coke saw continuity, Levellers believed that the Norman conquerors had obliterated Anglo-Saxon liberty and on this basis condemned the common law as a Norman imposition. While Levellers and army agitators were prepared to argue that as 'men of the present age' they were free to redesign government without reference to the past, many clung to the belief that natural reason had been embodied in the Anglo-Saxon constitution.[85] In similar fashion through his rendering of the Anglo-Saxon golden age, Gerrald seeks quasi-historical ground for rational liberty.

However, there was little direct continuity between reformers of the 1790s and the Leveller tradition; with a few significant exceptions, Leveller works were not widely available or well known.[86] In contrast, Hampden, Sidney and Russell were the mythologised patriots of eighteenth-century Whig-libertarianism. Sidney's *Discourses* was available in a number of eighteenth-century editions and by 1794 D. I. Eaton was publishing an edition in cheap weekly instalments. Sidney's trial was reprinted in countless editions. Sidney was revered by both the American and French revolutionaries – busts of him were carried in French revolutionary processions.[87] To be sure, the Whigs had refigured Sidney

---

[84] David Simpson, *Romanticism, Nationalism, and the Revolt Against Theory* (Chicago, 1993), p. 4, and chapters 2 and 3.

[85] Hill, 'Norman Yoke', pp. 78–82; J. G. A. Pocock, *The Ancient Constitution and the Feudal Law: English Historical Thought in the Seventeenth Century* (New York, 1967), pp. 125–6. Cf. R. B. Seaberg, 'The Norman Conquest and the Common Law: The Levellers and the Argument from Continuity', *Historical Journal*, 24 (1981), pp. 791–806.

[86] Cf. F. K. Donnelly, 'Levellerism in Eighteenth and Early Nineteenth-Century Britain', *Albion*, 20 (1988), pp. 261–9.

[87] Karsten, *Patriot-Heroes*, p. 131; Worden, 'Commonwealth Kidney', p. 33; Caroline Robbins, *The Eighteenth Century Commonwealthman* (New York, 1968), p. 396; Alan Craig Houston, *Algernon Sidney and the Republican Heritage in England and America* (Princeton, 1991), chapter 6;

as a Whiggish supporter of the principles of 1688; they had long before drawn back from his republicanism.[88] But although Sidney wrote the *Discourses* between 1681 and 1683, his politics (like Milton's) were forged in the republican experiment of 1649–60 and shared much in common with the writings of Levellers like Edward Sexby with whom he was closely associated.[89] As Sidney declared just before his execution, he stood as a witness for 'that old cause in which I was from my youth engaged'.[90] Through Sidney Gerrald managed to reach out, however obliquely, to the experience of 1649 as opposed to that of 1688. He not only embraced Sidney as patriot-martyr, but re-engaged Sidney's classical republican argument for a frequent return to first principles, his contract theory and natural-law justifications for rebellion. Moreover, Gerrald reproduced a tension similar to that found in Sidney's own writings between claims based on natural law and those founded on the ancient constitution. Just as Sidney could not resist countering Filmer's arguments against the ancient constitution, Gerrald was drawn to rehearse the saga of 'our real constitution' and to link his counter-constitutionalist understanding to concepts of reason and natural right.[91]

My point is not that Gerrald somehow constructed a highly coherent political text or that he staged a systematic recovery of seventeenth-century republicanism; quite the contrary. But it is often the 'looseness', the openness and incoherences in a text, that renders political rhetoric persuasive. Moreover, it is not that one cannot imagine a Godwinian defence at law; indeed, Godwin's best friend Thomas Holcroft wrote one, although he was not allowed to deliver it after the government dropped charges of high treason against him.[92] What is difficult to imagine is a rationalist defence as compelling as Gerrald's actual argument. Indeed, in his own *Cursory Strictures* (1794) which set out the defence position for the English treason trials, Godwin argued along

Harold T. Parker, *The Cult of Antiquity and the French Revolutionaries* (Chicago, 1937), pp. 172–7. For the continued importance of a 'remembered Interregnum' to British radicalism, see Antony Taylor's contribution to this volume.

[88] Dickinson, *Liberty and Property*, pp. 61–2.

[89] Jonathan Scott, *Algernon Sidney and the English Republic, 1623–1677* (Cambridge, 1988), pp. 115–17, and chapters 6 and 7.

[90] 'The Apology of Algernon Sydney in the Day of his Death', *State Trials*, vol. IX (1682–4), col. 916.

[91] See Jonathan Scott, *Algernon Sidney and the Restoration Crisis, 1677–1683* (Cambridge, 1991), chapters 10 and 11. For connections between Locke and Sidney's political thought, see Mark Knights, 'Petitioning and the Political Theorists: John Locke, Algernon Sidney and London's "Monster" Petition of 1680', *Past and Present*, 138 (1993), particularly pp. 106–8.

[92] Thomas Holcroft, *A Narrative of Facts, Relating to a Prosecution for High Treason . . . And the Defence the Author had Prepared, if He Had Been Brought to Trial* (London, 1795).

strictly constitutionalist lines that the Treason Act of Edward III defined treason in narrow and precise legal fashion.[93] Possessed of the utopian desire for communication without restraint and for meanings that were transparent and stable, rationalist theories of expression were often devoid of practical force. Gerrald's trial defence may serve to underscore, therefore, a final point about the constrained and contextual nature of all meaningful speech. In a sense, Gerrald was 'free' to say whatever he wished. The physical violence of the law could not suppress a moment of unrestricted utterance. Such freedom was, however, limited by rhetorical conditions governing the occasion and by Gerrald's desire to persuade hearers and readers of his case. Rather than destroying the prospects for meaningful expression, this context was what made meanings possible.[94] To speak effectively was to speak according to the conventions of trial defence and within the contested, unstable boundaries of 'our real constitution'.

[93] William Godwin, *Cursory Strictures on the Charges Delivered by Lord Chief Justice Eyre to the Grand Jury, October 2, 1794* (London, 1794), reprinted in William Godwin, *Uncollected Writings* (Gainesville, 1968).

[94] See the title essay in Stanley Fish, *There's No Such Thing as Free Speech And It's a Good Thing, Too* (Oxford, 1994).

3

∾

The English people and their constitution after Waterloo: parliamentary reform, 1815–1817

JONATHAN FULCHER

The effects on British society of the return of peace in 1815 were profound, and have been well documented by contemporaries and historians. The impact of peace on political argument has been examined to a much lesser extent, either because political argument has been seen as a reflection of economic processes and therefore historians have sought to 'get beyond the rhetoric' to the 'real' economic processes at work, or because the later resurgent radical career from 1817 seemed more important as an object for analysis.

It is a pity that the political debates of those first heady months of peace have received little attention. Not only has this obscured the process by which radicalism took on its distinctive post-war features, but it has left us with an account of the post-war parliamentary reform movement which is overdue for revision. Despite the recent welcome attention to the language of radicalism in the post-war period, the character of the attendant parliamentary reform movement in the historiography has changed little. A resurgent radical press writing for a new self-conscious working-class audience, arguing more stridently than ever before for an overhaul of the whole aristocratic political system, a confrontationalist mass platform, a developing split between moral and physical force reformers and a demagogic leadership are the features of this movement highlighted in the historiography.[1] In an attempt to get beyond the language to the 'real' formation of consciousness going on

---

[1] J. Belchem, *'Orator' Hunt: Henry Hunt and English Working-Class Radicalism* (Oxford, 1985); E. P. Thompson, *The Making of the English Working Class*, (Harmondsworth, 1980); J. Dinwiddy, *From Luddism to the First Reform Bill: Reform in England, 1810–1832* (Oxford, 1986); H. Perkin, *The Origins of Modern English Society, 1780–1880*, (London, 1963); D. G Wright, *Popular radicalism* (London: 1988).

during this period, historians have neglected the way in which political language and argument shaped the aspirations, aims and objectives of the movement, and the way in which the political context is crucial for understanding these developments.[2] This essay seeks to flesh out this political context.

The 'fiscal-military' state reached its apogee at the end of the wars,[3] the pressure on the financial system was then at its greatest, and the demobilisation of regular and militia forces put even more strain on parochial rate-payers. Recent research has also suggested that the decade 1811–21 saw both tax revenue per capita and taxes as a share of the national income reach their peak of intensity.[4] An oppositional language which concentrated on taxation as the index of corruption and the necessity of reform to offset its baneful effects was peculiarly placed to mobilise powerful arguments and develop a large following in these circumstances. The role of other political groups in relation to the reformers was also important for the development of an extra-parliamentary reform movement. Whig reluctance to embrace any kind of constitutional reform, and their decision to press in parliament only for retrenchment, was to prompt radicals to look elsewhere for support for their reform agenda. Further, the revolutionary fears sparked by such radical moves galvanised the loyal. Their trenchant opposition to radical accounts of the constitution was to prove important for the course of the post-war parliamentary reform movement.

Also, the return of peace made it possible for reformers to say much more about domestic questions, without being taunted with accusations of harbouring disloyal French sympathies.[5] Reformers of the English constitution were more easily able to legitimate their political activity with assertions of their patriotism.[6] During the wars it had been difficult

2   E. Biagini and A. Reid, *Currents of Radicalism: Popular Radicalism, Organised Labour and Party Politics in Britain, 1850–1914* (Cambridge, 1991), p. 5

3   J. Brewer, *The Sinews of Power: War, Money and the English state, 1688–1783* (London, 1989); P. Harling and P. Mandler, 'From "Fiscal–Military" State to Laissez-Faire State, 1760–1850', *Journal of British Studies*, 32 (1993), pp. 44–70, esp. p. 52.

4   P. Mathias, 'Taxation and Industrialization in Britain, 1700–1870', in *The Transformation of England: Essays in the Economic and Social History of England in the 18th Century* (London, 1979), p. 122; see also P. O'Brien, 'The Political Economy of British Taxation, 1660–1815', *Economic History Review*, 2nd series, 41 (1988), pp. 1–32.

5   J. Dinwiddy, 'England', in O. Dann and J. Dinwiddy (eds.), *Nationalism in the Age of the French Revolution* (London, 1988), p. 70.

6   William Cobbett, in an article to the Merchants of England, argued that the supposedly 'French' principles he and other reformers had articulated were all English, see *Cobbett's Weekly Political Register* (hereafter *CPR*), 29 April 1815, *passim*. The *Independent Whig* argued this line even more forcefully on 16 July 1815, p. 229: 'We acknowledge the bravery, but cannot discover the glory of an English conquest over the principles of the English Constitution.'

to develop reform arguments, except at extraordinary moments.[7] 'Patriotic' activity was easily characterised as dubious unless directed towards winning the war: it was hard to separate the 'patriotic' and 'loyal' strands of national identity at a time when France was the enemy.[8] It was even harder to defend dissent as patriotic in such circumstances. The marginalisation of anti-war feeling was partially effected by imputations of disloyalty.[9] Simultaneously, it became more difficult for loyalists who wished to maintain the status quo in Church and state to tar the reformers with the taint of French ideas.[10]

I

The debates over the Corn Laws and the property tax demonstrated starkly how matters in Europe could overwhelm domestic concerns, and allow the government both to avoid discussion of domestic questions, and to taunt with cries of 'Jacobin and Leveller' those who would treat with Napoleon on his escape from Elba.[11] Playing the patriotic card was extremely effective in stifling not only opposition, but also debate.[12] A petitioning campaign against any protective legislative shield for farmers began in February 1815. The masses of petitions against government

[7]   Peter Spence, 'The Rise and Fall of Romantic Radicalism, 1800–1810' Ph.D, (Cambridge University, 1993), see esp. p. 17. For the massive impetus given by the war to the sale of newspapers, see J. Holland Rose, 'The Unstamped Press', *English Historical Review*, 12 (1897), pp. 711–26, p. 712.

[8]   L. Colley 'Whose Nation? Class and National Consciousness in Britain, 1750–1815', *Past and Present*, 113 (1986), pp. 97–117. On patriotism and its meanings in this period see M. Taylor, 'John Bull and the Iconography of Public Opinion in England c. 1712–1929', *Past and Present*, 134 (1992), pp. 93–128, p. 126. See also *idem*, 'Radicalism and Patriotism, 1848–1859' (Ph.D, Cambridge University, 1990). C. Emsley, *British Society and the French Wars, 1793–1815* (London, 1979), pp. 112 ff., writes of a 'general trend towards loyalty' during and after the invasion scare at the turn of the century, p. 118.

[9]   J. C. Cookson, *The Friends of Peace: Anti-War Liberalism in England, 1793–1815* (Cambridge, 1982), esp. pp. 116–117, 167–8, 174. See also *CPR*, 5 February 1814, col. 176: 'The friends of freedom, under the name of Jacobins, Levellers, Democrats, or what not, have often been accused of wishing success to the French ... This was a very foul and base way of opposing arguments in favour of a reform of notorious abuses.'

[10] [Francis Jeffrey] 'State and Prospects of Europe', *Edinburgh Review*, April 1814, p. 37.

[11] Reform of abuses, it was argued, should take place only 'when there is great tranquillity at home, and little engagement abroad'; R. Hunt, *Letter to Robert Pemberton, Mayor of Shrewsbury, on Preserving the Framework of the British Constitution, while Correcting the Vices of the Times* (Shrewsbury, 1809), p. 10.

[12] Reformers were tired of this labelling after twenty years of being on the defensive. George Ensor, the Irish radical, was annoyed that patriotism had almost come to mean hatred of all things French; see his pamphlet *On the state of Europe in January 1816* (London, 1816), p. 109. William Roscoe had complained of this vilification of any kind of dissent for some years, see for instance, his *Remarks on the Proposals Made to Great Britain, for Opening Negotiations for Peace in the year 1807* (London, 1808), p. xii, and his *Answer to a Letter from Mr John Merritt, on the Subject of Parliamentary Reform* (Liverpool, 1812).

interference in the corn trade far outnumbered those in favour, and exposed the depth of feeling in the community.[13] The prospect of disorder occasioned by high grain prices worried many.[14] But the strongest argument against the Corn Bill was made by linking such protection to the exorbitant taxation and high prices of the war years.[15] Nearly all anti-protection petitions published in newspapers and laid before parliament in early 1815 argued that privations had been cheerfully borne for many years in the interests of the state and the war effort. With the return of peace, a relaxation of burdens was expected and demanded.[16]

The discussion of the Corn Bill in parliament shattered this widely held expectation and riots resulted in the first week in March 1815.[17] Protests and petitions kept up the pressure on the government until, on 11 March 1815, it was announced with shock that Napoleon had escaped from Elba. By 13 March, the tumults against the Corn Bill had subsided and the government seized the initiative to pass the bill on 20 March without much further protest. The starkness of the alteration in the climate of opinion, particularly in London, was evidence of the power of the European situation to dominate the political terrain. *The Times*, an erstwhile sympathiser with those protesting the protectionist moves, argued that the possibility for war having greatly increased on Napoleon's reappearance, the attitude to the Corn laws ought now to be seen in a different light. Unanimity was needed to defeat the French.[18] Reformers, too, deemed it necessary to scale down some of their activities in the face of potential hostilities.[19]

The debate over the property tax suffered a similar fate. Petitions were raised against it in 1814, buttressed by arguments similar to those marshalled against the Corn Bill.[20] Vansittart's budget proposals of early 1815 acknowledged that the property tax and other war taxes

---

[13]   *The Times*, 7 March 1815.   [14]   *The Times*, 21, 27 February 1815.

[15]   David Buchanan, 'Corn Laws', *Edinburgh Review*, February 1815, p. 504.

[16]   *The Times*, 2 March 1815: see reports of meetings in Parish of Saint Mary Newington, Parish of St Mary, Whitechapel, 28 February 1815, *The Times*, 2 March 1815; St Clements Danes, Strand, 1 March 1815, *The Times*, 3 March 1815. See also *idem*, 3 March 1815, Ward of Bishopsgate, 28 February 1815.

[17]   See Eldon to Sidmouth, 6 March 1815, Public Record Office (PRO) HO 42/143, fo. 85. See also Eldon to Beckett, 8 March 1815, PRO, HO 42/143, fos. 83–4. *The Times*, 6–10 March 1815. Riots occurred in Birmingham and Norwich, Birmingham bench to Sidmouth, 2 March 1815, HO 42/143, fo. 19.

[18]   *The Times*, 21 March 1815; *Hansard's Parliamentary Debates*, 30, 1815, cols. 256 ff.

[19]   See, for instance, *Resolutions and Petitions Put Before the People of Nottingham by a Committee of Reformers*, 10 May 1815, HO 42/144, fo. 106.

[20]   *Hansard*, 30, 9 February 1815, col. 693

would have to be abandoned in peace-time, but once again called for their continuance after Napoleon had returned in triumph to Paris.[21]

II

Despite the failure of the agitation against the Corn Laws, another mass petitioning effort rejecting the property tax was mounted in early 1816. It marked the start of the hardening of differences amongst reformers about the extent of reform necessary, and the entrenching of positions over the effects such reform would have on the constitution as variously defined. Most importantly the agitation was about taxation. Since reformers directly related high taxation to the extent of 'Old Corruption', any additions especially to indirect taxation were significant in increasing the insistence and frequency of calls for reform.[22]

Even before the Treaty of Vienna was finally ratified, reformers were issuing pamphlets requesting a 'virtuous parliament materially to lessen those TAXES which bear most heavily on the GROWERS OF CORN, or on the LABOURING CLASSES OF THE COMMUNITY; namely the TAXES on CANDLES, SOAP, SUGAR, and LEATHER'.[23] According to Leigh Hunt, editor of the *Examiner*, 'the universal discontent amongst all classes', was due emphatically to the return of a 'spirit of courtly encroachment'.[24] For him MPs in the parliamentary session of 1816 had urgently to consider '1. Improvident Methods of Taxation 2. Arbitrary Methods of Taxation 3. An Over-Military tendency in the state'. Hunt listed other such items which ought now to be on the political agenda as the Prince Regent's 'System of Profusion', and the corruption of selling seats in the Commons.[25] Henry Hunt, Leigh's more radical namesake, also made this explicit connection between distress and politics.[26] Even the impeccably Whig *Edinburgh Review*, argued that 'This extravagant taxation is the weight which pulls the country down.'[27] All shades of early-nineteenth-century reformers repeated this argument *ad nauseam*: and it

---

[21] Whigs such as Whitbread, a vociferous opponent of government financial policy, accepted that the property tax would be justified in the event of a renewal of hostitities; *Hansard*, 30, 19 April 1815, cols. 669, 672.

[22] See quote from a letter from Liverpool to Peel, in J. Cookson, *Lord Liverpool's Administration: The Crucial Years*, (Hamden, CT, 1975), p. 110.

[23] [Sir F. Burdett] Hampden Club of London pamphlet, 'Glasgow, 1 September 1815. Affairs being now settled ABROAD, 'tis high time to look at HOME' (London, 1815). I am grateful to Peter Spence for this reference.

[24] *Examiner*, 14 January 1816, p. 29.

[25] *Ibid.*, 21 January 1816; see also *Independent Whig*, 15 January 1815, p. 21.

[26] Belchem, *'Orator' Hunt*, p. 50.

[27] Buchanan, 'Corn and Money', *Edinburgh Review*, 26, February 1816, p. 155.

seems right, as W. D. Rubinstein has suggested, that radical arguments about how the French wars and the 'Pitt system' 'materially increased the scale and dimensions of Old Corruption' should be taken seriously.[28] Nonetheless, despite a fair amount of agreement amongst the more or less reform-minded, they were divided over the extent of the political solution required to deal with 'Old Corruption'.

It must have been with some sense of trepidation, then, that Nicholas Vansittart, Chancellor of the Exchequer, announced in the House of Commons on 1 February 1816 that he would be continuing the income tax at 5 per cent, despite promises earlier that the government would abolish it at the end of hostilities. Whatever expectations he might have had, it is doubtful whether he or the government were completely prepared for the clamour which was raised around the country. This agitation began the post-war momentum for parliamentary reform. The political fallout resulting from repeal of the income tax shaped the movement, and the political crisis of 1817 had its origins in the aftermath of repeal. The success of the campaign for repeal, the manifest reluctance of the state to reform itself and the obvious lack of enthusiasm of the Whigs over the question of reform helped increase the urgency of the reform debate. Politics became reconstituted around constitutionalist language again.[29]

In vain, Viscount Castlereagh spoke strongly of 'an ignorant impatience for relaxation of taxation'.[30] The public were not to be put off. *The Times* believed that the honour of the government was at stake over its promises to abolish the income tax.[31] Privations had been borne during the war with some stoicism as a tacit acknowledgement that it could not be prosecuted without money. Now that it was over, relief was sought, despite the fact that the debt amounted cumulatively in 1815 to £832,197,004.[32] The competing pressures on ministers to maintain debt redemption while attempting to retrench became impossible to reconcile as the agitation out-of-doors forced the government's hand.[33] A change of financial policy from debt redemption to tax remission became necessary, in order to placate that wide body of 'respectable' opinion

[28] W. D. Rubinstein, 'The End of "Old Corruption" in Britain, 1780–1860', *Past and Present* 101 (1983), pp. 55–86, p. 63.

[29] A. Mitchell, *The Whigs in Opposition: 1815–1830*, (Oxford, 1967), p. 167.

[30] Quoted in S. Buxton, *Finance and Politics: An Historical Study, 1783–1885*, 2 vols. (London, 1886) vol. I, p. 13.

[31] *The Times*, 6 February 1816.

[32] E. Halevy, *England in 1815* (London, 1949), p. 370. N. Gash, '"Cheap Government", 1815–1874', *Pillars of Government* (London, 1986), pp. 43–54, p. 44.

[33] E. Halevy, *The Liberal Awakening, 1815–1830* (London, 1949), p. 7; See also B. Hilton, *Corn, Cash, Commerce: The Economic Policies of the Tory Governments, 1815–1830* (Oxford, 1977), pp. 31–3.

which the government considered essential for its ongoing success.[34] But consequent upon this change of policy, the government had to maintain duties on articles of consumption, or even increase them in some cases. These duties directly affected the pockets of those least likely to be able to pay them, and provided an eager audience for the reform movement. Reformers were able to make their analyses intelligible to this new constituency by articulating a sense of exclusion and injustice. The group appealed to by reformers was somehow missing out on the benefits conferred by a repeal of the income tax.

Once the government had lost the £14.5 millions of receipts from the income tax, it became essential to maintain existing levels of other taxes. The principal taxes on consumables were those on salt, sugar, raisins, currants, pepper, vinegar, beer, wine, spirits, tobacco, tea and coffee. As well, taxes on coal, and the raw materials for house construction and shipbuilding combined to provide a revenue from indirect taxation of £38 millions.[35] To offset the deficit created by the loss of the income tax, port excises were increased and an addition was made to the duty on soap. A satirical cartoon depicted Vansittart appearing in 'Betty' the laundry maid's washing tub asking her: 'How are you off for soap?' For reformers the message was clear: the government's financial policy affected everybody, even the servants.[36] They recognised a potential new audience which could be mobilised for the reform cause, an audience whose political consciousness the government itself had done much to raise out of necessity during the wars.[37]

Many of the indirect taxes directly affected those industries, such as shipbuilding, wool manufacture and shoemaking, which provided many of those who swelled the ranks of reform. Those 300,000 or so members of the armed forces 'demobbed' after the wars also had direct grievances against the state.[38] A sergeant of the local militia at Clapham reported during the Corn Bill riots that the 'most violent seem to be the lower orders particularly those discharged from the Army'.[39] The government had done little to find work for these ex-

---

[34] A. Acworth, *Financial Reconstruction in England, 1815–1822*, (London, 1925), p. 33. Cookson, *Lord Liverpool's Administration*, p. 12.

[35] S. Dowell, *A History of Taxation and Taxes in England: From the Earliest Times to the Year 1885*, 4 vols. (London, 1886), vol. II, pp. 252–4.

[36] See cartoon 'Leap Year; Or, John Bull's Peace Establishment', March 1816, George Catalogue, no. 12754.

[37] See L. Colley, *Britons* (New Haven, 1992), chapter 7, 'Manpower'.

[38] Emsley, *British Society and the French Wars*, pp. 173–6.

[39] March 1815, HO 42/143, fo. 1. See also the debates on Militia demobilisation on 9 and 28 November 1814, *Hansard*, 29, 1814, col. 89 ff.

soldiers and seamen.[40] Charitable organisations were set up to assist them, with illustrious benefactors, but the grievances remained. One did not need to be an arch-reformer like Henry Hunt, who attacked these charities as 'sinecure-soup project[s]',[41] to argue the state was responsible for relieving the worst of the distress which raged throughout 1816. *The Times* argued in July that 'where the bulk of the nation suffers, we know not any power except the state itself which can command effectually the materials of relief – Nor any wisdom but that of parliament to which the people can resort with safety'.[42]

But at a Westminster meeting to consider the best means of opposing the income tax a split was exposed between those advocating reform and those content with retrenchment. Henry Hunt, William Cobbett, Major Cartwright and Sir Francis Burdett believed that taxation without representation was the 'true tyranny'. When Hunt rose to speak, Henry Brougham, Henry Grey Bennet, Thomas Brand and J. G. Lambton, all part of the progressive arm of the Whig party, left the hustings. In response to Cobbett's denunciations of him as a 'hireling', Leigh Hunt described Hunt's language and tactics as tending to 'subvert the People'.[43] The agitation over the property tax, while reviving old reform divisions, marked the moment at which these divisions were to see the canvassing of a new constituency, mobilised by the war and unwilling to be passed over again. A debate as to the nature of 'the constitution' and the identity of 'the people' resulted from the clash of these contending groups.[44]

III

On 29 July the Clapham Sect's Association for the Relief of the Manufacturing and Labouring Poor convened a meeting in the presence of the Dukes of York, Kent and Cambridge, the Archbishop of Canterbury, the Bishop of London, Lord Kenyon, William Wilberforce and Vansittart, amongst many other luminaries. A resolution was proposed that distress was caused by a 'sudden transition from war to peace'.

---

[40] Samuel Birch, Lord Mayor of London, reported to Viscount Melville on 3 February 1815 that discharged seamen were very distressed and were seeking assistance from the Corporation of London; HO 42/142, fos. 140 ff.

[41] Belchem, *'Orator' Hunt*, p. 51. The impact of charitable provision on the ability of reformers to harness discontent for their cause has been assessed by R. Glen, *Urban Workers and the Industrial Revolution* (London, 1984), pp. 53–4.

[42] *The Times*, 31 July 1816.   [43] *Examiner*, 3 March 1816, p. 140.

[44] E. S. Morgan, *Inventing the People: The Rise of Popular Sovereignty in England and America* (New York, 1988), p. 233. See also L. Colley, 'Whose Nation?'

Lord Cochrane, sailor and one-time reforming MP for Westminster who had been charged with fraudulent stock-jobbing and lost his seat, proposed a counter-resolution which charged that 'The distresses of the country came from a profuse and lavish expenditure of its resources.'[45] The meeting divided down the middle over these opposing positions. While all agreed on the fact of distress, its causes and solution were far from clear.[46]

The activities and arguments of those loyal to government had a crucial effect on radical language and political activity. Radical politics can only be understood with reference to the behaviour and exertions of its opponents. Only then are the vicissitudes and triumphs of reform completely comprehensible. Although historians of the late eighteenth century have lately become aware of this,[47] early-nineteenth-century historians have long neglected this dimension; to the extent that it has been commonly assumed that radicals overwhelmingly won the propaganda battle after the wars.[48] Such an assessment is hardly surprising, given that existing work has concentrated almost solely on radicalism and largely ignored the loyalist response. Despite being on the defensive after the wars, unlike the mass loyalism of the 1790s, loyalists still attempted to meet reform arguments, and they were important for actively disseminating views which the reformers felt it necessary constantly to attack.

The success of the radicals depended on their ability to persuade a mass of potential supporters that their analysis – that the ills of society were fundamentally due to a lack of reform – was correct. To achieve this it was essential to evoke the constitution, and to defend their political activity on the basis of a desire to save both the constitution and the country from a ruinous government. The idea of 'the constitution' was therefore central to English political culture in these years.[49] It is,

---

[45] *Examiner*, 4 August 1816, p. 483.

[46] *CPR*, 3 August 1816; see also Francis Place to James Mill, 2 August 1816, British Library (BL), Add. MSS 35152, fo. 199.

[47] John Money, 'Freemasonry and the Fabric of Loyalism in Hanoverian England', in E. Hellmuth (ed.), *The Transformation of Political Culture: England and Germany in the Late Eighteenth Century* (London, 1990), pp. 235–71; R. Dozier, *For King, Constitution, and Country*, (Lexington, KY, 1983); J. Bradley, 'The Anglican Pulpit, the Social Order, and the Resurgence of Toryism during the American Revolution', *Albion*, 21 (1989), pp. 361–88; T. Schofield, 'Conservative Political Thought in Britain in Response to the French Revolution', *Historical Journal*, 29 (1986), pp. 601–22; M. Philp, 'Vulgar Conservatism, 1792–3', *English Historical Review*, 110 (1995), pp. 42–69.

[48] See E. J. Evans, 'The Premiership of Lord Liverpool: Another Long-Serving Prime Minister', *Modern History Review*, 1 (1990), pp. 13–14, p. 13.

[49] See E. Wasson, *Whig Renaissance: Lord Althorp and the Whig Party, 1782–1845* (New York, 1987), p. 122; M. Francis with J. Morrow, 'After the Ancient Constitution: Political Theory and

then, necessary to try to understand what reformers, Whigs and anti-reformers believed was at stake in their struggle over the meaning of the constitution. Some, like Canning, argued that only the blessings of a free constitution had saved Britain and Europe from Napoleon.[50] The British constitution was the 'envy and admiration of the world', and it explained the ability of the British government to wage war for so long and on such a large scale:

And if we look around us, and compare our revenues with those of the other nations of Europe, we shall be perfectly satisfied that we owe our superiority, in a great measure, to the freedom of our government and the blessings of our constitution.[51]

The Society of Spencean Philanthropists, on the other hand, had questioned the very notion of an English constitution. In 1815 Thomas Evans made it publicly clear that

every Englishman deceives himself, if he thinks we have a Constitution – a glorious Constitution – we have no such thing. Ours is, and has ever been a Government of *expediency*, partly constitutional, partly assumptive.

'[T]he only constitution the world has to boast' was America's, a 'settled, written compact and agreement.'[52] The gulf between these two positions is clear, yet the invocation of some version of the constitution was almost a given.

As George Dyer pointed out in the *Pamphleteer*, all classes of politician talked of 'rallying around the Constitution, like different religious sects, who all appeal to the same code'.[53] The pseudonymous 'Kent of Kent' argued similarly. It entirely depended on the interpretation put upon 'the constitution' as to which political camp one supported.[54] William Shadgett, retrenched exciseman and loyalist editor of *Shadgett's Weekly Review of Cobbett, Wooler and Sherwin*, announced his desire also to defend the 'civil and religious establishments'. In a common panegyric, he claimed a firm

English Constitutional Writings, 1765–1832', *History of Political Thought*, 9, 2 (summer 1988), pp. 283–302, pp. 283–4.

50 This was George Canning's constant refrain; see his Liverpool election speech of 1818 and the reply by Richard Carlile, *A Letter to George Canning on his Late Speech at Liverpool*, (London: 1818) esp. p. 7: 'England is indebted for escape from the power of France to some secret virtue in her constitution, under its present practice.' Carlile rejected this argument, countering that only geography had saved England from invasion.

51 Mr Graham, 8 November 1814, House of Commons, *Hansard*, 29, 1814, col. 39.

52 Thomas Evans to Henry White, *Independent Whig*, 10 September 1815, pp. 301–2.

53 G. Dyer, *Four Letters on the English Constitution*, 4th edn, *The Pamphleteer*, 12 (1816), p. 156.

54 'Kent of Kent', *A View of the Great Constitutional Questions, Addressed to the Electors of the United Kingdom* (Canterbury, 1818), p. 27.

attachment to that glorious Constitution, which in 'former days used to be the envy and admiration of the world'; as to Englishmen it was their pride, their consolation. By it they lived; for it they were ready to die.[55]

On the other hand, and at the same moment, T. J. Wooler, radical editor of the *Black Dwarf*, proclaimed 'England's fairest best renown was in her Constitution.'[56] This merely echoed Cobbett's intoning: 'We have great constitutional laws and principles, to which we are immovably attached.'[57] The idea of defending a particular version of the constitution to the death was a commonplace sentiment. The context of its utterance, at either a Pitt Club meeting or a mass reform meeting, or within an argument about the necessity or danger of reform, provided clues as to its meaning. The social context of the utterance could not guide the interpreter infallibly as to the meaning of such phrases precisely because all types of men and women, both rich and poor, could be either loyalist or various shades of reformer.[58]

The man whose intellectual reconnaissance had done the most to prepare 'the constitution' as the political bible and rallying cry for reform was John Cartwright. His role in articulating the reformist 'constitution' should not be underestimated.[59] For him, the struggle with the unreformed system was about defending 'the true principles of the English Constitution and to vindicate its antiquity, for defeating the purpose of those who call it a constitution *"as by law established"* '.[60] Reform was needed through annual parliaments, universal (manhood) suffrage and vote by ballot to restore the independence of the House of Commons, the People's House, which was being eroded by the overwhelming influence of the crown and the Lords through the sale of seats, places and pensions. Such 'boroughmongering' was destroying the spirit

---

[55] *Shadgett's Weekly Review* (hereafter *SWR*), 1 February 1818, p. 1; the quote within the quote was from one of Canning's speeches.

[56] *Black Dwarf*, 29 January 1817, col. 14.   [57] *CPR*, 2 November 1816, col. 568.

[58] Various popular anti-radical political clubs, such as the Pitt Clubs in many towns, sought to praise and defend 'the constitution'. The only records extant of Pittite Clubs for this period are as follows: Canning Club of Liverpool, Liverpool Central Library, 329 CAN 1/1; London Pitt Club, British Library Pamphlets; Sheffield Pitt Club, Sheffield City Library, Jackson Collection, 1296; Chelmsford Pitt Club, Essex County Record Office (Chelmsford), D/Z4/2, the members of this last club, particularly, were tradespeople, exactly the same social groups from which many reformers sprang; Manchester Pitt Club Records, Manchester Central Library Archive.

[59] Many reformers acknowledged his influence such as Bamford, Wooler, Cobbett and so on, Bamford, *Passages in the Life of a Radical*, p. 31; *Black Dwarf,*, 17 December 1817, col. 768: 'The "Father of Reform", as the venerable Major is so justly called ...'; Ensor to Place, 9 March 1819, Place Papers, BL, Add. MSS 35153, fo. 58: Cartwright 'is the father of reform'.

[60] Cartwright to Sir Robert Wilson, 23 August 1817, BL, Add MSS 30108, fo. 333.

of the ancient constitution through an oligarchy of interests inimical to those of 'the people'.[61]

The pillars of Cartwright's constitution were Magna Carta (in contemporary radical usage) and the Bill of Rights. These underpinned 'the assembly of laws, institutions and customs' derived from 'certain fix'd principles of reason', and directed to 'certain fix'd principles of public good', which together made up 'the constitution'. They composed the general system 'according to which the community hath agreed to be governed'.[62] Such an account distinguished between the government and the constitution. The former meant the 'Chief Magistrate, and the inferior magistrates under his direction', who held the 'administration of public affairs' at any one time. The conduct of the government ought to be determined within prescribed limits set by the constitution. Cartwright made this abundantly clear in a letter to Lord Holland:

That the authority of parliament is strictly limited within the scope of the Constitution, is clearly deducible from the writings of Locke, as well as from the still higher authority of reason.[63]

For Cartwright, historical rights and natural rights were appealed to simultaneously. He may well have regarded such a distinction as unhelpful. The usurpation of rights had been effected by the crown in a long historical struggle to control parliament, and increase its influence through boroughmongering. Those trafficking in seats had usurped the power of legislation as the means of enforcing constitutional precepts. In 1818 Cartwright drafted a Bill of Rights and Liberties which enshrined these distinctions and sought to offset the effects of corruption.[64] The 'fix'd principles' of the constitution, prior to government, ought to be referred to when government was to be reformed. The omnipotence of parliament, argued for by Lord Holland,[65] was incompatible with Judge Blackstone's maxim, regularly resorted to by the major, that 'England

---

[61] See I. Prothero, *Artisans and Politics in Early Nineteenth Century London: John Gast and His Times* (Folkestone, 1979), pp. 77–9, and note the similarity of Gast's political views to Cartwright's. See also D. A. Lambert, 'The Anglo-Saxon Myth and Artisan Mentality, 1780–1830' (Ph.D, Australian National University, 1984), who has an interesting angle on Cartwright's 'constitution'.

[62] *Black Dwarf*, 24 September 1817, col. 589.

[63] Cartwright to Holland, 4 September 1820, Holland House Papers, BL, Add. MSS 51831, fo. 112.

[64] *CPR*, 31 January 1818, col. 130 ff. See letter of Cartwright, *Black Dwarf*, 4 February 1818, col. 74.

[65] See Holland's notes on the back of a letter from Cartwright, stating that he does not concur with the sentiments of Cartwright's communication as they tend to deny the 'authority of parliament', Holland House Papers, BL, Add. MSS 51830, fo. 101.

was perhaps the only land in the universe, in which political or civil liberty is the very end and scope of the Constitution'.[66]

Figures and texts, like Blackstone and his commentaries' or Locke and the treatises, were given different meanings and put to opposing purposes by competing groups. So Shadgett quoted another piece of Blackstone back at Cartwright to counter these arguments. Parliament held, he declared, 'that absolute despotic power, which in all governments must reside *somewhere*, being placed by our constitution, in the three estates of the realm'.[67] In other words, instead of the people being the origin of sovereignty in the state, and so the state being created at their consent, as the radicals had it, Shadgett argued that the government was prior to the constitution. This original government took the form of the monarchy and the aristocracy:

In this country in particular, this *nation* or *people*, have sprung into consequence from concessions made by the kings and nobles; and the Constitution of England, formed by the Crown and barons, may, with great truth, be said to have produced the *people*.[68]

'The constitution' was designed, not to fashion the greatest possible liberty, but to resist the 'encroachments of the governed, and to prevent them from becoming ungovernable'.[69] Shadgett complained that the reformers were trying to redefine 'the people' to include those deliberately placed beyond the pale of the constitution. By so doing they were upsetting its balance. The *Anti-Jacobin Review* agreed: 'In the Legislature the People are a check upon the Nobility, and the Nobility a check upon the People ... while the King is a check upon both ... And this very executive power is again checked and kept within due bounds by the two Houses.'[70] Far from being an enhancement of liberty, the 'unconstitutional ascendancy ... aimed at by the people' actually threatened its existence.[71] This remained a constant theme with the *Anti-Jacobin*: 'Public opinion – that is, the democratic part of our constitution ... has grown too strong. It has actually overpowered the regal part, and the aristocratic part is almost neutralized.'[72]

---

[66] *Black Dwarf*, 4 February 1818, col. 73; See W. Blackstone, *Commentaries on the Laws of England*, 16th edn, 4 vols., ed. J. T. Coleridge (London, 1825), vol 1, p. 6. It is in turn a quote from Montesquieu's *Esprit d'Lois*.

[67] *SWR*, 19 September 1818, p. 266; the equivalent passage in Blackstone's Commentaries, vol. 1, pp. 160–2; see also N. Gash on this 'omnipotence of parliament' in 'The English Constitution in the Age of the American Revolution', *Pillars of Government* (London, 1986), pp. 3–15, 14.

[68] *SWR*, 5 April 1818, p. 74.   [69] *Anti-Times*, 20 November 1819, p. 3.

[70] *Anti-Jacobin Review*, February 1817, p. 634.   [71] *Ibid.*, p. 635.

[72] *Ibid.*, April 1819, p. 98. In this it merely echoed what the *Quarterly Review* had always

Anti-reformers thus turned reformist arguments about 'the constitution' on their heads. They argued against a Cartwrightian (or Lockean) state of nature, and against rights and principles antecedent to government. The origins of civil society in the family, argued Merle, in fact negated claims to these natural rights. '[T]he very association of men . . . was a tacit acknowledgement that the rights of nature themselves were to be subjected to the control of reason.'[73] Appropriating Blackstone once again, Merle rejected the social contract arguments of Cartwright, Cobbett and Wooler on the grounds that any society had always to be governed and fundamental principles did not have to inform it. A constitution developed out of the exigencies of governing civil society. 'The Warder' in *Blackwood's* presented perhaps the most sophisticated account of the primacy of government as the source of all order and authority. This writer stressed the importance of people obeying the authorities of the state. Reformers were wilfully and dangerously asking people not competent to do so to question their allegiance under the pretext of merely 'considering' the theory of their government.[74]

IV

While constantly contesting what was at stake, political groups also had to develop arguments about who they wished to support their differing versions of the constitution. Meetings of the Common Hall at the end of August, at Palace Yard, Westminster, in early September 1816, and various meetings in the north and midlands took reformist ideas about the constitution to the people.[75] But it was the activities of Major Cartwright and his petitioning campaign, organised around the Hampden Clubs and the radical press, which was crucial in creating a reforming public. A revival of Luddism, the 'Bread or Blood' riots in East Anglia,[76] and colliers in the midlands and the north dragging coal wagons with petitions attached around the countryside to seek public relief,[77] prompted Cartwright to seek an extension of the Hampden

---

asserted: 'Parliamentary Reform', *Quarterly Review*, 16 (1816), p. 252: 'At present it is the influence of the democracy which has increased, is increasing and ought to be diminished.' This in turn echoed with a twist Dunning's famous parliamentary motion of the 1780s.

[73] *White Dwarf*, 7 February 1818, p. 166; See Blackstone, *Commentaries*, vol. 1, p. 46.

[74] *Blackwood's Edinburgh Magazine*, December 1819, p. 333.

[75] *Examiner*, 25 August 1816, p. 541; 15 September 1816, p. 589; *The Times*, 22 August 1816; 12 September 1816; see also HO 79/2: Private and Secret Outletters, Becket to Colonel Fletcher, 30 August 1816, unfoliated, on the provincial effects of the livery meeting.

[76] A. J. Peacock, *Bread or Blood: The Agrarian Riots in East Anglia, 1816* (London, 1965).

[77] See *The Times*, 8 July 1816; Becket to Conant *et al.*, HO 41/1, fo. 92; Halevy, *Liberal Awakening*, p. 10.

Club membership qualification in order to 'direct insurrectionary discontent into constitutional forms'.[78] With Thomas Cleary, Cartwright embarked on a lecture tour in winter 1815. Francis Place remarked later that it 'was they who gave the tone to many places and revived the dormant desire for reform'.[79] The 'very remarkable growth of provincial Hampden Clubs or Union Societies in the last months of 1816' which resulted cannot be understood simply in social terms. Distinguishing between middle-class and working-class reformers in provincial centres directs attention away from the political divisions over the meaning of constitutionalist categories.[80]

Historians such as G. D. H. Cole, E. P. Thompson, Harold Perkin and John Belchem have seen the years 1816–20 as crucial to the development of working-class consciousness. Their accounts are framed by concepts derived from class analysis which do not adequately explain the *political behaviour* of working men and women. The appeal to 'journeymen and labourers', and the unrepresented more generally, was not a process fuelled in the last instance by changes in the economic system. Rather it was a contingent solution on the part of reformers to gain support for the cause of reform, after appeals to traditional sources of opposition, such as the gentry, produced little result.[81] Cartwright, Cobbett and Hunt reworked existing political categories to include the mass of the unrepresented. 'The people' was redefined to be inclusive.

Moreover, the development of class identity in this period, a consciousness of separateness and distinctiveness regarding property relations, was at best spasmodic and fitful, largely because of the overwhelming importance to the reform movement of political identities such as 'the people'. Social identity resulted from the developments in political identity, rather than the reverse. 'Journeymen and labourers', included by reformers as support for the cause of reform, responded because their political consciousness was raised by unprecedented state mobilisation during the wars,[82] and because constitutionalist categories enabled them to articulate their grievances. Francis Jeffrey's claim that radical doctrines were 'but exaggerations of very familiar propositions'[83] suggests that any attempt to re-interpret the

---

[78] Thompson, *The Making*, p. 666; *ibid.*, p. 678; Belchem, *'Orator' Hunt*, p. 53.
[79] Place's manuscript history of the years 1815–18, written 14 December 1829, Place Papers, BL, Add. MSS 27809, fo. 8.
[80] Thompson, *The Making*, pp. 705–6; Belchem, *'Orator' Hunt*, p. 54.
[81] See the comments in J. Brewer, *The Sinews of Power: War, Money and the English State, 1688–1783* (London, 1989), p. 243.
[82] L. Colley, 'Whose Nation?'; *idem, Britons*.
[83] [F. Jeffrey], 'State of the Country', in *Edinburgh Review*, October 1819, p. 295.

movements of these years must take the political language of constitutionalism as its starting-point.

Cartwright was dissatisfied with the existing political categories
because of the existing political arrangements. He believed the best way
to alter these was to extend the idea of the political nation to balance
the encroachments of 'arbitrary power'.[84] The property qualification
necessary for membership of the Hampden Clubs (£300 per annum)
was also unacceptable to him, for he believed that such a restriction
would damage the cause of reform by narrowing its potential supporters.
Mass support, with gentry leadership, was the only way to make the
cause 'unanswerable'. Lord Holland was exhorted by Cartwright not to
undervalue the lower classes of society as they now had a great deal of
political knowledge. They required only 'a small body of statesmen in
the higher ranks' who

shaking off all prejudice, and rising superior to the influence of prejudice in
others, should, both in and out of parliament, become the unreserved, bold and
inflexible advocates of the People's Right to complete Representation in the
legislature, would shortly have in their hands the irresistible means of
renovating the Public Liberty with peace and security.[85]

To triumph, reform needed only the backing of some substantial
gentry.[86]

But the Whigs were prepared no longer to take the lead in public
meetings calling for reform. Brougham's toying with the Westminster
committee in 1814–15 had come to nothing over this issue.[87] He fell into
line behind the cautious Whig leaders like Earl Grey. For them, it was
'nonsense' to see radical reform as the 'only relief we can look for'. Cries
of universal suffrage and calls for annual parliaments were a 'mischie-
vous absurdity' for many Whigs.[88] Those who tried to effect a 'cooperation between the Whigs and the people, in favour of more rational
and practicable measures', met with 'a cold, cautious, forbidding reserve
– almost indeed approaching the freezing point – an excess of delicacy –
a fear of being misunderstood – of standing committed – of their names
being used'.[89]

---

[84] On the manipulation of definitions of crucial terms, see I. Prothero, 'William Benbow and
the Concept of the General Strike', *Past and Present*, 63 (1974), pp. 132–71, p. 143.

[85] Cartwright to Holland, 14 May 1818, Holland House Papers, BL, Add. MSS 51829, fo. 84.

[86] Sir Charles Wolseley, *Address to the Country Gentlemen of England*, 2 October 1818, Stafford; See
also PRO, TS 11/157/543.

[87] Ann Hone, *For the Cause of Truth: Radicalism in London, 1796–1821*, (Oxford, 1982), pp. 257–8.

[88] Earl Grey to Holland, 6 January 1819, Holland House Papers, BL, Add. MSS 51546, fo. 6.

[89] Robert Waithman to Lord Holland, 15 January 1818, Holland House Papers, BL, Add. MSS
51829, fo. 6. On Waithman, see J. R. Dinwiddy, ' "The Patriotic Linen-Draper": Robert

The debate over universal suffrage became the focal point for discussions of the meaning of 'the people', which reformers were redefining in the face of Whig tardiness. An extensive addition to the franchise was posited by reformers as the effective solution to government corruption. Some property owners, however, saw another. They did not dispute the fact of corruption and over-expenditure, but argued that universal suffrage would worsen the situation. An increase in the franchise would simply add to the number of dependent voters capable of being bought. What was needed was an *increase* in the property qualification for both MPs and voters, so that neither could be bought.[90] This was an attempt to make the category of 'the people' even more exclusive than it had become for some politicians. Moderate reformers like Sir Philip Francis, a Friend of the People in the 1790s, spoke haughtily in 1817 of 'the people' as 'a name by which I never did nor ever will describe the populace'.[91] Holland House librarian John Allen argued in the *Edinburgh Review* of June 1816 that universal suffrage had never been the practice of the constitution. Originally, the people had been landed proprietors.[92] Sir James Mackintosh attacked the idea of universal suffrage by distinguishing between 'the People' with a capital P and 'the people' with a small p, in order to maintain the eighteenth-century distinction of 'the People' as 'the electors'.[93] Such assertions pointed up the Whigs' difficulties in treading a middle way between ministerialists and reformers in 1817, against the background of political crisis, reform insurgence, loyal reaction, 'gagging' bills and 'dungeon parliaments'.[94]

As a search for a middle way, this was as much a desire to win the

---

Waithman and the Revival of Radicalism in the City of London, 1795–1818', *Bulletin of the Institute of Historical Research*, 46 (1973), pp. 72–94. See also Belchem, *'Orator' Hunt*, p. 70 for the failure of Waithman's moderate 'Friends of Economy, Public Order and Reform' to gain support in 1817.

90 See *Reform without innovation* (London, 1817), in *The Pamphleteer*, 9 (1817), p. 404; It was also argued that universal suffrage would increase dependence on the part of the lower orders: G. F. Leckie, 'Essay on the Practice of the British government ...' (London, 1817) in *The Pamphleteer*, 11 (1818), p. 92; Sir John Jervis to Liverpool, 14 July 1817 BL, Add. mss 38267, fos. 296–300: Jervis sought an introduction of a £50 freeholder franchise in the counties, as the 40 shilling franchise was 'fixed so far back in the reign of H[enry] VI, when money was so much more valuable'. Jervis also wrote anti-reform articles for the *Morning Post*.

91 Sir Philip Francis, *Plan of a Reform in the Election of the House of Commons, Adopted by the Friends of the People in 1795 ...*, in *The Pamphleteer*, 9 (1817), p. 548.

92 [John Allen], 'The Constitution of Parliament', *Edinburgh Review*, June 1816, 26, pp. 338–83, 341; cf R. J. Smith, *The Gothic Bequest: Medieval Institutions in British Thought, 1688–1863* (Cambridge, 1987), p. 141.

93 Sir James Mackintosh, 'Universal Suffrage', *Edinburgh Review*, December 1818, p. 21.

94 For different interpretations of the 1817 repression, see Halevy, *Liberal awakening*, p. 25; and J. E. Cookson, *Lord Liverpool's Administration*, pp. 112, 114.

political argument against the government and reformers as it was 'tactical' or 'strategic'.[95] Whig attempts to define who 'the people' were need to be understood as part of the battle over crucial contested terms as much as a calculated desire to control radicalism. Where Lord Holland had difficulty in achieving his desired aim of 'preventing the triumph of the Court in Parliament & of Hunt & the rabble out of Parliament',[96] a Whig newspaper editor experienced the same problems in selling newspapers.

Sensibilities over exactly who the Whig 'public' was laid Whigs open to abuse from reformers as well as ministerialists.[97] Cartwright wrote and published six letters to the Marquis of Tavistock, eldest son of the Duke of Bedford, because he believed that public opinion would only be forceful if the aristocratic and democratic parts of the community acted in concert.[98] Arguments with other members of the Hampden Club, who did not wish to lower the qualification for membership, served only to convince Cartwright more strongly of the necessity of widening his appeals. Once these had failed to attract the gentry, and the very low membership of the club and Whig equivocation over reform were testament to this, Cartwright sought support elsewhere. His 'people' were no longer 'the electors'.[99]

While Cartwright and Cleary were exhorting 'all those of the Nobility, Gentry and others' to meet to call 'forth the Public Voice in the cause of parliamentary Reform',[100] Cobbett was addressing 'Journeymen and Labourers' on 2 November 1816.[101] Cobbett asked those he addressed: 'Are you not part of the people?' He wanted these men[102] included in the political nation:

---

[95] See B. Hilton, 'Whiggery, Religion, and Social Reform: the Case of Lord Morpeth' (unpublished paper, Cambridge, 1992), p. 1.

[96] Holland to Grenville, 13 January 1817, Dropmore Papers, BL, Add. MSS 58952, fo. 141.

[97] See letter from the editor of the Whig paper the *Edinburgh Reflector*, to Lord Holland asking for financial aid; J. A. Williams to Holland, Holland House Papers, BL, Add. MSS 51829, fo. 31.

[98] N. C. Miller, 'John Cartwright and Radical Parliamentary Reform, 1808–1819', *English Historical Review*, 329 (1968), pp. 705–28; idem, 'Major John Cartwright and the Foundation of the Hampden Clubs', *Historical Journal*, 17 (1974), pp. 615–19.

[99] See T. Tholfsen, *Working-class Radicalism in mid-Victorian England*, (London, 1976), p. 50.

[100] Report of proceedings, extraordinary general meeting of the Hampden Club, 18 May 1816, British Coffee House, Cockspur St, Place Papers, BL, Add. MSS 27840, fo. 281; See also Hampden Club Proceedings, 4 March 1815, and hand bill, 23 March 1816, Bodleian Library, G. Pamph. 1987(7).

[101] A letter from Cobbett to Hunt, 5 June 1816, suggests that Cobbett was considering as early as June publishing the leader article from his *Political Register* in very cheap form, Cobbett Papers, Supplementary Box, Nuffield College, Oxford.

[102] Cobbett never believed women to be part of 'the people', and loyalists exploited this difficulty in radical calls for universal suffrage; see J. Fulcher, 'Gender, Politics and Class

The Bill of Rights declares, that the Laws of England and the Rights and Liberties secured thereby are the birthright of the people. It does not say, of the rich, of the nobles, of the priesthood, the yeomanry cavalry, the members of corporations, the borough voters, but of THE PEOPLE.[103]

Although the Bill of Rights was framed by aristocratic rebels, whose notion of 'the people' equated with 'the electors', it was possible for Cobbett and Cartwright to redefine the term and include the unrepresented in the way that they did because the mobilisation of the war years had aided the legitimation of the claims to citizenship of those who had manned the ships, fought the battles, supplied the troops and borne the heavy taxation.

Popular journalists flocked to the presses to defend this identity of 'the people' as inclusive. David Vincent has remarked upon the great expansion 'of all forms of popular printed commentary on the state of the nation and its institutions' at this time.[104] Wooler, William Hone, as well as the *Manchester Political Register,* took Cobbett's lead and published in cheap weekly form. The *Birmingham Inspector* hoped that its main readership would be 'the respectable and valuable Artizans of Birmingham'. Its editor lamented that the 'Gentlemen' of the town of Birmingham had neglected the cause of economy, retrenchment and reform. Everything in the power of Birmingham reformers had been done 'to induce the 'Magistrates, Gentry, Clergy, Merchants, and Manufacturers' of the town to promote and take the lead' at meetings.[105] Throughout January and February 1817 a battle raged between reformers and loyalists over the conduct of public meetings called to investigate the distress. Artisan political activity was again defended in terms of abandonment by 'Gentlemen' of their proper place on the hustings.[106]

But this was not all. A new claim in defence of political activity was cited. Legitimate public agitation in favour of the constitution had always been part of an Englishman's duty, irrespective of riches or station.[107] Since gentlemen had refused to come forward and take the lead in defence of popular rights and privileges, artisans had to fill the breach. 'You will readily admit', the editor of the *Birmingham Inspector* suggested to its 'Fellow Townsmen'

    in the Early Nineteenth-Century English Reform Movement', *Historical Research* (February 1994), pp. 58–74.
103 *CPR,* 23 November 1816, col. 669.
104 D. Vincent, *Literacy and Popular Culture: England, 1750–1914* (Cambridge, 1989), p. 245.
105 *Birmingham Inspector,* 15 February 1817, p. 66.   106 *Ibid.,* supplement to no. 2, p. 2.
107 Colley, 'Whose Nation?', p. 101; Emsley, *British Society and the French Wars,* pp. 112 ff.

that wealth will and should have its suitable weight and influence in society, but at the same time you will contend that the protection of the Laws, and the decent comforts of Life, are what all classes are entitled to expect, so long as they shall strive to deserve them.[108]

As Linda Colley has recognised, the government knew that such appeals to patriotic defences of the law were double-edged.[109] David Eastwood has also pointed to the tension inherent in denouncing reformers for their democratic claims while yet calling for mass participation to defeat them.[110] Such appeals could be used equally to galvanise the loyal and the disaffected.

Anti-radicals made similar appeals to the gentry with opposite intent. Gibbons Merle, editor of the *White Dwarf*, a journal set up to denounce Cobbett, Wooler and other radical writers, argued that appeals to artisans and others such as those made by the *Birmingham Inspector* were illegitimate. By appealing to a wider 'people', reformers were neglecting the ties of society which were the people's best protection in times of distress. While not condoning their tactics, Merle could understand the reformers' search for mass support. The 'abdication on the part of the governors' was the cause of at least some of the distress.[111] He was not alone. 'The Warder' in *Blackwood's Edinburgh Magazine* also believed it 'too evident that the upper orders of society have been tending, more and more, to a separation of themselves from those whom nature, providence and law, have placed beneath' them. Worse, the 'rich and the high have been indolently and slothfully allowing the barriers that separate them from their inferiors to increase and accumulate'.[112] Individuals as well as governments had to tighten their belts in times of distress, and maintain their ties with their tenants and labourers. 'In times like the present', wrote the *Anti-Jacobin Review*, 'the Noblemen, as well as private Gentlemen, should be more frequently resident on their estates.'[113]

Conservatives, then, set out to deny radical redefinitions of 'the

---

[108] *Birmingham Inspector*, 29 March 1817, pp. 131–2.

[109] Colley, 'Whose Nation?', p. 117; see also Vincent, *Literacy and Popular Culture*, p. 232.

[110] D. Eastwood, 'Patriotism and the English State in the 1790s', in M. Philp (ed.), *The French Revolution and British Popular Politics*, (Cambridge, 1991)

[111] *White Dwarf*, 13 December 1817, p. 35; the phrase was Thomas Carlyle's: H. Perkin, *The Origins of Modern English Society*, p. 183. See also the discussion in W. Stafford, *Socialism, Radicalism and Nostalgia: Social Criticism in Britain, 1775–1830* (Cambridge, 1987), pp. 20–1; P. Langford, *Public Life and the Propertied Englishman, 1689–1798* (Oxford, 1991), pp. 367–9, takes these fears about absenteeism and slothful landowners back into the late seventeenth century, and see the chapter 'Rural Duties' more generally, pp. 367–436.

[112] *Blackwood's Edinburgh Magazine*, April 1820, p. 92.

[113] *Anti-Jacobin Review*, February 1817, p. 640.

people' while reaffirming a desire to return to a more paternalistic and deferential social order. A long-neglected aspect of the political culture of these years has been the popular *conservative* response to radicals by means of the press as well as associations. Journals published by loyalists used the same format and were sold at the same price as radical weekly offerings, in order to capture a similar audience. It was also important for the rallying of the loyal. John Lloyd the Stockport magistrate attested to this: 'the press employed for the loyal and just cause – will be everything towards reviving the spirits of those who possess the latent spark of patriotism – I very much admire a writer in the *Leeds Intelligencer*.'[114] The *Detector: An Occasional Paper*, begun around February 1817, outlined the reasons for attacking Cobbett by employing his methods:

I have waited in the hope that some hand, more able than mine would have asserted their progress, but now that the *disorder* spreads so widely, and with such dangerous symptoms, I will no longer restrain myself from the duty of calling upon my countrymen, to resist and expose their absurdities and machinations[115]

Like the *Detector*, the *Anti-Cobbett* was set on foot specifically to attack Cobbett, 'the head of those worthies who spread abroad this poison'.[116] Addressing the journeymen and labourers was 'diabolical wickedness' on Cobbett's part. It was well known that these men 'were tempted to engage in secret associations of the most dark and dangerous nature'.[117] Loyalists demonstrated in their choice of metaphors that they believed reformers rather than boroughmongers were responsible for the corruption and decay in the body politic.

A paradox was evident in the publication of these writings, which perhaps explains why the government was reluctant to give other than

---

[114] Lloyd to Sidmouth, 7 January 1817, HO 40/3 part 1, fo. 12. A member of the Norwich Brunswick Club sought financial assistance from the Home Office for a new publication entitled, predictably, *The Brunswick*, Thomas Coldwell to Sidmouth, 21 January 1817, HO 40/9, fo. 5. One Edward Clarkson was constantly employed writing *jeux d'esprit* for the *Anti-Gallican* in late 1816 and early 1817. Its editor, Lewis Goldsmith, had been requested by Becket of the Home Office to circulate thousands of pamphlets whose purport was the 'defence of Social Order and English principles'. See HO 42/174, fos. 32, 38 and 58 for Clarkson and Goldsmith's correspondence of early 1818 demanding financial reward for their exertions in the previous year. Fo. 32 holds Clarkson's *Heroic Epistle to William Cobbett* (London, 1817).

[115] *The Detector* (London, 1817), p. 1.   [116] *Ibid.*, p. 2.

[117] *Anti-Cobbett: Or the Weekly Patriotic Register* (London, 1817). The use of 'patriotic' was designed to catch the unsuspecting buyer, because radicalism had used this word to such an extent that it was tainted for loyalists. See also J. Glanville to Liverpool, 23 June 1817, BL, Add. MSS 38267, fo. 163, and the anti-Cobbett tract *The Friend of the People ...* (London, December 1816).

token support to them.[118] These conservative journalists, by aping the reformers' journalistic practice, were simultaneously reluctant to admit the importance of the new constituency the radicals were creating, while trying to win the new audience over to their version of the constitutionalist language. The reactive nature of these conservative journals clearly suggests that the reformers, initially at least, set the agenda and determined the tone of Regency political culture. The government was wary of opposing this agenda openly, simply because reference to any new political audience at all raised the possibility that eventually that constituency would have to be accommodated in the political system. But conservatives understood, much to their chagrin, that it was the new definitions of constitutionalist categories which prompted reformers' initial success. *The Age* sought to explain how radical journals 'were unfailing sources of success'. It was precisely because of their reliance on the 'assistance of a few words, *Boroughmongers*, National Debt, Universal Suffrage, etc, etc.'[119]

Conservatives were terrified of the power of the press. Robert Southey's urgent tone in a letter to Canning of March 1817 echoed the universal lament amongst ministerialists. 'You must curb the press', he warned, 'or it will destroy the Constitution of the country.'[120] Many pamphlets, loyal resolutions and government proclamations like Sidmouth's notorious circular letter of March 1817 highlighted the danger.[121] W. J. Richards, alias 'Oliver' the spy, believed that pamphlets 'so industriously circulated throughout the country' was the main part of the danger facing the state.[122] '[T]he *Black Dwarf*', he warned, 'had done much mischief all over the Country.'[123] The files of the Treasury Solicitor reveal the number of attempts by government to prosecute seditious material. Their subsequent failure to convict or even begin an action merely increased anxiety over the 'licentiousness of the

---

[118] The government was only prepared to give some financial assistance, and this secretly. They were much more interested in supporting the 'respectable' press, London and provincial dailies and quarterlies. See A. Aspinall, *Politics and the Press* (1949; Brighton, 1973). See Home Office attempts to promote anti-radical literature, J. H. Addington to Boroughreeve of Manchester, 21 October 1816, and *idem* to Fletcher, 26 November 1816, HO 41/1, fos. 180 and 245.

[119] *The Age*, 24 January 1819, p. 2.

[120] Southey to Canning, Canning Papers, Leeds City Archives, Packet 66A.

[121] For the text of this letter, which commanded magistrates to prosecute the vendors of what they themselves considered 'seditious' literature, see G. Pellew, *The Life and Correspondence of the Right Hon. Henry Addington, First Viscount Sidmouth*, 3 vols. (London, 1847), vol. III, p. 174.

[122] Richards to Hobhouse, 4 May 1817 [from Wakefield], HO 40/10, fo. 221.

[123] *Ibid.*, 8 May 1817, HO 40/10, fo. 225; Boroughreeve and Constables to Sidmouth, 3 March 1817, HO 40/5/4A, fo. 7.

press'.[124] The ambiguities of constitutionalist categories were very evident in the courts.[125] Since the press was the main vehicle for the dissemination of the new reform definitions, reformers delighted in playing upon constitutionalist categories with impunity.

The government had few if any qualms about supporting publications like the *Courier* or the *Quarterly Review*. The latter equated 'the people' with the reformers: 'By *the people*, of course, the discontented faction is meant – the deceivers and the deceived – according to that figure of speech by which a part is put for the whole – a political synecdoche.'[126] This was in October 1816; by January 1817 the *Quarterly*'s worst fears had been realised. It marked 'the great and momentous change which the public press has produced in the very constitution of society. Formerly the people were nothing in the scale – we are hurrying on towards the time when they will be everything.'[127]

The effects of such an inclusive definition of 'the people' would be 'rapine, republican revolution and bloodshed'.[128] In March 1817, this paper noticed what it called an 'innovation' in the calling of County Meetings. 'The practice of including in the Requisitions for County Meetings the mass of the inhabitants was pregnant with dangerous consequences', wrote the editor, Daniel Stuart, at one time in the 1790s a Friend of the People, by 1817 a staunch ministerialist. 'Formerly', he went on, 'the Requisition ran thus – 'the Nobility, Gentry, Clergy, and freeholders' – none but the freeholders were summoned. Now the call is extended to the Inhabitants in General, of whom the Freeholders must be a minority.' Stuart and the *Courier* were vehemently reaffirming that 'the people' were equivalent to the independent part of the community, 'the natural representatives of the whole population'.[129]

v

A concentration on the political context of battles over crucial constitutionalist terms and categories like 'the people' and 'the constitution' allows us to drop the 'proletarian' tag applied by the Thompsonian tradition to the Hampden Clubs and the risings at Folly Hall and

[124] See *Courier*, 14 January 1817.
[125] See O. Smith, *The politics of language, 1791–1819* (Oxford, 1984), chapter 5.
[126] [R. Southey], 'Parliamentary Reform', *Quarterly Review*, October 1816, p. 262. This article was republished and distributed as a pamphlet by the Manchester Pitt Club, *Anti-Jacobin Review*, 52, May 1817, p. 250.
[127] 'Rise and Progress of Popular Disaffection', *Quarterly Review*, January 1817, p. 513.
[128] *Courier*, 14 January 1817.   [129] *Ibid.*, 6 March 1817.

Pentrich.[130] From the accounts we have of Hampden Club meetings, it is clear that the broad-based membership of the clubs clearly accepted radical analyses of their distress as consequent upon the excessive number of places, pensions and sinecures requiring exorbitant taxation for their maintenance.[131] Government pensioners were the object of the Leicester Hampden Club's wrath. The role of these 'tax-eaters' as state agents enraged the members.

Thompson's oft-quoted sentence that 'In the years between 1780 and 1832 most English working people came to feel an identity of interests as between themselves and as against their rulers and employers'[132] deserves further examination in this light. 'The people' certainly developed a strong sense of identity against their rulers, but this was an undifferentiated 'people' which also sought to include their employers within the pale of the productive classes. Although this had the tendency to retard the development of an exclusively working-class identity, such an inclusive definition of 'people' could be revolutionary in obtaining reform by mass pressure. The unproductive classes were those living on government pensions, those whom William Hazlitt labelled 'state paupers'.[133] Wooler thought the people were the 'thinking and honest portion of all classes'.[134] The editor of *The People*, a shortlived reformist journal begun soon after Cobbett left for America in March 1817, was very explicit about his audience, who 'the people' were.

> Nor by 'THE PEOPLE' does he [i.e. the editor] mean *the labouring class* only ... He is anxious for the happiness of *all*; of the highest as well as the lowest; of the richest as well as the poorest.[135]

While blaming the government for their distresses, reformers and those they persuaded explicitly did not blame their employers. The second resolution passed at a Manchester meeting in late October 1816 unequivocally stated

---

[130] Thompson, *The Making*, p. 733.

[131] On suggestions as to the social heterogeneity of the membership of the clubs, see M. Thomis, *Politics and Society in Nottingham, 1785–1835* (Oxford, 1969), p. 199.

[132] Thompson, *The Making*, p. 11; see also postscript, p. 939; *idem*, 'The Peculiarities of the English', *The Socialist Register* (1965), pp. 1–54.

[133] W. Hazlitt, 'What is the People?' first appeared in the *Yellow Dwarf*, ed. L. and J. Hunt, 14 March 1818; reprinted in Hazlitt, *Political Essays*, (London, 1819). See E. P. Thompson, *The Making*, pp. 819 ff., who compares the styles of Hazlitt and Cobbett. Interestingly, he argues that Cobbett used 'the people' as a kind of shorthand to mean the working classes, p. 819. Cf. K. Gilmartin, ' "Their Nature Contradiction": [Leigh] Hunt, Cobbett, Hazlitt and the Literature of Independent Opposition, 1800–1830' (Ph.D, University of Chicago, 1991).

[134] *Black Dwarf*, 12 February 1817, col. 37.   [135] *The People*, 19 April 1817, 2 col. 5.

That we are convinced this state of things [the distress] does not arise from causes which are under the control of the Farmer, the Tradesman, the Manufacturer, or the Merchant; because we find all these classes suffering under the losses and privations which are without parallel, and in numerous instances completely ruinous.[136]

Reformers like W. T. Sherwin sought to convince his readers that the real problem was bad government not self-interested employers. Sherwin separated the Nation from the Government in his *Political Register* in order to support the argument that economic discontent was not the fault of employers but of a corrupt government:

[The poor] are convinced that it is no fault of the persons accustomed to employ them, that they are not ... maintained [with the necessaries of life]. They know that the cause rests with the Government, and that if the expenses of the Government were reduced to the proper standard, they should have the means of subsistence restored to them again.[137]

Connections with government (and therefore corruption) were ruthlessly exposed locally and nationally by reformers.[138] Red Books,[139] Black Books, '*People's Mirror[s]*',[140] and countless other reform pamphlets, resolutions at meetings and speeches showed the extent to which constitutionalist language and its interpretation of distress were highly successful in recruiting people to the cause.[141] Not only did many Hampden Club members, and others present at reform meetings during 1816–17, accept radical explanations of their distress, they also agreed that parliamentary reform was the only appropriate solution. John Knight of Oldham wrote to fellow reformer John Kay of Royton enthusiastically recommending Cartwright's initiative for reform meetings and petitions. The '[l]anguage used should be mild and constitutional, but firm and clear'. Knight also urged that reformers should seek to 'gain considerable numbers of the upper classes (as they are called)', by open meetings and constitutional activity.[142] Support for the constitutional mass platform grew apace.

---

[136] HO 42/154, fo. 479.
[137] *Sherwin's Political Register*, vol. I, p. 222.
[138] *A Letter to the Inhabitants of Manchester ... by 'Algernon Sidney'*, 21 January 1817, HO 40/9, fo. 45. See also Chippendale to Sidmouth, 20 January 1817, HO 40/10, fo. 10.
[139] [R. J. Richardson] *The Extraordinary Red Book: A List of All Places, Pensions, Sinecures ...* (London, 1816), Goldsmith Library.
[140] Liverpool local variant of the Red Book, HO 42/154, fo. 463.
[141] *Petitioning Weavers Defended in Remarks on the Manchester Police Meeting of 13 January 1817* (p. 6), HO 40/9, fo. 54.
[142] Enclosure in Colonel Fletcher to Hobhouse, 23 November 1816, HO 40/3 part II, fo. 8.

VI

Loyalists, magistrates and ministers believed reform activity was simply a thinly veiled disguise for 'commotion and convulsion',[143] the Hampden Club meetings a mask for revolutionary designs.[144] Exactly *what* was revolutionary about reform clubs and meetings needs to be carefully examined. It is not necessary to disagree with the idea that there was physical force activity amongst Hampden Club members and Spa Fields rioters in order to take issue with the idea that this activity was in any important sense proletarian in origin or consciousness. The Thompsonian tradition, while making necessary qualifications as to the moral force/physical force dichotomy inherent in the earlier work of the Hammonds, has other dichotomies of its own which need to be questioned. In Thompson, Parsinnen and Belchem, constitutionalism is separated from republican revolution as a different kind of political behaviour and attitude,[145] one determined by the supposedly different class identities of their constituencies of support, the former middle class, the latter working class. As John Belchem has put it: 'Like the great crowds at Spa Fields, the victims of 1817, the participants in the various risings and conspiracies, were overwhelmingly working-class.'[146]

Instead of stressing social origins, the revolutionary or reformist versions of constitutionalism ought to be understood with loyalist denunciations of radical activity in mind. Without the blanket loyalist condemnation of their arguments and activity, some reformers would not have felt the need to stress their non-violent credentials, while at the same time keeping their options open as to 'resistance to tyranny', as all good constitutionalists did. Although anti-reformers defended the right of people to express their grievances as allowed by the petitioning clause in the Bill of Rights, they argued it was wrong to seek representation by extending the idea of 'the people' under the rubric 'universal suffrage'. As one loyal journalist put it, to look to '*the people as power to subvert*' the constitutional representation was to court revolution and anarchy.[147] In a post French Revolution context, such redefinitions were easily construed as subversions of property. 'The question of reform has been coupled by its enemies with the question of property', wrote Thomas

---

[143] Sidmouth to Mundy, [January 1817], HO 41/2, fo. 96.
[144] Enclosure in letter from Rutland to Sidmouth, 24 January 1817, HO 40/3 part 1, fo. 26.
[145] For example, Thompson, *The Making*, p. 735, and pp. 683–5 for a discussion of moral and physical force; T. Parsinnen, 'The Revolutionary Party in London, 1816–20', *Bulletin of the Institute of Historical Research*, 45 (1972), pp. 266–82.
[146] Belchem, '*Orator' Hunt*, p. 77.
[147] Gibbons Merle, *White Dwarf*, 13 December 1817, p. 35.

Hodgskin to Francis Place. 'Almost every man of more than 1000 a year looks on reform as the cover to spoliation.'[148] Reformers who denied this, men like Sir Francis Burdett, Leigh Hunt, John Thelwall, Francis Place and Henry White, were the moderates.[149] Cartwright was the link between this tradition and the more radical reformers: men like Henry Hunt, Sir Charles Wolseley, John Knight of Oldham, William Benbow, John Kay and William Fitton of Royton, Robert Pilkington of Bury, John Johnston and John Bagguley of Manchester, Samuel Bamford of Middleton and Samuel Drummond of Stockport. A revolution in meanings was effected as a direct result of appeals to 'natural leaders' – Whigs and country gentlemen – falling largely on deaf ears.

Despite the fact that Whigs paid lip-service to the revolutionary tradition inherent in constitutionalism they were not prepared to promote threats of violence as a legitimate tactic available to those with strong grievances against government. Such practices were dangerous to Whigs because they questioned the sovereignty of parliament, a central tenet of Whig doctrine. However, the 1688 Revolution had created ambiguity. The act of resistance to the Stuarts had set the precedent for 'resistance' to become an 'immutable' Whig principle. The 'Bloodless Revolution' created an ambivalence among reformers regarding the actual use of physical force at all.[150] Reformers found it nearly impossible to decide how much and what kind of oppression constituted a scenario for resistance. The category of 'resistance' within the language of constitutionalism had developed in specific circumstances; its meanings were not automatically clear under different conditions.

Loyalists knew about the possibility of resistance because they spoke the same language as reformers with a different accent.[151] They did not 'misunderstand' radical catch-cries. They believed that radicals were perpetrating violence on the categories of a discourse in which they had as much invested as reformers.

Until the Spa Fields meetings at the end of 1816, the loyalists were very much on the defensive in the face of a mass radical movement of active clubs and vociferous journalists. Thereafter, while the riots in

---

[148] Hodgskin to Place, 12 October 1819, Place Papers, BL, Add. MSS 35153, fo. 89. For examples of such denunciations of reform, see [Henry Matthews], 'Thought on the Present Political Prospect of the Times', *Blackwood's Edinburgh Magazine*, 8, February 1821, p. 492; *Anti-Jacobin Review*, February 1817, pp. 633, 642.

[149] Thelwall was editor of the *Champion*. White was editor of the reformist *Independent Whig*.

[150] See F. K. Donelly, 'Levellerism in 18th and Early 19th Century Britain', *Albion*, 20 (1988), pp. 261–69.

[151] See the toasts cited scathingly by Cobbett when noticing a Revolution Club dinner in Manchester, *CPR*, 20 June 1818, col. 720.

London on 2 December merely confirmed the interpretation put upon radical activity by supporters of 'the Constitution as by law established', loyalists were under no illusions about the danger posed by the radical threat, or about the necessity of publicly responding to it.[152] On the other hand, John Belchem has claimed that the three Spa Fields meetings of 1816–17 'transformed' popular radicalism.[153] They initiated the 'mass platform' under the tutelage of Henry Hunt, establishing him 'in importance as a rival to Burdett'.[154] Without disagreeing that these meetings were an important stage in the development of extra-parliamentary activity, it is necessary to suggest a further dimension to their significance. Not simply the occasion for government repression, these meetings prompted a national loyal response which was inimical to the fortunes of radicalism in the short term. By expressing public outrage, the loyalists provided the ammunition for government to justify an offensive policy against reform. Sidmouth wrote to Liverpool, arguing that the meeting at Spa Fields on 15 November 'has done us no Harm', in terms of strengthening the government's position in parliament and in the country.[155]

The spectre of 'the Terror' and the Gordon Riots haunted the loyal.[156] When announcing the extraordinary general meeting of the Hampden Club, the famous delegate meeting of late January 1817, the *Courier* made explicit the connection between these clubs and revolutionary ardour. 'They are anxious for the Destruction of the Constitution, and they are labouring for a Republic one and indivisible.'[157] Fear of this revolution was everywhere; the *Quarterly Review* spoke of reform as 'this endemic moral malady of this distempered age'.[158] Before Spa Fields, Robert Southey had called on the 'government and parliament' to 'save both the poor and the rich from the common curse and misery of Revolution'.[159] After Spa Fields, something more was obviously necessary. No longer was it just the government's job to save the country; the malignancy had exposed itself at the meetings and was clearly too dangerous merely to rely on the efforts of state. An attempt to rally the loyal was made: 'What is required of us is that we

---

[152] *St James's Chronicle*, 9208, 9210, 30 November–3 December 1816, 5–7 December 1816.
[153] Belchem, *'Orator' Hunt*, p. 58.   [154] Prothero, *Artisans and Politics*, p. 95.
[155] 20 November 1816, Sidmouth Papers, 152/OH Unrest etc., Devon County Record Office, Exeter.
[156] For references to the riots of 1780 during the Corn Bill riots of 1815, see Eldon to Beckett, 8 March 1815, HO 42/143, fo. 83; Arthur Morris, Bailiff of Westminster, to Sidmouth, 9 March 1815, HO 42/143, fo. 88.
[157] *The Courier*, 14 January 1817.
[158] 'Rise and Progress of Popular Disaffection', *Quarterly Review* (January 1817), p. 552.
[159] 'Parliamentary Reform', *ibid.* (October 1816), p. 278.

be as active in good as the malevolent are active in evil; let each man do his duty in his respective station ... and it will be found that the good principle is mightier than the evil one.'[160] The rise of the 'mass platform' had prompted not only a government reaction but also a loyal one.[161]

VII

But the momentum of the Hampden Clubs in the provinces had also been increased by the Spa Fields agitation. In Manchester John Bagguley, Samuel Drummond and John Johnston spoke in vehement threatening tones throughout January and February about extricating the people 'from an odious and tyrannical Government'.[162] The escalation of the tone and stridency of language at meetings in Manchester and elsewhere at the beginning of March is incomprehensible without an awareness of this corresponding escalation in government and loyalist activity. The march of the blanketeers was the last attempt to petition parliament before the government suspended habeas corpus and instituted repressive legislation. The coincidence of a London Hampden Club delegate meeting and the attack on the Prince Regent in January 1817 was too much for a government many of whose members had served their political apprenticeships during the 1790s. Much of the Pittite repressive legislation of that decade was re-enacted. The Habeas Corpus Suspension Act passed the two Houses of parliament by 1 March 1817. Bills were passed which restricted the right of public meeting and banned the election of delegates by provincial and metropolitan clubs.[163] Sidmouth defended these bills in the Lords on the grounds of defending the constitution. He 'required the suspension of the Habeas Corpus Act, in pity to the peaceable and loyal inhabitants of the Country, for the protection of the two Houses of parliament, for the maintenance of our liberties, and for the security

---

[160] 'Rise and Progress ...', *ibid.* (January 1817), p. 552.
[161] *The Declaration of the Merchants, Bankers, Traders and Inhabitants of London at a Meeting Held the 31st Day of January 1817 ...*, HO 55/34. See also W. H. M. to Sidmouth, 22 January 1817, HO 40/3 part I, fo. 57; Address of the Grand Jury at Manchester Quarter Sessions, 25 January 1817, HO 40/3 part I, fo. 128; 20 January 1817, Manchester Pitt Club records; Norwich produced Brunswick clubs to oppose the Hampden Clubs, 17 December 1816, HO 40/3 part II, fo. 47.
[162] Deposition of S. F. before Rev. C. W. Ethelston, 28 January 1817, HO 40/3 part I, fo. 140.
[163] The acts were 57 George III cap. 3 (Habeas Corpus Suspension), 57 George III cap. 6 (extension of Act to Protect King's Person to Regent), 57 George III cap. 19 (Seditious Meetings, 31 March 1817) and 57 George III caps. 38 and 50.

of the blessings of the Constitution'.[164] The resort to meet for the purpose of petitioning parliament was no longer available. The only option left was revolution.

Those engaged in the attempted insurrections were persuaded that the social contract binding governors and governed had been broken by the rulers. As Thompson himself points out, on the evidence of William Stevens, a Nottingham needlemaker, resistance to tyranny was a definite option for many reformers in the face of the treatment meted out by parliament. But this was more than simply a 'rhetoric'[165] or a 'style'.[166] It was a real possibility; and, as importantly, a point of debate at which radicals could undermine the constitutionalism of conservatives, for whom 1688 was a 'Glorious Revolution' also. Precisely these ambiguities surrounded the question of the legitimacy of these risings. All the constitutional authorities, like Blackstone, were vague about the moment when resistance became a duty. The defence of Brandreth and the Pentridge rebels as the dupes of 'Oliver' the *agent provacateur* in part avoided the whole question of the solidity of the social contract by denying that revolution had ever been the rebels' aim. The Whiggish historiographical tradition, particularly the Hammonds, by believing and elaborating these radical arguments about 'Oliver', obscured the possibility of violence always available in the constitutionalist tradition.[167] While the Thompsonian tradition has criticised the Whiggish tradition, they have stressed what was modern ('proletarian') about such rebellion by concentrating on the social position of the rioters. The justification for the risings was never made on the basis of class oppression. The government was at fault; it was the enemy, as Brandreth repeated in verse on the night of 9 June 1817:

> Every man his skill must try
> He must turn out and not deny;
> No bloody soldier must he dread,
> He must turn out and fight for bread.
> The time is come you plainly see
> The government opposed must be.

Brandreth tried to persuade his followers that 'they should proceed from Nottingham to London, and wipe off the National Debt.'[168] To identify a corrupt government as the enemy in the minds of these men

---

[164] *Annual Register*, 1817, p. 24.   [165] Thompson, *The Making*, p. 684.
[166] *Ibid.*, p. 685.
[167] *Ibid.*, p. 713: see the strictures here on the Hammonds, and Cole and Postgate.
[168] Both quoted in *ibid.*, p. 724.

is to show that political identity was the motivating factor in their behaviour. If we accept such a re-interpretation, the explanation of the failure of these risings and of the course of the reform movement can then be based on an examination of the activities of other political groups and the state.

4

⁓

Public opinion, violence and the limits of constitutional politics

DROR WAHRMAN

In June 1820 Robert Isaac Cruikshank (brother of the better-known George Cruikshank) produced an unusually elaborate political print, titled *The Time Piece! & C^{u}nning Jack O' Both Sides* (figure 4.1). The issue which prompted this print, and which famously dominated politics throughout the summer and autumn of 1820, was the notorious 'trial' of Queen Caroline, namely the proceedings in the House of Lords through which the new king George IV attempted to divorce his wife Caroline of Brunswick on the grounds of adultery, and thus to prevent her from taking her place as queen. Cruikshank's remarkable image could be read on two levels. Explicitly, as the print's title indicated, it was a stab at George Canning, a former friend of the queen who now retreated into ambiguous dithering; and as such it was an intervention in the current political debate, expressing a pro-queen stance.[1] But this appears to have been a secondary objective of Cruikshank's production, as is evident in the relegation of the hesitant Canning to a relatively inconspicuous place at the bottom of the composition. Rather, this print maintained a fairly neutral outlook overall, distant and critical towards

I am grateful to David Armitage, David Bell, Ian Burney, Richard Davis, James Epstein, Philip Harling, Stephen Larsen, Peter Mandler, Lawrence Stone and James Vernon for comments on earlier versions of this essay; and to Marcus Daniel for conversations he might no longer remember.

[1] The print was probably occasioned by Canning's parliamentary speech on 7 June in which he defended the proceedings against the queen while also paying tribute to her 'fascinating manners'; a speech which according to Charles Greville 'is said to have given as great dissatisfaction to the Queen as to the King'. (*Hansard's Parliamentary Debates* n.s., vol. I, cols. 950 ff. *The Greville Memoirs 1814–1860*, eds. L. Strachey and R. Fulford, 18 vols. (London, 1938), vol. I, p. 96). Canning was notorious for unprincipled political wavering: in Hazlitt's words in October the same year, 'with him inversion is the order of nature' (in the *London Magazine*, reprinted in *Complete Works of William Hazlitt*, ed. P. P. Howe, 21 vols. (London, 1930–4), vol. XVII, p. 20; I am grateful to Philip Harling for this citation).

Fig. 4.1. Robert Isaac Cruikshank's *The Time Piece! & Cᵘnning Jack O' Both
Sides*, June 1820.

all participants in the political scene – a noncommittal stance which Dorothy George has long ago noted as unusual.[2] Taking advantage of this detached viewpoint, and (characteristically) packing into the design as much as it could bear, Cruikshank's prescriptive political message was overshadowed by an ambitious symbolic representation of politics and the political process as a whole; and it is in (one possible reading of) this comprehensive portrayal of politics in mid-1820 that we are interested here.

Cruikshank portrayed the political system as a large clock. The clock's dial represented the foundations of the British constitution – 'KING, LORDS, COMMONS'. The dial's hands, the central focus of the composition, were the stretched hands of Queen Caroline. The rest of the image reproduced starkly the oft-noted political polarisation of those years; a point driven home time and again by the clever use of symmetrical antitheses – between the similarly shaped cornucopia and cap of liberty supporting the dial, between the queen's supporters and opponents vainly attempting to seduce her on both sides of the dial, between Brougham and Castlereagh fighting beneath it, between the crown and the cap of liberty luring Canning in the pendulum, and (in every detail) between the two upright supports of the clock – the one representing the army and navy, the crown and the church, and the other representing the radicals.

And yet, polarised as politics might have been, Cruikshank did not see its centrifugal pressures sending it out of control. Thus the armed soldiers and radicals at the base of both supports did not threaten or in any way engage with each other. Indeed the very layout of the image, separating them safely to its two extremes, controlled their potential for violent encounter: there was no visual contact between them, let alone a more direct interaction (a point reinforced further by the secure harnessing *en masse* of the potentially destructive arms of both sides – bayonets and pikes – in support of the upper beams). Instead, the only violent interaction in this representation of politics was that between

---

[2] M. D. George, *Catalogue of Political and Personal Satires Preserved in the Department of Prints and Drawings in the British Museum* (hereafter *BMC*), vol. IX (London, 1949), no. 13738, and p. xxii. Indeed, the political message of Cruikshank's *Time Piece* was not too clear to contemporaries: it could thus be found represented in another print, a few weeks later, as part of the display in an *anti-queen* publisher's shop-window (*BMC* 14206). It is also worth noting that a year later Robert Cruikshank inserted himself into one of his prints in a similarly non-committed way, meditatively smoking a pipe in whose smoke appeared the words 'Much may be said on both sides' (*BMC* 14194). Still, a hint of his sympathy for the queen can be seen in Castlereagh's defensive pose when attacked by Brougham (underneath the dial of the *Time Piece*); and compare *BMC* 13730, also of June 1820, in which Cruikshank paid tribute to a dignified queen for resisting ministerial bribery.

Brougham and Castlereagh at the base of the clock's dial. But this was not an outburst of unbridled violence: quite the contrary, it was a pugilistic match, that is to say a stylised and controlled exchange of blows, the regulated orderliness of which was visually underscored by the boxing gloves worn by both combatants, and by the seconds that duly accompanied them.

Of course, the 'violence' exchanged between Brougham and Castlereagh was not physical, but that of *words*; a distinction of which viewers of this print were well aware. Cruikshank's point was clear – verbal altercations between rival politicians in-doors, controlled and stylised like the pugilistic match, stood vicariously for the potentially more violent and uncontrolled clashes between political adversaries out-of-doors; clashes like those that had been etched in national memory by the bloody events of Peterloo, less than a year earlier, between soldiers and radicals much like those at the two sides of this image. The threatening shadows evoked by that explosive confrontation were unmistakably present in the image (note 'PANDORA's BOX' beneath the radicals' feet), but ultimately Cruikshank's vision of politics allowed no place for such destabilising eruptions. Rather, the same symmetrical oppositions that were the visual rendering of political polarisation served at the same time to highlight the balanced and stable equilibrium of the structure as a whole. Despite Cruikshank's obvious suspicion of the ragged radicals, he still assigned the two opposing sides, complete with their symbols, flags and arms, an equal role in supporting the whole edifice; both were equally necessary to turn it into a unified interconnected mechanism.

Moreover, the mechanism that Cruikshank chose for his symbolic representation of politics was *a clock*; an image that had long been associated in European culture with harmony and order.[3] God's universe was often likened to a clockwork mechanism. Likewise, the political process in Cruikshank's print was a complex mechanism, one that despite its complexity – or rather because of it – could be depended upon to work in a controlled and disciplined manner. And just like the omnipresent divine clockmaker, remote and infinite, overlooking the smooth interaction and coordination of the numerous parts of his providential clockwork universe, so Cruikshank's political clockwork had its own elevated overseer. This supreme presence was the wide-eyed head – much larger than any other in the image – crowning the

[3] See Otto Mayr, *Authority, Liberty and Automatic Machinery in Early Modern Europe* (Baltimore, 1986).

composition, for which the curved arms of the clock structure served as surrogate arms embracing the whole political universe: the head, as the caption explained, of 'Chief Justice Bull – Jurisdiction – ad Infinitum'.

This was a new position for John Bull. In the 1790s – according to John Brewer, 'the decade of John Bull' – the numerous portrayals of this symbolic Englishman had endowed him with little dignity, power or authority. Typically, as Brewer has noted, John Bull had turned out to be a broad-grinning buffoon, a dim-witted glutton or a child-like simpleton; a helpless and hapless victim of the real powers to be.[4] But the John Bull of 1820 now found himself placed in a rather different situation, that of a magisterial overseer presiding over the whole constitutional edifice and political playing field – over the opposing political camps, and even over king, Lords and Commons (note the crown significantly placed beneath John Bull's chin). His claimed role of ultimate arbiter was symbolically embodied (here as in others of Cruikshank's images at that time) in the huge judge's wig, extended over his dominion. His supposedly supreme authority was moreover reinforced by the metaphor of the clock, which had had a long history of association with representations of authoritarian political structures.[5] But at the same time that Cruikshank placed John Bull in such a position of paramount importance, he also subverted it by representing him as cross-eyed and befuddled: the satirist, from his detached and critical perspective, apparently had his doubts about John Bull's ability to fulfil this august role.

As Miles Taylor has recently pointed out, John Bull was frequently – and in this case, undoubtedly – a metaphorical device for talking about *public opinion*.[6] And indeed, in analogy to the role assumed by John Bull in Cruikshank's print, political debates in the years immediately preceding its publication were characterised by a striking prominence of appeals to and invocations of 'public opinion', placing it in a similarly elevated metapolitical position as the ultimate constitutional arbiter and

[4] John Brewer, *The Common People and Politics 1750–1790s* (Cambridge, 1986), pp. 41–3.
[5] Indeed, as Otto Mayr (*Authority, Liberty and Automatic Machinery*) has shown, because of this close affinity between the clock metaphor (with its inherent preordained order, and its prerequisite omnipotent clockmaker) and representations of authoritarian regimes (notably in France and Germany), it had been relatively rare in England, where the flowering of a constitutional monarchy encouraged a series of very different mechanical metaphors, based on equilibrium systems of 'checks and balances'. Against this background, Cruikshank's choice of a clock image, and the authoritarian position of John Bull in it, are all the more remarkable. For John Bull as a wigged judge, exercising his jurisdiction over the king, see also Robert Cruikshank's *Half-a-Crown Lost!* of October–November 1820: *BMC* 13939.
[6] M. Taylor, 'John Bull and the Iconography of Public Opinion in England c. 1712–1929', *Past and Present*, 134 (1992), pp. 93–128.

adjudicator; a phenomenon that provides the starting point for what follows. Moreover, just as John Bull occupied the apex of the unified central axis of this otherwise bifurcated image, so 'public opinion' will be seen to have been widely presented as a unified, univocal entity, set above political divisions and capable of checking their centrifugal tendencies. But this understanding of the role of 'public opinion', it is then suggested, despite some assertions of contemporaries and latter-day historians to the contrary, was not at all a natural, self-evident or inherently plausible one – a point underscored by Cruikshank's ridicule. Establishing this claim requires a broader perspective on the uses of 'public opinion' in political debates before and after the specific moment discussed here: through a survey of the ways in which 'public opinion' was invoked between the 1790s and the 1830s it becomes evident that the role assigned to it in the late 1810s was quite extraordinary. It is not, therefore, to attributes inherent to the concept of 'public opinion' that we should look to explain the unusual part it played in the political language of the late 1810s, but rather to the specific and indeed unusual circumstances of that particular moment.

Furthermore, by unravelling the specific logic of the post-war prominence of 'public opinion' we are able in turn to enrich our understanding of the peculiarities of politics at that juncture. As suggested by Cruikshank's *Time Piece*, emphasising 'public opinion' in this particular way involved an understanding of the political process in which the possibility of violence was limited and disciplined within the overall dependable operation of an orderly political mechanism, a mechanism capable of absorbing pressures of disintegration. In August 1819, however, the pressures generated by the violent confrontation at Peterloo (following alarming signs during the previous months) appeared to expose the unsound foundations of this benign picture. The subsequent Queen Caroline affair, by contrast, is seen below to have been a powerful recuperative moment, triumphantly reinstating and reinforcing this benign view of the political process. By linking, therefore, these two major eruptions of national energy (which cannot be adequately understood apart from each other), the final section of this essay shows the resulting climax of the 'public-opinion'-based understanding of politics that was induced by the agitation for the queen. By the end of this journey, therefore, we might have a better insight into how the queen and John Bull came to be coupled together as the linchpins of Cruikshank's representation of the mechanics of politics in mid-1820, constituting in tandem the unifying axis that provided direction and guidance (after all, it was the queen's hands that fulfilled the intended function of the clock – telling time), and that prevented the polarised extremes from tearing the social and political fabric apart.

Building therefore on the picture of post-war British politics as it has been drawn by many able historians, the purpose of this essay is to tease out certain links between political language and political action; namely, to show how political circumstances induced specific understandings of the constitution and the political process (in this case, understandings focused around the role and nature of 'public opinion'), and how those understandings, in turn, imposed certain directives and constraints on further political behaviour. Along the way, this essay also questions some of the assumptions that historians – more often historians of France than of Britain – have recently made with regard to the historical meanings and uses of 'public opinion'.

One disclaimer might also not be out of place, with regard to what this essay does *not* do. The conventional textbook account of this period inevitably gives much due to the continual growth of public opinion throughout the late eighteenth and the first half of the nineteenth centuries. What follows does nothing to challenge (or, for that matter, to confirm) this prevailing account, which was already noted by many contemporary observers. It is not concerned with the development of public opinion as a social scientist would gauge it (based on parameters such as the growth of the press and of popular political mobilisation), but with the development of contemporary understandings of what 'public opinion' meant and what role could it be expected to play. At the end of the day, however, we might conclude that the correlation between these two developments was far less simple or straightforward than what one might have initially been led to expect.

I

On 11 October 1819 a popular meeting was held in Newcastle upon Tyne to discuss the notorious 'massacre of Peterloo', that event which more than any other worked to exacerbate and entrench post-war political polarisation. In Newcastle, the local manifestation of this polarisation was the pitting of reformists and radicals against the town corporation, together with placemen and pensioners – the loyalist elite of the town and their followers. 'These men', complained the 'official' account of this popular meeting, '[who] have generally taken the lead in all public affairs in this town ... deem themselves not only the most respectable part of the community, but *the regular channels of public opinion*.' But in fact, it continued, nothing was further from the truth; what they say 'gives no view whatever of the state of public opinion', since 'the great bulk of the people has long had the misfortune to be misrepresented' by this self-proclaimed elite, a misrepresentation abetted by the corporation's corrupting influence throughout the town. 'Little has therefore been known, generally, of the state of public opinion in this place'; an unfortunate deficiency which the October popular meeting was supposed to rectify.[7]

At the same time that this account set the scene for political disagreement, however, it also offers us a glimpse of the ground that the opposing adversaries *shared* – a common ground underscored by insistent reiteration: namely, the importance attached to the authority and verdict of 'public opinion', resulting therefore in a struggle over who could claim to represent it. As one pamphlet put it shortly thereafter, 'we hear from all quarters appeals to the shelter and countenance of public opinion'; though it still remained necessary 'to demand from those who so loudly magnify the value of public opinion, whom they mean by the *public*'.[8] John Bull's verdict was considered paramount by all sides; a shared consensus that generated competing claims for the recovery of this verdict, as in the case of the contest over the mantle of the 'genuine' herald of 'public opinion' between the conservative *John Bull* newspaper (launched by Theodore Hook in December 1820) and its radical rival *Real John Bull* (counter-launched a month later by William Benbow).[9]

Indeed, however people chose to define it, there is little doubt that the post-war years saw an extraordinary outburst of confidence in 'public opinion' as the ultimate key to the political process – an omnipotent, infallible, supreme arbiter; a development which culmi-

---

[7]   *A Full Account of the General Meeting of the Inhabitants of Newcastle upon Tyne and the Vicinity ... on Monday the 11th of October, 1819 ... for the Purpose of Taking into Consideration the Late Proceedings in Manchester* (Newcastle upon Tyne, 1819), p. [2] (my emphasis).

[8]   *Statement of the Question of Parliamentary Reform: With a Reply to the Objections of the Edinburgh Review, No. LXI* (London, 1821), pp. 125–9.

[9]   See Taylor, 'John Bull and the Iconography of Public Opinion', p. 106. Taylor however seems intent (despite some assertions to the contrary) on providing a single narrative for the evolution of John Bull, presuming him at any given moment to represent 'predominantly' one unified meaning. Given the contradictory political agendas for which John Bull (as a symbolic vehicle for 'public opinion') was in fact enlisted, therefore, the result is necessarily a diluted compromise, an 'average' of opposing political stances, that divests him of political potency and leaves him with an ambiguous and ineffective political identity. 'By 1820', Taylor concludes, 'John Bull was neither loyalist nor radical.' But we might gain more from seeing John Bull as emphatically and committedly *both*, thus restoring his political relevance (a relevance attested to by the vigorous contestation over the right to represent him); though this could be the case precisely because John Bull, while gaining increased consequence for all political contenders, stood at the same time for mutually exclusive and irreconcilable positions that *cannot* be harmoniously synthesised into a unified compromise nor incorporated into a single coherent narrative.

nated with particular force in the Queen Caroline affair, as we shall presently see. 'This is not a time at which PUBLIC OPINION can be trifled with', John Lambton (later Lord Durham) told parliament in 1821. 'The all-conquering power of PUBLIC OPINION', he declared, 'is making rapid and mighty progress throughout the world.'[10] In the late 1810s such statements flowed from all sides in tireless repetition: 'The great security of the Constitution, then, [is] the vigilance of public opinion'; 'a new Leviathan has grown up, called Public Opinion'; 'the *Borough-mongers* [will] vanish in the unanimous, aweful, and omnipotent voice of public opinion'; 'Public opinion, [is] that great ultimate arbiter of all human merit'; 'a tribunal which cannot err … its decision being the only standard of right and wrong'; 'public opinion is never long misled'; and it has 'never-failing corrective power'.[11] In order to express this inordinate power, writers were combing the natural world in search of an analogous force: 'The march of public opinion … is more stronger than the waters that sweep from the *Nile* to the oceans'; 'public opinion has … electric force'; 'it is as vain to oppose its commands as it would be to order the earth not to revolve upon its axis'. For others, who saw it as an inevitable byproduct of the progress of civilisation, the analogy had to be to a power man-made, such as an 'all-powerful and ever acting engine'.[12] To be sure, such pronouncements rolled more readily off the tongues of reformists, liberals and radicals than off those of their adversaries; but (as was suggested by the report of the Newcastle meeting) the grip that this notion achieved over political language in the late 1810s was such that the more conservative voices were no less eager to harness 'the power of public opinion' to their own anti-reformist agendas. 'Everyone, who has the slightest regard for the constitution', declared the *Anti-Jacobin Review and Magazine* in one instance, should

---

[10] Speech of 17 April 1821; in *Speeches of the Earl of Durham, on Reform of Parliament* (London, 1835), p. 41. On the role of 'public opinion' in the political debate of the late 1810s see also D. Wahrman, *Imagining the Middle Class: The Political Representation of Class in Britain, c. 1780–1840* (Cambridge, 1995), pp. 190–9.

[11] Henry Brougham in the *Edinburgh Review*, 27, September 1816, p. 250 (and see also 245, 249); *Examiner*, 472, 12 January 1817, p. 17 (and see similarly, among virtually innumerable examples, 480, 9 March 1817, pp. 146–7; 535, 29 March 1818, p. 193; 654, 9 July 1820, pp. 433–4); *The Gorgon*, 7, 4 July 1818, p. 50; 17, 12 September 1818, p. 129 (and see also 10, 25 July 1818, p. 73; 26, 14 November 1818, p. 205); Charles Maclean, *The Triumph of Public Opinion: Being a Standing Lesson to the Throne, the Parliament, and the People … in the Case of Her Majesty Caroline, Queen of England* (London, 1820), p. [1]; *The State of the Nation at the Commencement of the Year 1822 …* , 2nd edn (London, 1822), p. 193; *Examiner*, 719, 14 October 1821, p. 642.

[12] William Benbow, *The Whigs Exposed: Or, Truth by Day-Light. Addressed to the Reformers of Britain* (London, 1820), p. 12. *Black Dwarf*, 4, 12 January 1820, p. 3. J. Nightingale (ed.), *The Spirit of the Addresses Presented to the Queen, with Her Majesty's Answers* (n.p., [1820?]), p. 30. *Examiner* 556, 23 August 1818, p. 520 (letter to editor).

'now rally around the throne, lest public opinion respecting it be perverted'; while another writer of similar convictions pronounced his confidence that the 'Sovereign public opinion', despite the deluding efforts of unprincipled radicals, 'would soon right itself'.[13]

Reminiscent of the position assumed by John Bull in Cruikshank's *Time Piece*, 'public opinion' was presented in the late 1810s as the fount of authority and legitimation, most evidently by those numerous pamphleteers and journalists who appealed to it (often in their opening paragraphs) in justification of their writing. Like Cruikshank's John Bull, the power of 'public opinion' was asserted to be superior to that of King ('The crown is dependent upon the public opinion'), Lords ('That House [of Lords] will have to appear at the bar of public opinion') and Commons ('the re-appearance of public opinion, influencing the conduct of that assembly, may justly be considered as one of the various changes, now passing in the world'); as well as to all other branches of government ('In opposition to public opinion, the wig of the judge and the feather of the soldier are alike powerless').[14] Like the claims of Cruikshank's John Bull, 'public opinion' was now endowed with infinite jurisdiction as the ultimate metapolitical arbiter; a role underscored by the frequent use of legal language (as in 'the Tribunal of Public Opinion shall try, convict, and ... *punish* you'; or, 'every one recognises its jurisdiction, and courts it as a tribunal ... from whence a righteous verdict is sure to emanate'). Alternatively, 'public opinion' was also

---

[13] [Rev. Lionel Thomas Berguer], *A Letter to the Gentlemen of England, upon the Present Critical Conjuncture of Affairs* (London, 1819), p. 9. *Anti-Jacobin Review and Magazine*, 59, September 1820, p. 34. [John Wilson Croker?], *A Letter from the King to his People*, 12th edn, (London, [1820]), pp. 2–3. For some conservatives this sudden need to acknowledge 'public opinion' was in obvious tension with an habitual disdain for the political understanding of the people; as was the case for one anti-reformer, who while taking apparent pride in the then-fashionable observation that 'in this country, no Minister can long maintain himself' against the bar of 'public opinion', could also ask a few pages later: 'What is so fluctuating as public opinion? Who so liable to be dazzled by glitter, and led away by false lights, as the people?'; W. J. Ching, *England's Danger: Or, Reform Unmasked* (London, 1819), pp. 23–4, 31. And note Peel's oft-cited begrudging acknowledgement of the influence and liberality of 'public opinion', combined with deep distrust: 'Do you not think that the tone of England – of that great compound of folly, weakness, prejudice, wrong feeling, right feeling, obstinacy, and newspaper paragraphs, which is called public opinion – is more liberal ... than the policy of the Government? ... It seems to me a curious crisis – when public opinion never had such influence on public measures, and yet never was so dissatisfied with the share which it possessed'; Peel to Croker, 23 March 1820; in *The Croker Papers: The Correspondence and Diaries of the Late Right Honourable John Wilson Croker*, ed. L. J. Jennings, 2 vols. (New York, 1884), vol. i, pp. 155–6.

[14] [Thomas Attwood], *Prosperity Restored: Or, Reflections on the Cause of the Public Distresses, and on the Only Means of Relieving Them* (London, 1817), p. 133. Queen Caroline's response to an address from Hammersmith, quoted in the *Anti-Jacobin Review and Magazine*, 59, September 1820, p. 71. *Remarks upon the Last Session of Parliament: By a Near Observer*, 2nd edn (London, 1822), p. 1. *Black Dwarf*, 4, 12 January 1820, p. 3.

discussed in constitutional language (as, in one high Tory exhortation, 'a powerful check on Parliament'), highlighting its perception as a keystone in the edifice of the constitution. It was the 'greatest excellence' of 'our glorious constitution'; it was the constitution's 'corrective for any mistaken principle or diseased action in the conduct of power'. And ultimately, just like the analogy suggested by Cruikshank's *Time Piece* between John Bull and the divine clockmaker, so Henry Bathurst, the Bishop of Norwich, declared 'public opinion' in a sermon that same year to be the expression of 'the favouring aid of Divine Providence', 'righting the vessel of state', which was 'ample cause for calling on the public to unite in thankfulness towards Heaven'. 'Public opinion', then, was perceived as divinely ordained, the manifestation of the hand of providence in human affairs; as one speaker put it with unbound confidence, these were indeed 'magic words'.[15]

II

But perhaps all this is not very surprising. After all, isn't it simply one more example of that reign of 'public opinion' that was the inevitable culmination of the transformation wrought upon politics by Enlightenment reason? Some historians would have us believe so. The key example of this supposed transformation, or at least the one studied most closely in recent years, is that of the French ancien régime in its final decades before the French Revolution; it is thus there, perhaps more than anywhere else, that historians' assumptions and expectations with regard to 'public opinion' have been formed and can be examined.

As David Bell has summarised it, the basic argument of this recent spate of historical work is that 'a new, critical attitude' developed among the French in the second half of the eighteenth century, and that 'the application of this rational criticism led men and women to identify political legitimacy less with the sovereign himself than with "public opinion", which had lost its earlier reputation for instability and irrationality, and had come to be considered the embodiment of reason'.[16] Thus Roger Chartier, for instance, in an influential account

---

15   *The State of the Nation at the Commencement of the Year 1822*, p. 2. *Black Dwarf*, 4, 12 January 1820, p. 3. *Examiner*, 654, 9 July 1820, p. 433 (and see also 745, 5 May 1822, p. 280, for 'the gibbet of public opinion'). *Statement of the Question of Parliamentary Reform*, p. 125. Rev. Melville Horne, *The Moral and Political Crisis of England: Most Respectfully Inscribed to the Higher and Middle Classes* (London, 1820), p. 6. *Examiner*, 556, 23 August 1818, p. 520. Henry Bathurst, *A Sermon, Intended to Have Been Preached before Her Majesty the Queen ... 29th of November, 1820 ...* (London, 1820), pp. 10–12.

16   D. Bell, *Lawyers and Citizens: The Making of a Political Elite in Old Regime France* (New York,

of the 'cultural origins' of the French Revolution, places much emphasis
on a new sceptical attitude towards received authorities, linked to such
developments as critical habits of reading and the desacralisation of the
king. A key element in this 'progress of critical modes of thinking',
according to Chartier, was a 'new political culture' that 'transferred the
seat of authority from the will of the king alone' to 'the judgment of an
entity embodied in no institution, which debated publicly and was more
sovereign than the sovereign'; this was 'public opinion, set up as a
sovereign authority and a final arbiter, [which] was necessarily stable,
unified and founded on reason'.[17]

Chartier, like many other 'public-opinion' enthusiasts, has followed
here the path suggested by Jürgen Habermas in his field-shaping *The
Structural Transformation of the Public Sphere*. Poised between the state and
civil society, this bourgeois public sphere – a historically specific
phenomenon of the European Enlightenment – was 'the sphere of
private people com[ing] together as a public', 'making use of their
reason', and thus turning it into 'a sphere of criticism of public
authority'. 'The self-interpretation of the function of the bourgeois
public sphere', Habermas continues, 'crystallized in the idea of "public
opinion"'. Importantly, according to Habermas the key to the formation of 'public opinion' (somewhat indiscriminately both as a political
authority and as a concept representing this authority) was the conditions under which it was formed: the closer it came to being generated
by public discussion between informed individuals exercising freely their
critical reason, communicating in a sphere where social hierarchies and
dependencies were suspended, the closer it necessarily came to that
ideal 'true opinion', unified, enlightened and ultimately infallible, the
only source of legitimate authority. Habermas measures the conditions
prevailing in various historical moments against this ideal, and often
finds them lacking to a lesser or greater degree – especially after the mid

1994), p. 10. Compare also D. Goodman, *The Republic of Letters: A Cultural History of the French
Enlightenment* (Ithaca, 1994), pp. 235 ff.; M. V. Becker, *The Emergence of Civil Society in the
Eighteenth Century* (Bloomington, 1994), p. 5.

[17] R. Chartier, *The Cultural Origins of the French Revolution* (Durham, 1991); quoted pp. 27, 30,
134. See also K. M. Baker, 'Public Opinion as Political Invention', in his *Inventing the French
Revolution* (Cambridge, 1990), pp. 167–99. There was more than one way to derive this
image of 'public opinion' from Enlightenment beliefs – either as embodying the absolute
power of reason, or as replacing the absolute authority of divinely-ordained kings: see F.
Furet, *Interpreting the French Revolution* (Cambridge, 1981), pp. 38–9. B. Nathans, 'Habermas's "Public Sphere" in the Era of the French Revolution', *French Historical Studies*, 16
(1990), pp. 620–44, pp. 637–8. J. Popkin, 'The Concept of Public Opinion in the
Historiography of the French Revolution: A Critique', *Storia della Storiografia* 20 (1991),
pp. 77–92.

nineteenth century.[18] But the basic ideal scenario is not put in doubt: under favourable circumstances, the emergence of 'public opinion' as a supreme arbiter, unified and omnipotent – that is, precisely as it was heralded throughout England in the late 1810s – appears by this view immanently reasonable, an inevitable concomitant of a properly functioning public sphere.

But perhaps we should not be so quick to accept this notion of 'public opinion' as immanently reasonable. As Daniel Gordon has pointed out, theorists of 'public opinion', from those who articulated the concept during the period in which Habermas locates its origins down to Habermas himself, have not provided a theoretical justification for this view of 'public opinion' as an attainable, intelligent and beneficent consensus.[19] When Chartier posits the emergence of 'public opinion' as the culmination of the Enlightenment application of critical reason, one might ask whether this very belief itself, in the existence and possible recovery of a unified infallible verdict of 'public opinion', was not in truth a testimony to the *limits* of Enlightenment reason. Or perhaps it is better to see it not as an unfortunate limitation of Enlightenment reason, but rather as an *enabling contradiction*, in that it allowed the suppression of irrationality in order to maintain ostensible coherence.[20] But be that as it may, such a confident belief, absolute and uncondi-

---

[18] J. Habermas, *The Structural Transformation of the Public Sphere: An Inquiry into a Category of Bourgeois Society*, trans. T. Burger (1962; Cambridge, MA, 1989), quoted pp. 27, 51, 89, 95. See also K. M. Baker, 'Defining the Public Sphere in Eighteenth-Century France: Variations on a Theme by Habermas', in C. Calhoun (ed.), *Habermas and the Public Sphere* (Cambridge, MA, 1992), pp. 181–211; and D. Goodman, 'Public Sphere and Private Life: Toward a Synthesis of Current Historiographical Approaches to the Old Regime', *History and Theory*, 31 (1992), pp. 1–20, esp. p. 5.

[19] D. Gordon, 'Philosophy, Sociology, and Gender in the Enlightenment Conception of Public Opinion', *French Historical Studies*, 17 (1992), pp. 882–91, p. 886; and *idem*, *Citizens without Sovereignty: Equality and Sociability in French Thought, 1670–1789* (Princeton, 1994), pp. 174, 200–1, where Gordon refers to the Enlightenment notion of 'public opinion' as a 'myth', 'a lie or a fantasy'. It should also be noted that Enlightenment philosophers, *pace* Chartier, were themselves not always blinded by a reverence to 'public opinion' to the problems inherent in the concept: in addition to Gordon, see for example M. Ozouf, ' "Public Opinion" at the End of the Old Regime', *Journal of Modern History*, 60 (1988), supplement, pp. s1–s21.

[20] The spectre of irrationality might lead us even further (and into a discussion beyond the scope of this essay), by raising doubts about the very ideal of an attainable, universally accepted standard of reason, an ideal which of course underlay the confident belief in 'public opinion'. As Wendy Motooka has intriguingly suggested (in 'The Age of Reasons: Quixotism and Sentiment in Eighteenth-Century Britain' (Ph.D, University of Michigan, 1992)), this was a doubt that haunted Enlightenment writers time and again, surfacing persistently (if not always self-consciously) through the ubiquitous figure of Don Quixote – the most eloquent embodiment of an alternative standard of reason. Indeed, it even surfaced – albeit inconspicuously – on one of the bars in the pendulum of Cruikshank's *Time Piece*; and see also figure 4.4.

tional, certainly placed 'public opinion' itself beyond the bounds of critical reasoning.

More important to our discussion than the question of the theoretical justification for the Habermasian view of 'public opinion', however, are the ways in which contemporaries themselves perceived it and made use of it: whether theoretically justified or not, did they hold to this supposedly quintessential Enlightenment belief in the power of 'public opinion'? We have seen that during the post-war years (Cruikshank's satirical reservations about the competence of John Bull notwithstanding) 'public opinion' did indeed achieve a consensual elevated position in political debate, remarkably close to that anticipated by Habermas. But was this role assigned to 'public opinion' a 'natural' outcome of an enlightened age? Or was it in fact unusual, the distinctive product of peculiar circumstances specific to this historical juncture? In order to answer this question we need to take a longer-term perspective: the next two sections therefore sketch (albeit briefly) the uses of 'public opinion' in political debates before and after this particular moment, thus providing a broader picture within which the specificity of the late 1810s can be assessed.

III

A reasonable place to begin such a survey might be the 1790s, given the profound effects that the events in France had on the British political scene.[21] Indeed, following late ancien régime France, Britain in the 1790s similarly witnessed a marked proliferation in the uses of the notion of 'public opinion'. But the ways in which British speakers invoked 'public opinion' were in some important respects quite different from those of the French.

Most significantly, for the British speakers of the 1790s 'public opinion'

---

[21] What follows is based on the reading, prompted by another project (see n. 10), of more than 2,000 publications from the 1790s to the 1830s, primarily political, as well as several hundreds of volumes of periodicals and newspapers; and thus, though admittedly impressionistic (as well as constrained by limits of space), is informedly so. Moreover, it is intended as a sketch of the uses of 'public opinion' in political debate over a given span of time, not as an intellectual-historical genealogy of a concept whose origins go back a long way. For some starting points on the latter project see J. A. W. Gunn, 'Public Spirit to Public Opinion', in his *Beyond Liberty and Property: The Process of Self-Recognition in Eighteenth-Century Political Thought* (Kingston, 1983), pp. 260–315; *idem*, 'Public Opinion', in T. Ball *et al.* (eds.), *Political Innovation and Conceptual Change* (Cambridge, 1989), pp. 247–65. Gunn notes a peak of interest in 'public opinion' around the elections of 1784, which might provide an interesting prelude to the 1790s in that comprehensive history of the uses of the concept which still remains to be written.

largely turned out to be not an elevated metapolitical concept, occupying a position *above* the humdrum of adversarial politics, but rather very much a part of it. In modern times, wrote one moderate, '*public opinion* has risen to the rank of a fourth estate in our constitution' – one, that is, that contends with the other three. The consequence of this development, explained another (of a more conservative bent), was that 'public opinion and the voice of the people should be considered of some moment': *some* moment, not more.[22] And if 'public opinion' was simply one of several contenders in politics (usually, as here, synonymous with the popular or radical voice), it had – like all others – its own interests, its grievances, its enemies, even its own biases and myopias. Of course, it is hardly surprising to find radicals enlisting 'public opinion' on their side in the Manichean struggle between 'aristocracy' and 'people'.[23] What is more interesting is that so many speakers – from across the political board – were willing to accept the limiting consequences of this understanding of 'public opinion' for its possible role and power.

Outside radical circles, the most conspicuous consequence was a widespread scepticism, not to say outright suspicion, towards this 'public opinion'. Moderates were afraid of its demotic nature. Pitt's mistake, complained one, has been to 'float upon [the] surface' of 'the stream of public opinion', rather than to 'direct its course where wisdom or patriotism might suggest'. Political leaders should not 'chase the caprices of public opinion', echoed another member of the respectable non-radical opposition; those 'sudden revolutions of public opinion' which threatened political stability. The source of these apprehensions was never far away: the bloodier stages of the French Revolution were an ominous reminder, even to a writer who had initially been sympathetic to it, of the possibility that 'public opinion, the strongest sanction of moral law, will be depraved, and will afford all its authority to recommend as examples, those excesses and crimes which are committed, or may be pretended to be committed, in the fury of an ungovernable patriotism'.[24] James Mackintosh, in his famous response

---

[22] James Currie in letter of 8 April 1789; in William Wallace Currie (ed.), *Memoir of the Life, Writings, and Correspondence of James Currie, MD FRS of Liverpool*, 2 vols. (London, 1831), vol. II, p. 24. Thomas Hearn, *A Short View of the Rise and Progress of Freedom in Modern Europe, as Connected with the Causes Which Led to the French Revolution ... with a Vindication of the English Constitution ... in Answer to the Calumnies of Thomas Paine ...* (London, 1793), p. 7.

[23] 'A PEOPLE ARE FREE IN PROPORTION AS THEY FORM THEIR OWN OPINION', wrote Coleridge in the prospectus for his radical newspaper, *The Watchman* (*The Collected Works of Samuel Taylor Coleridge: The Watchman*, ed. L. Patton (Princeton, 1970), p. 4). Among many other such examples see also John Thelwall, *The Natural and Constitutional Right of Britons to Annual Parliaments, Universal Suffrage ...* (London, 1795), p. 19.

[24] Charles Faulkener, *An Enquiry into the Merits of Mr Pitt's Administration ...* (London, 1796),

to Edmund Burke in 1791, similarly displayed tensions in his writing
between wishful thinking ('public opinion' as 'infallible') and sobered
observation ('public opinion' as 'a mild authority ... of slow operation',
and readily corruptible). By the end of the decade one disillusioned
moderate cynically summed up the 'paradox' of 'the tyranny exercised
by means of public opinion': whereas in principle 'public opinion' and
liberty should go hand in hand, in practice 'all great changes of public
opinion have proceeded slower in this country, considering its freedom,
than in any other, because the government has been watchful to check
or promote them according to its own pleasure'. The unfortunate truth,
in short, was that 'a government may stand for a long time against
public opinion, while it has the power of the sword'.[25] And moving
further to the right, one can find side by side attempts to appropriate
'public opinion' for conservative agendas (like the 'Antidote against
French Poison' that distinguished the poisoned minds of the lower
orders from 'the general trend of public opinion ... set strongly and
decisively' in support of 'our present invaluable constitution'), and
dismissals of 'public opinion' as comprising 'the most contradictory
sentiments', as 'fickle', and as claiming to represent a unity not derived
'from any thing really existent in nature'.[26]

p. 65; also quoted in William Belsham, *Remarks on a Late Publication, Styled the History of the
Politics of Great Britain & France, &c. &c.* (London, 1800), p. 120. [Samuel Parr,] *A Sequel to the
Printed Paper Lately Circulated in Warwickshire by the Rev. Charles Curtis* ... (London, 1792),
pp. 67, 88. James Workman, 'A Letter to the Duke of Portland; Being an Answer to the
Two Letters of the Right Honourable Edmund Burke, against Treating for Peace with the
French Republic', January 1797; in his *Political Essays, Relative to the War of the French Revolution*
... (Alexandria, 1801), p. 117.

25 James Mackintosh, *Vindiciae Gallicae: Defence of the French Revolution and Its English Admirers,
against the Accusations of the Right Hon. Edmund Burke* ... (London, 1791), pp. 163, 333–4; and
see also 340. William Burdon, *Various Thoughts on Politics, Morality, and Literature* (Newcastle,
1800), pp. 8–10. Compare also another moderate who acknowledged the former role of
'public opinion' as 'umpire' between parties, but who argued that following the accession of
George III, 'a great part of this [role] has been since done away': Brooke Boothby, *A Letter
to the Right Honourable Edmund Burke*, 2nd edn with additions (London, 1791), pp. 97–8.

26 *The Miracle: An Antidote against French Poison* (London, 1793). [William Laurence Brown,] *An
Examination of the Causes and Conduct of the Present War with France* ... (London, 1798), pp. 3–4.
Jackson Barwis, *A Fourth Dialogue Concerning Liberty: Containing an Exposition of the Falsity of the
First and Leading Principles of the Present Revolutionists in Europe* (London, 1793), p. 8. Burke
himself attempted to appropriate 'public opinion', for example in *An Appeal from the New to
the Old Whigs* ... , in *The Works of Edmund Burke* (Boston, 1839), vol. III, pp. 424–5. Note also
the complaint about this tendency of ministerialist speakers in Thomas Bigge, *An Address to
the Inhabitants of Northumberland and Newcastle upon Tyne, who Petitioned against the Two Bills Lately
Depending in Parliament* (Newcastle, 1796), p. 3. Finally, compare Mark Philp's comments on
the ambivalence of 1790s conservatives towards the plebeian public, part distrusting, part
wooing: M. Philp, 'Vulgar Conservatism, 1792–3', *English Historical Review*, 110 (1995),
pp. 42–69, esp. pp. 44–5.

Overall, these examples (to which many more could be added[27]) should suffice to convey how confused, and often contradictory, were the understandings and assessments of 'public opinion' in the 1790s. And this is precisely the point: in contrast with its apotheosis in the post-war period, the notion of 'public opinion' in the 1790s did not become the centre of a widespread consensus regarding its political or constitutional role. Moreover, in contrast with the largely metapolitical and metacritical position which 'public opinion' attained in the post-war period, in the 1790s it was seen primarily as a contender in the political struggle, and as such – like other contenders – not immune to political mud-slinging. Public debates of the 1790s were therefore studded with expressions of scepticism about this 'public opinion', casting doubts on its efficacy, its power, its consistency, its unity, its incorruptibility and its rationality – that is to say, on all those aspects of 'public opinion' that supposedly marked it as the beneficent political embodiment of reason. The 1790s, in sum, presented a very different picture of the understandings and uses of 'public opinion' from that of the late 1810s; and it was quite befitting, therefore, that the typical John Bull of the 1790s (as John Brewer has noted), the metaphorical representation of this 'public opinion', did not command much respect, but was rather plebeian, dense, and more often than not led through the nose by some crafty politician (see figures 4.2a–c).

IV

From the 1790s we can turn to the 1820s and early 1830s, a period of radically different political circumstances (a significant distinction to which we shall return). As these were the years immediately following the post-war heyday of 'public opinion', they are of particular interest here. Beginning in the mid-1820s one can find a stream of sobered voices – first a trickle, then more of a torrent – expressing disillusionment with the optimistic view of 'public opinion' as the omnipotent panacea for all political woes. Take for instance the mid-decade writings of the Irish landowner turned socialist and feminist William Thompson: writing in 1824, Thompson repeatedly contrasted his vision of an ideal society – where 'public opinion' lived up to the most sanguine expectations – and 'general society' as it existed around him, in which 'public opinion' was in fact fragmented, contradictory, tension-ridden, even

---

[27] Compare the variety of the sources cited in Gunn, 'Public Spirit to Public Opinion', pp. 288–94, 303–8.

Fig. 4.2a. Representations of John Bull in the 1790s.

Fig. 4.2b. Representations of John Bull in the 1790s.

Fig. 4.2c. Representations of John Bull in the 1790s.

oppressive. In the ideal society, Thompson wrote, 'public opinion' would be the expression of 'reason', and thus become 'the arbiter of public affairs, as well as of the private transactions of life'; in actual society, however, misery created a 'public opinion of suffering', that 'wage[d] war against the public opinion of the well-fed and the powerful'. A year later, in the feminist tract which he wrote in cooperation with Anna Wheeler, Thompson took up the case against the 'barbarous public opinion' much more forcefully: in truth, he now repeated insistently, it was 'the public opinion of the oppressors, of the males of the human race in their own favor', the 'fruit of the selfish conspiracy of men' against women.[28] By now, 'public opinion' had no redeeming features left.

This change can also be suggestively (if not as angrily) illustrated through the pages of the *Edinburgh Review*, the leading enlightened liberal organ which one could expect to have been a major proponent of 'public opinion'. Indeed in the 1810s the *Edinburgh Review* often took up this role, presenting 'public opinion' as 'the great and ultimate barrier against corruption, oppression, and arbitrary power', 'the only sure and ultimate guardian either of freedom or of virtue', 'a commanding and uncontroulable power in every enlightened community'.[29] 'The great security of the Constitution', Henry Brougham told the *Review*'s readers in September 1816, was 'unquestionably the influence of Public Opinion'; 'a corrupt Judicature and a venal Parliament may in vain combine with a despotic court, in defiance of public opinion'.[30] But compare these assertions of Brougham's – resonating so well with the general tenor of the late 1810s – to what he wrote in the *Edinburgh Review* exactly a decade later. Paraphrasing Jeremy Bentham's confidence in the control of the tribunal of 'public opinion' over parliamentary abuse, Brougham was now found to have had his doubts: 'Neither can we quite admit, that if things were so very bad within the walls of Parliament, there would be any great deference very long shown towards the

[28] [William Thompson], *An Inquiry into the Principles of the Distribution of Wealth Most Conducive to Human Happiness* ... (London, 1824), pp. 223, 261–2, 497, 505–8, and *passim*. Idem, *Appeal of One Half the Human Race, Women, against the Pretensions of the Other Half, Men, to Retain Them in Political, and Thence in Civil and Domestic Slavery* ([London?], 1825 (repr. edn, London, 1983)), *passim*; quoted, pp. 35, 61, 68–9.

[29] These expressions were mostly those of Francis Jeffrey: *Edinburgh Review* 17, February 1811, p. 278; 21, February 1813, p. 7; 23, April 1814, p. 29. The *Edinburgh Review* was often the bellwether of the liberal camp, prefiguring developments that were to attain wider currency shortly thereafter.

[30] *Ibid.*, 27, September 1816, pp. 245 ff. Compare also Brougham's confident recourse to 'public opinion' in *ibid.*, 30, June 1818, pp. 181 ff., as well as Jeffrey's in 30, September 1818, pp. 275 ff.

"tribunal of public opinion" established without.' The previous year, another essay (perhaps also attributable to Brougham) insisted that 'the rules of evidence on which public opinion proceeds are defective, and its decisions are capricious. Its condemnation frequently spares the guilty, and falls on the innocent ... At best it is a feeble check to wickedness, and at last it becomes its most powerful auxiliary.'[31] This was quite a long way from the bulwark of the constitution that the *Edinburgh Review* had celebrated earlier, that 'great and ultimate barrier against corruption, oppression, and arbitrary power'.

Towards the end of the 1820s, side by side with familiar celebrations of 'public opinion' (like William Mackinnon's repetitive *On the Rise, Progress, and Present State of Public Opinion* of 1828), one can readily find more expressions of distrust, ranging from calls to 'giv[e] to the public opinion that wholesome direction, of which it stands in so much need', to outright denunciations of 'public opinion' as prone – in the words of Robert Southey – to 'tyranny' and 'usurpation'. 'The more loudly and confidently Public Opinion is expressed', Southey wrote in 1829, 'with the more reason ought it always to be distrusted!'[32] That year, which witnessed the showdown on the thorny issue of Catholic Emancipation, was indeed a significant moment in the ebbing of confidence in 'public opinion'. Supporters had entertained high hopes that 'the Catholic claims are to be carried by no force, but the force of public opinion, which ultimately bears down all before it'; and their disappointment was therefore just as great when it turned out (as was the common observation) 'that the mass of public opinion is so hostile to the Roman Catholics, that it has overruled the national sense of justice'. These were the words of William Empson in the *Edinburgh Review*, still striving to exonerate 'public opinion' from this charge. But this was a lost cause: in the subsequent issues of the periodical 'public opinion' was repeatedly denounced as oppressive, fallible, and adverse to moral liberty.[33] 'Public

---

[31] *Ibid.*, 44, September 1826, pp. 468–70; 41, January 1825, pp. 474–5 (Brougham or Macaulay).

[32] *Picture of England at the Close of the Year 1826: Her Colonies; Her Manufacturers ... Her Starving Population*, 2nd edn (London, [1827]), p. 9. R. Southey, *Sir Thomas More: Or, Colloquies on the Progress and Prospects of Society*, 2 vols. (London, 1829), vol. II, p. 203. [William A. Mackinnon,] *On the Rise, Progress, and Present State of Public Opinion, in Great Britain, and Other Parts of the World* (London, 1828). It should be noted that both Southey and Mackinnon were Tories: again, such statements did not necessarily follow partisan political lines.

[33] Alexander Mundell, *The Influence of Interest and Prejudice upon Proceedings in Parliament Stated ...* (London, 1825), p. 56 (appropriately, Mundell dedicated his book to 'the Public'). *Edinburgh Review*, 49, March 1829, p. 241 (Empson); June 1829, pp. 456–7 (Carlyle); 50, October 1829, pp. 132–3 (Hazlitt); January 1830, p. 549 (Macaulay). Only a few years earlier, the *Edinburgh Review* too had expressed hope that 'public opinion' would be 'strongly manifest' in favour of Catholic Emancipation: *ibid.*, 43, November 1825, p. 126 (Parnell). The pressure felt by

opinion', it now seemed, did not necessarily come down on the 'progressive' side; John Bull could turn out to be selfish and hard-hearted (see figure 4.3).

The effects of this sudden realisation were particularly striking in the pages of the London *Examiner*, whose heights of uncritical faith in 'public opinion' at the beginning of the decade were matched only by the depths of its critical disillusionment by the decade's end. In autumn 1828, in the context of the Catholic question, the *Examiner* first hinted (following the *Morning Chronicle*) that 'public opinion' might 'operat[e] to prevent the display of individual opinion'. The Tory *Standard* did not fail to capitalise on its rival's predicament, commenting on the *Examiner*'s 'horror' when faced with 'public opinion, which is admitted to be Anti-Catholic'. 'We remember the time', continued the gleeful Tory newspaper, 'when *Vox populi vox Dei*, was the motto of our friends of the people'. The *Examiner* responded defensively: 'As for the maxim, *Vox populi vox Dei* ... we must beg leave to repudiate it ... The minds of the many are not competent to form opinions on questions, the grounds of which often lie entirely out of the sphere of their knowledge, or within the range of their inherited prejudices.' A week later the *Examiner* admitted again that indeed 'there were some grounds for our apprehensions of taint in the mass of the popular sentiment with regard to the Catholic question' (note the transmutation of 'public opinion' into the less dignified 'popular sentiment'). And by the time the Catholic issue had been settled, there remained little doubt in its editorial mind: 'It is the fashion of our day to over-estimate the influence of public opinion, which is capable of much, but not of all that is supposed of it. Public opinion is one of those giants that die on the cast of the stone; and we see that whenever it is boldly defied, it is conquered.'[34] So much for that 'never-failing corrective power of public opinion' of which the *Examiner* had spoken so highly a decade earlier.[35] 'Public opinion' thus entered the 1830s knocked down from the shortlived pedestal from which it had triumphantly overlooked politics at the beginning of the 1820s. The

Empson to exonerate 'public opinion' of the charge of anti-Catholic bigotry manifested itself at exactly the same moment also in the liberal *Manchester Guardian* (409, 28 February 1829): 'To take the names of clod-hoppers, carters, children, drunkards, paupers, and people who cannot even write their names,' the *Guardian* protested, 'as indicative of the state of public opinion ... is quite preposterous.'

[34] *Examiner*, 1077, 21 September 1828, p. 610 (quoting the *Morning Chronicle*); 1082, 26 October 1828, p. 689 (quoting the *Standard*); 1083, 2 November 1828, p. 705; 1138, 22 November 1829, p. 737. And note also 1109, 3 May 1829, p. 274 ('There are, indeed, many curious solecisms in public opinion'); and 1147, 24 January 1830, p. 50 ('public opinion too often acts with the whim of our justice').

[35] *Ibid.*, 719, 14 October 1821, p. 642; and see many more examples in nn. 11, 12 above.

Fig. 4.3. John Bull and Catholic Emancipation: one of the relatively few prints of 1829 favourable to Catholic Emancipation, and one which was *critical* of John Bull's selfishness.

THE LIMITS OF CONSTITUTIONAL POLITICS

decade of reform, rather, resembled more the 1790s, when the role and importance of 'public opinion' were in themselves bones of contention (though not necessarily following partisan lines). In the imagery used in one 1831 confrontation, was 'public opinion' a 'mighty river', or 'not a spoonful's splash of dirty water' with 'no constitutional existence'?[36] For every voice declaring 'the force of public opinion – the triumph of national morality and intelligence ... [which] like gravitation and electricity ... exerts its stupendous powers', another could be found declaring that 'public opinion is, and has always been, very often quite wrong', or 'a mere animal impulsion', or simply 'impotent'.[37] And finally, the Reform Act itself hammered one more nail into the coffin of that unified and just 'public opinion', by sealing its identification with the proclaimed political winner of the day – the 'middle class'. Like so many other things, 'public opinion' too became absorbed in the triumphant 'middle-class'-based vision of the world; as Edward Bulwer-Lytton put it in 1833, the 'middle classes interest themselves in grave matters: the aggregate of their sentiments is called OPINION'.[38] Visually, this narrowing of the meaning of 'public opinion' was manifest in the transformation of the pictorial characteristics of John Bull, now depicted in popular prints as prosperous, contented, and with a rapidly expanding waist-line. John Bull was made into a member of the 'middle class' ('the middle class ... has usurped almost the entire force of what is called *public opinion*', the *Poor Man's Guardian* observed indignantly), that is into a member of one limited sector of society; and in the process he lost – at least in the eyes of the political losers of this moment – whatever

[36] *What the Lords Will Do: Stated in a Letter from a Peer of Parliament* (London, 1831), p. 13; quoting and responding to *What Will the Lords Do*.

[37] Thomas Bailey, *A Discourse on the Causes of Political Revolutions* (London, 1830?), p. 18; parts of which were lifted word for word by William Carpenter in his *A Political Letter*, 1831, p. 2. John B. Walsh [Baron Ormathwaite], *Popular Opinions on Parliamentary Reform Considered* (London, 1831), p. 14 (and see through p. 16). Edward Bulwer-Lytton, *The Present Crisis: A Letter to a Late Cabinet Minister*, 15th edn (London, 1834), p. 22. *A Plain Man's Estimate of the State of Affairs* (London, 1835), p. 23. Even those who acknowledged the force of 'public opinion' appeared now more savvy about its limitations: 'public opinion, whether right or wrong, must and will prevail – to resist it is impossible – all that we can hope to do is to control and regulate it' (Wentworth Holworthy, *The Book of Reform ... Humbly Submitted to the Consideration of Honest Men of All Parties* (London, 1833), pp. iv–v). For each position demonstrated here, many more examples – crossing partisan lines – can be readily adduced. And see John Burrow's comments on the mid-century loss of confidence in 'public opinion', in his *Whigs and Liberals: Continuity and Change in English Political Thought* (Oxford, 1988), pp. 70, 75–6.

[38] Edward Bulwer-Lytton, *England and the English*, 2 vols. (New York (also London), 1833), vol. I, p. 87. In some cases – notably, that of William Mackinnon (see n. 32) – the move to equate 'public opinion' with the 'middle class' dated back to the 1820s.

Fig. 4.4. The abduction of John Bull in 1832: John Bull as a fat Sancho Panza duped by Lord Grey into the folly of reform. Three days after the passing of the Reform Act, he was now identified with the political winners of the day, who (in his words) believed they 'know how to govern' Britain. The Quixotic metaphor (note the windmills on the horizon) highlighted the possibility of an alternative – and unsatisfying – standard of reason on which 'public opinion' was supposed to have been predicated, to which John Bull had now succumbed (see p. 20).

claims he might have still had to the title of the supreme metapolitical arbiter of British society (see figure 4.4).[39]

V

Let us now resume our original inquiry. What this quick detour into political rhetoric before and after the post-war years has shown is that the introduction of 'public opinion' into political debate was not in itself a rational self-evident move with a single inevitable meaning. Rather, it could be construed in very different ways, and thus introduced into politics quite differently: as part of the constitution and the very structure of politics, or as an interested and aggressive contender within it; as a beneficial source of infallible truth and judgement, or as a malleable and fallible force, even a dangerous one; as the bellwether which politicians ought to follow, or as an inchoate mass which politicians ought to direct. Seen against this background, the apotheosis of 'public opinion' in the late 1810s appears to have been quite unusual, indeed unique within the series of historical moments surveyed here, spanning almost half a century.

It might also be helpful to consider the nature of the political circumstances at these different historical moments. A priori, one might have expected the ups and downs of the notion of 'public opinion' to follow upon those of actual public expression, that is upon those political circumstances in which expressions of public opinion (understood heuristically as some socio-political entity assessable by the distant analyst) were more frequent and effective. Following this logic, one should have found those circumstances that were more conducive to free speech and public political expression – or perhaps, alternatively, those characterised by political harmony and consensus – to engender the peaks of confidence in 'public opinion' (as a socio-political entity, and thus as a concept). But such correlations are in fact not borne out by the actual patterns of usage of 'public opinion' as sketched above. Thus

---

[39] *Poor Man's Guardian*, 126, 2 November 1833; (repr. New York, 1968), vol. ii, p. 349. Miles Taylor has noted this visual transformation of John Bull, presenting it as the sapping of his political meaning. In Taylor's view this meaning always had to do basically with the fiscal complaints of 'the collective taxpayer', and now that John Bull no longer embodied these complaints, he became politically irrelevant (Taylor, 'John Bull and the Iconography of Public Opinion', pp. 108–9, 118). However, one might pursue further the possibility that the political uses of John Bull had changed over time; and thus that his mid-century depiction as a heavy and rotund armed man aggressively guarding his pudding together with his viciously loyal dog (reproduced in *ibid.*, p. 115) was no less a loaded political statement than his earlier more popular depictions, stumbling miserably under excessive tax burdens.

we saw parallels between the savvy and sceptical understandings of 'public opinion' (side by side with more sanguine ones) in the 1790s and in the 1820s, periods that politically could hardly have been more disparate – the former a decade of extreme political turmoil and conflict, the latter (in the words of E. P. Thompson) 'strangely quiet'.[40] And by contrast, whereas the political scene in the late 1810s did resemble that of the 1790s in important ways – both characterised by turbulent agitation, intensive public expression, and strong repression – the meanings and uses of 'public opinion' during these two moments were very different.

What appears to have influenced the political understandings of the nature and role of 'public opinion', then, was not so much (or not necessarily) the prevailing conditions of communication and speech – that is to say, those circumstances (underscored by Habermas) that we tend to associate with our own heuristic notion of public opinion. Instead, we need to focus on the prevailing political alignments and struggles – that is to say, those circumstances that provided the logic for and the stakes in the mobilisation of 'public opinion' in political argumentation. 'Public opinion' became a meaningful coin of political language when circumstances made it a potentially effective rhetorical device, not an accurate depiction of the political playing field (though at times the two could powerfully coincide, as we shall see shortly). We are converging here, therefore, with Keith Baker's insistence that 'the significance of public opinion [was] as a political invention, rather than as a sociological function'.[41] And thus, just as Baker and others following him have been led to search for explanations for the uses of 'public opinion' during the final decades of the French ancien régime in the specificities of the political debate at that point, so the present argument requires that we link the extraordinary post-war heyday of 'public opinion' in Britain to the specific configuration of the political map at that particular moment. The question now is this: why was 'public opinion' assigned such a distinctive and unusual role in the representation of politics in the late 1810s?

The key to answering this question, it seems to me, has already been suggested in the work of several historians on the nature of politics at this juncture, and in particular on the nature of post-war radicalism. As John Belchem and James Epstein have pointed out, it was precisely during those years that radicalism assumed most widely the forms of

---

[40] E. P. Thompson, *The Making of the English Working Class* (London, 1963), p. 711.
[41] Baker, 'Public Opinion as Political Invention', p. 168.

popular constitutionalism. 'What is striking about early-nineteenth-century British political reasoning, both elite and popular,' Epstein has written recently, 'is how rooted debate remained within a discourse about the "real" meaning of the English constitution and its history.'[42] For most radicals this meant recourse to the Cartwrightian constitutional language, drawing on historical precedents and on interpretations of constitutionally sanctioned forms of political action, rather than to the Paineite language of natural rights (though the latter did not altogether fade away). The outcome, especially significant during the spate of radical activity and government repression in the late 1810s, was a political language that crossed party lines – a 'constitutionalist idiom' drawn upon by all participants in a deeply polarised political struggle. Constitutionalism allowed radicals to claim legitimacy for their demands and their actions, a legitimacy sanctioned by standards recognised nationwide; which was why their rivals could not allow them to monopolise this idiom, but had to contest their uses of it and reappropriate it in support of their own agendas, in order to defend their own grounds.

It is as part of this contestation over the ability to claim the backing of the constitution, played out within shared rhetorical game rules, that we should understand the unusual appeal to 'public opinion' so widespread during these years, as well as its specific form. Unlike the French case, the hold of 'public opinion' over British political rhetoric was not primarily due to its representation (whether rightly or wrongly) as *reasonable*, but to its representation as *constitutional*. Far from riding on the triumphant waves of Enlightenment reason, it in fact belonged more to the *retreat* of Paineite rationalism in face of popular constitutionalism. 'Public opinion' was the ultimate constitutional sanction, which could be claimed by all political adversaries but which belonged to none. This was of course a very particular construction of 'public opinion' – precisely the one we have seen as prevalent in the late 1810s: portraying it as fair, just, metapolitical, a non-partisan arbiter or tribunal set above the political affray. 'Public opinion' (in this particular constitutional guise) could therefore be shared across the political board, while maintaining – like 'constitution' itself – enough malleability to be appropriated by all sides and moulded to fit their own differing political

---

[42] J. A. Epstein, *Radical Expression: Political Language, Ritual, and Symbol in England, 1790–1850* (New York, 1994), p. 9; and see his whole introduction. Also see J. Belchem, 'Republicanism, Popular Constitutionalism and the Radical Platform in Early Nineteenth-Century England', *Social History*, 6 (1981), pp. 1–32. *Idem, 'Orator' Hunt: Henry Hunt and English Working-Class Radicalism* (Oxford, 1985), pp. 3–5, 107–9, and *passim*.

agendas. Thus it could help maintain an imaginary common ground for discussion and at the same time sustain the (mutually exclusive) political hopes of all sides for shaping British society in their own image. In short, it was perfect for the moment.

More speculatively, the question can perhaps also be linked to a broader social context. This particular understanding of 'public opinion', it might be suggested, was further reinforced – or at least rendered more plausible – by concurrent developments of a very different kind. The post-war years were a key moment – perhaps *the* key moment – in British society's coming to terms with its new face as a commercialising and industrialising society, transformed irreversibly by social change; a realisation manifested in a variety of developments after 1815 – including the far-reaching popularisation of political economy, the intense debate on machinery and its social effects, and the reshaping of government policy (notably, *Tory* government policy) to take these irreversible social transformations into account.[43] At the same time, the expressions of obeisance to 'public opinion' during these years frequently registered a sense of recent and radical social change, one that could account for this 'new Leviathan' that 'has grown up' in modern times, linking 'the march of public opinion' with 'the progress of knowledge'.[44] The sharpened awareness during those years of social change and its implications, therefore, could lend credibility to the narrative of change underlying the concept of 'public opinion' and the sudden realisation of its power.

VI

Let us take stock of the argument so far. We began by noting the extraordinary confidence with which 'public opinion' was invoked during the latter years of the second decade of the nineteenth century, presented widely as the supreme constitutional authority and arbiter. In order to explain this phenomenon, we first considered the oft-repeated assumption that such a confidence in 'public opinion' was the likely outcome of Enlightenment reason, and found it theoretically question-

---

[43] These developments are discussed, *inter alia*, in M. Berg, *The Machinery Question and the Making of Political Economy 1815–1848* (Cambridge, 1980). N. W. Thompson, *The People's Science: The Popular Political Economy of Exploitation and Crisis 1816–1834* (Cambridge, 1984). B. Hilton, *Corn, Cash, Commerce: The Economic Policies of the Tory Governments 1815–1830* (Oxford, 1977). *Idem, The Age of Atonement: The Influence of Evangelicalism on Social and Economic Thought, 1795–1865* (Oxford, 1988). And see a fuller discussion in Wahrman, *Imagining the Middle Class*, chapter 7.

[44] Quoted above, p. 91; and note other examples there. For 'the march of public opinion' as 'the progress of knowledge' see Benbow, *The Whigs Exposed*, p. 12.

able. We then proceeded to show that historically, too, this assumption cannot be maintained, and that in fact the paramount importance that was conferred upon 'public opinion' in the late 1810s was distinctly unlike any of its uses in the decades before or after. Given, therefore, that this phenomenon was not self-explanatory through some properties inherent in the concept of 'public opinion', and that it was idiosyncratic to this particular political moment, it required an explanation based on the circumstance-specific peculiarities of that moment. It was then suggested that the key characteristic of late 1810s politics which could provide the missing explanatory link was its specific rhetorical game rules, whereby all participants placed such a high boon on the constitution; game rules which made this confident representation of 'public opinion' a valuable strategy for all sides, at the same time that simultaneous social developments – the increased awareness of intense social change – rendered it more readily credible.

Having arrived thus far, then, we can now turn to the final goal of this essay – namely, exploring the *consequences* of this particular situation, and how they might help us understand other peculiarities of politics in the era of Peterloo and Queen Caroline. Such consequences can lead us in different directions. Elsewhere I have proposed that the claims of political adversaries to speak for 'public opinion' imposed certain constraints on the drawing of lines of exclusion and inclusion in the demarcation of political camps. Such claims for a universalist voice required that one's political camp would manifestly encompass more than any single self-interested social group; which worked to subvert any neat correlation between perceived social groups and perceived political camps, like that which had characterised the 1790s.[45] What follows here goes in another direction, considering briefly the consequences of this situation for the ways in which people conceptualised the political process itself, and in particular for the interplay between the post-war vision of 'public opinion' and attitudes towards political violence.

For the elevation of the tribunal of 'public opinion' was not only a statement about the static structure of the constitution, but also about the dynamic workings of politics. The recognition of the metapolitical jurisdiction of 'public opinion' entailed an acceptance (in theory) of a process of arbitration, a manner to resolve political controversies within

---

[45] As a consequence, both radicals and conservatives in the late 1810s (and unlike the 1790s) repeatedly tried to show that their respective positions were supported by the 'middle class' – a social group without a manifest corollary in the binary polarised political map, whose alliance therefore could prove that one indeed spoke for 'the people' rather than simply for one's own self-interested social camp. See Wahrman, *Imagining the Middle Class*, pp. 195–9.

shared game rules and under the shared umbrella of the 'public'. Though there could be much disagreement about where to find this 'public opinion' and who might speak for it, the conviction that such an arbiter in principle could be found was not put (at this moment) in serious doubt. Moreover, it was this presumed capability of the political process to subsume conflict – its built-in shock absorbers – that ensured that it will always further the public good. 'Public opinion', according to Henry Brougham, prevented those extremes that threatened to pull society asunder: because of 'the vigilance of public opinion', he asserted in the *Edinburgh Review* in late 1816, 'tyranny will dread going beyond a certain length, and this fear will supersede the necessity of applying the ultimate check' – namely, revolution. And again: 'As long as Parliament and the Courts of Law are retained in the line of their duty by the force of public opinion, no necessity ever can arise for bringing the Crown and the People into immediate conflict.' This was the key: 'public opinion' prevented a possible 'necessity' of recourse to non-constitutional, violent action. 'Public opinion', Brougham insisted, 'operates by its preventive influence, and *renders it unnecessary to employ force*.'[46]

Of course this too was not an inevitable understanding of the function of 'public opinion': only a few years earlier Francis Jeffrey had written in the *Edinburgh* that 'little deference is paid to public opinion, except when it threatens to indicate itself in tumult and disorder', while Francis Horner had characterised 'public opinion' (in France) as 'violent'. But Jeffrey's and Horner's disorderly and violent entity had been that previous incarnation of 'public opinion' that participated in the political struggle, not Brougham's 'public opinion' of the late 1810s that adjudicated above it. By this moment, even a much more radical voice like T. J. Wooler's *Black Dwarf*, when it talked about 'public opinion' as the 'bastion' against which 'the mighty Duke of Waterloo' can in vain 'marshall his forces for a trial of strength which he has not yet experienced'; even then, in the midst of all this combative military language, the *Black Dwarf* made it clear that this was not a war with force, but rather with the *moral authority* of 'public opinion'.[47] Much has been written about the effectiveness of the radical 'strategy of forceful intimidation', that is the assertion of the right to arm and to use force, but at the same time 'the interdiction of any violent act until all

---

[46] *Edinburgh Review*, 27, September 1816, pp. 249–50 (my emphasis).

[47] *Edinburgh Review*, 14, July 1809, pp. 292–3; on Jeffrey's position see also Burrow, *Whigs and Liberals*, pp. 43–4. Horner to J. A. Murray, 25 February 1814; in *Memoirs and Correspondence of Francis Horner*, ed. L. Horner, 2 vols. (Boston, 1853), vol. II, p. 159. *Black Dwarf*, 4, 12 January 1820, pp. 3–4.

constitutional channels had been explored'.[48] 'Public opinion' was such a channel, an especially valuable one as long as it maintained its reputation for imperviousness to political machinations. 'Had Charles the First, and James the Second shewn a becoming deference for public opinion', argued a key radical remonstrance in 1819, 'the one would have not lost his head on a scaffold, nor the other have been driven from the throne by an insulted and justly enraged People.'[49] 'Public opinion' – now stronger than ever (an observation which few doubted, despite the characteristic invocation of historical precedent) – was there to prevent revolution, to provide substitutes for the political recourse to force. Its elevated position as supreme arbiter was expected to guarantee a basic measure of political stability.

But this benign scenario itself was not very stable. From the mass Spa Fields meetings of late 1816 and the March of the Blanketeers and the Pentridge Rising of 1817, it had been in constant tension with a more ominous and potentially violent political screenplay. And then, nothing undermined this benign scenario more than that nation-shocking confrontation that blatantly failed to follow its prescribed stage directions – namely the 'massacre of Peterloo', when a meeting encompassing tens of thousands of Lancashire reformers at St Peter's Fields in Manchester was dispersed violently by the yeomanry cavalry, at the order of local magistrates, leaving eleven dead and hundreds injured. Peterloo was often portrayed by radicals (and by later historians) as, in the words of Wooler and Cartwright, 'our most glorious victory', a heroic moral victory exposing the corruption of the anti-reform camps.[50] But it also remained true that Peterloo posed a serious problem for the radical and reformist camp, in foregrounding the concern that in fact the political process – in particular, oppositional politics – did not lead ultimately to the public good, but rather to the violent undoing of the social fabric. The mechanisms of political arbitration – capped by that omnipotent and omniscient 'public opinion' – appeared to have failed. For many respectable propertied reformists this was the sign for retreat. And for mainstream radicals it became crucial that such an eruption of violence would not be repeated: were it to happen again, it would have proved this derailment of the political process to have been not an aberration

---

[48] Belchem, 'Republicanism, Popular Constitutionalism and the Radical Platform', p. 11.

[49] Remonstrance of the Manchester meeting of January 18, 1819; reprinted (from the *Manchester Observer*) in D. Read, *Peterloo: The 'Massacre' and Its Background* (Manchester, 1958), appendix A (quoted, p. 215).

[50] Quoted in Belchem, *'Orator' Hunt*, p. 122.

but somehow an inevitable result of the radical engagement with national politics.

Consequently, as many historians have noted, immediately following Peterloo mainstream radicals – who 'could have filled the streets of London, the Midlands, the north and Scotland with demonstrations' – cautioned against any further exercise of forcible intimidation, and in particular wished to ensure that (in the words of one radical resolution) 'the Spirit of Violence [be] repressed as much as possible'.[51] The fact that some extreme radicals appeared ready now to embrace violence did little to help. And therefore, when events that *could* readily have been constructed as replays of Peterloo did take place in Scotland a few months later (like the confrontation between soldiers and working-class demonstrators in Paisley in mid March 1820, 'inflict[ing] a good many bayonet wounds'), the reactions of the English radicals and reformers consisted predominantly of a surprising ability to look the other way.[52] And that, to come to this essay's final argument, was why the Queen Caroline affair was such a godsend. If, as John Belchem has written, 'after Peterloo, it was the weaknesses and not the strengths of popular constitutionalism that were revealed', then now its strengths could prevail once more.[53]

Much has recently been written about this affair of 1820. Historians have repeatedly tried to explain how the defence of Queen Caroline against George IV's attempts to divorce her became the most widespread popular agitation of the early nineteenth century, forging – in the words of one recent account – 'unlikely alliances across class,

[51] Quoted in *ibid.*, p. 127, and see 121 ff. Thompson, *The Making of the English Working Class*, p. 700.

[52] As reported in the conservative *Edinburgh Evening Courant*, 16974, 25 March 1820, followed by similar reports over the next several weeks (I am grateful to Geert van den Bossche for assistance in tracking them down); and see J. D. Young, *The Rousing of the Scottish Working Class* (London, 1979), p. 60. P. Berresford Ellis and S. Mac a' Ghobhainn's *The Scottish Insurrection of 1820* (London, 1970) presents this silence on the part of English radicals as a consequence of the peculiarly Scottish content of this political unrest. But given the previous cooperation between English and Scottish radicals (as seen for example in James Epstein's contribution to this volume), this explanation may be insufficient. It should also be noted that the confrontations in Scotland had overall a less orderly and more brawl-like appearance than that in Manchester; a fact which undoubtedly contributed further to the English radicals' embarrassed silence. See also M. I. Thomis and P. Holt, *Threats of Revolution in Britain 1789–1848* (Hamden, 1977), pp. 65–82. And compare Hazlitt's observation on the selective radical interests during the Queen Caroline agitation: 'At the very time when all England was mad about the poor queen', he wrote, 'a man named Bruce was sent to Botany Bay for having spoken to another man who was convicted of sedition; and no notice was taken' (quoted in T. W. Laqueur, 'The Queen Caroline Affair: Politics as Art in the Reign of George IV', *Journal of Modern History*, 54 (1982), pp. 417–66, p. 418).

[53] Belchem, 'Republicanism, Popular Constitutionalism and the Radical Platform', p. 14; and see through p. 16.

ideological, and cultural lines'.[54] The problem here is twofold: first, this widespread enthusiasm was roused by a rather unlikely royal figure, whose predicament could just as easily have been dismissed by an unsympathetic opposition as a trivial squabble within a scandal-prone monarchical family. Second, it was an agitation which foregrounded matrimonial issues and family values, manifestly overshadowing those constitutional issues that had dominated the post-war public debate. 'Men still demand licenses for themselves', went the *Examiner*'s utterly typical pro-queen argument against the sexual double standard, 'which they do not allow for women. They will scatter in other families a confusion, which they protest against being brought into their own.' 'I would tremble for the fate of every woman in this country', echoed another of countless such statements, 'whilst an example is held up to every ruffian in the land to abuse and insult the wife, that he promised to cherish and protect.'[55] A priori, it seems, these were not the usual materials of which the English popular political movement had been made.

Thus, for E. P. Thompson this enigma was an embarrassment to the radical record, one that was best ignored as much as possible. Other historians have incorporated this episode into the well-established narrative of struggle against 'Old Corruption', though at the price of leaving out its most unusual and interesting features. Thus Iorwerth Prothero has seen its importance not in the 'ostensible aim' of the agitation, but in its form, in that it helped dissipate the constrictions of the Six Acts and re-establish open political campaigning; while J. Anne Hone's conclusion, within the expectations set by the same narrative, is that the affair 'can be seen as leading nowhere'. Craig Calhoun has seen it as proof of the inherent backward-looking tendencies of radicalism, here coming out in favour of 'traditional images of the family'; Thomas Laqueur sees it ultimately as a popular radical failure, since the political potential of the affair was diffused and 'rendered harmless' by 'domestic melodrama' – 'a play about marriage, about women, home and family'; Catherine Hall and Leonore Davidoff see it as a key public affirmation of quintessentially 'middle-class' values (which, presumably, reaffirms

[54] A. Clark, 'Queen Caroline and the Sexual Politics of Popular Culture in London, 1820', *Representations*, 31 (1990), pp. 47–68, p. 49.
[55] *Examiner*, 662, 3 September 1820, p. 561 (editorial). *The King's Treatment of the Queen Shortly Stated to the People of England*, 2nd edn. (London, 1820), pp. 31–2. For many more examples and further discussions of the 'moralistic' contents of the Caroline agitation, see L. Davidoff and C. Hall, *Family Fortunes: Men and Women of the English Middle Class, 1780–1850* (London, 1987), pp. 150–5. Clark, 'Queen Caroline'. A. Clark, *The Struggle for the Breeches: Gender and the Making of the British Working Class* (Berkeley, 1995), pp. 164–74.

the perception of the popular enthusiasm for the queen as a failure, a kind of bourgeoisified false consciousness); and for Anna Clark – who wants to rescue the popular agitation from the condescension of fellow historians – this was indeed a plebeian victory, but one whose 'primary significance ... is that it provided the occasion for a *style* of politics independent of middle-class parliamentarism'.[56] What all these interpretations have in common, however, is the sense that enthusiastic support for Queen Caroline, especially in a cross-class alliance, could not really serve (in terms of its content) a true popular political agenda.[57] Nevertheless, perhaps it could. The present argument might enable us to add an explicit *political* function to the widespread support for Queen Caroline on such moralistic ('domestic') grounds, by pointing to another unique characteristic of this affair – namely, the extraordinarily passionate expression of this support as the triumph of 'public opinion'.

For if the violent eruption at Peterloo demonstrated the dangerous possibility of a derailment of the political process, the Caroline agitation (historians' critical judgements of its political goals and success notwithstanding) was perceived as its triumphant rehabilitation. What popular politics needed at this point was to demonstrate its commitment to consensual moral causes in support of the fundamental social order, unobjectionable causes that could prove the effectiveness of 'public opinion' rather than expose its weaknesses. Already before the queen so conveniently turned up, William Cobbett, for one, that astute radical tactician, had understood this well. In January 1820, after weeks of shying away from stance-taking in the wake of Peterloo, Cobbett suddenly announced 'A PLAN'; only that his plan (as E. P. Thompson has noted with the same scorn with which he has dismissed the Caroline agitation) turned out to be not a vigorous comeback of

---

[56] Thompson, *The Making of the English Working Class*, pp. 708–9 ('Into the humbug of the Queen's case we need not enquire. It displayed every vice of the radical movement ... on the largest scale.') I. Prothero, *Artisans and Politics in Early Nineteenth-Century London: John Gast and His Times* (Folkestone, 1979), p. 141 (in reviewing Prothero's book, E. P. Thompson acknowledged his mistake in ignoring this affair and accepted Prothero's judgement of its tactical value for the radicals, but continued to dismiss the actual contents of the agitation as a 'glorious ebullition' of humbug: *New Society*, 3 May 1979, pp. 275–6). J. Ann Hone, *For the Cause of Truth: Radicalism in London 1796–1821* (Oxford, 1982), p. 317. C. Calhoun, *The Question of Class Struggle: Social Foundations of Popular Radicalism during the Industrial Revolution* (Chicago, 1982), pp. 105–15 (quoted, p. 105). Laqueur, 'The Queen Caroline Affair' (quoted, pp. 418, 441, 463). Clark, 'Queen Caroline', p. 50. Davidoff and Hall, *Family Fortunes, ibid.*

[57] This remains true even for Anna Clark, for whom it was the 'style' of the agitation rather than its moralistic content that made sense in terms of popular politics; though she insists that at the same time this moralistic content did make sense in terms of another popular agenda of a different kind, namely the specifically plebeian concerns about the family.

constitutional radicalism, but an address 'To the Ladies', intended for 'Promoting Sobriety and Frugality, and an Abhorrence of Gaming' – that is to say, precisely the right kind of causes at this particular moment.[58]

But what Cobbett had had to invent, the fortuitous issue of the queen provided in abundance (not least for Cobbett himself, who immediately became one of her most adamant champions, putting his *Political Register* completely at her disposal). The queen's cause vindicated popular politics by demonstrating that a widespread agitation could be vehemently oppositional and at the same time protect the basic pillars of the social fabric; namely, those family and matrimonial values on which the opposition to the king was predicated. This was oppositional politics conspicuously in defence of fundamental social ties, not undermining them; and as such – here was the second gain – it had an obvious cross-class appeal, allowing for the renewed cooperation of radicals and moderate reformers. 'Public opinion' was therefore shown again to be a national entity above interested class lines. Better still, 'public opinion' was positioned now within a highly becoming narrative, reaffirming its constructive and unobjectionable social role as the collective embodiment of the chivalrous manliness of the nation, rising courageously to defend a wronged woman. And finally, having put the Humpty Dumpty of the shattered post-Peterloo 'public opinion' together again (*against* all the king's horses and all the king's men ...), this affair appeared to provide the necessary proof that this longed-for constitutional arbitration mechanism actually *worked*. Here, at last, was a moment when the peak of investment in the imagined 'bar of public opinion' coincided with a political development which seemed most indubitably to be determined by the opinions of an enraged public. (After all, it often goes unnoticed that the queen in fact

---

[58] *Political Register*, 22 January 1820. Thompson, *The Making of the English Working Class*, p. 700. Arguably, moreover, the same impulse was also behind the disproportionate emphasis in radical evocations of Peterloo on the attack on women (as noted recently in Linda Colley's *Britons: Forging the Nation 1707–1837* (New Haven, 1992), pp. 264–5). The innumerable examples include the Scottish banner that depicted Peterloo as 'a woman, with a child in her arms, under the murderous sabre of a Manchester yeoman'; the comment of the *Manchester Observer* that 'women seemed special objects of rage of these bastard soldiers'; and the versing of the *Nottingham Review*, 'When infants, borne in starving mothers' arms / Unlawful wounded by infernal arms' (quoted in Thomis and Holt, *Threats of Revolution in Britain*, p. 65; and in M. I. Thomis and J. Grimmett, *Women in Protest 1800–1850* (London, 1982), pp. 101–2). While surely a forceful means for condemning the cruelty of the yeomanry, such representations went further, turning the event in effect from a political confrontation over political rights (i.e. a derailment of the political process) to a defence of wronged women (i.e. a defence of fundamental social values) – much reminiscent, again, of the representations of the queen's case a short while thereafter.

lost her case in the in-doors tribunal of the House of Lords – but that defeat was completely drowned in the clamour raised by the out-of-doors tribunal of 'public opinion'.)

Small wonder, then, that the deliverance of the queen turned into such a catharsis in the celebrations of, as the title of one pamphlet had it, *The Triumph of Public Opinion*. William Hone published an ornamented sheet to commemorate 'that the base Conspiracy was defeated by the irresistible force of Public Opinion'.[59] 'The Minister turned pale', rejoiced another writer, 'that very moment [when] public opinion pronounced its verdict on the whole proceeding.' In the gleeful words of another, it was an 'almost unexampled exertion of Public Opinion', (and again) 'one of the strongest spontaneous expressions of public opinion that was ever evinced in any age or country'. The queen herself hurried to capitalise on this wave of excitement: 'the power of public opinion', she wrote in response to one of many addresses of support, 'is become so great, that every other must finally bend to its decrees', and her own struggle was evidence that 'public opinion must be ultimately omnipotent'. This ultimate triumph was also inscribed in popular prints, like those showing the scales of 'public opinion' weighted down in favour of the queen, or another (figure 4.5), in which a cherubic blast of 'PUBLIC OPINION', while overpowering a saturnine counterblast of 'PERSECUTION and MALICE', drove the crown off the king's head (indeed taking its place), and dimmed his half-crown in contrast to the bright half-crown of his wife.[60]

Perhaps most importantly for the rehabilitation of the political process, the queen's affair – especially once it had been safely over – was reverberating proof, as the *Examiner* put it, 'of what public opinion,

---

[59] Charles Maclean, *The Triumph of Public Opinion: Being a Standing Lesson to the Throne, the Parliament, and the People*; for this and other examples, see above, nn. 11–12. *The Printer's Address to the Queen, and Her Majesty Tribute to the Press, in Answer*, London, printed for William Hone, [c. October–November 1820]: *BMC* 13947. Hone related this triumph of 'public opinion', as always, to the power of a free press; an important aspect which cannot be followed here.

[60] *The King's Treatment of the Queen Shortly Stated to the People of England*, 2nd edn (London, 1820), p. 21 (and compare p. 17). *Examiner*, 683, 4 February 1821, p. 66; 685, 18 February 1821, p. 105. J. Nightingale, (ed.), *The Spirit of the Addresses Presented to the Queen, with Her Majesty's Answers*, pp. 29–30 (and also p. 39). See also Bathurst, *A Sermon, Intended to Have Been Preached before ... the Queen*, pp. 11–12. And see Laqueur, 'The Queen Caroline Affair', pp. 430–2; Prothero, *Artisans and Politics*, p. 139; and for the ministers themselves being forced to 'finally come to terms with the "rise of public opinion"', J. E. Cookson, *Lord Liverpool's Administration: The Crucial Years 1815–1822* (Hamden, 1975), pp. 267, 270. For the scales of 'public opinion' in popular prints, see T. L. Hunt, 'Morality and Monarchy in the Queen Caroline Affair', *Albion*, 23 (1991), pp. 697–722, p. 699. The flip-side of these celebrations of the tribunal of 'public opinion' was perhaps the peak during those very months in radical parody trials (as noted in M. Wood, *Radical Satire and Print Culture 1790–1822* (Oxford, 1994), p. 149) – that is to say, in radical mockery of lesser and corruptible tribunals.

Fig. 4.5. The triumph of 'public opinion' in the Queen Caroline affair.

without physical force, can effect against established corruption'.[61] This is not to say that the Queen Caroline agitation saw no outbursts of 'physical force', which of course it did. But, as Laqueur puts it, 'these kinds of protest' – booing and pelting aristocrats, window-breaking charivari processions, effigy burning, etc. – were manifestly secondary, 'in all their eighteenth-century innocuousness', to the real display of popular power in the form of 'public opinion'. Moreover, like the exchange of blows between pugilists, these were controlled and stylised forms of violence, forms that had long before established themselves as a familiar and legitimate part of the political process, and quite unlike its undoing in the traumatic eruption of violence at Peterloo. It is also telling that when confronted with one instance of such stylised violence, the *Examiner* hastened to characterise it as *feminine* ('It was observable that the women took the most violent part'), and thus as distinct from and antithetical to the key political player of the moment, the explicitly masculine 'public opinion'. Overall, then, it appeared that Brougham's ideal scenario, of 'public opinion' as the ultimate constitutional arbiter that would put unbridled political violence beyond the pale as well as make it unnecessary, had been achieved; a rare political achievement indeed. And it was this achievement, we may recall, that was evoked so suggestively (despite the satirist's sceptical irony) by Robert Isaac Cruikshank's pictorial representation of politics of June 1820.[62]

---

[61] *Examiner*, 673, 19 November 1820, p. 741 (my emphasis).

[62] *Examiner*, 654, 9 July 1820, p. 442 (in the context of a riotous reception of the Italian witnesses brought to testify against the queen). Laqueur, 'The Queen Caroline Affair', pp. 422–7. And note Calhoun's observation about the calm tone that prevailed in almost all communications of the authorities during this agitation, including those of well-known alarmists (*The Question of Class Struggle*, p. 109). On the masculine construction of 'public opinion' at this point see D. Wahrman, ' "Middle-Class" Domesticity Goes Public: Gender, Class, and Politics from Queen Caroline to Queen Victoria', *Journal of British Studies*, 32, (1993), pp. 396–432, pp. 404–5.

5

∾

Making room at the public bar: coroners' inquests, medical knowledge and the politics of the constitution in early-nineteenth-century England

IAN BURNEY

On 10 September 1830, two taverns in the vicinity of London's Clerkenwell Green served as outposts for rival candidates in an election that the leading radical politician Henry Hunt professed 'more important than that [for] members of parliament'.[1] The Crown Tavern was festooned with 'handsome red banners' recommending William Baker, a Limehouse solicitor and Vestry Clerk to St Anne's parish, to the attention of the Middlesex freeholder electorate. At the nearby Northumberland Arms, rival blue notices touted Baker's better-known opponent, the surgeon and redoubtable public man, Thomas Wakley. Shortly after 9 am Sheriff Sir William Henry Richardson, flanked by county officials ranged in front of the Sessions House, opened the contest by congratulating the crowd on being assembled in the exercise of 'one of those invaluable privileges with which the laws and constitution invested the people of this country'.[2]

In so doing, Richardson opened a ten-day contest remarkable in many respects, for the modern reader perhaps in no way more so than that the high office to which Hunt referred was that of county coroner, the privilege Richardson exhorted his audience to exercise that of choosing a replacement for the late incumbent John Unwin. Richardson and Hunt were not alone in ascribing profound importance to the choice of a Middlesex coroner. Wakley's cause drew the active support not only of Hunt but of the most influential of his radical colleagues,

I thank Mario Biagioli, Sue Grayzel, Tom Laqueur, Jeff Lena and James Vernon for comments on early drafts of this essay. Special thanks to Tom Green, Joan Scott and Dror Wahrman for giving me the benefit of their observations at several stages in its production.

[1]   *The Times*, 14 September 1830, p. 4.
[2]   *Morning Chronicle*, 10 September 1830, p. 3.

including Joseph Hume, Francis Place and William Cobbett. Cobbett, for one, concurred in Richardson's assessment of the coronership's constitutional significance, describing it in another context as 'a part, and a most important part of the *"ancient institutions"* of the country.'[3] Baker's backers, though less famous, were no less numerous, with the recently defeated parliamentarian Samuel Charles Whitbread heading a list of local worthies.

What political and constitutional stakes were supposed to be involved in such a contest? What could lead two men occupying such polar political positions as the honourable Sheriff of Middlesex and William Cobbett, the veritable embodiment of the radical assault on 'Old Corruption', to agree on the form, if not the meaning, of the link between the office of coroner and the rights and privileges of Englishmen? These questions are interlaced with further ones raised by the professional claims upon which Baker and Wakley based their candidacies. For the 1830s, Baker's credentials as a lawyer well connected to parochial administration made him an archetypal candidate for the coronership, whereas Wakley's bid to capture the office on the strength of his medical credentials was a decidedly novel one.[4] From an historical perspective, however, Wakley's stance might well seem the more predictable of the two, his campaign representing one instance among many of the steady expropriation by professionalised medicine of hitherto lay spheres of competence and judgement. Yet the Wakley–Baker contest oversteps the conventional limits of this 'medicalisation' analysis by encompassing the very discourse of legitimation commonly taken as antithetical to the claims of scientific expertise – that of participatory democratic politics. Far from unfolding neatly within a space cleared by these ostensibly polarised historical trajectories, the

---

[3] *Cobbett's Political Register*, 80, 10, 8 June 1832, pp. 624–5 (emphasis original). In a later number Cobbett elaborated, informing his readership that 'the coroner's court has always been a great favourite of mine: it is the institution for the protection of life and limb, as old as the laws under which we live, and a part of the constitution of which we ought to be particularly jealous.' (*CPR*, 80, 9, 1 June 1832, p. 538). The pretext for these panegyrics was the verdict of justifiable homicide returned upon the death of a policeman killed while attempting to disperse an 1832 political demonstration in London. The story of the 'Calthorpe Street Affair' and its relation to the constitutional standing of the inquest tribunal cannot be explored in the space of this essay.

[4] Though in 1830 the link between medicine and the coronership was at best weak in practice, the arguments for it were quite familiar, due in large measure to the efforts of Wakley himself: as founding editor of the *Lancet* (est. 1823) Wakley had made the need for medically qualified coroners one of the more prominent of the journal's reforming causes, and a central plank of its broader campaign against the 'corrupt' medical establishment. See my 'Decoding Death: Medicine, Public Inquiry, and the Reform of the English Inquest, 1836–1926' (Ph.D, University of California 1993) for further discussion.

election provided a pretext for articulating a complex, and in many senses an unstable, set of connections between the narrative of science's inexorable march onto the public stage on the one hand, and of the stalwart defence of the rights of freeborn Englishmen on the other.[5]

This is expressed, in terms recognisable both to contemporary observers and to modern historical sensibilities, by the four slogans Wakley chose to represent himself to the electorate. Two of them, 'Wakley and Medical Reform' and 'Reason and Science against Ignorance and Prejudice' sit comfortably with the logic of 'medicalisation'. 'Wakley and the Sovereignty of the People' and 'Wakley and an Open Court', on the other hand, are more surprising rallying calls coming from the camp claiming to embody the cause of scientific progress. These, after all, seem to resonate with precisely the sort of conceptual vagueness that scientific objectivity promised to purge from the realm of public affairs. Yet in making himself available to the Middlesex freeholders, Wakley offered an alliance between expertise and popular politics, proposing science in the service of the popular constitution, the coronership as a fulcrum of reform, and the inquiry into the causes of accidental, suspicious or otherwise 'unnatural' death as an extension of radical politics.

This essay is concerned with the possibilities of forging such links, and with the instabilities inherent in such a project. My aim in this endeavour is to extend the reach of constitutional 're-readings' beyond the 'political' as it has been traditionally construed, by demonstrating its relevance to the historical negotiation of a role in public institutions for scientific expertise. In so doing I do not wish to reify either politics or science, but to suggest their contingent and relational standing, anchored at this historical conjuncture in a shared recourse to constitutionalism. Two central and overlapping themes are therefore pursued in the pages that follow: the reasons for investing the early-nineteenth-century coronership with constitutional significance; and the extent to which constitutionalism could serve as a framing discourse for articulating competing conceptions of the past, present and future standing of

---

[5]   In its most trenchant form, the medicalisation thesis holds public passivity to be an essential concomitant of the rise of expertise: see for example Ivan Illich, *Limits to Medicine* (London, 1976). Even more historically nuanced accounts of the connections between English political and medical reform, however, tend to ignore the implications of the alliance between the cultural chauvinism of popular radicals like Cobbett and the supposed 'continental' rationalism of scientific reformers like Wakley. Thus in Adrian Desmond's superb analysis of the world of London radical medicine in the era of reform, Wakley is depicted without comment as being both a protégé of the rabidly anti-Gallic Cobbett and a French-sympathising 'ultra'. See Desmond, *The Politics of Evolution: Morphology, Medicine, and Reform in Radical London* (Chicago, 1989), e.g. p. 107.

the inquest. No one doubted that medicine, politics and the constitution were in some way implicated in the selection of the Middlesex coroner – the question at issue was precisely how. For Wakley's part, they were linked by a struggle against the forces of 'Old Corruption': medical and political reform were in his view not only compatible with but essential to the integrity of the inquest's rightful place as a constitutional bulwark of popular liberties. Yet the confidence with which Wakley promoted a vision of 'constitutionalised' science belied its vulnerability to an entirely different interpretation: by aligning expertise with a regime of secret knowledge, Wakley's opponents depicted the prospect of a medical coronership as antithetical to the true foundations of English liberties – ultimately to the principle of jury independence itself.

I

The banner 'Wakley and an Open Court' contains in a condensed form each element of this thematic compound. From the perspective of inquest law, Wakley's pledge raised a number of controversial issues (though in isolation hardly controversial enough to attract the attention of radicalism's leading lights). The inquest's 'openness' was neither a matter of definitive statutory declaration nor of settled judicial precedent, and was thus subject to the operations of interpretation and translation that characterised the fluid discourse of constitutionalism. On one side stood a string of recent judicial decisions tending towards a limitation of public access to legal proceedings. The Court of King's Bench focused particular attention upon accounts of *ex parte* proceedings appearing in the newspaper press, finding that such reports perverted the course of justice by prejudicing jurors.[6] Lord Chief Justice Ellenborough epitomised this train of thought at the 1811 libel case of *Rex* v. *Fisher*, when he declared: 'If anything is more important than another in the administration of justice, it is that jurymen should come to the trial of those persons on whose guilt or innocence they are to decide, with minds pure and unprejudiced.'[7] The legality of publishing testimony from an ongoing inquest was itself the main issue of contention in *Rex* v. *Fleet* (1818), at which the court similarly decided in favour of suppression.

---

[6] Law dictionaries of the period commonly defined an *ex parte* proceeding as one in which only one party is heard, or one conducted for the benefit of one party only, and without notice to, or contestation by, any person adversely interested. As will be seen, the questions of whether inquests were *ex parte* proceedings, and whether publication of such proceedings were necessarily prejudicial to the public mind, were central to the debate about openness.

[7] *Rex* v. *Fisher* (1811), 2 Camp. 563–72, p. 570.

Justice Bayley considered that such publication 'may influence the public mind', rendering it impossible for jurors to 'decide solely on the evidence which they hear on the trial'.[8] Bayley's colleague, Justice Abbott, weighed in with a more epistemologically venturesome comment: 'Every person who has attended to the operations of his own mind must have observed how difficult it is to overcome preconceived prejudices and opinions, and that more especially in matters of sentiment or passion.'[9] The judicial argument against the open inquest was thus framed largely in relation to the influence of the press in the formation of public opinion, and was of course part and parcel of the broad restrictions placed upon the circulation of politically sensitive information in the revolutionary and post-revolutionary eras.

Many commentators, however, were not convinced of the merits of such decisions in relation to inquest law. At the most general level, they questioned the modern justices' conception of the inquest as an essentially preliminary investigation convened with an eye to further action in civil or criminal law. Matthew Hale's posthumously published classic, *Pleas of the Crown* (1736), provided the surest grounds for constructing an alternative version of the inquest: 'The coroner's inquest', Hale had written, 'is to inquire truly *quomodo ad mortem devenit*, and is rather for information of the truth of the fact as near as the jury can assert it, and not for an accusation.'[10] Arguments for the inquest's inherent openness could draw further support from the vestigial signs of ancestral intent still legible on the early-nineteenth-century inquest. At the level of procedure, the inquest was commonly regarded as looser than other forms of judicial inquiry, referred to (both in praise and scorn) as a 'rough and ready' proceeding. This rested in part on the proposition that the inquest's purpose was an open-ended one of information gathering, rather than a formally structured proceeding against a named suspect. The absence of an accusatorial framework made for a more amorphous standard for instigating inquiry – an inquest might legitimately address itself to 'suspicion' or 'rumour' that a death had occurred in some way out of the ordinary course of nature without needing to specify the object of such suspicion. Accordingly, rather than limit itself to the merits of a particular charge, Sir John Jervis' authoritative nineteenth-century treatise on inquest law asserted, it was proper for the inquest to 'inquire of all the circumstances of the party's death, and also of all things which occasioned

---

[8] *Rex* v. *Fleet* (1818), 1 B. & Ald. 380–85, p. 384.   [9] *Ibid.*
[10] Matthew Hale, *The History of the Pleas of the Crown*, 2 vols. (London, 1800), vol. II, pp. 60–1.

it'.[11] The ambiguous legal standing of the material generated at inquests added to the tribunal's air of indeterminacy: 'According to the best opinions,' Jervis noted, 'the Coroner's inquisition is in no case conclusive.'[12]

The role of the inquest jury at the proceedings was at least theoretically in keeping with 'rough and ready' inquiry. Contrary to the trend in English legal procedure towards jury passivity, for example, coroners were advised to encourage jury participation in the questioning of witnesses.[13] Inquest jurors furthermore qualified for service solely on the basis of their standing as local men 'lawful and true', being explicitly excluded from statutorily imposed standards of property eligibility. Finally, inquests were themselves marked by certain features in both their object and performance which were specific to them and which could readily be placed under the rubric of 'openness'. Inquests were both locally and swiftly convened, proceeding in general within days of an inquirable death, and paced in no small part by the sure onset of putrefaction in its primary evidentiary and symbolic referent (the dead body). This meant that inquests were seen as episodic, contingent affairs, dictated to by circumstance rather than legal form. The inquest's relationship to the physical body involved the proceedings in a further enactment of 'openness' peculiar to it: in order to be a valid inquiry, the jury and coroner had to 'view' the body. Though the rationales given for this requirement varied over time and between different commentators on inquest law, the view of the body unambiguously located a rite of access at the heart of the inquest.[14]

---

[11] Sir John Jervis, *A Practical Treatise on the Office and Duties of Coroners* (London, 1829), pp. 29–30. Jervis did not write as an advocate of an open court, but was merely setting out the terms of the debate.

[12] *Ibid.*, p. 216. Yet at the same time, and as an exception to the developing rule against admitting hearsay, testimony taken before the coroner could be treated as 'evidence' for the purposes of further proceedings even though the individual to be placed on trial might not have been in attendance at the inquest to engage in cross-examination (p. 217).

[13] *Ibid.*, p. 292. The active part accorded the jury in some respects followed from the lack of an accusatorial framework at inquests, which largely shielded inquests from the very innovations (such as the introduction of advocates) tending to formalise evidentiary procedure and the jury's relationship to evidence. For a more general discussion of these developments, see John Langbein, 'The Criminal Trial before the Lawyers', *The University of Chicago Law Review*, 45, 2 (winter 1978), pp. 263–316; Thomas Andrew Green, *Verdict According to Conscience: Perspectives on the English Criminal Trial Jury, 1200–1800* (Chicago, 1982), esp. parts II and III; Stephen Landsman, 'From Gilbert to Bentham: The Reconceptualization of Evidence Theory', *The Wayne Law Review*, 36 (1990), pp. 1149–86; J. M. Beattie, 'Scales of Justice: Defense Counsel and the English Criminal Trial in the Eighteenth and Nineteenth Centuries', *Law and History Review*, 9, 2 (autumn 1991), pp. 221–67.

[14] Legal authorities prescribed differing degrees of openness in declaring the view as an absolute requirement. Britton's 'Summary of the Duty of Coroner' warned thirteenth-century coroners not to omit causing the body to be 'openly viewed'; Britton's

It was to these sorts of characteristic signs, rather than express legal opinion, that commentators could turn for legitimation of the open inquest. But again it was not the conflicting interpretations of the fine points of inquest law that made Wakley's pledge to keep his court 'open' a loaded one. In early-nineteenth-century discussions about the purpose of the inquest, its 'openness' brought history, epistemology and political event into a common, though contested, frame. This is so because for at least two decades after the autumn of 1819, it was next to impossible to broach the subject of an open inquest, and the role played by the press in making it so, without confronting the legacy of Peterloo. Accordingly, my analysis of the connections between the coronership and the narrative of popular constitutionalism must step some ten years back from the scene at the Clerkenwell Green hustings, to an inquest at the Duke of York public house in Oldham on 8 September 1819, convened to inquire into the death of John Lees.

II

John Lees was an Oldham cotton spinner and a veteran of Waterloo who, along with at least ten others, was fatally wounded during the violent suppression of the 16 August mass meeting at St Peter's Fields, Manchester. Lees' was (and is) by far the most notorious of the inquests held in connection with the 'Peterloo Massacre', due in no small part to his own strong constitution, which enabled him to live a full three weeks with his injuries. Lees' tenacious grip on life allowed time for two radical solicitors, James Harmer of London and Henry Dennison of Liverpool, to appear at the opening day of the inquest accompanied by several coachloads of witnesses prepared to testify to the legality of the meeting and to the excessive force used by Manchester authorities in dispersing it. As a consequence of the organised case presented on behalf of Lees' family and the national conscience, between 8 September and 1 December the cause of his death was a matter of formal, though episodic, inquiry before Thomas Ferrand, the County Coroner for the district of Rochdale, and a jury of twelve local men *probi et legales*.

The proceedings, which have been described in broad outline in

pseudonymous contemporary, 'Fleta', declared that the body 'must be seen naked.' Standards had loosened by the eighteenth and nineteenth centuries, Jervis agreeing with Blackstone that it was no longer necessary for the body to be 'lying before the jury and the Coroner during the whole evidence'; Jervis, *Practical Treatise*, p. 28. For a discussion of the view's place in inquest procedure, see my 'Viewing Bodies: Medicine, Public Order, and English Inquest Practice', in *Configurations*, 2, 1 (winter 1994), pp. 33–46.

numerous historical works on Peterloo, were as acrimonious as they were protracted.[15] They were also inconclusive, effectively terminated by a decision of the Court of King's Bench not to grant an order requiring Ferrand to reconvene the inquest following his final declaration of adjournment. The request for re-opening had been submitted to the court by the prominent Whig barrister, Thomas Denman, who presented an affidavit charging that the adjournment was illegal, the result of collusion between Ferrand and the Manchester magistrates. Denman was opposed in court by the government attorney Mr. Serjeant Cross, who posed several objections to the motion, most emphatically that the inquest had degenerated into nothing more than a set-piece for radical agitation. In arguing the illegitimacy of the Oldham proceedings, Cross invoked the very features that others took as indices of a viable, open inquest. The inquiry owed its very existence to nothing more than a 'rumour' that Lees 'had suffered in a tumult at Manchester, about three weeks before, some injury – no matter what.'[16] The public, informal nature of this 'humble department of the law' – taking place in a tavern 'filled with multitudes of turbulent people, hooting and hissing, or applauding the witnesses' – confirmed its dubious legal standing. The end and effect, if not object and meaning of the inquiry, Cross concluded, 'was fairly to suspend and paralyze the law of England through the whole of that populous district, and put all the Justices of the Peace, all the Constables, and all the civil and military authorities, under the accusation of murder ... Since the great trial of the seven bishops, there has never been a trial pending in this court containing a charge half so important to the interests of the public as was left to the consideration of the helpless Coroner.'[17]

The arguments put forth by Denman and Cross as to the merits of the Lees inquest in principle, however, ostensibly played no part in the court's decision. Instead, Denman's motion was refused on a technicality – that Ferrand had failed to view the body of the deceased in the company of his jurors. The court's ruling outraged government opponents across the political spectrum, and has subsequently provoked a similar response from historians, who for the most part have regarded the Lees inquest as an exemplar either of political corruption in general

---

[15] The proceedings were suspended at several points by the coroner, the last of which halted proceedings for seven weeks. As a result there were only twelve days in which the inquiry was actually in session. The most complete record made of the Lees inquest was Joseph Augustus Dowling's 580-page *Whole Proceedings before the Coroner's Inquest at Oldham, etc., on the Body of John Lees . . .* (London, 1820).

[16] *Ibid.*, appendix: 'The King versus Ferrand', p. 6.   [17] *Ibid.*, pp. 8–10.

or of the lowly standing to which the nineteenth-century inquest itself
had sunk.[18] Others have taken a more nuanced approach. E. P.
Thompson, for instance, has taken note of some informal results of the
hearings, especially the widely publicised letter signed by seven of the
twelve jurors declaring their opinion that the meeting had been peaceable, and that Lees had been wilfully murdered. In Thompson's
estimation, such a show of independence in defiance of official collusion
makes the Lees inquest an example of the complex standing of 'English
liberties': 'I will allow that the "freeborn Englishman" congratulated
himself too far upon his liberties ... What I will not allow is that these
liberties created no difficulties for authority.'[19]

Despite the anti-climactic termination of the Lees inquest – the fact
that the High Court chose to decide on a point of procedure rather than
on the political and constitutional issues it raised – Thompson's assessment of its links to the ambiguities of English liberties is surely correct.
Nor is this a matter of historical judgement alone: during the course of
its proceedings, and in the years that followed, the Lees inquest served
as a focal point for discussing fundamental points of law and governance. Among the more prominent issues raised, both in and out of the
inquest room itself, was that of publicity and the limits of open justice.

At the inquest itself, controversy over the extent and meaning of
openness reigned from its very first, confused, day. The inquest was
convened on 8 September by the coroner's clerk, Mr Battye, who
peremptorily terminated the proceedings soon after learning that
potentially culpable violence ('cutting' rather than mere 'crushing') was
the likely cause of death. During his brief stewardship of the case,
however, Battye managed to highlight the vexing issue of publicity.
Having noticed Harmer and Dennison amid the crowd of witnesses,

---

[18]   The contemporary radical reaction emerges in the subsequent analysis, but it is worth
noting that condemnation also came from the likes of Henry Brougham, who declared in
the House of Commons that the case compelled him to break with his usual attitude of
deference to English justice: 'when he saw a bare-faced collusion like that which had long
been exhibited in the face of the country, when he saw a coroner questioning his own
irregularity, and availing himself of his own breach of the law, to escape from the necessity
of executing the law, he could not think of dignifying such a mockery of the people of
England with the name of justice'; *Hansard's Parliamentary Debates*, 41 (November–February
1819–20), p. 1184. As for historical comment, Donald Read's standard account of Peterloo
considers that the proceedings demonstrated Ferrand's 'clear bias' towards the local
Manchester authorities. Read, *Peterloo: The 'Massacre' and its Background* (Manchester, 1958),
p. 148. A less measured appraisal characterises them as 'a tragi-comedy with moments of
farce'; Joyce Marlow, *The Peterloo Massacre* (London, 1969), p. 161.

[19]   E. P. Thompson, *Writing by Candlelight*, (London, 1980), p. 205. Yet in the end Thompson
returns to the inquest's unsatisfactory formal results, remarking that due to the lack of a
verdict the people of Oldham 'remain today in suspense'; *ibid.*, p. 208.

spectators, and newspaper reporters, Battye ventured an opinion that they had no right to be present. He further professed confidence that when the real coroner took over the case, he would close the proceedings to the public altogether. Responding to this challenge, and setting the terms of controversy for the duration of the inquest, Harmer stated:

Mr Ferrand could not legally exclude us; for, as this is a public court of justice, instituted for the purpose of inquiring into the cause of death of a fellow subject, who met his death by violence, if all the people of England could be so compressed, they are entitled to be present.[20]

Thomas Ferrand's assumption of control on 25 September did not bring the clarity promised by his beleaguered clerk, though not for want of trying. His first action was to issue an order prohibiting the publication of accounts of the proceedings in the press until the completion of the case, justifying his ban with reference to the recent string of court decisions against the publication of *ex parte* proceedings. Ferrand did, however, concede the right of representatives of local and national newspapers to attend and take notes for future publication. The conflict erupted in earnest on the fifth day of the inquest. Ferrand entered the Duke of York brandishing an account of the previous day's testimony published in *The Times*, and proceeded to upbraid the offending reporter for ignoring his directive. The reporter's protests that he had merely transmitted his notes to London, and was not responsible for their publication, did nothing to placate the enraged coroner: 'Notes have gone, that is certain; and you must know it is extremely wrong, that publicity should thus be given to the proceedings, as it is not an open Court.' This provoked Harmer to respectful disagreement, calling to his side the authority of ancient procedure: 'You must be aware, Sir, that, formerly, Inquests of this kind were, and very properly too, held in the open air, in order that there might be no secrecy in an investigation respecting the death of one of the King's subjects.'[21]

---

[20] Dowling, *Whole Proceedings*, p. 3.

[21] *Ibid.*, p. 106. Harmer derived this notion of the 'open-air' inquest of yore from Sir Thomas Smith's sixteenth-century legal classic, *De Republica Anglorum*. Smith had observed that in his day the impanelling of the Coroner's inquiries, and the view of the body, 'is commonly in the streete, in an open place, and *corona populi*'; Sir Thomas Smith, *De Republica Anglorum*, ed. Mary Dewar (Cambridge, 1982), p. 108. In so doing, Harmer was engaging in the mode of interpretive anachronism that characterised appeals to the ancient constitution: Harmer cited Smith not merely to indicate that the sixteenth-century inquest was a public affair, but further to suggest that the terms of Smith's description were directly accessible and applicable to the modern debate. Effecting a kind of conceptual and spatial conflation, Harmer was making the rather dubious (though powerful) claim that the physical 'openness' of Smith's outdoor inquest might serve to elucidate questions about the inquest's relationship to 'the public' in all its nineteenth-century connotations.

The participants in the simmering debate over publicity were joined later that afternoon by a Manchester barrister named Ashworth. Ashworth informed the inquest that he appeared in the name of the local authorities, and listed as first among his several objectives, 'to prevent *ex parte* evidence from getting abroad, or garbled and imperfect statements from being published, for the purpose of producing particular impressions on the minds of the people'.[22] While protesting his sincere desire for the public to get the truth, Ashworth argued that the very procedural openness of the coroner's court made the question of publicity a delicate one. The publicity associated with the present inquest, involving as it did such highly charged political and social issues, was driven by party spirit seeking to agitate the public mind. Because the witnesses gathered by Harmer and Dennison were testifying first, the direction of such agitation, in his view, was inevitable: 'Do we not know how susceptible the human mind is of first impressions, and naturally prone to receive them as truths', Ashworth demanded in terms reminiscent of Justice Abbott in *Rex* v. *Fleet*, 'so that no subsequent evidence can hereafter remove them?'[23] This being the case, Ashworth urged Ferrand to renew his resolve to prohibit the daily publication of evidence. Harmer rejected this assessment, offering an alternative model for the circulation and reception of knowledge in rebuttal: 'It would be more conducive to the ends of justice and far more satisfactory information would be conveyed to the public', he argued,

if reporters were allowed to take down fully what passes, and publish it daily, than that the mixed audience which are here assembled should each go hence and give publicity to his own imperfect and confused account, made up from recollection, and tinctured with mistaken impressions and party bias. The former mode would give the public a correct statement, on which they might with propriety exercise their reason and judgment; the latter would only mislead and perplex them, and make them form false and erroneous opinions.[24]

Ferrand declined to avail himself and his court of these services. In the specific matter of the breech by *The Times*, he took the curious, and much ridiculed, step of allowing the offending reporter to remain in the room on the provision that he desist from all further note-taking. Not surprisingly, this did nothing to settle the matter, and similar exchanges were repeated for the duration of the inquest: Ferrand continued to issue orders against publication before a verdict was reached; Harmer continued to defend the principle of openness on constitutional grounds; and the press continued to criticise, and in some instances ignore,

---

[22] Dowling, *Whole Proceedings*, p. 118.   [23] *Ibid.*, p. 120.   [24] *Ibid.*, pp. 125–6.

Ferrand's efforts to keep the inquest off its pages. From the outset, the radical press in particular took exception to Ferrand's prohibition. 'The Inquest at Oldham on the body of John Lees', thundered Wooler's *Black Dwarf*, 'has exhibited every feature of the system in its strongest light.' It had begun with the attempts of Battye, a 'blundering blockhead', to dismiss the inquiry out of hand, an attempt considered 'too gross, even for the [Manchester] faction to countenance'. Next had come Ferrand, 'a smooth-tongued gentleman, a mild and cautious practitioner', who had nonetheless used all possible means to further the cause of the 'Manchester murderers'. With the broad features of the inquest's failings thus sketched, Wooler concluded with a declaration of fundamental principle: 'Every court of law is an open court, into which every man has a legal right to enter, if he can find room.'[25]

Similar views were expressed – with varying degrees of vehemence – in the other leading opposition newspapers. The *Examiner* upheld the principle of public access while dismissing as 'absurd' the supposition that the public mind would be irrevocably prejudiced by the first evidence reported.[26] The *Cap of Liberty* seconded this assessment: the public would form a firm opinion based on conclusive evidence alone, and if early reports of the Lees inquest served to convict the Manchester magistrates in the court of public opinion, this was indicative not of prejudice but of the clarity of the issues under inquiry. The only real effect (and intent) of suspending daily press reports, the editorial concluded, was to confine publication to lengthy and expensive retrospectives, thereby depriving the greater public 'of the knowledge of most important concerns to every individual in the community'.[27]

The issues raised at Oldham brought the link between the inquest and popular constitutionalism to the fore, and provided those arguing the cause of openness with a potent and enduring referent. Ferrand's manoeuvrings struck critics as part of a broad-scale assault on the foundations of English liberties, of which Peterloo was itself the most obvious and flagrant instance. Inquiry into the violent dispersal of a peaceable demonstration convened in the name of the ancient right of petition was being covered up by the machinations of a 'wretched imbecile Administration' and its agents. The combination, a correspondent to the *Examiner* continued, presented opponents of despotism with a constitutional crisis of epic proportions:

---

[25] *Black Dwarf*, 3, 41, 13 October 1819, p. 661.   [26] *Examiner*, 3 October 1819, p. 634.
[27] *Cap of Liberty*, 1, 6, 13 October 1819, p. 93.

As if the atrocious sabring of an unarmed inoffensive population were not sufficient of itself to mark the triumph of arbitrary principles, supported by military power, over the constitutional rights of the people, we are doomed to witness the scandalous perversion of judicial proceedings in support of that system of state policy which will either destroy this country, or it must be destroyed by the spirit of the British nation.[28]

In 'Vindicator's' view, there was no question that even so 'humble [a] department of the law' as the coroner's inquest was a weighty enough feature of popular liberty to merit such a judgement. Citing authorities ranging from thirteenth-century statute law to Blackstone, he concluded: 'the political consequences of this conduct of the Coroner are of such importance to our liberties, that every man who values his own, who prefers security by law to the wild attempts of persons in authority arbitrarily to suspend its operation, should come forward and unite in the determination to maintain what yet remains good or valuable in our Constitution, against the machinations and attempts of a jesuitical, daring Administration to destroy it'. The next issue of the *Examiner* carried a further contribution from 'Vindicator', who expanded his argument's constitutional pedigree by invoking Coke, the Magna Carta, and 'the sublime language of the 35th Institution of our noble Saxon Monarch, Edward the Confessor' in calling right-thinking Englishmen to their duty: 'When a tremendous ruin appears ready to burst upon our devoted country, and to sweep away in its devastating torrent our laws, ancient customs, rightful privileges, and personal liberties, all inferior considerations give place to that of safety – all must unite to resist the meditated destruction – or all will perish in it.'[29]

III

During and in the immediate aftermath of the Lees proceedings, it was figures like Hunt and Wooler who were at the forefront in arguing its

[28] *Examiner*, 24 October 1819, p. 686 (letter from 'Vindicator'). 'Vindicator's' position had been foreshadowed by the *Examiner*'s editorial of the previous week, warning that a successful suppression of inquiry would usher in an era of true continental despotism, with 'the police of this country reduced to the mixed laxity and severity of old Lisbon itself – lax as far as the people's lives are to be secured, and severe only in behalf of Government'.

[29] *Ibid.*, 31 October 1819, pp. 702–3. Nor was 'Vindicator' by any means alone in articulating this critique: the *Cap of Liberty* considered the authorities as 'classed in the ideas of the people with the horde of Usurpers and Traitors to the Constitution with which our unfortunate country has too long abounded'; I, 7, 20 October 1819, p. 101; a *Manchester Observer* editorial (reprinted in the *Cap of Liberty*) concluded that victory for the authorities would amount to demonstrative proof that 'Englishmen are no longer free – the Constitution no longer exists'; I, 13, 1 December 1819, p. 208.

connection to a fundamental assault on the popular constitution. Indeed, the Oldham inquest retained its place as a signal instance of liberties in danger and as a rallying cry for the radical cause into the 1830s at the very least. The case's ramifications were evident to a wider spectrum of observers, however: for a decade after its abrupt termination, the Lees inquest figured as an element in a broader discussion of the relationship between open justice, anti-despotism, and coroner's court, involving Whig reformers and 'philosophic' as well as 'political' radicals, and guided on the theoretical plane by the vision of no less a figure than Jeremy Bentham.

Bentham may well appear out of place in this discussion. No friend of the ancient constitution, his penchant for systematising and rationalising place him squarely on the side of trends in early-nineteenth-century legal theory and practice away from the principle of open judicial procedure.[30] And yet, precisely because of this apparent contradiction, Bentham's presence is critical here, as his framing of the imperatives of publicity, both radically different from and yet formally related to the inquest's place in the popular constitutionalist conception of justice, neatly illustrate the flexibility of the constitutive conceptual elements of the constitutionalist discourse itself.

Public access to the workings of authority at all levels was a central feature of Bentham's formula for open, rational and moral government. 'The fittest law for securing the public confidence', he declared in his *Essay on Political Tactics*, '... is that of *publicity*.'[31] Bentham developed this law of rational governance using the very same set of terms that marked contemporary discussions of the inquest: openness, suspicion, judgement, mystery, participation. Bentham's public, like that of the inquest,

---

[30] These trends included the formalisation of rules for excluding evidence, the increasing importance of the lawyer as an intermediary between defendants, witnesses and jurors, the hardening of the law–fact distinction and the reform of penal sanctions, tending towards limiting jury mitigation and thus the role of lay intuition. Bentham's position on the different levels of openness appropriate to legal proceedings was a complicated one, however. He consistently argued for what might be described as a regime of 'virtual' openness secured by press representations. Yet at the same time he pointed to the limits of such a regime, recalling the intangible, ephemeral evidence available only to a truly 'open' (i.e. participatory) proceeding. While in his *Rationale of Judicial Evidence* he concluded a chapter on publicity by praising newspapers for their ability to fix evidence 'by signs of an unevanescent and imperishable nature', earlier in the same chapter he had warned that 'it is not the whole of the evidence that is capable of being expressed by writing. Deportment (an article constituting a considerable branch of circumstantial evidence, and itself distinguishable into a considerable number of varieties) is an article not communicable but in a very imperfect manner, to any that are not at once auditors and spectators'; *The Works of Jeremy Bentham*, ed. John Bowring (Edinburgh, 1843), vol. VI, p. 377 and 371. I am grateful to Tom Green for sharing his considerable insight into these issues with me.

[31] Bentham, *Works*, vol. II, p. 310 (emphasis original).

was both subject and object of the scrutinising function of publicity. On the one hand, publicity acted as a lever for exposing real corruption and abuse resulting from irresponsible power. The regime of public opinion, activated through publicity, was, Bentham frankly admitted, one founded on suspicion:

Is it objected against the regime of publicity, that it is a system of *distrust?* This is true; and every good political institution is founded upon this base. Whom ought we to distrust, if not those to whom is committed great authority, with great temptations to abuse it?[32]

For Bentham such distrust was both constructive and inevitable: constructive as a check on abuse; inevitable because of the natural response to secrecy in the social and political world. To those who would argue that the public is an unfit judge of the workings of the state, that publicity inevitably leads to misjudgement, Bentham countered with another maxim:

This objection would have some solidity, if, when the means of judging correctly were taken from the popular tribunal, the inclination to judge could be equally taken away: but the public do judge and will always judge.[33]

Given that the public would always judge, irrespective of the wishes of its governors, Bentham urged disclosure as a principle of self-protection. In an economy of ever-present suspicion, innocence, virtue and truth were the real victims of secrecy:

Suspicion always attaches to mystery. It thinks it sees a crime where it beholds an affectation of secrecy ... In proportion as it is desirable for improbity to shroud itself in darkness, in the same proportion is it desirable for innocence to walk in open day, for fear of being mistaken for her adversary.[34]

Truth, then, was both induced through and stabilised within mechanisms of public access. But Bentham did not consign society to a regimen of perpetual suspicion; instead, he looked to this process as a way of effecting a rationalisation of the public mind, and ultimately of creating a new social subject. The habit of participation and access to the whole of the evidence in question ultimately produced a citizenry capable of *withholding* judgement where appropriate:

A habit of reasoning and discussion will penetrate all classes of society. The passions, accustomed to a public struggle, will learn reciprocally to restrain themselves; they will lose that morbid sensibility, which among nations without

---

[32] *Ibid.*, p. 314 (emphasis original).   [33] *Ibid.*, p. 313.   [34] *Ibid.*, p. 310.

liberty and without experience, renders them the sport of every alarm and every suspicion.[35]

This was the ultimate answer to those who would deny the virtues of publicity. Publicity was the route to a disciplined, responsible public. In its objective, it should be noted, Bentham's vision of open, participatory judgement was somewhat ambiguous. Openness was a virtue, a necessity, and an interim phase in the development of truly rational government. Tribunals of participatory judgement encouraged truth, detected abuse, enacted and demonstrated transparency, *and* ultimately taught the public the limits of its capacities for judgement. In his prescription for open government, then, Bentham had left space for expertise, and its problematic relationship to lay knowledge.

It was these connections between public opinion, tribunals of inquiry and specialist knowledge that made Bentham's views apposite to discussions of the political and constitutional issues raised by the Lees inquest, and ultimately to the 'professional' stakes posed by the Wakley–Baker contest. One of the more sustained efforts to explicitly articulate the former set of links appeared in the March 1824 issue of the *Edinburgh Review*, in the form of a forty-page analysis of Bentham on legal evidence. The reviewer was Thomas Denman, who, as a leading figure in the Bentham-inspired circle of legal reformers and as a direct participant in the legal battles arising from the Lees inquest itself, can be seen as the veritable embodiment of the historical and conceptual network now being considered.

Denman devoted the final quarter of his article (singled out by the *Dictionary of National Biography* as one of his most influential legal essays), to the proper role of publicity in legal procedure. He began by professing discomfort at some of Bentham's more radical views on evidentiary admissibility (in particular his acceptance of anonymous information), but took comfort in Bentham's stipulation that publicity must be at the root of all legal procedure, a stipulation in full keeping with the historical principles of English jurisprudence: 'Secret tribunals', Denman observed, 'have ever been odious.'[36] Having established both the rationale for and the historical confirmation of the principle of open justice, Denman proceeded to describe – in terms clearly resonant of his experience with the late controversy surrounding the inquest's public standing – the harmony between the interests of the public and the press

---

[35] *Ibid.*, p. 311.
[36] *Edinburgh Review*, 40, March 1824, review of *Traité des Preuves Judiciares: Ouvrage extrait des Manuscrits de M. Jeremie Bentham* . . ., by E. Dumont (1823), p. 195.

in legal cases, and the evil which inevitably befell any attempt to interfere with this relationship:

If the transaction has been of such a nature as to arouse the public attention, every one present at the audience has carried away and disseminated his own report; the whole town is in possession of the tidings in one little hour. Partial, garbled, exaggerated, full of error and falsehood and rash suspicion, as all these rumours must inevitably be, the means of securing a faithful narrative are, in our times, fortunately always at hand; for it happens that the ministers of public curiosity find their account in being present at the examination, and recording every part of it with an accuracy beyond all dispute. The gossip flies abroad neglected; But every one waits for the next journals, which correctly represent the truth, and instantly convey it with the rapidity of beacon-lights to the most distant corners of the land.[37]

Denman's confidence in the contemporary press's capacity to both embody and transmit rational public knowledge allowed him to depict it as an essential supplement to legal inquiries, especially to those like the inquest.[38] As a tribunal convened in many cases to manage the effects of 'rumour', 'gossip' and 'curiosity' which posed a potential danger to the reign of reason, the inquest was in particular need of the press's 'beacon-lights'. Indeed, Denman can be seen as arguing that the press might eventually replace inquests, imagining along the lines of Bentham an informed social body transparent to itself and thereby rendered immune to the ill-effects of rumour.

Such an age of rational tranquillity grounded upon unimpeded publicity, if ever seriously imagined by Denman, was in his assessment far removed from the realities of England in the 1820s. And for Denman, it was the inquest itself that served as a reminder of how far English justice had deviated from its pure constitutional foundation. In principle, he declared, the inquest was the exemplary institutional embodiment of the reign of publicity:

The English law has one provision of the general security, which has been justly extolled, – the Coroner's Inquest. In every instance of sudden death, a jury of the neighbours is summoned by a known officer, and information as to the cause is invited and solicited from every quarter ... This is essentially a public court ... Its whole merit, indeed, consists in its publicity.[39]

Thus despite the inquest's lowly standing (the coroner being 'rarely a

[37] Ibid., pp. 196–7.
[38] 'The press', Denman wrote, 'is not like the stage, which "echoes back the public voice," for it is the public voice. It is the organ of public opinion, but of public opinion acting upon facts selected and conveyed by the same organ'; ibid., p. 202 (emphasis original).
[39] Ibid., pp. 200–1.

person of high legal attainments'), it properly served as a bulwark against the twin dangers of despotism and suspicion. Yet, in an unmistakable reference to the Lees inquest, Denman adverted to recent attacks on this principle: 'In some counties, however, it seems that [the coroner] has formed splendid notions of his own authority; his reading has informed him of the high misdemeanour [of publicity]; and he has taken upon himself to prohibit and prevent its commission, by ordering persons present to take no notes of the proceedings. He does not object to the efforts of memory; but to a correct report, his objections, in point of law, are insurmountable!'[40] The stakes in such manoeuvring, in Denman's view, could not be higher, and he concluded his essay with the following exhortation:

For the honour of the law of England, we hope it will not be found to sanction a claim so inconsistent with the due administration of justice, and so destructive of all just confidence in it. But if this should turn out differently, the Legislature itself, we trust, will for once interfere, for the protection of the liberty of the subject.[41]

Some eight years later, the Whig-led House of Commons attempted just such a defence of English legal honour. On 20 June 1832, members considered amendments to a bill whose primary aim was to alter the method of paying for inquests. The bill itself was ultimately rejected, but not before it served as a vehicle for articulating, on the national political stage, the full gamut of positions on public access to coroners' courts. Henry Warburton, another Benthamist reformer with ties to both Whig and Radical parliamentarians, proposed that the inquest be declared an open proceeding by statute, making the theoretical lineage of his position quite clear in the process: 'In the words of a great man lately deceased, "publicity is the soul of justice." '[42] Echoing these sensibilities, the liberal legal moderniser John Campbell (later Lord Chief Justice and Lord Chancellor) exhorted his fellow members to view the issue as a matter of public good rather than as one of political partisanship: 'for the sake of individuals and the public, it was of the last importance that there should be no appearance of secrecy in the proceedings of Coroners' Inquests'.[43]

But for Radicals in parliament, the matter could not be adequately appreciated without taking note of its traumatic political heritage. The open inquest was not a question of abstract legal theorising, but resided at the heart of the popular constitution. Daniel O'Connell invoked the

---

[40] *Ibid.*, p. 201.   [41] *Ibid.*, pp. 206–7.   [42] *Hansard*, 13, May–July 1832, p. 925.
[43] *Ibid.*, p. 937.

Lees inquest as a prime example of the true stakes of the debate, declaring 'the impunity of those who were concerned in the celebrated murders at Manchester to have been secured by the imperfection of the law respecting the Coroner's Court'. He further denounced as 'new, and Judge-made law' the trend over the past decade or so for coroners to claim the right of excluding the public.[44] Having marked the issue with the stamp of popular constitutionalism and located it unambiguously within radical political memory, O'Connell drew the broader lesson: 'There ought to be no secrecy before a Coroner, for it was a Court of Inquiry, and, like every Court of Justice, that Court ought to be an open one. Publicity was a great corrective of abuse, which otherwise would creep in were Courts kept closed.'[45] Henry Hunt lent the authority of first-hand experience to O'Connell's assessment of closed inquests' illegitimate legal and historical standing: 'The right of excluding the public from Coroners' Inquests', Hunt assured the House, 'was first assumed, twelve years ago, at Manchester.' He concluded by likening modern, *in camera* inquests to the archetypal absolutist perversion of the true constitution: 'a Coroner's court, as the law now stood, was little better than the Star Chamber or the Inquisition'.[46]

Tory members rallied in defence of limiting public access to inquests, several objecting to the proposed amendment on the grounds that it would injure private sensibilities while merely gratifying the prurient.[47] But the most pointed attack came immediately after passage of Warburton's amendment (by a 94–54 vote), when Frankland Lewis invoked the inquest's constitutional lineage to *denounce* the amendment. Describing the inquest as 'one of the oldest institutions of the country', Lewis charged the Whig ministers in attendance with dereliction of their governing responsibility to protect the foundations of constitutional order from the vagaries of mere politics. Lewis professed profound surprise and disappointment 'that his Majesty's Ministers had taken no decided part in the discussion of a question of so much importance, and one brought under the consideration of the House at a time when all the institutions of the country were undergoing such extensive and fundamental changes'.[48] Stung by this rebuke made in the name of the inquest's ancient standing, government representatives quickly and

---

[44] *Ibid.*, pp. 926–7.   [45] *Ibid.*, p. 931.   [46] *Ibid.*, p. 927.

[47] Alexander Baring, for example, demanded to know whether a statutory declaration of openness would make it necessary 'to throw open the doors of any house where a catastrophe might occur, and let all the blackguards in the street have entrance?'; *ibid.*, p. 936.

[48] *Ibid.*, p. 932.

categorically denied Lewis' imputations of the amendment's radical
pedigree, describing it instead as a felicitous marriage of rational reform
with solid constitutional principle. Lord Althorp, as Chancellor and
leader of the House, and the Solicitor-General, Sir William Hone, both
rose to affirm that the vote represented not an innovation but merely a
declaration 'in perfect conformity with the acknowledged practice'. The
fact that of late 'some uncertainty over the matter' had arisen made it
perfectly reasonable, in Hone's opinion, to have 'a clause in an Act
which went to declare that to be the law which, as a lawyer, he had
always held to be the law'.[49] Warburton closed the discussion with an
attempt to rhetorically reconcile the grounds upon which the Whig and
Radical victory rested, declaring himself pleased to hear the government's legal counsel concur that his amendment 'was consistent, not
only with general reason ... but was also consistent with the old
constitutional law'.[50]

The parliamentary debate evinced not only the temporary confluence
of Whig and Radical versions of the inquest's legal standing, but the
broader availability of the constitutionalist idiom in such debates as
well. Lewis's declaration of the legitimacy of closed inquests rested on
the same historico-political foundations upon which his opponents
argued the case for openness. While the nature and function of the
inquest was a matter of disagreement, the framework within which any
such delineation was to be worked out most certainly was not. As a
general proposition, this observation should come as no great surprise,
the flexibility of recourse to the ancient constitution being acknowledged
by practitioners and commentators alike as one of its primary features.
But, as is amply demonstrated in the essays of this volume, the
recognition of an available formal fluidity is only the first part of the
story. The ancient constitution could be invoked from any number of
positions, but only according to strict rules of genre. The analytical
payoff in juxtaposing such narratives is to test their limits, and to
interrogate the grounds of their mutual construction. This is what I
propose for the final section of this essay. Having demonstrated the
components of a framing discourse within which the inquest could be
legitimised – those of openness, publicity, participation and authority of
historical precedent – we can now return to the hustings of the 1830
election for the East Middlesex coronership, and attempt a more precise

---

[49] *Ibid.*, p. 934.
[50] *Ibid.*, p. 936. Hunt too 'expressed satisfaction at hearing the Attorney-General's confirmation of the old law of the country'; p. 937.

analysis of the issues at stake, and the thematic web within which they were suspended.

IV

Recall in particular the four slogans emblazoned on Wakley's blue banners: 'Wakley and Medical Reform'; 'Wakley and the Sovereignty of the People'; 'Reason and Science against Ignorance and Prejudice'; and 'Wakley and an Open Court'. The first two drew attention to Wakley's credentials as a public man: Wakley the outspoken champion of wholesale reform in the medical and the political realms; Wakley the crusading editor of both the Lancet and the (shortlived) Ballot, who conceived of journalism as properly concerned with 'opening' the closed, corrupt worlds of medicine and politics.[51] They indicated Wakley's conviction, and that of his fellow radicals, that medical reform was not a mere derivative of politics, but was coextensive with it. Power and abuse collected in places which were closed and secret. It was left to the searchlight of publicity to expose to the general intelligence the prejudices and irrationalities of 'Old Corruption'. Wakley's version of the inquest drew directly on a conception of participatory democratic politics grounded in popular constitutionalism, but with a crucial proviso – in order to realise its public mission, the inquest required the assistance of medical science.

Hence Wakley's third slogan. Science, in his estimation, was an extension and an exemplar of the searching rational eye. Wakley's cause, as one of his supporters declared at the hustings, was that of 'enlightenment and humanity'; it represented the forces of advanced knowledge in both its scientific and political applications.[52] But even as a representative of this progressive epistemology, Wakley was not exempt

---

[51] Wakley the medical journalist used the Lancet as a tool for prising open the 'closed,' patronage-bound world of the London medical elite. In the words of one Wakley enthusiast, the pre-Lancet medicine was the undisputed province of 'men who obtained their offices by intrigue, with whom all depends upon influence and favour, and nothing upon intelligence, knowledge, or capability ... But THE LANCET appeared – threw open its pages for the publication of every act of injustice or oppression that was committed, and afforded that best shield against the tyranny of the powerful – publicity'; Lancet, 1, 1830–1, 2 October 1830, p. 43. Wakley the political spokesman advocated the full range of radical causes; he frequently attended, and occasionally chaired, meetings of organisations like the National Union of Working Classes, and took such opportunities to preach the virtues of a government open to the scrutiny and influence of the people. The Ballot's inaugural editorial announced that 'The TITLE which we have adopted, declares, in ONE word, our political creed. It announces that we are Reformers in the fullest acceptation of the term'; 2 January 1831.

[52] Morning Chronicle, 10 September 1830, p. 3.

from constitutionalism's generic dictates. This is evident in the most problematic of his campaign themes, the pledge to keep his court 'open'. Though heralding his allegiance to the inquest of the popular constitution, radical memory and reformist politics, 'Wakley and an Open Court' was to many an oxymoron, emblematic of liberties endangered by the overreaching grasp of science.

Henry Hunt's ubiquitous presence by Wakley's side at the hustings should have been enough in itself to make clear the intended resonance of his candidate's vow of openness. Not content simply to embody the link between his candidate and the inquest's recent history, however, Hunt more than once during the contest recalled the Lees inquest in endorsing Wakley's vision of participatory democratic politics guaranteed by medical knowledge.[53] This was the way Wakley represented himself as well. His first campaign advertisement, printed in the 24 August issue of the *Morning Chronicle*, began:

Gentlemen, The Coroner's Court is an institution of such great antiquity that its origin is not discoverable in the pages of the history of our country. Founded upon the immutable basis of public justice and security, it has, throughout the succeeding ages, resisted the devastating influence of corruption; and, in the nineteenth century, you have still handed down to you, unrestricted and uncontrouled, the invaluable prerogative of electing its presiding officer; if, however, the sound and pure principles upon which this Court was established remain unchanged, it must be confessed that the advantages which might have been expected from such an institution have not been altogether realised, because men who by education and habit were utterly inadequate to the fulfilment of the duties connected with the Coroner's office have been elected for its Presidents.

Having embraced the ancient lineage of the institution and tied it to the righteous struggle against 'Old Corruption', Wakley connected these causes to that of a medical coronership: 'What is the chief duty of a Coroner', he asked? 'To inquire into the obscure and endless causes of death, produced, or supposed to be produced, by events out of the usual course of nature. The investigation, therefore, which the Coroner has to conduct often involves the most complicated questions in anatomy, physiology, surgery, and chemistry'. The consequences of coroners bereft of medical knowledge, Wakley warned in closing, had already

---

[53] At the hustings and at other public events Hunt invoked the memory of the 'Manchester Massacre'. Before one gathering, for example, Hunt contrasted Wakley's radical credentials – his 'determination to resist power in high stations, when that power was in his opinion exercised to the oppression of others' – to Hunt's own experience of 'the reverse of this conduct in the case of the Oldham inquest'; *Lancet*, 2, 1829–30, 28 August 1830, p. 875.

been experienced to the cost of liberty: 'Innocent men have been consigned to dungeons, dragged to the felon's bar, branded for life, or even executed upon the scaffold, while the guilty, exulting in the imperfect administration of the law, have escaped the punishment so justly demanded by their crimes.'[54]

Given that this campaign notice was addressed to a general newspaper readership, perhaps there was nothing remarkable in Wakley's use of the language of constitutionalism in announcing his intention to capture the coronership in the name of medicine. Yet Wakley paid an equally lyrical tribute to the venerable standing of the inquest in the other main public notice of his candidacy, published as a lengthy editorial in the 21 August issue of the *Lancet*. This piece began with the demand, by then familiar to *Lancet* readers, that coroners be medically qualified, and ended with Wakley offering his services to the cause as candidate for the vacant Middlesex position. In the process, Wakley described the nature of the office:

The Coroner's Court, in the nature of its constitution, is one of the best institutions of the country; it is calculated, and ought, to confer inestimable advantages upon the public. The greatest Law authorities have ever spoken of this Court in terms of high commendation, and the freedom of inquiry of which it admits, has always been deemed a source of great protection to the subject. There are no technicalities, there are no fettering, unreasonable forms, the Court is opened by proclamation, and there is an invitation to all who are acquainted with any circumstances relating to the matter under investigation, to come forward with their evidence. [55]

This passage is of interest on two counts. As a substantive statement it contains the essence of Wakley's criticism of the legal coronership. Because the inquest was a rough and informal forum, reminiscent of a wiser, purer age, because it was convened for the purposes of free public inquiry devoid of constricting legalism, the case for a legal coroner was a nullity. It was in the subject matter of the inquest, rather than its form, that technical expertise was required.[56] But as significant as the

---

[54] *Morning Chronicle*, 24 August 1830, p. 1.

[55] *Lancet*, 2, 1829–30, 21 August 1830, p. 835.

[56] This point was underscored at a meeting of Wakley supporters a week later, when the London medic Thomas King remarked from the chair: 'The forms of [the coroner's] court are simple; but he has not only to call witnesses, to take depositions, – to collect evidence, but it is his duty to judge in some degree of the validity of testimony, to see that it is complete, to strip it of its technicalities and lay it plainly before the jury'; *ibid.*, 2, 1829–30, 28 August 1830, p. 867. That a medical man was the only person qualified to perform this vital translation was reiterated by several speakers during the evening's proceedings, and not by doctors alone. Hunt for one considered Wakley's medical training to be as important as his radical credentials in qualifying him for the post: surgeons, Hunt noted, were barred

substantive claim is the audience to which it was addressed. Wakley invoked the idiom of constitutionalism to underscore to a scientifically minded readership the necessity for a medical coronership. This was by no means an isolated instance. The pages of the *Lancet* in the weeks surrounding the election were replete with such overlapping of constitutional and scientific concern. In the report of a pro-Wakley meeting at the infamous Crown and Anchor tavern, for example, an observation that it made as much sense to elect a coroner ignorant of medical science as 'to employ a butcher to shave, or a lawyer to cure a brain fever' sat next to, and in ostensible harmony with, one heralding the inquest's participatory basis as 'one of the greatest blessings of this country'.[57] A discussion of a fine point of post-mortem evidence followed immediately on from a declaration that 'all the institutions we have derived from Alfred are essentially good; my ears are gratified by the wholesome and old English sound, "O yez, O yez." '[58] The intertwined discourses of expertise and popular constitutionalism were thus as much a staple for readers of the *Lancet* as for the sizable crowds massed at Clerkenwell Green on successive days of the election.[59]

Wakley's name was placed in nomination on the first of these gatherings by the Reverend George Evans, a last-minute substitute for Wakley's more noteworthy supporter, the Middlesex MP Joseph Hume.[60] Evans opened his address to the freeholders by reminding them of the election's formal stakes: in choosing 'a person to fill the office of Coroner, they were exercising one of the most precious and important privileges with which the Constitution invested them'. Invoking the recent 'downfall of tyranny in France', Evans went on to exhort the electorate to set an example for the rest of the nation and

from serving as jurors, leaving juries destitute of medical information. 'If the coroner is also uninformed', he inquired, 'how is the true cause of death to be discovered? It is true the jury have in many cases the benefit of medical evidence, but there ought to be a medical mind (if I may so express it) to estimate the value of that evidence'; *ibid.*, p. 874.

[57] *Ibid.*, p. 867. These remarks were King's, who contrasted the English situation favourably to that obtaining on the more despotically inclined continent. The contrast with the centralised, bureaucratised and expert-oriented procedures of death investigation in France, Germany and even Scotland, was a dominant feature of the inquest idiom, one which obviously participates in the broader discourse of constitutionalism. This further illustrates the limitations of describing figures like Wakley as straightforward 'Francophiles' (see above n. 5).

[58] *Ibid.*, p. 872.

[59] Estimated by the *Morning Chronicle* to at times have reached upwards of 40,000, and declared by Hunt in his experience to have been the 'larg[est] crowd of his fellow-countrymen brought together within so small a compass' – denser, he observed, than the Manchester meeting itself; *Morning Chronicle*, 21 September 1830, p. 3.

[60] Hume had earlier written a letter of support to Wakley which was subsequently published in the *Lancet* and printed up as election posters. No reason was given for his absence.

'put down the tyrant prejudice' favouring a legal coroner.[61] Sir John
Lilly followed with the starkest possible argument in favour of a medical
coroner; one of the first things a coroner must be able to do, Lilly
observed, was 'to ascertain whether the body be dead at all, or whether it
be not merely a case of suspended animation', a nicety which he declared
had been frequently proved as beyond the competence of legal coroners.[62] Colonel Jones, another of Wakley's supporters, made his case by
denouncing lawyers as 'the creatures of precedent, and precedent was
the pretext for all abuses'. Jones then reminded the voters that as 'an
open Court', the inquest was a tool in the struggle against abuse, and
thus urged them 'to reject all prejudices and perform their duty to
themselves and the public openly, honourably, conscientiously'.[63]

But Wakley was himself the most ardent and articulate advocate of
his cause, on this as on each successive day of polling. In numerous
speeches delivered from the hustings, he claimed the coronership on the
strength of the investigative method and professional epistemology at his
disposal, and its potential for furthering the cause of popular liberty.
Legitimate, uncorrupted medicine was in his formulation first and
foremost a science, one that had a different relationship to truth than
did lay professions such as the law. Where a lawyer was 'fettered by
legal sophistry and precedents', a doctor cared only for unencumbered
and socially unmediated evidence.[64] While a lawyer's trade was irredu-
cibly social, embedded in contingent vested interests, a medical man was
connected to the social realm only at a removed level, in that he might
read out of his object of professional investigation signs of dysfunction,
abuse or corruption (but not himself be their cause).[65] And as a
guarantee of his benign, yet thoroughly populist intentions, he spelled
out the substance behind the slogan 'Wakley and an Open Court':

His Court should be at all times open to the Press; in the fullest publicity would
be found that open and severe scrutiny, without which substantial justice would
not appear to the public to be done. He was resolved that everything he did
should be in the open face of day.[66]

---

[61] *Morning Chronicle*, 10 September 1830, p. 3.   [62] *Ibid.*, p. 4.   [63] *Ibid.*

[64] *The Times*, 14 September 1830, p. 4.

[65] Wakley laid several charges of interestedness: against lawyers in general (that they had a
professional interest in verdicts of manslaughter, for example); and Baker in particular
(dismissing him as a mere creature of vestry politics); *Morning Chronicle*, 21 September 1830,
p. 3; and 18 September 1830, p. 4.

[66] This pledge was often referred to in the subsequent days of the campaign, especially by
Hunt. Hunt ridiculed Baker's belated promise (on the fifth day of the election) to keep an
open court, by invoking a scientifically sensible public which would turn Baker's openness
to account: 'If he did only keep an open Court for three months, it would suffice to show his
incompetency, and he would be discharged'; *ibid.*, 15 September 1830, p. 1.

Wakley's promise of an objective medical coroner looking only to the people's interests, however, was far from self-evident to all. Baker supporters countered with an attempt to disaggregate the proposed amalgam of science, politics and constitutionalism, and to reconstitute it as a harbinger not of enlightened liberty, but of faction and despotic prejudice. For them a medical coroner contradicted the very essence of the inquest's constitutional standing, by negating both the role of lay jurors and the possibilities of public access to evidence at a conceptual level. How, they asked, could inquests be both scientific and popular? How could a medical coroner respect the common sense of lay jurors? Could medical knowledge be credibly represented as an extension of public knowledge? Could the freeholders of Middlesex really expect to have both Wakley and their sovereignty?

In pressing their case, the 'friends of Baker' sought in the first instance to turn Wakley's radical credentials into a liability. Samuel Charles Whitbread, recently dislodged from his parliamentary seat, placed Baker's name in nomination on the strength of two observations: first, that 'dead men required no assistance from a surgeon – there was no knowledge requisite for a Coroner of which Mr Baker was destitute'; and second, that the selection of a man suitable to discharge the duties of coroner 'had nothing to do with politics'. Frederick Hodson, in seconding Baker's nomination, underscored Whitbread's somewhat paradoxical injunctive against politics: 'as to the business which brought them together, he must take leave to say, that they had not met for the purpose of procuring an opinion upon the French Revolution, but simply to fill the vacancy in the office of Coroner'.[67] Baker himself, on the fifth day of the election, cast his opponent as a politicising subversive: the question of fitness for the office, he declared, had been displaced by 'a political contest, and to the disgrace of the county of Middlesex, the standard of rebellion had been raised within its limits'.[68]

This challenge to the association of inquests with radical politics was

[67] *Ibid.*, 10 September 1830, p. 3.
[68] *Ibid.*, 16 September 1830, p. 4. The response from Wakley's camp was unapologetic in reasserting the inseparability of the political issue from that of qualification. Wakley demanded: 'Why should it not be political? The Coroner was the people's Judge ... In good old times the people created the office for their own use and for their own protection, and the man who filled it should be incapable of being intimidated by the Crown or machinations of any Minister – nay, even if that Minister were a Field Marshal.' Hunt, for his part, declared that 'nothing could be more correct and proper than that the election should assume a political character, for the office of Coroner, with that of the Sheriff of London, was the only office of which the people retained the appointment'. As to Baker's charge of 'rebellion', Hunt agreed: 'There was a rebellion against the old system, and assertion of the people's rights, but that was all'; *ibid.*

joined by careful critiques of the supposed common purpose of science and the constitution. The leading figure in this effort was George Frederick Young, a London shipping merchant who entered the House of Commons in 1832 as the member for Tynemouth. In his appearances for Baker at the hustings Young drew attention to the seams of Wakley's position, as in the following observation made on the fourth day: 'They had heard much during the present election of Coroners, as if the Coroner constituted the whole Inquest. Surely there was a Jury sworn to find a true verdict upon their oaths. It was rather remarkable that amongst Reformers they should have heard so little about the Jury.'[69] But it was in a letter appearing as a Baker advertisement in *The Times* of 13 September that Young most fully made his case. Young's notice opened with a sarcastic reference to Wakley's political pretensions: 'Sir, – As it has pleased the "majesty of the people" now daily assembled in front of the hustings at Clerkenwell, to grant their present idol, Mr Wakley, a full opportunity for the expression and consequent promulgation of his absurd opinions and libellous reflections ... I trust you will allow me a corner of your valuable columns for the consideration of a subject deeply interesting not only to the freeholders of Middlesex, but to the public in general'. It then proceeded to characterise the substance of Wakley's bid as a campaign for 'the reform of medical jurisprudence', predicated on the 'the identification of that reformation with political reform' and put into operation by 'the foul and atrocious calumnies uttered against medical opponents, – the pantomimic exhibitions of medical supporters' aimed at 'pandering to the passions of the multitude'.[70]

In place of this politicking noise, Young asked for a dispassionate consideration of the implications of a medical coronership – a consideration within the very terms of the Wakley campaign: liberty versus tyranny, objectivity versus professional prejudice. Viewed in the cool light of reason, Young predicted, Wakley's claims would be exposed as paradoxical, contradictory and subversive. If Wakley were to honour his protestations of respect for the independence of the jury, Young observed, 'his medical knowledge is useless'. If, on the other hand, Wakley were to lead the jury through the evidence on the basis of his own medical knowledge, Wakley's coronership would become worse than useless. In the first place, it would introduce a 'pernicious' form of professional prejudice. Medicine, in Young's estimation, could lay no

---

[69] *Ibid.*, 15 September 1830, p. 1.   [70] *The Times*, 13 September 1830, p. 4.

legitimate claim to universalist truth; instead, it occupied the decidedly more mundane space of self-interested sectarian conflict:

> There is no unerring standard on medical questions. The judge will bring to that bench where strict impartiality should preside, his own dogmas and prejudices, and prepossessions. He will draw the attention of the jury from the plain and straightforward investigation of facts, into the labyrinths of his own scientific inquiries.

Medical science, then, was itself unfit to sit in objective judgement. There was no such thing as Medical Knowledge, only knowledg*es* emanating from located and interested sources. In the hands of a medical man, the coronership would become a public pulpit for preaching the virtues of a particular medical regime cloaked in the language of scientific objectivity. In this sense the inquest would serve medical, rather than public, interest. Indeed, the public would become the object of medical professionalising strategies, medical propaganda and medical curiosity. A medical coroner thus represented tyranny rather than liberty, prejudice rather than truth, and exploitation of the public rather than its protection and enlightenment.

At a deeper level, Young maintained, a coroner dispensing expert medical advice to the jury from the bench threatened the essence of the inquest's constitutional standing. In such a case, Young argued, the verdict would 'be returned, not, as the jury have sworn, "according to the evidence," but according to the opinion of the judge'. Wakley's candidacy ultimately represented nothing less than 'an insolent attempt to unite in one the offices of judge, witness, and jury, and virtually to abolish in this portion of our judicial institutions one of the most cherished bulwarks of rational liberty'. 'I cannot refrain from remarking', Young wrote,

> that, making every allowance for popular facility and credulity, it does still appear marvellous that the friends of political reform should have in any degree sanctioned a pretension based on the destruction of one of the most valuable and popular portions of our institutions, – the free and independent exercise of judgment according to evidence on the part of a sworn juror.[71]

---

[71] *Ibid.* The constitutional stakes of a medical coronership were posed with greater theoretical precision, but with no less force, at the hustings. Baker's seconder, Frederick Hodson, presented the following scenario for the voters' consideration: 'Suppose [Wakley] were elected to the office of Coroner; suppose a case came before him in which it was necessary to examine three or four medical witnesses; suppose Mr Wakley's opinion differed from theirs, but, being a matter of opinion, he might possibly be in error, and the three or four equally competent men in the right. Unconscious as he would be of the error under which he was labouring, he would naturally impart to the inquiry a peculiar character, and so direct its course, as that his own opinions would appear the best founded, and those of his

Having exposed the fallacy of medical claims to objectivity, and raised the spectre of the constitution in danger, Young concluded with a powerfully resonant plea to the sensibilities of the electorate:

I call, then, on the freeholders, as they value the decency and decorum of a court of justice, as they prize the institutions of their country, as they would prevent the inquisitorial investigation before the coroner from being rendered, indeed and in a different sense, an inquisition of the most tyrannical nature, as they would save the country from the stain and disgrace of seeing its inquest rooms converted into dissecting theatres, and into arenas for the unseemly display of scientific contention, – to come forward promptly and unitedly, and by their votes and exertions to place Mr Baker in the office, whose qualifications are as undisputed as his character is unblemished.[72]

In warning the electorate of the consequences of a Wakley victory – inquest rooms as 'dissecting theatres' and sites of 'unseemly display' of medical factionalism – Young linked the 'openness' promised by Wakley to some of the less attractive facets of medicine's public image.[73] In place of the publicly edifying performance of legal process, a Wakley court promised an on-going invasive and debilitating rite of violence against the social body.

V

Wakley lost. Baker's majority was a narrow one (136 from a total of 7,204 ballots cast) and though Wakley initially contested the results, he and his supporters eventually yielded to what Hunt descried as the 'corrupt power, arbitrary and unjust influence ... cant hypocrisy, fraud, perjury, bribery, and every species of falsehood' that had conspired to thwart a righteous cause.[74] In this assessment, 'Old Corruption' had for the time being staved off the progressive alliance of medical science and democratic politics. Not for long though, Wakley promised in conceding

---

opponents the least rational. With the authority, the experience and the adroitness, which a combination of the professional and official character could not fail to impart, he must of necessity have great weight with any Jury ... A lawyer, free from medical theories and preconceived opinions, would sum up the evidence to the Jury with the clearness and the indifference proper to his profession, and leave them to form their judgment, not on his opinions, but on the evidence upon oath.' Wakley, he concluded, would 'naturally try to impress his opinion on the Jury', and thereby 'overpower the plain common sense of the Jury'; *Morning Chronicle*, 10 September 1830, p. 3.

72 *The Times*, 13 September 1830, p. 4.

73 In particular to the highly charged issue of procuring subjects for anatomical study. For a stimulating discussion of the controversial standing of anatomy in this period, see Ruth Richardson's *Death, Dissection and the Destitute* (London, 1988).

74 *Morning Chronicle*, 21 September 1830, p. 3.

defeat: not only would he run again at the next available opportunity, but the strength of his showing despite the forces ranged against him guaranteed that Baker, as an attorney-coroner, would be 'the last of his race'.[75]

Wakley kept part of this pledge when in 1839 he was returned as coroner for Middlesex's Western District, though his prediction about the extinction of the attorney-coroner has not to this day been realised. More important from the perspective of this essay, however, are the analyses offered for Wakley's failure by different participants and observers. In Wakley's estimation, his defeat paradoxically reaffirmed the true confluence of medical and political reform, and the identity of interests between the legitimate scientist and the cause of popular liberty. A medical coroner would ensure discovery and exposure of vested interest institutionalised in public bodies, and it was precisely this prospect of openness that had roused the combined forces of medical and political corruption to deny the natural alliance of politics and science.

But his defeat was explained differently by others. Baker supporters like Young and Hodson, for their part, could simply celebrate the defeat of medicine's pretensions to unseat law as the dominant discourse of public order. A more delicate post-mortem, however, had to be performed by those advocating medical ascendancy at inquests, though one stripped of its radical trappings. Here the need was to use the same analysis as Wakley's – that his interlacing of medical and political reform had been the cause of his defeat – to draw a diametrically opposed conclusion. The *London Medical Gazette*, the leading organ of the 'respectable' members of the profession, argued that Wakley's defeat showed not the fallacy of a medical coronership, but of radicalism in either its medical or political incarnation. The inquest was indeed both a blessing bestowed by the constitution and a predominantly medical tribunal. But the *Gazette*'s was a constitution of order, and its medicine insular and thoroughly apolitical. The inquest's proper constitutional role was as an 'instrument towards securing the detection and punishment of great crimes', declared its editorial announcing Wakley's defeat. The constitutional standing of the inquest construed in this way undoubtedly did require a leading role for medicine, but for the medicine of the establishment. Wakley was thus not wrong because he claimed the coronership in the name of medical science, but because he did so in the name of an illegitimate hybrid of politics, medicine and a

[75] *Ibid.*

popular constitution. 'As yet', the *Gazette* editorial concluded, 'we deny that the question of a medical or non-medical coroner has been tried ... No man, possessing the slightest observation can fail to have perceived that the late contest was merely a political one ... The cry was not, Mr Wakley shall be coroner, because he is a medical man, but because he is avowedly a "radical" – the friend of Hunt and the protégé of Cobbett'.[76]

For the most part, the future lay with the *Gazette*'s version of a public role for medicine, at inquests as in other institutions of social order. Notwithstanding its failure to wrest the coronership itself from the lawyers, the medical profession did undoubtedly come to play an increasingly determinant role in the conduct of inquests.[77] And while the more expert-oriented inquest never completely disowned its constitutional heritage, it was a heritage in which the memory of Peterloo had no part to play.

[76] *London Medical Gazette*, 6, 25 September 1830, p. 1019.
[77] For a fuller discussion of this process, see my 'Decoding Death'.

6

∾

Republicanism reappraised: anti-monarchism and the English radical tradition, 1850–1872

ANTONY TAYLOR

In recent years the view of the plebeian classes as relatively unsophisticated 'monarchists' has become one of the stereotypes of English political culture. It is now quite simply accepted by historians. For E. P. Thompson the absence of any significant current of opposition to monarchy is a defining feature of the 'Peculiarities of the English' that measures the success of the political system created by the governing accord between aristocracy and industrialists.[1] The presentation of such crude monarchism as the all-pervasive attitude of the nineteenth-century audience precludes any discussion at all of plebeian criticism of monarchy when it occurred, and closes off the very conception of a 'republican'-style movement *per se*. I hope to challenge this notion and suggest that, far from being a rarity, opposition to monarchy was actually a strong feature of nineteenth-century movements of political protest, one, importantly, that was contained within established discursive modes relating to the constitution.

In support of this view this essay seeks to reshape our understanding of republicanism by highlighting the non-monarchical models encoded within the traditions of the British reform movement through potent images of 'Old Corruption' and the experience of the Commonwealth period. It suggests that these, rather than natural rights doctrines, provided the validity for much of the nineteenth-century opposition to the power and status of monarchy itself.

Opposition to monarchy within the British radical tradition has

---

[1] See E. P. Thompson, 'The Peculiarities of the English', in his *The Poverty of Theory and Other Essays* (London, 1978), pp. 245–301.

received relatively little attention from historians.[2] The little literature that exists is either outdated or dismisses British critics of the throne as entirely marginal to the political mainstream.[3] Partly this is a fault of the model used to define the position of those who criticise monarchy itself. British historians writing on this subject have looked to the French example, and sought in particular an equivalent to the French republican tradition in the British context. Working backwards from Charles Bradlaugh's involvement in the republican campaign of the 1870s, and grounding their ideas in Thompsonian orthodoxy, Edward Royle and Fergus D'Arcy associate criticism of monarchy almost exclusively with the ideas of Thomas Paine, who was the British radical most strongly inspired by the French example.[4] In this sense they have quite uncritically accepted the loyalist propaganda of Paine's contemporaries who sought to portray all opponents of the throne as foreign-inspired natural rights theorists.[5] By assuming an 'ideal type' of republican thought in this way, their argument takes on a 'Whig' aspect that does not allow for other forms of anti-monarchist display. British republicanism has therefore been made marginal by association. Traditionally, pure Paineism, as it survived into the later nineteenth century, has been discounted as nothing more than an attenuated, sect-like creed. According to this view its emphasis upon doctrines of natural rights, the cult of citizenship and a written, non-monarchical constitution on the French model, never translated effectively into a radical medium that, rather than providing a blueprint for change, sought instead the alleviation of immediate, short-term grievances. Seen in these terms republicanism can be represented as merely an offshoot of the freethought/infidel legacy, rooted originally in the Paineite tradition, passed down through Carlileism and ultimately marginalised by its connections with Bradlaughite secularism. This perception has been upheld by recent work that emphasises the

---

[2]   The standard introduction to this subject is N. J. Gossman, 'Republicanism in Nineteenth Century England', *International Review of Social History*, 7 (1962), pp. 553–74.

[3]   See, for example, J. Belchem, 'Republicanism, Popular Constitutionalism and the Radical Platform in Early Nineteenth Century England', *Social History*, 6 (1981), pp. 1–35.

[4]   This idea is first set out in detail in E. P. Thompson, *The Making of the English Working Class* (London, 1968), p. 88, but also see for its implications for later interpretations of anti-monarchism E. Royle, *Radicals, Secularists and Republicans: Popular Freethought in Britain 1866–1915*, (Manchester, 1980), pp. 198–206 and F. A. D'Arcy, 'Charles Bradlaugh and the English Republican Movement', *Historical Journal*, 25 (1982), pp. 367–83.

[5]   This theme is addressed in S. Cottrell, 'The Devil on Two Sticks: Francophobia in 1803', in R. Samuel (ed.), *Patriotism: The Making and Unmaking of British National Identity*, 3 vols. (London, 1989), vol. 1, pp. 259–74.

incompatibility of Paineism with agitations that adopt a popular constitutional mode of political expression.[6]

Disatisfaction with this view of the legacy of Paine has led to a reassessment of his influence that now emphasises the diverse interests of his followers, and the intersections of Paineism with the broader current of British radicalism. Against this background older notions of the Paineite movement as an insulated sect have broken down.[7] Existing definitions of British republicanism therefore require considerable reworking. Republicanism read purely and simply as Paineism is now clearly inapplicable. Once freed from this misconception, it becomes necessary to look elsewhere for the basis of British opposition to monarchy.

At the 1993 Charter 88 conference on the monarchy, traditional British opposition to the throne was labelled 'vulgar' or 'crude' republicanism,[8] but the term anti-monarchism captures the essence of it as well as any other. In keeping with the long-established spirit of British radicalism, anti-monarchism has no blueprint for change, nor does it present a broader agenda for the overhaul of the constitution. Its opposition to the throne is based simply upon a stock of long-standing radical images of corrupt practice in British politics. By drawing attention to these it suggests that aristocratic and kingly rule is irredeemably flawed by the sloth, intrigue and dissoluteness of a leisured and pampered lifestyle. In platform rhetoric this conception is amplified as a broader metaphor for bad government in general. Moreover, it exposes the court as a place of scandal, sexual indiscretion and the misuse of wealth and power. Throughout this discussion I use the term 'republicanism' to denote this set of attitudes without necessarily implying that this posture proposed the model for a republican constitution.

Although such anti-monarchist images have occurred in other political contexts,[9] they lie at the heart of the British radical tradition. They

---

[6]   See for this view J. Vernon, *Politics and the People: A Study in English Political Culture c.1815–1867* (Cambridge, 1993), esp. chapter 8.

[7]   There is now a large literature on this subject, but see in particular: J. Fruchtman, 'The Revolutionary Millenialism of Thomas Paine', *Studies in Eighteenth Century Culture*, 13 (1984), pp. 65–77; I. McCalman, 'New Jerusalems: Prophecy, Judaism and Radical Restorationism in London 1786–1832' (paper presented to Manchester University Modern History Seminar, March, 1992) and I. Dyck, 'Local Attachments, National Identities and World Citizenship in the Thought of Thomas Paine', *History Workshop Journal*, 35 (1993), pp. 117–35.

[8]   A. Barnett (ed.) *Power and the Throne: The Monarchy Debate* (London, 1994), *passim*.

[9]   See for a comparison of such images in a British, Australian and European context W. D. Rubinstein, 'British Radicalism and the Dark Side of Populism', in his *Elites and the Wealthy in Modern British Society* (Brighton, 1987), pp. 339–73 and R. Darnton, 'The High Enlightenment and the Low Life of Literature in Pre-Revolutionary France', in D. Johnson (ed.), *French Society and the Revolution* (Cambridge, 1976), pp. 53–87.

also demonstrate the profoundly populist roots of many British radical forms. Their provenance can be traced back to the seventeenth century, and they display a durability that allowed their persistence into the 1890s and beyond.[10] The same sentiments that inspired William Cobbett to describe the panoply of aristocratic rule as 'the Thing' continued to infuse all the major mid-century movements of political protest. The Chartist press in particular exemplified this trend and like its predecessors traded heavily in anti-aristocratic lampoons and caricatures. It regularly made use of such events as royal weddings and christenings to highlight the broader inequalities of wealth and power underpinning society. In 1843 the *Northern Star* prefaced a description of the finery on show at the marriage of Princess Augusta, daughter of the Duke of Cambridge to the Grand Duke of Mecklenberg with the comments:

Who could imagine it possible that in the country where all this glitter and show is made, this ostentatious parading of costliness and gilt, handloom weavers, those who produce the richest white silk and the rich pink silk, who could imagine after harkening to this detail of Peacockism that those who made all the finery to deck the royal wedding are pining to death on four shillings and six pence a week.[11]

This critique of monarchy was heavily reliant upon the regular exposure of royal scandal to sustain itself. Details of marital infidelities, sexual intrigue and financial corruption ran like a thread throughout such rhetoric and provided a salacious, semi-voyeuristic quality intended to titillate and entertain a wider audience. As part of this process the staple features of previous celebrated scandals were endlessly rehearsed and re-examined. In the first half of the century radicals made much play of the strong anti-Hanoverian images of the later eighteenth century, alluding in particular to the many clandestine affairs of George IV, his divorce from Queen Caroline in 1820, and the evil reputation of Victoria's uncle, the Duke of Cumberland, suspected of the murder of his footman.[12] During Victoria's reign, however, most radicals transferred their attention to the heir to the throne ('Edward the Caresser' as he was dubbed by the popular press). His exploits resurrected strong

---

[10] I disagree with W. D. Rubinstein's assertion that the power and coherence of such images was beginning to fade by the 1860s. See 'The End of Old Corruption in Britain, 1780–1860', in Rubinstein, *Elites and the Wealthy in Modern British Society* (Brighton, 1987), pp. 265–303.

[11] *Northern Star*, 1 July 1843, p. 5.

[12] For an examination of these themes see I. McCalman, *Radical Underworld: Prophets, Revolutionaries and Pornographers in London 1795–1840* (Cambridge, 1988), pp. 204–231.

memories of George's minority and enabled the many images of
Regency dissoluteness to be recycled. In 1869–70 such sentiments
crystallised around Edward's apparent involvement as co-respondent in
the Mordaunt Divorce Case. Although exonerated of any direct involvement with Lady Mordaunt, the case nevertheless spawned a considerable ballad literature that accused the prince of cuckolding other
members of the aristocracy,[13] and prompted a searching examination of
his lifestyle by the radical press. The former Chartist W. E. Adams
remarked in the *Newcastle Weekly Chronicle*:

It is morally impossible that men can lounge through a lifetime without
experiencing a great deal of misery and perhaps receiving a great deal of injury.
A life of idleness is of all lives the most wretched and the most worthless.
Without duties to discharge, without occupations to engage the time and
attention, the lounger necessarily seeks relief in a succession of excitements. And
the excitements that are sometimes relished the most are not always the most
innocent or the most intellectual.[14]

Dorothy Thompson has questioned the centrality of such highly
personalised lampoons. She sees them having little validity in their own
right and as merely reflective of the strong contemporary note of satire
in Victorian politics.[15] Yet, amongst rank-and-file Chartists they were
commonly held ideas that served to mark out a populist radical terrain.
In many senses opposition to monarchy was part of an inherited belief
system that was passed down through the generations. In later life
Andrew Carnegie, who came from a strongly radical/Chartist family in
Dunfermline, recalled the republican sentiments uttered by both his
father and his uncle in 1842:

As a child I could have slain king, duke or lord, and considered their deaths a
service to the state and hence an heroic act ... All this was inherited of course. I
only echoed what I heard at home ... I developed into a violent young
republican whose motto was 'death to privilege'. I did not know what privilege
meant, but my father did.[16]

Thompson's disregard for the central place of such anti-monarchist

---

[13] See the ballad 'A New Song on the Mordaunt Divorce Case' (Q 821 04 B2) in the
Manchester Central Reference Library, Broadside Collection. For images of cuckoldry and
their place in the criticism of monarchy more generally see T. L. Hunt, 'Morality and
Monarchy in the queen Caroline Affair', *Albion*, 23 (1991), pp. 697–722.

[14] *Newcastle Weekly Chronicle*, 5 March 1870, p. 4. The Mordaunt divorce proceedings received
considerable exposure in other surviving radical papers; see in particular *Reynolds's
Newspaper*, 6 March 1870.

[15] D. Thompson, *Queen Victoria: Gender and Power* (London, 1990), p. 98.

[16] A. Carnegie, *Autobiography* (London, 1920), pp. 9–12.

ideas within Chartism and her reduction of their exponents to a 'tendency', relegates republicanism to the margins of the movement. In many ways, however, she wilfully ignores the relevance of such sentiments to the large stock of memories of the English Civil War period that came to occupy such an important place within movements of radical protest during the nineteenth century.[17] Such reliance upon a remembered Interregnum provided a means whereby a critique of the throne might be introduced into the myth of a popular constitution. Celebrations of the Commonwealth, like such radical themes as the 'Norman Yoke' or the experience of 1688, provided a collective historical memory of the past that contextualised events in the present (by demonstrating the viability of non-monarchical government) whilst at the same time satisfying the desire for continuity that inspired conceptions of a mythic constitution under Alfred or Canute. The presence of such memories as a staple of anti-monarchist rhetoric therefore serves to rescue republican sentiment from the fringes of radical culture, and places it instead in the mainstream of radical arguments about the British past.

Memories of the Interregnum were, however, never the exclusive preserve of any one political grouping. They were for example especially dear to the Dissenting community. It was their vision of the Civil War as primarily a struggle to liberate Dissent that Joseph Arch and John Bright articulated when they exalted the role of Milton or of Coke and Pym.[18] Yet at the same time these images held a particular fascination and provided a unique moral example for radicals. Lecturing at Bristol in 1850 on the Civil War period, the former Chartist leader, Henry Vincent, remarked:

He had selected this splendid passage in the life of our country because he felt that it not only brought them into contact with virtue of the noblest kind, with intelligence of the most useful order, but also into close relationship with some of those great principles of liberty in which the people of this country so justly boasted, the supremacy of just laws over anarchy and despotism, of freedom from the prerogative of princes and – what was of greater importance to all who felt the truths of Christianity – of the non-right of human powers to inflict pain

---

[17] The central importance of memories of the English Revolution for a later generation of reformers is emphasised in M. C. Finn, *After Chartism: Class and Nation in English Radical Politics 1848–1874* (Cambridge, 1993), pp. 13–59.

[18] For Joseph Arch's invocation of the legacy of the English Commonwealth see his reminiscences, *From Ploughtail to Parliament: An Autobiography* (1898; repr. London, 1986), pp. 3–4. John Bright also drew extensively upon memories of the Civil War period in his speeches, see W. Robertson, *The Life and Times of John Bright* (1877, repr. London, 1912), p. 228 and p. 279.

and penalties upon a man because of his religious belief and, by inference, the necessity of the entire disseverance of the secular and religious power.[19]

Such sentiments contained the clear message that the most virtuous forms of government were to be found outside the rule of princes. It was for this reason that the Interregnum period occupied such a central place in English radical thought, providing both inspiration and political example to a later generation of reformers.

This package of notions taken from the Commonwealth period placed the constitutional idiom at the heart of the debate on government and made heroes out of those who opposed the excesses of autocratic monarchs. Hampden and Sidney are crucial here, but its main icon was Oliver Cromwell. Alan Smith has pointed to the demonisation of Oliver Cromwell in popular folk traditions from the seventeenth century onwards. This feeling was never, however, universal and in many areas, especially the radical West Riding, a more positive image of him persisted. There, as in other localities, he came to assume the status of a golden age monarch who had presided over a period of unparalleled justice and prosperity.[20] In the 1840s such notions drew upon renewed interest in the Interregnum period following the bi-centenary of the Civil War, and grew out of Cromwell's rehabilitation in Carlyle's 1846 biography.[21] Carlyle's image of a Tory Cromwell whose government was characterised by the values of decisiveness and firm leadership demonstrates that he also had a contemporary incarnation for Conservatives.[22] Amongst radicals, however, Cromwell was chiefly exalted as a 'plain man ... who unmade kings', for his opposition to excessive executive power and, above all, for his refusal to don the crown.[23] In accordance with his central position, nineteenth-century radical rhetoric was absolutely saturated with references to Cromwellianism. Amongst the Chartists Henry Vincent was perhaps the chief custodian of his memory and lectured widely on his career in the 1850s. His lectures were so vividly evocative of his life and times, that J. B. Leno recalled

[19] *Bristol Examiner*, 9 March 1850, pp. 1–2.

[20] These conflicting images of Cromwell are examined in A. Smith, 'The Image of Cromwell In Folklore and Tradition', *Folklore*, 79 (1968), pp. 17–39.

[21] P. Karsten, *Patriot Heroes in England and America: Political Symbolism and Changing Values Over Three Centuries* (Wisconsin, 1978), pp. 139–55 and Finn, *After Chartism*, pp. 42–3. There was a previous outbreak of Cromwell worship in the 1790s when many radicals referred to him in connection with events in France; see McCalman, 'New Jerusalems', *passim*.

[22] Images of a Tory Cromwell are discussed in R. Samuel, 'Puritanism and Democracy: Some Nineteenth and Twentieth Century Perspectives' (paper presented to Manchester University History Department Democracy Seminar, January 1994).

[23] There is an account of Cromwell's career that makes these points in the *National Reformer*, 30 April 1876, p. 273.

'you could hear the sound of the great man's jackboots'.[24] Cromwell also featured strongly in the work of the Chartist poets. In 1854, W. J. Linton appealed for the sight and spirit of Cromwell's sword-arm once more to revive flagging radical ardours, whilst at a reception for John Frost in 1856, Ernest Jones, reciting from his poetry, asked for 'one glorious day of Cromwell's time' as an antidote to aristocratic misrule in the present.[25]

Such images of the Commonwealth were not necessarily irreconcilable with the ideas of 'golden age' constitutions under Anglo-Saxon monarchs that feature elsewhere in radical thought. Despite the presence of agendas for monarchical and non-monarchical forms of government in such rhetoric, the two viewpoints were compatible and interchangeable. A reliance upon memories of the Commonwealth period merely demonstrates the elasticity of the language of popular constitutionalism itself, and suggests that such discourses need not always be interpreted in excessively loyalist or patriotic ways.[26] The fractured continuity of the replacement of a monarchy by a republic, and later a restoration, was barely noted by such commentators as Ernest Jones, who represented the Puritan revolution as part of the same trajectory towards a corrective to the excesses of an unchecked, centralised executive. In this sense Jones saw the Chartists of the 1850s operating in a tradition that dated back to the peasant revolt of 1381. Their battle he saw as:

That struggle which the men of Kent, Lincoln and Essex began ... which the Puritans of Cromwell brought nearer to its issue, which the revolution which seated Orange on the throne developed in its middle-class aspect, and which the Chartists of today, if true to their mission, are destined to complete.[27]

Other radicals who adopted a strongly anti-monarchist stance, teased out an alternative interpretation of the Anglo-Saxon constitution that emphasised the elective nature of Anglo-Saxon kingship, and the significance of the 'folkmoot' as an integral part of the compact between monarch and his subjects.[28] Equally a radical squib in the *Poor Man's Guardian* for 1832 illustrates the infinite malleability of the imagery of the

[24] J. B. Leno, *The Aftermath* (London, 1892), p. 79.
[25] See the *Northern Tribune*, 1, 5, 1854, p. 147, and the *People's Paper*, 20 September 1856, p. 1.
[26] For a recent assessment of popular constitutionalism that seeks to define it almost entirely in loyalist terms, see L. Colley, *Britons: Forging the Nation 1707–1837* (New Haven and London, 1992), esp. pp. 283–308.
[27] *People's Paper*, 22 May 1858, p. 1.
[28] G. Claeys, 'Thomas Evans and the Development of Spenceanism 1815–1816: Some Neglected Correspondence', *Bulletin of the Society for the Study of Labour History*, 48 (1984), pp. 24–30.

'ancient constitution' by making its contempt for monarchical forms vividly felt in the present, while showering praise upon 'Just Monarchs' in the past:

> Let knaves and fools in raptures sing
>   Till they are hoarse 'God save the king!'
> I pray – may heaven in mercy keep all
>   From kings and priests, God save the people,
> I'm not an advocate for kings
>   – such haughty, empty, useless things,
> The greater number, strange to tell –
>   Their characters are black as hell!
> I find but two without a blot
>   Great Alfred and brave Castriot
> But William Guelph, Britons caress him
>   He is the perfect king, God bless him!
> Disloyal people tell us that
>   He is a – hush, I'll say not what
> My gentle muse with truth in view,
>   Must give to royalty its due!

Yet the same poem says of the historical King Alfred:

> Illustrious sovereign! In thy reign
>   No abject poverty was seen
> No sluggish priests who fleece the fold
> No bishops wallowing in gold
> No evil from which luxury springs
> No panders to the lusts of kings . . .[29]

It is therefore possible to discern a far greater degree of anti-monarchist sentiment than hitherto acknowledged amongst radicals of the pre-1860 period, and even to detect a republican tinge amongst those reformers not commonly acknowledged as such. These rhetorical forms remained a constant, and acted as a political background noise that underlined other reform activity, and came to the fore strongly during later agitations.

Anti-monarchism was still, for example, an undercurrent in the reform agitation of 1866–7. Malicious 'To Let' notices appeared on the gates of Buckingham Palace in 1864 in the wake of the reform sentiment generated by Gladstone's 'Pale of the Constitution' speech. By using the royal statutes governing public recreations in Hyde Park to prohibit popular demonstrations there in 1866, the Home Office placed the

---

[29] *Poor Man's Guardian*, 30 June 1832, p. 445.

throne in collision with the reform community at the height of the agitation. Subsequently unease about the throne's custodianship of the public lands assumed by the crown after the Norman Conquest became a major popular issue.[30] Even Victoria noticed the lack of public warmth towards her as she drove through London in these years.[31] In keeping with the style of previous reform agitations, the Reform League couched much of its rhetoric in the accepted radical form of the constitutional idiom. In August 1866, for example, the Reform League activist W. G. D'Gruyther responded to Victoria's refusal to receive a League deputation by reminding her in an open letter of the flight of James II in 1688, and suggesting that her own refusal to see her subjects amounted to a similar abrogation of authority.[32] At branch level the Reform League also resuscitated memories and the nomenclature of the Interregnum period. Cromwell and Hampden featured in the long titles of local branch associations, and addresses on the theme of the Commonwealth became staples of the lecture circuit repertoire.[33] More-over, in 1868 the Reform League executive confirmed its republican sympathy by issuing statements welcoming the rebellion against Queen Isabella's authority in Spain and the subsequent declaration of a republic.[34]

Nevertheless, anti-monarchism did not achieve the status of a mass platform agitation in its own right until the 1870s, when radicals and reformers sought a new direction following the passage of the 1867 Reform Act. By this stage the main radical grievances concerning the franchise had been satisfied, leaving only the hitherto submerged discontent with monarchical power as the basis for a popular agitation.

The campaign against the queen of 1870-2 not only demonstrates the degree of support anti-monarchism could command at the height of its power, but also provides a useful indicator of the relative strengths of my own model of a non-Paineite 'populist' republican form, and Paineism proper. Throughout, the leaders of this campaign described themselves as 'republicans', but although they used this term frequently

---

[30] It is referred to by Sir Charles Dilke in his 'Cost of the Crown Speech' at Newcastle in 1871, see the *Newcastle Weekly Chronicle*, 11 November 1871, p. 5.

[31] The opposition that emerged towards Victoria during the 1866-7 reform campaign is examined in R. L. Arnstein, 'Queen Victoria Opens Parliament: The Disinvention of Tradition', *Historical Research*, 113 (1990), pp. 178-94.

[32] *Manchester Examiner and Times*, 20 August 1866, p. 3.

[33] See on this point *A List of the Departments and Branches of the National Reform League 1867*, in the Howell Collection, Bishopsgate Institute (henceforth HC, BI). For James Finlen's lecture on Cromwell to the Holborn branch of the Reform League see *The Commonwealth*, 29 September 1866, p. 8.

[34] *The Beehive*, 3 October 1868, pp. 4-5.

they never put forward an effective model for a non-monarchical constitution, and their concerns were overwhelmingly those of an older generation of anti-monarchists.

The reasons for the emergence of a popular current of opposition to the throne in the 1870s are well known. Queen Victoria's withdrawal from public life and, in a marked break with parliamentary precedent, the government's application for donations from the civil list to support the royal children and Princess Louise's new husband, the Marquis of Lorne, prompted a major debate about the nature of the state's financial commitments to the upkeep of royalty. During this period it was widely believed that Victoria had added the money saved on public ceremonials to her personal wealth.[35]

The resultant campaign precipitated a stronger popular response than any previous anti-royal agitation. Contemporaries compared it to the later Tichborne movement which evoked an equally strong public response in favour of the claims of a pretender to the estates and titles of the Tichborne family who was seen as unfairly dispossessed.[36] It was certainly the largest popular campaign of the 1870s prior to the emergence of the Tichborne agitation itself. It was also the first since the 1866–7 reform agitation to unite reformers in the metropolis with their counterparts in the provinces. Significantly the geography of the campaign closely adhered to older areas of radical strength. There were republican conferences in Newcastle, Sheffield and Birmingham, the first regional radical assemblies held there since the 1840s, and active republican cells were also established in Leicester and Nottingham. This strong organisation in the east and west midlands was almost certainly connected with the prominent part played by the trio of Midlands MPs, Henry Fawcett, P. A. Taylor and Auberon Herbert in the republican campaign in parliament.[37] In the north-west, Bolton became the organisational focal point of the region after the establishment of a republican club boasting three hundred members in 1871. George Howell also noted the presence of republican clubs in Peterborough, Portsmouth, Norwich, Cambridge and Exeter.[38] In addition there was a

---

[35] See for an account of the controversy surrounding Queen Victoria's private income in the 1870s W. M. Kuhn, 'Ceremony and Politics: The British Monarchy 1871–1872', *Journal of British Studies*, 26 (1987), pp. 133–62 and Kuhn, 'Queen Victoria's Civil List: What Did She Do With It'?, *Historical Journal*, 36 (1993), pp. 645–65.

[36] See S. Gwynn and G. M. Tuckwell, *The Life of the Rt Hon. Sir Charles W. Dilke* (London, 1918), vol. I, p. 140.

[37] See the *National Reformer*, 26 February 1871, p. 139 and 12 March 1871, p. 171 for the opening of the Birmingham republican club, and *ibid.*, 2 April 1871, p. 220 for the activities of the Leicester republicans.

[38] Howell–Goldwin Smith, 25 February 1871, HC, BI.

strong republican outpost in the north-east with clubs formed in New-castle, Bedlington and Sunderland.[39] In London republicans mounted major demonstrations in all the capital's public spaces, particularly Hyde Park and Trafalgar Square, where they reasserted the right of metropolitan reformers to gather in the open spaces that had been established by the reform campaign of 1866–7.[40] Furthermore, the republican movement highlighted existing political divisions at local level and proved so divisive that it provoked counterblasts which turned its meetings into battlegrounds. With the collusion of the local authorities there was sustained disruption at Charles Dilke's constituency meeting in Chelsea and at his addresses in Leeds and Derby. Moreover, George Odger was seriously injured by loyalists in an ambush at the station at Reading, whilst at Bolton a republican was killed by a Tory mob during a visit by Dilke to the town.[41] This event prompted stronger government interest in the movement than had been expressed in any agitation for reform since the Hyde Park riots of 1866.

Like commentators writing of the radicals of the 1790s, contemporaries were only too eager to ascribe this surge of anti-royal feeling to the direct importation of foreign and ultimately 'un-English' ideas and models of government into an inappropriate setting (see figure 6.1). The campaign was therefore represented in the press as wholly derivative and slavishly Francophile. The *Saturday Review* wrote: 'The Commune only represents in a more practical form the doctrines of the Land and Labour League, the International Association and the other Jacobin Clubs of London.'[42] This sense of the republican campaign of the 1870s as purely an imitative offshoot of events abroad has pervaded even recent historical accounts of the events of these years and served to minimise, or even deny, those elements that placed it within the radical constitutional mainstream.[43] In reality this campaign was profoundly

---

[39] There are accounts of the formation of the Tyneside and Sunderland republican clubs in the *Newcastle Weekly Chronicle*, 4 March 1871, p. 3 and 5 August 1871, p. 3.

[40] See on this theme *ibid.*, p. 4 and for details of a meeting in Hyde Park in opposition to the Prince of Wales's tour of India in 1875, the *National Reformer*, 25 July 1875, p. 50.

[41] The disturbances at Dilke's constituency meeting are described in *The Times*, 29 November 1871, p. 10, but also see for the disorder at Derby the *Manchester Guardian*, 5 December 1871, p. 8 and for the riots at Reading and Bolton the *Newcastle Weekly Chronicle*, 16 December 1871, p. 4 and the *Bolton Evening News*, 1 December 1871, p. 4. There are Home Office files on these events in the Disturbance Books (HO 45/939/2/) at the Public Records Office.

[42] *Saturday Review*, 22 April 1871.

[43] See Finn, *After Chartism*, pp. 273–303. A more eclectic approach locating republicanism in the context of previous radical agitations is followed in a new study of Tyneside radicalism by N. Todd, *The Militant Democracy: Joseph Cowen and Victorian Radicalism* (Tyne and Wear, 1991).

A FRENCH LESSON.

Britannia. "IS *THAT* THE SORT OF THING YOU WANT, YOU LITTLE IDIOT?"

Fig. 6.1. *Punch* and the other popular satirical journals ignored the traditional radical components in English opposition to the throne and portrayed
anti-monarchism as a French-inspired import. In this cartoon by John
Tenniel Britannia admonishes a foolish-looking George Odger wearing a
cap of liberty for his desire to emulate the French republican model.

English in its reworking of the constitutional idiom, and in the uses it made of the images of 'Old Corruption'.

As in the radical movement of the 1790s the key text of this agitation was never solely Paine. Rather its preoccupations serve to locate it more properly in the tradition of Edmund Burke's speech on 'economical' reform from 1780. This provided the inspiration and the framework for Sir Charles Dilke's 'Cost of the Crown' speech in Newcastle in October 1871, and featured in his address in Leeds a few weeks later.[44] By choosing Burke's line of attack on executive power, it raised questions of excessive royal interference, the use of money to influence the complexion of government through placemen, and concentrated attention upon the unjustifiable state expenditure on the ornamental and excessive outward trappings of monarchy itself.

In its origins this was a debate purely about finance, but it rapidly assumed the proportions of a broader attack upon the power, privilege and prerogative of the queen herself. In many ways it bears the hallmarks of previous attacks upon the expense of monarchy at the time of the coronation of William IV and Victoria's marriage to Prince Albert in 1840.[45]

As in these previous campaigns, the emphasis placed by reformers upon the Germanic origins of the House of Hanover allowed them to connect strongly with broader currents within English popular culture. Xenophobia has an established pedigree within the English radical tradition, and stigmatising monarchs by association with 'alienness' was a long-standing populist tactic of all the major post-Napoleonic War movements of political protest. In this instance it also enabled opponents of monarchy to exonerate themselves from the charge that they harboured unpatriotic aims. In the 1870s such attitudes drew strongly upon the images and language employed by previous reform movements. In the 1830s William IV had been dubbed 'Mr Guelph' by the *Poor Man's Guardian* and particular venom was reserved for his German-born wife, Queen Adelaide, who was booed at public meetings during the reform crisis.[46] In practice most of these chauvinistic assaults upon

---

[44] See Kuhn, 'Ceremony and Politics: The British Monarchy 1871–1872', pp. 140–1. The full text of Dilke's speech at Newcastle and initial responses to it are in the *Newcastle Weekly Chronicle*, 11 November 1871, p. 4 and p. 5 and *The Times*, 9 November 1871 p. 6 and p. 9; Dilke's speech at Leeds is reported in the *Leeds Mercury*, 24 November 1871, pp. 2–3.

[45] For radical opposition to the expense of William IV's coronation ceremony see the *Poor Man's Guardian*, 18 July 1831, p. 1.

[46] James Aytoun recalled the dislike of Queen Adelaide made apparent during the reform crisis of the 1830s in his article in *The Beehive*, 11 November 1871, pp. 1–2. Edmund Baines' role in leading the booing of the queen at Meetings in 1832 was also recalled by the press

royalty tended to concentrate upon the German antecedents of the royal line. Even the Prince Consort was not immune to criticism on these grounds. In the *People's Paper* in the 1850s, Ernest Jones, who was himself German by birth, strongly attacked the Coburgs for buying 'English land with English money' following Albert's purchase of the Osborne estate on the Isle of Wight.[47] By establishing the link in the popular mind between Prussianness, which carried strong undertones of continental despotism, and the marked German anti-liberal tradition, reformers were also able to damn the British monarchy by association. Such attitudes surfaced strongly during the 1866–7 reform crisis that acted as a bridge into the republican campaign of the 1870s. At the Trafalgar Square meeting of June 1866, Osborne of the Clerkenwell branch of the Reform League vigorously attacked the queen's new son-in-law, the Crown Prince Frederick William, husband of the Princess Royal, for his decision to take up a commission in the Prussian army in the impending war against Austria. In his remarks, and in Lucraft's responses to them, radical rhetoric blended the themes of opposition to continental despotism, the civil list pensions issue and memories of the Interregnum:

And as a sign of the times, let it be borne in mind that a certain Prince recently married to an English royal princess was according to the evening papers going this week to fight in the cause of despotism [groans]. That was one way of rewarding Englishmen for the willingness with which they saw a Royal Dower given, which was wrung out of the sweat of their brow.

The chairman Benjamin Lucraft added:

My friends, Charles the First was executed at Whitehall gardens. On Monday next we hold a meeting there [tremendous and prolonged cheering].[48]

In the 1870s Charles Bradlaugh, who was the republican leader most strongly influenced by the Paineite inheritance, omitted almost all references to Paine in his pamphlets and, embracing the mainstream radical tradition, concentrated his fire on the Germanic connections of the British throne. The very title of his pamphlet, *The Impeachment of the*

following his patriotic outbursts against Dilke in 1871, see the *Bolton Evening News*, 27 November 1871, p. 3.

[47] *People's Paper*, 4 October 1856, p. 4. Popular ballads of the Crimean War period also sought to discredit Prince Albert's peace mission to the Russians by suggesting that there was a conspiracy between the Coburgs and the Tsar to dismember Turkey and convert it into a Russian protectorate. See on this theme the ballad 'Lovely Albert' in the Manchester Central Reference Library, Broadside Collection, vol. 5 (BR F 821 04 BAI), p. 296.

[48] *The Commonwealth*, 30 June 1866.

House of Brunswick, resonates with patriotic hostility to the alien connections of the royal house:

When her Majesty travels in England great precautions are taken to prevent her from coming into contact with the common people who are her loyal and devoted subjects. When her Majesty is abroad, the natives of foreign parts being much superior to the ordinary type of Briton, are allowed greater indulgence. In England railway stations are cleared, piers and docks are carefully purged of the presence of the vulgar British subject. In Germany her Majesty is amongst those she loves, and there the same rigid exclusiveness is not maintained.[49]

Public sympathy for the infant French republic during the Franco-Prussian War converted this anti-Prussian sentiment into a popular cause, and precipitated a wave of hostility towards the openly pro-Prussian sympathisers at court, including the queen, that fed into, and in turn reinforced, the republicans' campaign.

In common with the radical movements of the earlier part of the century the republican platform of the 1870s also held a strong appeal for a female audience. Recently Anna Clark has drawn attention to the language of domesticity used by Chartist orators in the 1840s to provide a point of contact within the movement for the National Charter Association's female following.[50] As Clark points out, such references were really about existing structures of sexuality and power which remained unchallenged by the movement, but metaphors of the hearth, the home and the domestic environment more generally, served to augment the main Chartist message and made complicated political ideas explicable in purely household terms. A similar element is discernible in the republican campaign of the 1870s. *Reynolds's Newspaper* and the figureheads of the movement placed the marriage of Victoria's daughter, the Princess Louise, to the Marquis of Lorne in 1871 at the heart of the debate on the monarchy. Her application for a Civil List donation for her husband and the government's decision to meet the cost of her dowry from the public purse, spawned a wave of popular slogans, scurrilous songs and disrespectful alphabets on the Regency model. Thomas Wright recalled:

'The rattle of the royal begging boxes'; 'outdoor relief'; 'able-bodied paupers'; 'royal leeches'; 'royal spongers'; were the mildest terms of contempt employed in speaking of the subject. It became a stock workshop joke to speak of setting up the Marquis of Lorne as a greengrocer, or teaching him this or that

[49] C. Bradlaugh, *The Impeachment of the House of Brunswick* (London, 1871), p. 129.
[50] See A. Clark, 'The Rhetoric of Chartist Domesticity: Gender, Language and Class in the 1830s and 1840s', *Journal of British Studies*, 31 (1992), pp. 62–88.

handicraft to enable him to earn an honest living for himself and wife without coming upon the public.[51]

The image of the aristocratic Marquis of Lorne and his household contained here provides a striking example of such domestic comparisons. By highlighting the Marquis' lack of practical skills, and making the ironic comparison between the everyday privations of many poorer families and his own exalted status, it injected a note of outrage into the agitation inspired particularly by the plight of poor, working-class women living under the threat of the Poor Law. It also compromised his manhood by challenging his ability to provide for his family.

The *Newcastle Weekly Chronicle* detected in these issues a strong overlap with the contemporaneous agitation for a bill allowing sisters and husbands of deceased spouses to marry each other. This latter legislation was rejected by the House of Lords in the same sitting in which it approved a civil list pension for Lorne, causing the *Chronicle* to remark:

Thus the Peers in a double sense insult the people. First by refusing their consent to a measure that is loudly called for, not only to make hundreds of homes happy by legalising morally lawful unions, and also to legitimise and make heirs-at-law thousands of children actually born in wedlock ... Secondly by agreeing with an unseemly and defiant haste to an unnecessary increase of the public burdens.[52]

Such stark representations of the everyday inequalities afflicting women in Victorian society enabled republican agitators, like previous generations of reformers, to address the concerns of a female audience. Most republican associations accordingly had a mixed membership, although women were still often relegated to the purely support capacity of providing refreshments and stitching banners common in the political culture of the day.[53]

That such attitudes were in fact part of the radical constitutionalist mainstream is made apparent from the almost wholesale transfer of both branch associations and personnel from the earlier Reform League into the republican movement. The most fertile ground for the emergence of the new movement was thus in London's radical club circles which had provided the bedrock for popular reform agitations since the 1820s and before. Charles Bradlaugh presided at the formal inaugura-

---

[51] T. Wright, *Our New Masters* (1873; repr. London, 1969), p. 171.

[52] *Newcastle Weekly Chronicle*, 4 March 1871, p. 4.

[53] The controversy surrounding the republican riots in Bolton meant that the activities of the republican club there were closely monitored by the local press which noted these aspects of female involvement in the movement in its reports. See the *Bolton Evening News*, 1 December 1871, p. 4 and 2 December 1872, p. 4.

tion of the London republican club at the secularist Hall of Science, Old Street, in March 1871.[54] The hall was a long-standing radical meeting place and became the headquarters for all republican operations in the capital at the start of the campaign. Republican branches were never, however, simply updated secularist associations. Both the Eleusis Club in Chelsea and the Patriotic Club, Clerkenwell Green, which comprised survivors of the Reform League, also made the transition from League to republican branches during this period.[55] In practice most branches of the kindred Land and Labour League were also interchangeable with republican organisation, and the Mile End Branch, the Sir Robert Peel branch and the Hackney Road branch were all re-activated as republican associations.[56] This pattern was repeated in the provinces, and in Bolton the former secretary of the local Reform League, John Bramwell, occupied the same post for the republican club, which was based in the old Reform League premises at the Temperance Hall.[57] Republicanism's role as the successor to the parliamentary reform cause meant that its style was conditioned by the cultural milieu in which a previous generation of radicals had operated. In many ways its success lay in its ability to breathe new life into this political culture. As with its predecessors the club lay at the heart of the British republican experience. Like the Chartist and Reform League clubs, republican groups sought to erect a total radical environment that placed them outside Liberalism and perpetuated older radical styles and forms. The Birmingham republican and former Chartist, C. C. Cattell wrote to the *Republican Chronicle* on this theme:

Republican should be the name to cover the whole ground of political and social reform. Public or concerted action no doubt would be somewhat limited at first because a majority must be obtained to assist any great principle effectively. But this would be more easily arrived at by people meeting each other and discussing things desirable and practicable. These clubs would then become National Schools and a power in stimulating the governing bodies of the country. Nothing is of more importance in a free country, than an intelligent public opinion outside the elected administrative powers. This is the safeguard of personal liberty and free institutions. If such institutions as these were

---

[54] There is an account of the formation of the London republican club in the *National Reformer*, 23 April 1871, p. 271.

[55] The Eleusis Club, Chelsea was the site of a conference of metropolitan republicans in April 1871 reported in *Reynolds's Newspaper*, 30 April 1871. See A. Rothstein, *A House On Clerkenwell Green* (pamphlet, 1976; new edn, London, 1983), pp. 44–8 for the conversion of the Patriotic Club into a republican branch.

[56] See for the incipient republicanism of the Mile End and Sir Robert Peel branches of the Land and Labour League the *National Reformer*, 13 November 1870, p. 318.

[57] *Bolton Evening News*, 7 November 1872, p. 3.

established, the election of such persons as are now in our municipal and parliamentary councils would be impossible.[58]

Given the paucity of information relating to these clubs and the generally hostile environment in which they operated, it is difficult to chart the course of individual organisations. Nevertheless, it seems clear that they were intended to fulfil a basically convivial, yet at the same time educative, role. The London republican club amassed a library of books and materials relating to past republican movements.[59] The Mile End Branch enjoyed excursions to Rye House, Sussex.[60] There were lectures on improving topics such as land reform or aspects of the history of the British Commonwealth, and songs were composed and performed in public to honour particular leaders.

One marked feature of these clubs was the use of republican paraphernalia and even separate styles of dress to create a distinct identity.[61] Meeting places were decorated with tricolours; sashes and tricolour rosettes were worn; a white, green and blue banner based upon W. J. Linton's designs for a republican flag was produced and used at republican conferences, whilst the 'Marseillaise' became the most popular of the English republicans' repertoire of songs.[62] These outward trappings were more than just displays of arrant Francophilia and were intended to create the basis for a counter-culture that would make republicans recognisable to each other and instantly recognisable in society at large. Thomas Wright wrote of: 'The stagey, fanfaron-nading republicans who hoist red flags, address each other as "citizen" and indulge in high-sounding revolutionary talk.'[63] In many ways there are parallels with the Spenceans here, who also adopted different styles of dress, and even speech to emphasise their apartness.

As with previous movements of reform, republicanism during the 1870s also sought to cement an alternative centre of loyalty through the

[58]   *Republican Chronicle*, 1 April 1875, pp. 1–2.   [59]   *Ibid.*, p. 8.
[60]   See the *International Herald*, 10 August 1872.
[61]   These features of republican meetings were reinforced by the constant police scrutiny and harrassment to which republican branches were subject. For an example of a police presence at a meeting of the Republican League in the Wellington Tavern, Brook Street, London, see *Reynolds's Newspaper*, 9 April 1871.
[62]   The decorations at the inaugural meeting of the London republican club are described in the *National Reformer*, 23 April 1871, p. 271. The design for Linton's republican banner is described in F. B. Smith, *Radical Artisan: William James Linton 1812–1897* (Manchester, 1973), p. 108, and its presence at the Sheffield conference of 1872 is noted in the *International Herald*, 30 November 1872, p. 3. For an example of a republican meeting ending with the singing of the 'Marseillaise' see a report of the Mile End branch of the Land and Labour League in the *National Reformer*, 29 May 1870, p. 349.
[63]   Wright, *Our New Masters*, p. 178.

creation of martyr figures who reflected the twin themes of dedication and self-sacrifice in the service of the cause. Attempts to turn the victim killed by a royalist mob during Dilke's visit to Bolton into a martyr were reminiscent of previous martyrdoms of the radical dead during the post-Napoleonic War reform movement and Chartism. William Scholefield, a Bolton man with no previous history of attachment to radical causes, was on the slenderest of evidence elevated to the pantheon of those who had given their lives for reform. This process bears many of the characteristics of the martyrdom of John Lees, who died from wounds received at Peterloo, and of Samuel Holberry, the Sheffield Chartist who died in gaol in 1842. Like Lees and Holberry, Scholefield was given a public funeral that attracted 5,000 participants and spectators, received radical accolades to his dedication and commitment and was commemorated annually at a public soirée.[64] George Odger saw his death as linked to the same spirit that had inspired the mob attacks made on Joseph Priestly in 1792, but also drew the wider message from his life that:

Once more the old spirit of persecution has raised its hideous head and in so called free England men's lives are endangered by the expression of an honest conviction in favour of republicanism. In Bolton a victim has already fallen to this accursed spirit; at Reading I myself, by an almost imperceptible margin, escaped death from the hands of an infuriated host of savages, while Sir Charles Dilke has been subjected to no end of dangers.[65]

Allegations of partiality on the part of the coroner, and the subsequent acquittal of eight accused members of the mob at trial, lent weight to Odger's remarks, and ensured that the affair attracted considerable press attention.[66]

Other features of an older radical culture also lingered in republicanism. The custom of naming children after prominent radical heroes was still strongly observed. In this case the anti-monarchy campaign of the 1870s threw up its own new generation of heroes that could be employed expressly for this purpose. The Bradlaughite coal merchant, William Chenery, for example, named his son Taylor Dilke Fawcett Chenery after the three middle-class radicals who voted for an inquiry

---

[64] These aspects of the martyrdom of William Schofield are reported in the *Bolton Evening News*, 5 December 1871, p. 3; 14 December 1871, p. 3 and 2 December 1872, p. 4. His funeral is reported in the *Bolton Journal*, 16 December 1871, p. 3 and there is further radical comment on the affair in the *International Herald*, 30 March 1872, p. 4 and 17 August 1872, p. 3.

[65] G. Odger, *Odger's Monthly Pamphlets On Current Events No. 1: Republicanism Versus Monarchy* (London, 1872), p. 3.

[66] See for these aspects of the case the *Bolton Evening News*, 9 December 1871, p. 3.

into the civil list in 1872. Subsequently he emblazoned the names on his coal-trucks and they became a well-known local landmark in the area of the Elephant and Castle in London.[67]

The radical cult of leadership was similarly well represented within the campaign against the throne. James Epstein has noted the importance of the demagogic style of popular agitation in shaping the structure of British radicalism in the period between 1815 and 1848.[68] Central to this process he argues was the role of 'gentlemen leaders', men of a privileged position in life who forsook their natural allegiances, posed as the representatives of the poor and dispossessed and showed themselves prepared to sacrifice family, friends and influence as the price of their radical commitment. More recently historians have extended the significance of the gentleman leader into the post-Chartist period, and seen the concept as influential in shaping the appeal of both John Bright and H. M. Hyndman, the two main platform orators of the period.[69] Republicanism threw up a new generation of radical leaders in this mould, amongst them the charismatic John de Morgan, who fused the twin themes of republicanism and defence of the open spaces to form the basis for a broad radical populism. In particular de Morgan's opposition to enclosure, personal interventions in defence of threatened moorland and willingness to break the law on behalf of the cause of public access, echoed similar events in Oliver Cromwell's career and, appropriately for a republican agitation, allowed his followers to emphasise this connection strongly.[70]

Nevertheless, the leader who most strongly captured the spirit of an earlier generation of radical leaders was the titular head of the movement, Sir Charles Dilke. A baronet, landowner, and Cambridge-educated lawyer, Dilke's was the distillation of all previous radical leadership styles. In the 1860s he developed the first tentative contacts with the plebeian reform movement, and by 1868 was working actively with radical clubs in Chelsea to create a popular constituency organisation that secured his successful return for the borough in 1874. He was a

[67] I am grateful to the National Museum of Labour History, Manchester, for sight of an election photograph of George Odger's by-election committee at Bristol in 1870 which contains this information.

[68] See J. Epstein, *The Lion of Freedom: Feargus O'Connor and the Chartist Movement 1832–1842* (London, 1982), esp. pp. 90–3 and 216–20.

[69] For my own work on this theme see A. D. Taylor, 'Modes of Political Expression and Working-Class Radicalism 1848–1874: The London and Manchester Examples' (Ph.D, University of Manchester, 1992), esp. chapters 1–4.

[70] For details of John de Morgan's career see S. St. Clair, *A Sketch of the Life and Labours of John de Morgan* (pamphlet, Leeds, 1880), esp. pp. 1–2; and D. Nicholls, *The Lost Prime Minister: A Life of Sir Charles Dilke* (London, 1995).

fine orator, a much-respected parliamentarian and a stern critic of unfair government who showed considerable courage in bringing the issue of the monarchy before the public.[71] On a number of occasions he risked serious injury at stormy meetings, but impressed his supporters by his nonchalant disregard for his own personal safety and his coolness under fire. At the Bolton meeting he refused to seek cover from missiles, or wear a hat to protect him from head injuries.[72] Contemporaries also made much of his dedication, and portrayed him in true gentleman leader fashion as both martyr and saint, unjustifiably reviled by an ungrateful press who ignored his work on behalf of the people. George Odger remarked on this theme at Bolton:

An attempt had been made in the press to create a feeling in the minds of the working-classes that would mitigate against one of the most able men in the country, who had travelled wide and gained experience of no ordinary kind. While other men were idle he was searching out information for the people of this country and every other country, and yet the man who had had the moral courage to do what he had done, had been calumniated and maligned. He did not attack the queen, but those who spent the money, and Sir Charles Dilke deserved the sympathy of every honest man in the world.[73]

In the event Dilke's contact with the republicans was shortlived, but in later years he remained a popular figure within the broader context of radicalism.

Republicanism's greatest contribution to nineteenth-century radicalism was, however, the degree to which it helped define a sphere of operations independent of, and outside, mainstream Liberalism. At a time when the forces of ultra-radicalism were contracting or becoming absorbed by the Liberal party, it helped provide a focus for those unrepentant radical activists who remained stubbornly outside the Gladstonian consensus. During the 1870s republicanism and Liberalism were irreconcilably opposed. This rift was emphasised by the degree to which Liberalism had shed the strong association with republicanism and other Commonwealth values that had characterised eighteenth-century Whiggery.[74] As a consequence, under Gladstone's ministries the

[71] See for these aspects of Dilke's career, Gwynn and Tuckwell, *The Rt. Hon. Sir Charles Dilke*, vol. I, esp. pp. 94–168.
[72] See the *Bolton Evening News*, 1 December 1871, p. 4.
[73] See George Odger's remarks at Bolton in *ibid.*, 27 November 1871, p. 3.
[74] For a sense of Liberalism's move away from Whiggery's past associations with republicanism see J. G. A. Pocock, *The Ancient Constitution and the Feudal Law: A Study of English Historical Thought in the Seventeenth Century* (Cambridge, 1957, revised 1987), esp. pp. 229–51. This theme is developed in J. Parry, *The Rise and Fall of Liberal Government in Britain* (New Haven and London, 1993), esp. chapters 2–4.

Liberal assault upon privilege stopped far short of outright abolition of monarchy and the hereditary principle. The dismay at royal interference expressed by Liberals as different in outlook as Palmerston and John Morley derived only from the frustrations of working with the cantankerous Victoria, and implied no broader programme of reforms in this direction.[75] Even Joseph Chamberlain, who did briefly advocate this course in the 1870s, sought to distance himself from such notions in later life, and by the 1890s in his new Tory incarnation had become one of the chief advocates of an imperial-style monarchy. Plebeian republicanism therefore acted as a conduit for the expression of disillusionment with Liberalism on issues of the hereditary principle, inherited monarchy and aristocratic misgovernment. It gained its strongest support during the trough of the unpopularity of the Liberal government of 1868–74, and made particular targets of the great doyens of Liberalism, Gladstone and John Bright.

Its vehemence in targeting these former working-class icons of the 1866–7 reform campaign reflected a much broader groundswell of radical disapproval of the Liberal party on trade-union and social-reform issues, which has conventionally been seen as transferring working-class radical support to Toryism, rather than channelling it back in the direction of an independent radical position. The person of Gladstone bore the brunt of these attacks. He was especially loathed for the part he played in drawing up the special bill, which he personally steered through the House, that allowed the Marquis of Lorne and the royal children to receive donations from the civil list in 1871–2. In addition he was strongly attacked for his role in devising the special service of thanksgiving to celebrate the recovery of the Prince of Wales from typhoid in 1872 that did much to restore the popularity of the Royal House.[76] Fierce criticism was also, however, levelled at John Bright and reflected a wider sense of disillusionment with middle-class radical politics following his transfer from the role of critic to that of pillar of the establishment. Radicals bemoaned his failure to satisfy the working-class expectations he had aroused in 1866–7 in his new position as President of the Board of Trade, or indeed to seek to ameliorate the lot of his former supporters in any way at all. In 1872 John de Morgan declared of him at a meeting at Middlesbrough: 'John Bright has turned flunkey and does not speak out for the

---

[75] The best account of the difficulties Palmerston experienced in working with Victoria remains Lytton Strachey, *Queen Victoria* (London, 1921), pp. 130–61.

[76] See on these points F. Harcourt, 'Gladstone, Monarchism and the "New Imperialism" 1868–1874', *Journal of Commonwealth and Imperial History*, 14 (1985), pp. 20–51.

people.'[77] Bright's own strongly affirmed support for the queen and refusal to consider approaches from republicans to put his name forward for the presidency of the first British Republic,[78] reinforced these radical doubts about him, and prompted particularly vicious criticism of his failure to oppose a special parliamentary grant awarded to the Prince of Wales to enable him to tour India in 1875. Scurrilous verses appeared in the radical press condemning Bright for his association with this measure

> His Royal Highness, Prince of Wales,
>   To India Would go,
> To gratify some dream of life
>   He held since long ago.
> John Bright was by to sanction
>   And support the royal grant,
> Though many thousand people,
>   Pine in poverty and want.[79]

The mid-1870s therefore marked the final fragmentation of the links between Bright and the broader working-class radical constituency that had formed the bedrock of his support in 1866–7.

The single most enduring legacy of the campaign against the throne of the 1870s was this association between republican ideas and a theatre of operations that was both independent of, and outside, Liberalism. In later years British republicans continued to organise apart from the Liberal party, and the anti-monarchist stance itself came to denote a stubborn refusal to compromise with the consensus of the existing party system. A thin republican strand therefore links together those movements which sought their rationale in opposition to the forces of Liberalism, and emerged particularly strongly in groups which worked towards independent working-class political representation. Republican sentiments were strongly represented within the Tichborne movement, which was the only mass working-class agitation to mobilise apart from, and in some senses in opposition to, Liberalism during the period of the late 1870s and early 1880s. For its leader, Edward Kenealy, the court of Victoria was a thinly disguised Jesuit conspiracy presided over by her lover, the arch-Papist John Brown, that sought to deprive the Claimant

---

[77] *International Herald*, 27 July 1872, p. 5.

[78] See Bright's strongly worded defence of Victoria at a meeting at St James's Hall reported in the *Beehive*, 8 December 1866. His letter in reply to invitations to assume the position of President of the British republic is recorded in Robertson, *The Life and Times of John Bright*, p. 299.

[79] *People's Advocate*, 18 September 1875, p. 6.

and his honest Protestant champions of the natural rights of justice.[80]
Tichbornism therefore fused ultra-Protestantism with established
images of 'Old Corruption'. At the end of the century republicanism
still routinely resurfaced in *Reynolds's Newspaper* and the new labour
periodicals.[81]

In the nineteenth century British anti-monarchism offered a populist
assessment of the evils of monarchy and of royal government in keeping
with the British radical tradition of popular constitutionalism and the
nature of British radicalism itself. It differs strongly, for example, from
the contemporary French model. The British anti-monarchist tradition
had its own lineage, its own martyrs and was strongly represented within
the mainstream radical movement. It was certainly never simply Paine,
although the two have been confused. This confusion has misled
scholars and allowed republicanism to be discounted as an effective
force within radicalism itself. In the 1870s, however, it was able to
organise a highly effective and popular campaign that drew attention to
many of the weaknesses of the throne under Victoria. Subsequently it
came to occupy a permanent place within the radical traditions of
Labourism and helped in turn define a broader radical stance outside
Liberalism.

[80] See on this theme D. Woodruff, *The Tichborne Claimant: A Victorian Mystery* (London, 1957),
pp. 392–93.
[81] See, for example, *Reynolds's Newspaper*, 27 March 1887, p. 1 and *The Clarion*, 19 March 1892,
p. 1.

7

∾

The constitution and the narrative structure of Victorian politics

PATRICK JOYCE

It is ironic that historians, so much concerned with the deployment of narrative, have for the most part been so little aware of how the concept of narrative has come to have a central place in the epistemological frameworks of a whole range of disciplines, spanning the natural as well as the human sciences.[1] In particular, the shift from representation to ontology in recent understandings of narrative indicates the centrality of narrative to the formation of social identity (though, it could be added, those like Hayden White who see narrative as representation also conceive of it as coterminous with the cognitive process, part of the human condition in which knowing occurs through telling, knowledge through narrative). Whatever theoretical understanding we have of narrative it clearly invites us to dissolve the traditional dichotomies of a realist epistemology in which representation and the 'real' are kept at arm's length, the former being understood as representing or reflecting the latter.

The concept of narrative is particularly relevant to questions of politics. Geoff Eley has recently chided historians of class for dealing with identity as fixed.[2] Versions of class consciousness do not usually,

---

[1] Margaret R. Somers and Gloria D. Gibson, 'Reclaiming the Epistemological 'Other': Narrative and the Social Constitution of Identity' in Craig Calhoun (ed.), *Social Theory and the Politics of Identity* (Oxford, 1994). See also Theodore R. Sarbin (ed.), *Narrative Psychology: The Storied Nature of Human Conduct* (London, 1980); Victor Turner and Edward M. Bruner (eds.), *The Anthropology of Experience* (London, 1986); J. Shoffer and K. J. Green, *Texts of Identity* (London, 1989), esp. part III, 'Drama and Narrative in the Construction of Identities'; and the synoptic Christopher Nash and Martin Warren (eds.), *Narrative in Culture* (London, 1989), covering many disciplines.

[2] G. Eley, 'Is All the World a Text? From Social History to the History of Society Two Decades Later', in T. McDonald (ed.), *The Historical Turn in the Human Sciences* (Ann Arbor, 1996).

as he says, turn on the idea that identity is fractured, unstable, mobile. As Eley says, 'We need an opposing concept of identity which stresses its unfixity and sees it as an unstable ordering of multiple possibilities whose provisional unity is managed discursively.' Talking of politics – which is what I largely talk of in this study – he suggests 'that politics is usually conducted *as if* identity is fixed. The issue then becomes, on what bases, in different places and at different times, does identity's non-fixity become temporarily fixed in such a way as to enable individuals and groups to behave as a particular kind of agency, political or otherwise? How do people become shaped into acting subjects, understanding themselves in particular ways?'

Narrative is a very important answer to the question. What, then, are the dominant or master-narratives that can be held to have underpinned popular politics? There are many sorts of narrative, personal and social, but what appears to matter most are these dominant, unifying, stories that cut across and concert the often contradictory multiplicity of narratives in people's lives. Only the most open and unfixed narratives can secure the fixity necessary to achieve coherent identities and a workable sense of political agency. To encompass different and some-times competing narratives, and the instabilities inherent within narra-tive itself, stories are needed that do not foreclose options. Only by allowing multi-vocality can a measure of uni-vocality be achieved. Far from being too vague and unwieldy for useful analysis, the masternarra-tives, and grand identities, discussed here are important because of, not despite, their very open-endedness.

Questions about the constitution of social and political identities involve the creation of a sense of purpose, agency, and empowerment. To have identity, at least in the senses pursued here, is to have a sense of purpose. Narrative in its very nature confers purpose, in that it involves a sense of motion and direction. To tell, or be in, a story, involve a sequence, a movement, from inaugural, to transitional, to terminal motifs. The extent to which this sense of motion conferred purpose depended on what story was told: the stories that I am concerned with were of a kind which were exciting, and which therefore transformed motion into purpose. Twentieth-century stories were not always as exciting as their nineteenth-century counterparts: often they did not involve the drive to a limitless future, the optimism of the characteristic Victorian narratives. For instance, around the time of the First World War irony can to some extent be said to have replaced romance as a dominant mode of narrative,[3] an earlier assuredness of purpose being shattered in the process.

The situation I describe in nineteenth-century England can be said therefore to have brought into the most active being the sense of motion involved in all stories. My story is therefore about the power of exciting stories to move people. It is also in large part about how politics, in order to function, depended on creating a sense of movement, and so of purpose. It is about political *movements* in fact, above all popular Liberalism, and its absolute dependence on exciting stories. And it is about a culture grounded in the exciting story itself, the optimistic, utopian narrative.

I

Narrative is always a matter of the aesthetic. The thinking and framing of the social shape of power is valuably approached through an understanding of the 'structures of imagination' apparent in the aesthetic realm. Fredric Jameson and others have argued the significance of this realm and shown some of its effect.[4] If narrative is as powerful a principle of ontology as theorists of narrative tell us, then it follows that it may be a productive means of reconstituting the imaginative structures in question. It is in this hope that the aesthetic is explored here. The social world is categorised in certain ways, and indeed can only be present to us as some kind of configuration of categories. These configurations are always changing, yet there are decided limits to how we see our worlds. One example, drawn from Walkowitz's recent work on sexual narratives in Victorian London, is that of melodrama. The melodramatic constructions of feminist propaganda in the 1880s were only capable of imagining women in a certain way, as a victim, exhibiting modesty and so on.[5] And this way was extraordinarily important over a long period. Yet it too in the end lost effectiveness as other aesthetic frames displaced the melodramatic, chiefly that of realism.

Walkowitz's emphasis on melodrama is apposite, for as cultural historians are now beginning to realise melodrama was one of the

---

[3]   Paul Fussell, *The Great War and Modern Memory* (London, 1975).

[4]   A work of particular interest in respect to the kinds of material studied here is that of a student of Jameson's, Michael Denning, *Mechanic Accents: Dime Novels and Working-Class Culture in America* (London, 1987).

[5]   Judith M. Walkowitz, *City of Dreadful Delights: Narratives of Sexual Danger in Late Victorian London* (London, 1993), p. 92.

central aesthetics of the nineteenth century, particularly at a 'popular' level. So, it may be that melodrama offers us a singularly revealing way of getting at the configuration or framing of the political that we seek to understand. Peter Brooks' account of melodrama has been singularly influential.[6] Brooks argues that this form of imagination represented the attempt to re-sacralise the world after the dissolution of traditional forms of the sacred at the end of the eighteenth century, particularly in the French Revolution, where in fact melodramatic theatre was born. With the invalidation of earlier certainties about religious and socio-political cohesion, the literary forms that depended on these certainties went too. Melodrama was in important measure a response to the loss of the tragic vision. It inhabited a world in which truths were violently questioned, yet one too in which moral imperatives were still felt to be of overwhelming concern. As Brooks puts it,[7] melodrama sought to expose these imperatives by making the moral accessible and legible to all. Its appeal lay in the reassurance that there was a moral purpose and order to the world.

What light can this aesthetic throw on the framing of the social and political in Victorian England? The shape of melodrama's aesthetic frame has been described by Brooks and others, and can be given summary form here. First, in making the moral legible it dealt in clearly delineated moral contours, expressed in unambiguous modes of presentation (emphatic, for us exaggerated diction, gesture and so on). Second, and working from the same need, it dealt in a polarised world of moral absolutes, in which reality was rendered as a Manichean struggle of good and evil in their countless expressions. These moral categories were invariably personalised, though this imagination had nothing to do with psychological realism. Therefore, third, it was 'pre-psychological' in character, while moral attributes were nonetheless individuated (as such it was situated between older forms like allegory, and newer ones like realism). It follows therefore that this mode of imagination can not be judged by the tenets of realism. It frequently is, however, and dismissed as wish-fulfilment and fantasy. Of course, this is precisely why it is interesting.

Fourth, its mode of emplotment gave a singular shape to the aesthetic framing of the social and political. Unlike comedy it did not posit the emergence of a new society, formed around the reconciliations emerging

[6] Peter Brooks, *The Melodramatic Imagination: Balzac, Henry James, Melodrama, and the Mode of Excess* (London, 1976); also his *Reading For the Plot: Design and Intention in Narrative* (Oxford, 1984).
[7] Brooks, *The Melodramatic Imagination*, chapters 1–3, and see pp. 204–6.

out of the plot. Unlike tragedy, which partook of the sacrificial body of the protagonist, it did not involve participation in a newly sacred order, one higher than man.[8] It was in fact very close to romance, in its desire that evil be transcended by the good, but unlike it to the extent that it desired less a transcendence of the world of experience, a new utopia, than an old utopia, a return to a previous state of innocence. It was the drama of restoration, concerned with driving out what threatened primal innocence. As such, it had a close kinship with the 'golden-age' motifs so evident in many forms of popular literature, especially ballads, and so evident too in popular politics. The plot structure of melodrama concerned virtue extant, virtue eclipsed and expelled, virtue tested (in struggle), virtue apparently fallen and virtue restored and triumphant. The emplotment of the prelapsarian narrative form concerned a similar process of primal virtue, loss, usually in the form of dispossession, struggle and restoration. The 'golden-age' form was too widespread to be realised in melodrama alone, but melodrama expressed its sentiments with particular force. The practical consequences of these formal characteristics will be evident in due course.

Finally, as Brooks and others have argued,[9] the aesthetic–cognitive frame of melodrama carried its own political message, implicit in its form as it were. This message was a democratic one: recent work has suggested that the form was 'falsely democratic' but this is irrelevant to my consideration,[10] for whether 'conservative' or 'progressive' (whatever these terms may mean) what matters is how it made possible the imagining of the social order, in this case in its 'democratic' form. It is not so much the democratic ingredients of presentation that matter here, for example the tendency to make merit and not privilege the sign of virtue, or the casting of the hero from 'low' society, the villain from 'high' (by no means always the case, of course). Rather, and here I elaborate Brooks' argument in my own way, it can be suggested that simply by receiving the conventions of melodrama those who received them were being constituted as political persons.

Melodrama sought to make the good legible to all. Given that the

[8]   *Ibid.*, p. 32.
[9]   David Grimsted, 'Vigilante Chronicle: The Politics of Melodrama Brought to Life' (paper presented to the British Film Institute Conference, 1992); D. Grimsted, *Melodrama Unveiled: American Theatrical Culture 1800–1850* (1968; Berkeley, 1987); for a contemporary condemnation of the 'jacobinical' tendencies of melodrama, the 'affectation of attributing noble and virtuous sentiments to persons least qualified by habit or education to entertain them', see Sir Walter Scott, 'Essay on the Drama', *Supplement to the Encyclopaedia Britannica*, London, 1819.
[10] Julia Przbos, *L'Enterprise mélodramatique* (Paris, 1987).

truth was unambiguous, all could have direct access to it. Melodrama appealed to all, irrespective of social condition, as equally able to read the signs of moral legibility. Further, because the moral law was absolute, it actively enjoined readers and audiences to partake of this reading. The 'democratic' implications are clear. All were potentially equal in the task of interpretation and there could no longer be an appeal to the court of tradition and the sacred. Rather, the appeal was to the moral law and to a demos that sanctioned it. But if the idea of the moral absolute was thereby sanctioned, the content of this law in fact always lay in the assumptions and values of the audience. There was no other source of legitimation. The eternal verities of melodrama were in fact the shared, mundane moral conventions of those to whom it spoke. Therefore, simply by partaking of the melodramatic aesthetic, audiences were being spoken to and hence constituted as social subjects, ones varying always by the context of the audience but at a general level very much akin, in this aesthetic egalitarianism, to the imagined communities that made up a 'democratic' culture, including the political community itself.

Melodrama spoke to a socially mixed audience in England, at least until the late nineteenth century.[11] The virtue in which it dealt was absolute, above differences of social circumstances. Its triumph showed that all might be virtuous. The lowly were however often closest to virtue – their friendlessness and helplessness represented best the help-lessness of virtue expelled and tested. The triumph of the helpless meant the truest of all restitutions of virtue, for only with the low made morally high could the victory of virtue be most fully assured. On the one hand, the melodramatic imagination can be seen as deeply implicated in the construction of categories often cutting across classes, like 'the people', 'the audience', the theatre 'public' and so on, categories closely linked to the democratic imperative. It addressed a socially undifferentiated 'popular' audience, and was indeed important in itself in creating the idea of 'the popular'. But on the other hand, it can be said to have made a particular appeal to the lowly, the excluded and the powerless.

Melodrama was about symbolic reassurance. In assuring its audience that there was a moral purpose and order to the world it can be regarded as speaking most eloquently to those whose circumstances exposed them to the fear that there might not be. Historians of the form have in fact noted its special appeal to the powerless, not least, in the nineteenth century, women.[12] The representation of the lowly and

[11] Michael Booth, *English Melodrama* (London, 1965).
[12] Martha Vicinus, 'Helpless and Unbefriended: Nineteenth-Century Domestic Melodrama', in J. L. Fisher (ed.), *When They Weren't Doing Shakespeare: Essays on Nineteenth-Century British and*

powerless in fact became translated into an appeal to that condition. It has been observed how the empowerment brought by melodrama involved the ability to say the truth out loud: the eternal verities could be named without embarrassment, and the crust of convention, fear and silence broken. The powerless could be given a voice: a poor, persecuted servant girl could confront her rich oppressor with the truth about their moral condition.[13] It is this twin function of speaking to both demos and the powerless, inserting the latter in the former, that to my mind gives it its fascination as a means of understanding the political unconscious, particularly in its Victorian realisations as popular radicalism and popular Liberalism.

Melodrama is equally suggestive in constituting collective *social* identities, sometimes outside, sometimes within, political ones. If the eternal verities were in fact simply the shared moral conventions of audiences, then it follows that this aesthetic is a privileged point of access to these conventions. And, as these conventions are clearly so deeply involved in what 'communities' and collectivities felt themselves to be, it follows that melodrama is directly implicated in the very construction of the sense of 'community' and social identity itself. Melodrama was implicated in the moral being of audiences, and the moral being of audiences was implicated in their social being. It is therefore the case that the melodramatic aesthetic was powerfully evolved in the broader cultural life of popular audiences. This is particularly apparent in the links between melodramatic framings of the social and the notion of the 'golden-age', so widely dispersed in the popular culture of the time.

The notion of a lost golden-age, linked to the restoration of the lost reign of virtue, simply permeates the broadside ballads and the culture of the poor more widely. In previous work I have explored this theme in great detail, dwelling not only on the ballads but the ways in which in the industrial regions of northern England the transition from domestic to factory production was accompanied by a mythologising of the 'good old days' of yore.[14] The extraordinary force and longevity of the myth of the golden-age of the handloom weaver is a case in point. The influence of such golden-age notions was felt far beyond dialect literature, and the ballads (with their talk of the 'good old days', 'the

---

American Theatre (Georgia 1989). See also the discussion of melodrama in P. Joyce, *Visions of the People: Industrial England and the Question of Class* (Cambridge, 1991), chapters 9, 13.

[13]   Brooks, *The Melodramatic Imagination*, p. 44.

[14]   Joyce, *Visions of the People*, chapters 9, 11–14, and 6, 8, but esp. 7 on 'The Sense of the Past'.

good old town', 'old England', the 'fine old English gentleman', the 'old-fashioned farmer' and so on).

Keith Thomas has dwelt on a dominant form of the golden-age narrative, that of 'Merrie England'.[15] He has shown how, progressively up to the mid Victorian period, this 'old England' was positioned increasingly nearer the present, until by that time it was almost too vague to be placed at all. As the container of all sorts of concerns about the present, the content of this imagined past varied enormously. Thomas indicates how it was diffused in all sorts of cultural artefacts. The same can be said of the 'Norman Yoke' story, though its political cast was nonetheless clear. Christopher Hill has explored this motif, though, contrary to his marxist teleology, which sees these 'historicist' notions giving way to more 'modern' natural right theories, and to class, it was in fact widely prevalent in the later nineteenth century.[16]

But if apparent throughout society, it can be suggested that the 'golden-age' form had a special salience for the poor and powerless. Its drama of dispossession, lost virtue, struggle, and eventual triumph spoke most urgently to those who had felt loss and dispossession. To those engaged in struggle it gave hope, precisely that sense of agency spoken of earlier. Early-nineteenth-century popular radical politics fed on this narrative. It did this directly, or by linking itself to other social movements themselves imbued with the prelapsarian narrative form. The Factory Reform movement is a good example of the latter,[17] the idea of the labourer's 'cottage economy' symbolising opposition to aspects of the factory system through its emphasis on a supposedly 'natural' rhythm of labour and family life which obtained in the past; a time (not so long distant in the mythology of the handloom weavers) when the independence of the labourer was assured, an independence closely linked to conceptions of manhood.[18] Chartism itself drew directly on such ideas (one thinks of O'Connor on the 'artificiality' of modern society), but also on the language of the Bible, above all the story of the exiled Israelites, Moses and the Promised Land.[19] Indeed, the golden-

---

[15] Keith Thomas, 'The Power of the Past in Early Modern England', Creighton Trust Lecture, 1983.

[16] Christopher Hill, 'The Norman Yoke', in *Puritans and Revolutionaries: Studies in Interpretation of the English Revolution of the Seventeenth Century* (London, 1965).

[17] For some interesting observations on this see R. Gray, 'The Languages of Factory Reform in Britain, c. 1830–1860', in P. Joyce (ed.), *The Historical Meanings of Work* (Cambridge, 1987).

[18] Sally Alexander, 'Women, Class and Sexual Differences in the 1830s and 1840s: Some Reflections on the Writing of Feminist History', *History Workshop Journal* (spring 1984), pp. 125–49.

[19] James Epstein, *The Lion of Freedom: Feargus O'Connor and the Chartist Movement 1832–1842* (London, 1982) and Joyce, *Visions of the People*, pp. 31–4, 95–102, and ff.

age form had its most extensive and perhaps most profound formulations in this religious character: for instance, Keith Snell has recently shown how for agricultural workers throughout the entire nineteenth century, images of society were articulated primarily through biblical exegesis.[20] The Promised Land had, of course, a very immediate meaning in the nineteenth century, and not for agricultural workers alone: if religion was perhaps the chief instance of the golden-age narrative form,[21] then the land itself was of great significance too, a matter of practical interest and reform but at the same time one which carried an enormous emotional charge, as historians are now beginning to discern more clearly.

That charge was in large part delivered through the conductive element of the golden-age narrative form. This form was in turn closely linked to the general cultural characteristics of the society in which it was imbedded. It can be understood as speaking to a 'popular' culture that still retained, up to the late nineteenth century, pronounced customary characteristics. Custom looked to precedent to regulate present social practices and social relations. In so doing the affinity with the golden-age form is clear. What, then, do melodrama and the golden-age narrative pattern have to tell us about popular politics at this time?

II

The second half of the nineteenth century saw the emergence and consolidation of mass, party-political democracy in Britain.[22] The Second and Third Reform Acts, of 1867 and 1884, still left sizeable proportions of the male electorate unenfranchised, and women were of course not enfranchised until after 1918. Nonetheless, mass democracy was real enough, albeit mass male democracy. Handling the problems posed by this new democracy involved handling narrative, for narrative

---

[20] Keith Snell, 'Deferential Bitterness: the Social Outlook of the Rural Proletariat in Eighteenth- and Nineteenth-Century England', in M. L. Bush (ed.), *Social Orders and Social Classes in Europe since 1500: Studies in Social Stratification* (London, 1992), esp. pp. 173–4, on the theme of deliverance and the Promised Land. See also J. F. C. Harrison, *The Second Coming: Popular Millennarianism 1780–1850* (London, 1979), p. 24.

[21] In forthcoming work Iain MacCalman dwells on the great importance of hebraism in early-nineteenth-century popular radical politics. Paineite rationalism, constitutionalism and 'radical restorationism' were often happily combined in a utopian politics unified by the narrative pattern of a lost golden-age. See I. MacCalman, 'New Jerusalems: Radicalism and Prophecy in Britain 1786–1832', paper given at Manchester University, May 1992.

[22] M. Pugh, *The Making of Modern British Politics 1867–1939* (1982, new edn, London, 1993), for a useful overview.

conferred what the new democracy needed, namely political subjectivities which created agency and legitimacy. This was so for the politicians
and the people alike: the latter acquired a sense of political identity, a
sense that enabled politics to go forward in the hands of the former. Out
of the imaginative projections of leaders and led, in their interaction,
was produced the democratic imaginary of the time. Parties, leaders,
issues and ideas certainly produced this, but these were only effective
within particular patterns of narrative.

Consideration of these narratives suggests that the legitimation of
mass democracy involved existing political narratives drawing on the
resource of narratives lying beyond the purely political sphere, in
particular those narrative elements so far considered, the narrative
patterns or framing evident in melodrama and the golden-age form. In
this process what was usable in existing political narratives was refur-
bished, and adapted to new circumstances. The most evident, pre-
existing political narrative was that of the constitution (usually the
'English constitution') the nearest thing to a political masternarrative of
its day. The story of the constitution had a force and literalness it is
perhaps difficult to appreciate today. One example must suffice here,
though a very representative and influential one. John Bright's words,
from a speech of the 1860s, show how strongly contemporary narrative
was historicised, and how the resulting certainty assumed an almost
mystical clarity when it came to politics:

I am in accord with our ancient Constitution. I would stand by it, wherever it
afforded support for freedom, I would march in its tracks. That track is so plain
that the way-faring man, though a fool, need not err therein. I would be guided
by its lights. They have been kept burning by great men among our forefathers
for many generations. Our only safety in this warfare is in adhering to the
ancient and noble Constitution of our country.[23]

In the warfare of which Bright spoke, that of the 1860s reform
struggle, it becomes apparent that while the old narrative of the
constitution continued powerfully, it is its changed meanings and
functions that are apparent. Bright inaugurated and Gladstone followed
a process whereby, on the one hand, the constitution became increasingly moralised and linked to notions of 'respectable' behaviour and, on
the other, it became associated with the cause of progress, itself
increasingly emblematised in moral conduct. Progress, in the characteristically Victorian form of 'Improvement', was perhaps the major

---

[23] Speech cited in J. Page Hopps, *John Bright: A Study of Character and Characteristics* [1880s?],
     p. 11.

masternarrative beyond politics at this time, and the story of the fusion of the narrative of the constitution with this narrative is the story of a good part of the party history and the popular politics of this period.

This fusion of narratives gathered force in the agitation preceding the Second Reform Act. Gladstone's was one major voice: his reform speech of 1866 dwelt on the 'pre-eminently rich and fruitful' institutions and traditions of England.[24] These 'institutions' were a shorthand for the constitution in the political discourse of the day, the plasticity of the constitution being its defining characteristic, so that in some readings one might include the ancient universities besides parliament, which nonetheless remained the jewel in the crown. For Gladstone, England had inherited more of what was 'august and venerable than any other European nation', but it was uniquely modern too.[25] Its modernity was above all apparent in the advance of 'progress', and progress itself received its most characteristic expression in the 'improvement' of the people themselves. In his Liverpool speech, designed to reach a wide public but also to win over his propertied audience in the city, he contrasted 1832 with the present day. Now industry was advanced, institutions – like the Church – were reformed, and the people were restrained and educated.[26] The people increasingly figured as the leading character in the story of improvement, and the need was to connect this people, and hence the improvement narrative, to the story of all that was good in English institutions. One link, in this speech, was the story of 1832 itself, and this was broadened out to the splendid array of the constitutional past, and its valuable legacy in the present. In Gladstone's speeches the overwhelming theme was that by virtue of their improvement the people should now have a right to share in the institutions of the nation.

This was all given an increasingly moralistic slant. The language of duty is one instance, the people needing to be brought to a level where they could exercise public duty, but – even more urgently – the institutions of this country if they were to survive needed to pay their debt of honour to the people, whose moral worth (but also economic contribution) had made them a proper part of this institutional realm. One sees in this an instance of a general phenomenon, the shift in popular politics from historical and natural to moral rights. Accompanying this, in Gladstone's 1860s speeches, there is the beginning of what

---

[24] Rt Hon. W. E. Gladstone, *Speeches on Reform in 1866*, 2nd edn (London, 1866), p. 85.

[25] *Ibid.*, pp. 89–90.

[26] 'Speech at a Public Meeting in the Amphitheatre, Liverpool, 6 August 1866', *Speeches on Reform*.

will later be over-mastering, namely the embodiment of the people as the moral law, as well as the law of improvement. The two in fact became synonymous, the narrative of providence coming in turn to the aid of the politicised narrative of improvement.

In 1866 Gladstone dwelt on how the truths of improvement were manifest around one every day, and how these bore an irresistible political witness: the idea that 'the signs of the times' must be seized in order to make political progress was evident in all Gladstone's public pronouncements at the time, for instance in the 1868 speeches that preceded the first general election under the new democratic dispensation.[27] Also evident was the by then familiar refrain that the Liberals were the true guardians of the constitution in both its venerable and progressive aspects.[28] Bright's view of the constitution was more concrete and historicised, but he too spoke of the constitution as mystically dispersed in a wide range of English institutions and codes. This attempt to bring the 'working class' and 'people' within the pale of the constitution by appealing to the spirit of improvement was not evident in Disraeli, even though it was the Tories that passed reform. Gladstone connected political reform to improvement as much within as outside the House of Commons.[29] By contrast Disraeli, inside and outside the House,[30] could not rise to this occasion of the 'signs of the times', so forfeiting the chance of capitalising on the sense of forward motion imputed to politics by this powerful narrative thrust.

In the reform agitation it was Bright and not Gladstone who did most to narrativise politics in these ways. At his October 1866 speech in Leeds Town Hall Bright dwelt at length on how 'you', 'the working class', have built up the country to what it is. The cities, industries and railways that were the material signs of progress were all due to the contribution of the people.[31] A fortnight before, in Manchester, he dwelt at similar length on all the usual signs of intellectual and moral progress; schools built, ignorance banished and cultivation triumphant (1867 was for Bright the culmination of his youthful efforts in the Manchester Athenaeum). He spoke in the evening of the day following a reputed

[27] *Speeches of the Rt Hon. William Ewart Gladstone, MP, in South West Lancashire, October 1868* (Liverpool, 1868).

[28] *Ibid.*, speech at Liverpool, 14 October 1868.

[29] W. E. Gladstone, *Speeches on Great Questions of the Day* (London, 1870), e.g. 'The Representation of the People', House of Commons, 12 April 1866.

[30] John F. Bulley (ed.), *Speeches on Conservative Policy of the Last Thirty Years* (1869), 'Representation of the People', February and March 1867 speeches.

[31] John Bright, *Speeches on Parliamentary Reform, by John Bright, Edited by Himself* (London, 1866), 8 October speech in Leeds.

gathering of over 100,000 people on the Knott Mill fairgrounds, in the city: the fact that so vast a throng had gathered without trouble was the most eloquent testimony of all to the people's advancement he said.[32]

Bright, unlike Gladstone, was happy to reveal the iron fist within the velvet glove of improvement. As he put it in Manchester,[33] 'It is not more immoral for the people to use force in the last resort, for the obtaining and securing of freedom than it is for the Government to use force to suppress and deny that freedom.' The people's role in the advancement of the nation had given them such an incontrovertible moral case for the vote that even force might be threatened. This force was all the more justified given that the institutions of England were prone to 'every form of corruption and evil'. In particular, they were corrupted by materialism, by 'Mr Money Bags MP' in the House of Commons.[34] The accent on material progress was always accompanied by this deep distrust of materialism.

The notion of a moral right sanctioned by progress received its most telling expression in the idea that the constitution might at last be restored to the people, who were in fact its rightful custodians. Life might be restored to a corrupt constitution by the people. At the Free Trade Hall in September 1866, we again find him speaking in the afterglow of the 'transcendentally great' open-air meeting at Knott Mill, this time on the same day.[35] The House of Commons was to be again what its name implied, the house of the common people. It was to be restored to them, their struggle in the present being part of the great struggle for liberty begun by their forefathers in the Civil War, two hundred years ago. Because the constitution was so indelibly the English constitution, it followed that their nation was being restored to them along with their constitution. The idea that a lost golden-age was being restored was also central.

In his famous Glasgow speech of October,[36] extolling the unity of the people above the divisiveness of 'class rule',[37] justice would not be got from a class, only from the nation, the whole people. The reign of justice would restore properly functioning institutions to the country, and these would bring about the profound changes he sought. These changes were imaged in the explicit terms of a restored Eden,

I am convinced that just laws and an enlightened administration of them, would change the face of the country. I believe that ignorance and suffering might be

[32] *Ibid.*, 25 September 1866.   [33] *Ibid.*, p. 20.   [34]*Ibid.*, 8 October 1866.
[35] *Ibid.*, 24 September 1866.   [36] *Ibid.*, 16 October 1866.
[37] Joyce, *Visions of the People*, pp. 54–5.

lessened to an incalculable extent, and that many an Eden, beauteous in flowers and rich in fruits, might be raised up in the waste of wilderness which spreads before us. But no class can do this ... Let us try the nation. This it is which has called together these countless numbers of the people to demand a change; and, as I think of it, and of these gatherings sublime in their vastness and in their resolution, I think I see, as it were, above the hill tops of time, the glimmerings of the dawn of a better and a nobler day for the country and for the people that I love so well.[38]

We see here far more than the confluence of the narratives of improvement and the constitution. The whole aesthetic edifice by which the social and the political were framed is in full evidence. The melodramatic shape of the political unconscious emerges with great clarity: this is the struggle of moral opposites, and moral absolutes, in which moral attributes are personified (not least in Bright himself). This is the melodrama of moral restoration, the golden age form characteristic of melodrama itself but of other aspects of popular culture too. The presentation of the reform agitation as a drama of lost rights (the constitution, the nation itself), of the struggle of the dispossessed and of the restoration of a vanished Eden mirrors exactly the narrative forms so apparent in popular fiction and popular drama. It does this, further, by the demonisation of the Tory, and the aristocrat, as the principle of evil.[39] The personification of this form of the demonic in 1866 was Robert Lowe, the reactionary Whig opponent of reform, who had referred to the people as 'the great unwashed', so denying their moral right as the great improved to enter upon their lost constitution. Men like Lowe had stolen England from the people.[40]

Even more in the political audience's response to Bright, and Gladstone, are we aware of this depiction of politics as a massive drama of struggle, movement and hope. The hope invested in Bright is conveyed by this description of his speech at the Free Trade Hall in September 1866. The Hall was under siege from early in the day. It filled up with 5,000 people, only one-quarter of the throng trying to get in, the streets outside swarming with people. Admission was by ticket, first come, first served, and tickets were changing hands on the black market for up to two guineas:

When Mr Bright stepped forward the scene was such as to baffle all attempts at description. The whole audience rose in his honour. The shouts were deafening

---

[38] Bright *Speeches*, 16 October 1866.   [39] *Ibid.*, 20 November 1866.
[40] For Lord Derby, the Tory Leader, as the man responsible for class conflict, and for separating the Commons from the people, see *ibid.*, Free Trade Hall Speech, 24 September 1866.

and long continuing. When the honourable gentleman rose to receive the address, the same enthusiasm was manifested, and when the time came for him to speak the whole audience listened with rapt attention.[41]

Vast as these indoor meetings were it is the great outdoor gatherings of these years which are even more striking. Bright did not speak at these, though he often attended. Even though not speaking he was the object of an undimmed popular veneration, and here we became aware of Bright as an icon. Although working men, and women, may never have heard him speak, and may only have read his words, or had his words read to them, he was still a cult object. The operation of the 'political unconscious' is amply apparent here in the sense of the 'visceral thrill' of politics, the emotional, 'pre-cognitive' delights of being in a narrative oneself and in a sense being that narrative, enacting it and being its subject at the same time.

The great Woodhouse Moor demonstration in 1866 is a good case: 200,000 were supposed to have gathered, walking from all over the region because the railway authorities refused to put on excursions (the authorities and employers in other British cities were, by contrast, actively cooperative).[42] Each cab and conveyance bore the Liberal colours. Every man and woman was also reported as carrying cards and rosettes, many of these in Chartist colours. The procession was divided between friendly society, reform organisation and trade society contingents, also 'non-electors' groups. There were also some individual colliery contingents. As was common at these meetings the trade societies marched in their trade attire and bore the regalia of their craft. The other contingents had their own identities conferred by banners and bands.[43] 'Rule Britannia' was sung repeatedly in the vast, two-hour long procession. There were five platforms in a great 'amphitheatrical' area on the moors, from which speeches were delivered by radical leaders and local Liberal potentates.

Gladstone, Bright and J. S. Mill, were the objects of this enthusiasm, but in homaging these the people were homaging themselves. Bright had revealed the iron fist of numbers with the glove of improvement, so calling into discourse the felt strength of the multitude. Occasions like Woodhouse Moor were in large part about feeling the intoxication of numbers, feeling the leashed power of the people and the working class. And this felt strength was expressed in narrative form: it was strength in movement, coming from a past of struggle and heading for the many

---

[41] *Reynolds News*, 30 September 1866.   [42] *Ibid.*, 14 October 1866.
[43] See also account of Birmingham reform demonstration; *ibid.*, 2 September 1866.

Edens promised by Bright. The banners of the crowd, like Bright's
oratory, reached back to a glorious heritage, telling the tale of liberty.
The Great Halton Reformers' banner ran thus: 'Freedom's battle once
begun / Bequeath'd from bleeding sire to son / Tho battled oft, will still
be won.' The essential narrative properties lay in this sense of being part
of an unfolding story, but strength also lay in the day itself, which was a
matter of joining this tidal movement of people, united in one cause and
moving inexorably towards it.

That inexorability was further conveyed by the figure of the Tory:
just as in Bright's oratory, the banners on the day defined the narrative
of liberty in terms of its vicious opponents, an 'other' that was all the
more effective in defining the radical self because of the knowledge that
it would imminently be destroyed.[44] The resources of comedy here
supplemented those of the romance and melodrama of politics: Lowe
was frequently derided for insulting the working class (showing and not
showing respect was a frequently elaborated theme at these meetings),[45]
one banner depicting the Tory cabinet as the Christy Minstrels, with
Disraeli ('Ass-man'), Derby and Lowe, and on the obverse a John Bright
earnestly engaged in disturbing the peace of the 'cave of Addullum', the
name given the anti-reform Tory conclave. At another meeting a
banner read 'Bright Cabinet Makers Wanted. No Addullumite Need
Apply', with on the other side, 'No more oligarchic rule. The people are
determined to be their own cabinet makers.' Fittingly, the banner was
carried by a contingent of cabinet makers.

III

When the Reform Act was passed in 1867 the politics of the excluded
began to become the politics of the included. The countryside remained
to be enfranchised, in 1884, so that the old narratives, which had taken
their bearings from the experience of political exclusion, still remained
important. Nonetheless, for large parts of the electorate the problem
became what to do with power once it was acquired. What happened
when the stake in the country asked for in 1866 was given, when
England was given back to the people? The politics of democratic
representation became the politics of democratic accountability and
action. What should the people do to justify themselves? What, also,
should the political parties do to be saved? For their task now became

---

[44] For the radical press equating the Tory and the aristocrat, *Reynolds News*, leader, 2
September 1865.
[45] On 'respect' see leader in *Reynolds News*, 9 February 1866.

that of allying the old, pre-1867, electorate with the new as the viable basis for the re-invention of party on the basis of a new demos. This alliance also depended on putting demos into action, on a politics of forward movement and accountability.

It was necessary that the old narratives be reworked if demos was to renew itself as the potent source of politics. The instability and limitations of the old narrative of progress and liberty become apparent in the new circumstances of politics described here. How might the narratives that drove politics be renewed? The conjuncture that helps us explore this is that of Gladstone's return to politics after 1876, and his attempt to shape the Liberal party in the image of his moral populism. The famous Midlothian speeches of 1879 were one of the vehicles by which the party's identity as the party of the moral crusade and of *vox populi* was deepened. They were also a vehicle for Gladstone's own return to power in 1880.[46] The roots of 1879 were themselves in the 'Bulgarian Horrors' agitation of 1876, but the Midlothian campaign is the best place to begin considering that renewal of narrative necessary if Liberalism was to prosper.[47] Both 'agitations' electrified the country, helping to launch the politics of democratic justification. With reform secured, there was a shift to external affairs as the ground on which a moral purpose might be exercised ('external affairs' of course included Ireland, for Gladstonian Liberalism perhaps the ultimate test of justice).

As in the previous decade the concern of Gladstone was to attach the constitution/institutions of the nation to the narrative of progress. In the first Midlothian speech Gladstone attacked the new-fangled changes proposed by the Tories: these would abrogate the constitution, going too far towards novelty. The constitution should be treated as adaptable but 'hallowed'.[48] Nonetheless, and again 1866 is echoed, there is the concern that parliament and party may fail the nation by falling into 'faction'. If 'hallowed', the constitution must renew itself. However, what had happened since the 1860s was an ever-deepening moralisation of the narrative of improvement and of its primary collective subject, 'the people'. In Midlothian what parliament and party had above all to comprehend was what Gladstone called 'the great human heart of this country': this heart beat outside parliament and parliament ignored it at its peril. What its beat reflected was consternation at the 'Bulgarian Horrors', the massacre of thousands of Christian Bulgarians by Muslim Turks. The 'great human heart of this country', in all its moral certitude,

---

[46] R. T. Shannon, *Gladstone and the Bulgarian Agitation 1876* (London, 1963), chapter 8.
[47] W. E. Gladstone, *Midlothian Speeches*, ed. M. R. D. Foot (Leicester, 1971).
[48] *Ibid.*, 25 November 1879.

was now to dominate politics; 'the country' and 'the people' becoming moral principle incarnate.

In the first Midlothian speech the fate of an enormous empire is in the hands of 'you', 'a great and free people'. It is not in the hands of an administration, parliament or a party. Britain is a self-governing country and 'man' is a citizen by nature, above all considerations of property rights. Man is more than the English or British, and we must not, like the Tories, think we are better than the rest of the world. Gladstone spoke, therefore, of the 'sisterhood and equality of nations', 'the absolute equality of public right among them'. What seems to be happening here was both dramatic and novel: 'the people' was slowly expanding until it became all people. The people could speak for all people, the British for the world, but also women for mankind.

'Woman' moved back to the spoken centre of politics. Earlier she is the absent trace, the implied presence in politics which defines in its absence, and by its silence, the all-pervasive 'masculinity' of politics. Gladstone had always addressed his audience as 'gentlemen', indeed this was one of his characteristic rhetorical ploys, evincing an equality between him and his invariably male audience, his peers in rational thinking and social worth (no matter how horny-handed they were). Because 'the people' had now been expanded to all people, this now required talk of an essential human nature which would describe, and hence embrace, all people. This nature could not be described without including women's special place in this encompassing unity that was humanity. This was all the more pressing because those who have been murdered, tortured and raped in their thousands by the Turks were women and children.

On Gladstone's second Midlothian day woman and the family came to the centre of attention.[49] On 26 November he went on from the Corn Exchange, Dalkeith, to the Foresters' Hall. Here he addressed 'women', not 'ladies'. 'Ladies' betokened rank, he said, whereas 'women' represented the essential principle of the human nature he wished to enunciate. Women were not 'abstract'. They were not interested in the 'harder, sterner, drier lessons of politics'. Their warmth and softness gave them access to what Gladstone termed the burden of sin, sorrow and suffering in the world, an access men did not have. He meditated publicly, communing with his female audience, on how the real meaning of 'Peace, Retrenchment and Reform' was to promote human happiness, and above all peace. Women touched the deepest chord of

[49] *Ibid.*, delivered Dalkeith, 26 November 1879.

the truly human, and in speaking to them Gladstone went on to develop an account of 'the horrors of war' that still reads with great force and must have been greatly moving to hear. His theme was 'Remember the rights of the savage, as we call him, remember the happiness of his home' (in Afghanistan, in South Africa). The sanctity of all human flesh must never be forgotten, in Europe no less than the Empire. The peroration ended with the affirmation that God had bound us in the law of mutual love and that this law governed all the earth. The vision was one of a suffering, bleeding humanity, joined by a love women had a peculiar knowledge of, and overseen by God in his providential wisdom.[50] The motive force in history, however, was perhaps not so much God as man-in-God, the narrative of improvement becoming the narrative of humanity at large, of all 'people'. A more religious and providential reading than hitherto is evident, but this is still demotic in its insistence on a Godhead realised in a law of human love, and what is more a human love the aim of which was to secure and exercise 'freedom'.[51] The message of 'freedom', as has been seen, spoke loudest to men. Women might testify to this freedom, by their human, unabstract warmth. But man exercised it. Thus while women were brought into the discourse of politics, this was without power.

The roots of 1879 lay in 1876 and the 'Bulgarian Horrors' agitation. Shannon has described this agitation:[52] horrific accounts of the Turkish massacres first appeared in the *Daily News* in late June, and were then circulated more widely in the press. W. T. Stead took these up and in his *Darlington Echo* began the systematic ignition of the public on the issue. In less than six weeks in August and September five hundred demonstrations were held throughout the country, with a concentration in the north and in Wales. Stead knew how to organise an agitation. The politicians and churchmen, who mostly did not, followed his lead. By late autumn Gladstone saw his chance, biding his time until he became fully convinced of the disinterestedness and spontaneity of the upsurge of 'the masses'.[53] He then began to ride the tumultuous tide of popular moral passion. The sequence of this agitation provides therefore a valuable chance of looking at narrative in action, but it also prompts some remarks on the action in narrative. Just, as was earlier suggested, a narrative was a kind of agitation, conferring in its intrinsic nature a sense of motion and direction, so can we think of the 'agitation' as in itself a narrative. The fact of the name, and of the name 'demonstra-

---

[50] *Ibid.*, see first Dalkeith speech.   [51] *Ibid.*, see 27 November speeches also.
[52] Shannon, *Gladstone and the Bulgarian Agitation.*   [53] *Ibid.*, pp. 100–1.

tion', which also came into vogue around this time, is a fact of the emerging democracy. The terms denoted the populace in movement, as a collective entity. In denoting demos thus, demos was constituted thus, as the implied subject and agent in this agitation. A subject in movement in turn implied its own narrative. In this particular example of the agitation W. T. Stead was perhaps the most important orchestrator of the people in narrative movement.

The primary audience Stead worked upon was a northern Nonconformist one. He spoke first to a religious memory looking back to a past of persecution. The seventeenth century again figured hugely, in the form of Milton and his support for the persecuted Vaudois, but also in the form of Cromwell, who was the object of a cult for Stead, and for many more, in these years. This Nonconformist narrative was accompanied by a similarly familiar one about the north of England as the true home of liberty. Both were centred upon a Liberal partisanship, casting the Tories as the villains of the piece.[54] Stead travelled to London in 1876, on his 'first political pilgrimage', to the Blackheath demonstration which was to bring Gladstone centre stage. He went sustained by visions of Hereward the Wake, the first, Saxon, 'Free Born Englishman', and of Cromwell. He saw Gladstone as the successor of both.[55] Born in Northumberland, his father was a Congregationalist minister. Like Josephine Butler and John Bright he was a crusader for democracy who detested the metropolitan elite.[56] Proud and vocal in his northernness, it is evident that his formation was the formation of many of his readers. The *Darlington Echo* was well named.

Stead stood at the beginnings of the 'popular press'. His attempts to 'democratise' the press have been seen, though what was understood as 'sensation' in some quarters was by Stead and his confrères seen as the 'Journalism of the Ideal': the newspaper had to be true to the facts, fulfilling its mission to educate, inform, but also to reform, the democracy. The alliance of entertainment and instruction earlier noted for the popular illustrated magazines of a generation before was continued in a new fashion, embracing Nonconformity this time. The narratives of an earlier popular fiction were continued in the *Pall Mall Gazette*: 1840s and 50s fiction on the theme of the 'mysteries' of the City was reflected in 'The Bitter Cry of Outcast London', running in 1883. This perpetuated an older melodrama, adding to it a more emphatic emphasis on social realism. There were other continuities with earlier 'popular' forms, and

[54] *Ibid.*, pp. 68–81.   [55] *Ibid.*, p. 116.
[56] Raymond L. Schultz, *Crusader in Babylon: W. T. Stead and the Pall Mall Gazette* (Lincoln, NE, 1972).

new departures arising from these, but what these amounted to in total can be regarded as a widening of the 'popular' itself, in the sense that a culture of the many earlier ostracised by the few was now, suitably scrutinised, brought within the remit of a still larger majority. In this process the populist tendencies of the 'popular' worked among new social constituencies and in new ways. Nonconformity is a good case in point. Brought within the remit of the popular in Stead's journalism, it developed its own populist tendencies, directing its traditional morality along populist lines: the defence of social purity,[57] described by Walkowitz, was democratically directed at all in society, high and low, rich and poor, with of course the greatest enemies being directed at the rich, the well-born and the powerful.[58]

Gladstone picked up the narrative motifs of Stead, the popular agitation and the *Daily News*, developing these in his own way. This is most of all evident in his *Bulgarian Horrors* pamphlet of 1876, which sold 200,000 shortly after publication.[59] The pamphlet was therefore itself a major element in the mobilisation of narrative described here. Gladstone's appropriations turned crucially around the central figure of the Turk: if ever there was an 'other' this was it, the Turk in his absolute evil defining the absolute good of an enraged moral populace. For Gladstone the Turk was 'the one great anti-human specimen of humanity'.[60] The Turk shaped that all-pervasive humanity which, as we have seen, came to re-fashion, in an enlarged form, earlier notions of 'the people'. Thus, the Turk made the moral self of an outraged moral democracy.

Gladstone's pamphlet begins by presenting the military Turks in the long historical narrative of Turk–Christian history. While drawing, gratuitously, from the antipathetic associations of this history, he is at pains to say it is not the religion of Muhammad that is his quarry (to do that would be to deny the brotherhood of man, existing under many versions of the Godhead). No, the Turkish variant is what is evil. And what is evil about it offends every sensibility of Christian liberalism. The Turk practises government by force, not by law. Fatalism is his guide in this life, and in the next, the prospect of a 'sensual paradise'. His is 'an

[57] For 'purity' as a rallying cry for Nonconformists, but for all sorts of radicals too, see Raphael Samuel, 'The Discovery of Puritanism, 1820–1914: A Preliminary Sketch', in Jane Garnett and H. C. G. Matthew (eds.), *Revival and Religion: Essays for John Walsh* (London, 1993).

[58] Walkowitz, *City of Dreadful Delights*.

[59] W. E. Gladstone, *The Bulgarian Horrors and the Question of the East* (London, 1876).

[60] *Ibid.*, p. 13.

elaborate and refined cruelty', 'the only refinement of which Turkey boasts'.[61] This is how the pamphlet ended:

But I return to, and I end with, that which is the Omega as well as the Alpha of this great and most mournful case ... Let the Turks now carry away their abuses in the only possible manner, namely by carrying off themselves. Their Zaptiehs and their Mudirs, their Bimbashis and their Yuzbachis, their Kaimakams and their Pashas, one and all, bag and baggage, shall, I hope, clear out from the province they have desolated and profaned. This thorough riddance, this most blessed deliverance, is the only reparation we can make to the memory of those heaps on heaps of dead; to the violated purity alike of matron, of maiden, and of child; to the civilization which has been affronted and shamed; to the laws of God or, if you like, of Allah; to the moral sense of mankind at large. There is not a criminal in a European gaol, there is not a cannibal in the South Sea Islands, whose indignation would not rise and overboil at the recital of that which has been done, which has too late been examined, but which remains unavenged; which has left behind all the foul and all the fierce passions that produced it, and which may again spring up, in another murderous harvest, from the soil soaked and reeking with blood, and in the air tainted with every imaginable deed of crime and shame. That such things should be done once, is a damning disgrace to the portion of our race which did them; that a door should be left open for their ever-so-barely possible repetition would spread that shame over the whole. Better, we may justly tell the Sultan, almost any inconvenience, difficulty, or loss associated with Bulgaria,

> 'Than thou reseated in thy place of light,
> The mockery of thy people, and their bane.'

We may ransack the annals of the world, but I know not what research can furnish us with so portentous an example of the fiendish misuse of the powers established by God 'for the punishment of evil-doers, and for the encouragement of them that do well.' No Government ever has so sinned; none has so proved itself incorrigible in sin, or which is the same, so impotent for reformation. If it be allowable that the Executive power of Turkey should renew at this great crisis, by permission or authority of Europe, the charter of its existence in Bulgaria, then there is not on record, since the beginnings of political society, a protest that man has lodged against intolerable misgovernment, or a stroke he has dealt at loathsome tyranny, that ought not henceforward to be branded as a crime. But we have not yet fallen to so low a depth of degradation; and it may cheerfully be hoped that, before many weeks have passed, the wise and energetic counsels of the Powers, again united, may have begun to afford relief to the overcharged emotion of a shuddering world.

What a mix of improvement and 'sensation' this is, the improvement

---

[61] *Ibid.*, p. 33.

of Gladstone's homiletic, reasoned cadences and locutions, the sensation that produces 'the overcharged emotion of a shuddering world'. The profane and the sacred confront one another, in a climactic melodrama. The 'moral sense of mankind' at large is here formed in the image of this sacred, and this is the sacred of purity, the purity of 'matron, maiden and child'. The most depraved of mankind, the criminal, the cannibal, recognise their humanity in the counter-figure of a Turk, the profaner of this sacrality. Three years later, before the 'women' of Dalkeith, Gladstone had summoned up a 'woman' who was not abstract to testify to the universal law of love, and the burden of sorrow, binding all humanity. The being of woman here testified to humanity. Three years before, it was the bodies of women that enunciated in their sacred purity the underlying moral sense of mankind, and hence established the people-become-humanity. The moral populism that triumphed in 1880 and thereafter was rooted in this moment of 1876.

The sensual, fatalistic and cruel Turk had 'sinned', and the soil was reeking in blood. This representation of the Turk and his 'atrocities' re-circulated images in fact already widely dispersed in the press. The 'eye-witness' reporting of the *Daily News* had already combined moralism and passionate outrage in its accounts. For instance, the report of the massacre at Panigurishti at which 3,000 were reported slaughtered, personalised the demonic Turk in the form of Hafiz Pasha, the perpetrator of events.[62] The report talks of horrors too awful to describe, and then goes on to describe them – the bayonetting of babies for instance, their little arms and legs hanging grotesquely down as they were carried aloft. The violation of women was very clearly indicated, and on a mass scale, though here prudence forbade the detail permitted in the accounts of children's deaths (in his speeches Gladstone did in fact counsel 'prudence' in public presentation of what clearly were mass rapes). Nonetheless, the accounts of rape were all the more telling for what was not said. Little was left in doubt.

Therefore, the mode of representation in the press was itself not a *tabula rasa* upon which Stead, Gladstone and others wrote their narratives. Rather, the pattern was circular, a diffused moral passion surfacing in the press, being re-circulated by the politicians, and thence returned again to the media of communication. In this process the bounds of the permissible in Victorian society were redrawn in novel forms. The discourse of 'the real' enabled these bounds to be transgressed with impunity. What could not in fact be said in fiction, except

---

[62] *Manchester Guardian*, 28 August 1876 for *Daily News* account.

of course in pornography, could be said in the press accounts of the atrocity. The ideology of the real was sanctioned by the idea of the press itself as impartial truth-teller and chronicler of events (in the 'eyewitness' account for example). It was sanctioned too by the weight attaching to the term 'atrocity': the awful reality of the atrocity demanded expression in the press, the new guardian of the real. A democratic press had arrived, and with it the unprecedented force of a fictive real was conscripted to the cause of the people.

Shannon's account of the Bulgarian agitation dwells on these aspects, also on progress: 'Two special aspects of the High Victorian moral sensibility contributed markedly to the atrocities agitation: the vision of progress and the veiling and exaltation of sexuality.'[63] The Turk exemplified everything that opposed progress, therefore he fortified its narrative, though in the newly moralised ways indicated here. Nor can the notion of progress be detached from hatred and fear of Islam, despite Gladstone's disclaimers.[64] 'The Turk' at this time did symbolise in his negation of progress a humanity 'cursed' to 'stagnate in evil'. As Shannon describes the sexual aspects: 'The dishonouring of chastity, the debauching of the conjugal union, and prostitution, undoubtedly touched on the most sensitive of Victorian nerves. And the accounts of the atrocities provided by the newspapers placed before the Victorian public, in unprecedented fullness of detail, thrilling accounts' (as the *Ross Gazette* put it) 'of rapine on a vast scale.'[65] In early 1877 Gladstone condemned the Turks by asserting that one of the first duties of government was the guardianship of the honour and sanctity of the family, and above all of women. The Turkish reputation for pederasty appears to have gained widespread currency from the agitation. The place of 'the harems of the dissolute Turks' in the imagination of the time is amply evident in W. T. Stead himself, who was reported as most affected in the agitation by the thought of outrages upon women 'in the form of his own mother'. Just as the roots of 1879 were in 1876, so too were the roots of Stead's sensational success with the demotic melodrama of 'The Maiden Tribute of Modern Babylon'.[66]

Not so far behind the Turk as moral Other was the Tory. The agitation helped further re-establish popular Liberalism in the counter-image of the Tory. At a Nottingham demonstration in September 1876 one speaker referred to a report that Disraeli had joked about the whole affair. For the speaker, 'Like a flash of lightning over an empty grave it

[63] Shannon, *Gladstone and the Bulgarian Agitation*, p. 30.   [64] *Ibid.*, pp. 30–3.
[65] *Ibid.*, p. 33.   [66] *Ibid.*, pp. 33–5.

suddenly revealed the heathen and hireling character of the man.' He then went into some detail on 'the blood-sucking apparatus of Constantinople', just as in the big Blackheath meeting around the same time speakers had dwelt on the Turk as a 'fiend', capable of 'fiendish barbarities'.[67] The vampire and the 'fiend', the flash of lightning over a grave, all these were directly taken from the melodrama of the time, particularly in its Gothic form, stage and fiction. The heathen, hireling Disraeli is the very opposite of the good, especially the good Gladstone. Much of the Liberal attack at this time, especially Gladstone's, dwelt on how the Tories had displayed lies, cunning and secrecy in keeping the true nature of the atrocities from the public gaze. At the Blackheath meeting Gladstone dwelt on the good press, the *Daily News*, and the bad, Tory, press.

The question of a lying press was closely related to the idea of a properly informed, and hence properly functioning, 'public opinion'. Again one is aware of this dimension of the 'democratic imaginary' of the time, the creation of a 'public' in the sphere of the mass circulation of news and knowledge. What is particularly interesting about the agitation is the association of this idea of an informed public opinion with images of a democracy at last awake, and increasingly empowered. At the Blackheath meeting Gladstone talked of driving that morning through the empty streets of London, being inspired by the knowledge that when the people awoke their earliest thoughts would be of the horrors in a far-off land.[68] It was, said Gladstone, useless to deny the unprecedented power of the agitation. It was not party, not Englishness, not the Christian religion even, which inspired the agitation but the 'greatest and broadest ground of all – the ground of our common humanity'. Here was the true voice of the people as all humanity. And how irresistible was the simplicity of this message; as a leading agitator in the cause put it at the time, 'Our party is just the people, of whatever way of thinking about anything else, who believe in right and wrong.'[69]

---

[67] *The Times*, 11 September 1876. [68] *Ibid.*
[69] Shannon, *Gladstone and the Bulgarian Agitation*, p. 23.

8

Narrating the constitution: the discourse of 'the real' and the fantasies of nineteenth-century constitutional history

JAMES VERNON

I arrived here by accident. When writing *Politics and the People* I stumbled across the now largely forgotten work of nineteenth-century constitutional historians and immediately realised that these were the histories for which I had so long searched in vain.[1] Histories which in speaking the languages of my subjects acknowledged that nineteenth-century politics was in effect a discourse about the historical meanings of the constitution. And so I began to plough my way through the voluminous constitutional histories long since hidden away in the library's store and quickly became fascinated with them as history, as political and literary monuments to their age. Perhaps monument is the wrong word for it implies passivity, permanence and solidity when, as we shall see, this was merely the effect they hoped to convey.

Given the privileged place afforded to the past in debates about the meaning of the constitution, it seemed sensible to explore the treatment of three foundational moments in English constitutional history by three of its founding texts, namely Macaulay's *History of England* (1848–55) on the 'Glorious Revolution' of 1688, Stubbs' *Constitutional History of England* (1873–8) on the Norman Conquest of 1066, and Maitland and Pollock's *The History of English Law* (1895) on Henry II's reforms and the Magna Carta of 1215.[2] Yet, increasingly my concern became less with how these

My thanks to Anthony Easthope, Patrick Joyce, Steve Rigby, Ros Wyatt and the Historiography Reading Group at the Institute of Historical Research for their comments on earlier drafts. Thanks too to those who commented on various versions of this at the Manchester Seminar in Cultural History, November 1993; and the History and Language conference at Warwick University, April 1994.

[1] James Vernon, *Politics and the People. A Study in English Political Culture, c.1815–1868* (Cambridge, 1993).

[2] All quotations from these works are cited in the text, they are taken from the following

texts endeavoured to write the unwritten constitution by interpreting these foundational moments as ones whose meanings were stable, secure and unproblematic, as with the ground upon which they claimed the authority to do so.

The history I wanted to write was not just a history of the political uses of constitutional history, but a history of the politics of the discipline of History itself. A history of how constitutional historians deployed a discourse of 'the real' both to establish the authority of History as an independent academic discipline which could police its epistemological borders against the excursions of 'Literature' and the 'Law', as well as to claim sole and authoritative access to the constitutional past at a time when demands for a redefinition of the constitutional present and future became increasingly shrill. I want to suggest that it was only through constructing a discourse of 'the real' that constitutional historians of the late nineteenth century were able to claim authority not only for History as a discipline but for their interpretations of the constitutional past and present. It was not just alternative conceptions of History that were foreclosed, but definitions of the constitution, and therefore democracy, as well.

This attempt to historicise the discourse of 'the real' in terms of both the politics of knowledge and the popular politics of the late nineteenth century is also in part a critique of those recent defences of the English historiographical tradition – by figures as diverse as Lawrence Stone, Geoffrey Elton, Arthur Marwick and Gertrude Himmelfarb – which have assumed that 'the real' was beyond discourse, that its essentialist categories were universal and ahistorical.[3] Invariably, such defences have taken the form of rather intemperate tirades against a 'postmodernism' whose apparent idealism, relativism and lack of empirical rigour threatens to kill off all that the English historiographical

editions. Lord Macaulay, *The History of England from the Accession of James the Second*, Vol. II (London, 1863); W. Stubbs, *The Constitutional History of England in its Origin and Development* Vol. I (Oxford, 1880); F. W. Maitland and F. Pollock, *The History of English Law before the Time of Edward I*, Vol. I (Cambridge, 1895). In the case of the latter text, I have taken Pollock at his word and assumed that Maitland was the principal author, often referring solely to him in the text. Pollock only wrote the first chapter and Maitland was supposedly anxious to finish the book before he could contribute any more. See Elton, *F. W. Maitland*, p. 50.

3   See Lawrence Stone, 'History and Post-Modernism', *Past and Present*, 131 (May, 1991), pp. 217–18; Gertrude Himmelfarb, 'Telling It As You Like It: Post-Modernist History and the Flight from Fact', *Times Literary Supplement*, 16 October 1992, pp. 12–15; Geoffrey Elton, *A Return to Essentials: Some Reflections on the Present State of Historical Study* (Cambridge, 1992); Arthur Marwick, 'Two Approaches to Historical Study: The Metaphysical (Including "Postmodernism") and the Historical', *Journal of Contemporary History*, 30, 1 (1995), pp. 5–36. A more thoughtful critique is provided in Joyce Appleby, Lynn Hunt and Margaret Jacob's *Telling the Truth About History* (London, 1994).

tradition has held most dear. Not only, as we shall see, are these anxieties largely unfounded but they rest upon the complacent assumption that historians alone do not need to historicise the categories within which they work – they alone are above history.[4]

I

So I want to suggest that these three histories by Macaulay, Stubbs and Maitland came to represent the founding texts of not just constitutional history, but the English historiographical tradition itself. The question is not whether these texts deserve such exalted status, but why they have been taken to represent a canon of English history – not that there is only one English historiographical tradition, with one omnipotent canon. And yet, as far as we know, constitutional history remained at the core of the curriculum in both schools and universities up to 1914, and possibly even 1945 – after all to many the Second World War was the finest hour in England's defence of constitutional liberty.[5] Arguably, it was even as late as the 1950s and 1960s when the empire struck back and Westminster ceased to be the mother of all parliaments, that the constitutional narrative of English history lost its resonance – the story of progress shifting to the growth of the welfare state and the forward march of labour for which historiographical traditions were hastily constructed around figures such as Toynbee, Power, Cole, Clapham and the Hammonds.[6]

The canonical status of Macaulay, Stubbs and Maitland is strikingly

---

[4] The works which I have found useful, and yet which are the object of such attacks, include Roland Barthes, 'The Discourse of History', and 'The Reality Effect', in his *The Rustle of Language* (London, 1986); Hayden White, *The Content of the Form: Narrative Discourse and Historical Representation* (Baltimore, 1989); Michel de Certeau, 'History: Science and Fiction', in his *Heterologies: The Discourse on the Other* (Minneapolis, 1986); Mark Cousins, 'The Practice of Historical Investigation', in D. Attridge *et al.* (eds.), *Post-Structuralism and the Question of History* (Cambridge, 1987), pp. 127–38; Joan Scott, 'The Evidence of Experience', *Critical Inquiry*, 17 (1991), pp. 773–97; Anthony Easthope 'Post-Modernism and the Historians: Romancing the Stone', *Social History*, 18, 2 (May 1993), pp. 235–49.

[5] Valerie E. Chancellor, *History for Their Masters: Opinion in the English History Textbook, 1800– 1914* (Bath, 1914); Peter Slee, *Learning and a Liberal Education: The Study of Modern History in the Universities of Oxford, Cambridge and Manchester, 1800–1914* (Manchester, 1986), chapters 5–7; Raphael Samuel, 'Continuous National History', in his edited collection *Patriotism: The Making and Unmaking of British National Identity. Vol. I. History and Politics* (London, 1989), pp. 9–17; J. A. Mangan (ed.), *The Imperial Curriculum* (London, 1993); Reba N. Soffer, *Discipline and Power: The University, History and the Making of an English Elite* (London, 1994).

[6] The history of social and economic history is only just beginning to be written; see Maxine Berg, 'The First Women Economic Historians', *Economic History Review*, 45, 2 (1992), pp. 308–29; Alon Kadish, *Historians, Economists and Economic History* (London, 1989); D. C. Coleman, *History and the Economic Past* (Oxford, 1987); David Cannadine, 'The Present and the Past in the English Industrial Revolution, 1880–1980', *Past and Present*, 103, 2 (1984), pp. 131–72.

apparent from two bibliographical guides to constitutional history published in 1929 and 1958 by that pillar of the English historical establishment the Historical Association. Intended for teachers and students respectively, these bibliographies can be taken to represent the *doxa* of English historiography. The first of these, Cam and Turberville's *Bibliography of Constitutional History*, rated Maitland's *Constitutional History* as the 'best textbook covering the whole period', while *The History of English Law* was deemed 'simply invaluable'.[7] Although his stock was beginning to fall, Stubbs too was still something of a colossus, his *Constitutional History of England* valued as 'indispensable' because although it was 'limited to some extent in interpretation by a nineteenth century outlook, its scholarly character makes it a safe guide to the facts'.[8] Macaulay was conspicuous by his absence, no doubt his literary imagination made him a decidedly unsafe guide to the facts.[9] Thirty years later little had changed. Chrimes and Roots' *English Constitutional History: A Select Bibliography* still eulogised both Maitland and Pollock's *The History of the English Law* and Stubbs' *Constitutional History* as 'the classic work', although sounding a cautionary note against the latter 'on matters of interpretation'.[10] Again Macaulay was excluded from the canon.

These reputations have remained remarkably unscathed. Only Maitland is still held up as a historian proper: recently revered for his scholarship by that patron saint of English empiricism Geoffrey Elton, and described by Norman Cantor as being 'in a class by himself – the standard by which others are judged'.[11] Ironically for those portrayed as great Whigs, Stubbs and Macaulay are now seen merely as staging posts in the development of 'history proper' Maitland style. Some even deny Macaulay that spurious honour, relegating his work from 'History' to 'Literature'.[12] Unable to qualify as proper historians Stubbs and Macaulay have most recently been held up as representatives of, if not active agents in, the great mythical story that was the Whig intellectual tradition.[13] Despite the subtlety of Burrows, his work often typifies that

---

[7] H. M. Cam and A. S. Turberville, *Bibliography of English Constitutional History: Historical Association Pamphlets. General Series* 75 (London, 1929), pp. 3 and 5.

[8] *Ibid.*, p. 4.   [9] *Ibid.*, p. 7.

[10] S. B. Chrimes and I. A. Roots, *English Constitutional History: A Select Bibliography. Helps for Students of History* 58 (London, 1958), pp. 6, 7 and 27. They thought Maitland's *Memoranda de Parliamento* the 'basis of most modern work on parliamentary history', p. 26.

[11] G. R. Elton, *F. W. Maitland* (London, 1985). Norman F. Cantor, *Inventing the Middle Ages* (London, 1991), p. 50. Of the three texts, Maitland and Pollocks's *History of the English Law* has best retained its popularity having been regularly reprinted in 1911, 1923, 1952 and 1968.

[12] John Hale, *The Evolution of British Historiography* (London, 1967).

[13] J. W. Burrow, *A Liberal Descent: Victorian Historians and the English Past* (Cambridge, 1981);

peculiarly English (or Cambridge) version of the history of ideas, with its concern for tracing the development of intellectual continuities and coherence, approaching the work of Macaulay, Stubbs and Maitland as reflections of wider intellectual and social contexts. Such an approach – which elsewhere I have argued has dominated the reception of 'the linguistic turn' in Britain, especially within political history[14] – remains trapped within the essentialist prison-house of the English historiographical tradition. Instead of historicising that tradition, it invariably reproduces its realist tropes and categories.

In contrast, a growing body of work on French (romantic) historiography has shown that if we concentrate upon the literary not the intellectual history of such histories it is possible to analyse the ways they work as texts; how they struggle to secure the boundaries of 'History' and 'the real' in order to convey authority and mastery to reading publics they were themselves constructing.[15] Here primacy is afforded to the text itself, to its internal contradictions and tensions, and the desire to resolve them rhetorically. This essay hopes to build upon this work by using the lens of literary history to explore the fantasies of nineteenth-century constitutional history for definitions of the constitution and of History as a discipline that were stable, secure and authoritative.

II

I want to start then at the end by examining how the invention of a discourse of 'the real' allowed historians from Stubbs and Maitland forwards to dismiss Macaulay as too literary to be a historian proper. To do so we must turn this discourse of 'the real' back upon itself, going backwards from its triumphal ascendancy in Maitland's work, through Stubbs' *Constitutional History*, to its troubled presence in Macaulay's *History*. I want to suggest that Macaulay's text can be read as a meditation on the nature of historical knowledge, a meditation whose anxieties about the relationship between 'the real' and the represented

P. B. M. Blaas, *Continuity and Anachronism: Parliamentary and Constitutional Development in Whig Historiography and in the Anti-Whig Reaction between 1890 and 1930* (The Hague, 1978).

[14] James Vernon, ' "Who's Afraid of 'the Linguistic Turn'?" The Politics of Social History and its Discontents', *Social History*, 19, 1 (1994), pp. 81–97.

[15] Hayden White, *Metahistory: The Historical Imagination in Nineteenth Century Europe* (New York, 1973); Stephen Bann, *The Clothing of Clio: A Study of the Representation of History in Nineteenth Century Britain and France* (Cambridge, 1984); Lionel Gossman, *Between History and Literature* (Cambridge, MA, 1990); Linda Orr, *Headless History: Nineteenth Century French Historiography of the Revolution* (Ithaca, 1990); Anne Rigney, *The Rhetoric of Historical Representation: Three Narrative Histories of the French Revolution* (Cambridge, 1990); Stephen Bann, *The Inventions of History: Essays on the Representation of the Past* (Manchester, 1990).

were largely disguised, repressed and edited out of the work of Stubbs and Maitland. In this way Macaulay can be used as a critique of history proper Maitland style, reminding us of what historians have ever since tried so assiduously to forget – the fragility of the discourse of 'the real' and the blurring of all its essential(ist) oppositions between history and literature, fact and fiction, context and text.

Thankfully, it is not difficult to recognise Maitland's use of this discourse of 'the real' for it was endlessly proclaiming its own authority and originality. Ironically, the more modestly these claims were made, the greater authority they incurred. Maitland made skilful use of this double discourse, dressing his ambitious claims for a new constitutional history in the language of professional respect for his predecessors and, in the process, doing much to create a code of honour for the new breed of professional historians.[16] Yet for Maitland, his constitutional history was the most real yet, not only because it represented an epistemological break from previous histories, but because it came at the subject from a new angle – the history of law. Indeed, his history defined itself against the abstractions of legal science and the politics of traditional constitutional history. It was solid, tangible and real, based on fact, experience and practice. In his own words, 'Law, such as we know it in the conduct of life, is matter of fact ... a thing perceived in many ways of practical experience' (p. xxv). It was this very desire to ground his account in 'the real' legal past of practice and effect that, for Maitland, made *The History of English Law* so original. It is the solidity of this historical experience of the law which defined the 'scientific frontier' of this new history, something which the ever expanding 'field' of constitutional history lacked. Although paying professional homage to the 'degree of accuracy and completion which constitutional history has attained in the hands of Dr Stubbs', there is a reassertion that 'we have kept clear of the territory over which they [constitutional historians] exercise an effective dominion' (p. xxxvi).

These images of 'fields', 'territories', 'dominions' and 'frontiers' recur again and again. It is as if Maitland saw himself, standing proxy for the figure of the professional historian, as part imperial explorer part detective; an Indiana Jones endlessly travelling across the subject in pursuit of 'the real' Temple of History – the very notion of a journey, a quest or a crime, implying that there was a destination, a goal, a just solution. One does not have to envisage a sweating, muscular, unshaven

---

[16] For an American parallel see Peter Novick, *That Noble Dream: The 'Objectivity Question' and the American Historical Profession* (Cambridge, 1988), pp. 58–60; Savoie Lottinville, *The Rhetoric of History* (Norman, 1990), esp chapter 8.

Harrison Ford cannily avoiding the cave's traps, securing its sacred
relic, before escaping a chasing horde of savages, to recognise the
masculine and imperial connotations of Maitland's quest. The preface
apologetically presents the text

well knowing that in many parts of our field we have accomplished, at most, a
preliminary exploration. Oftentimes our business has been rather to quarry and
hew for some builder of the future to leave a finished building. But we have
endeavoured to make sure, so far as our will and power can go, that when his
day comes he shall have facts and not fictions to build with.   (p. vi)

Only occasionally, alongside the confident predictions of discovery –
'We shall find … we find … we expect to find .. we expect to find … we
expect to find' (p. xxiv) – on a shared professional journey – 'the ground
we traverse has lately been occupied by' (p. xxxvii) – towards as yet
uncharted territories – 'Here, again, a remoter field of inquiry lies open,
on which we do not adventure ourselves …' (p. xxxiii) – are there
intimations of getting lost, of 'the real' being unattainable, of a journey
without end.[17]

The anxiety of falling into such an epistemological abyss was
continually offset by testing the solidity of the ground step by step for
what Maitland called the 'solid ground of known history' (p. xxx). No
historian had ever displayed such methodological rigour, had paid so
much attention to the 'materials' upon which his text 'stood', the
'sources of first hand knowledge' (p. xxxv). *The History of English Law* was
perhaps the first historiographical text to boast an exhaustively detailed
'List of Texts Used', although Geoffrey Elton is convinced that this
merely represented an edited version of publicly printed records available to all, not the mass of manuscripts he had consulted in the Public
Record Office[18] – a point which suggests that any attempt to historicise
the discourse of 'the real' must examine the role of the state in creating
a national (and imperial) archive. From the mid nineteenth century the
state began to publish parts of its archive in the form of the Rolls Series,
as well as training archivists at the Public Record Office and the British
Museum to catalogue the proliferating mass of information collected
by civil servants in order to govern at home and abroad.[19] It was a

---

[17] See, for example, the frequent laments for the lack of documentary evidence, p. 136 and
     p. 137.
[18] Elton, *F. W. Maitland*, p. 26.
[19] On the British Museum as imperial archive see Thomas Richards, *The Imperial Archive:
     Knowledge and the Fantasy of Empire* (London, 1993). On the Public Record Office, Rolls Series
     and private printing clubs see Slee, *Learning and a Liberal Education*, pp. 131–3; Phillipa
     Levine, *The Amateur and the Professional* (Cambridge, 1988), pp. 75–87.

project replicated privately with the emergence of a number of record societies and printing clubs committed to preserving, cataloguing and publishing local archives. As President of one such body, the Selden Society, Maitland was himself one of the leading publishers of archival documents. The development of the archive was arguably critical to the gradual dependence of the English historical tradition to the discourse of 'the real' from the mid-nineteenth century.

At this stage it is often objected that like Don Quixote I have set my sights on an imaginary target, that the realist discourse of English historiography is a straw man, that Maitland's contribution was precisely to make historians aware of the fallibility of their sources, their own subjectivity and the provisional nature of all historical knowledge and truth-claims.[20] Certainly, Maitland's extensive footnotes (itself an innovatory feature of his work) often cast doubt on the reliability of the sources he deploys, describing them as 'tales' or 'stories' before assuring us that 'they may be accepted as symbolically if not literally true' (pp. xxxii, 138, 145).[21] More usually his notes contain long Latin transcriptions followed by precise references in order to justify assertions, qualify doubts or anticipate objections. Maitland believed that he could self-consciously play one source against another, or even one source against itself, to make them correspond more closely to the reality of the past. The epistemological problem he denies is that archival sources are themselves discursive representations and that in using them historians call upon their own narrative strategies to endow them with significance and authority. As Roland Barthes reminded us thirty years ago, it is this

paradox which governs the entire pertinence of historical discourse ... fact never has any but a linguistic existence, yet everything happens as if this linguistic existence was merely a pure and simple 'copy' of *another* existence, situated in an extra-structural field, the 'real'. This type of discourse is surely the only one in which the target referent is envisaged as lying outside of discourse at the same time as it is impossible to reach it except through discourse.[22]

So if 'the real' can only be known through discourse there is no position from which we can assess how clearly that representation corresponds to 'the real' – except a transcendental one that not even Maitland, Elton or

---

[20] See n. 2.

[21] On the development of the footnote in western European historiography see Bann, *The Clothing of Clio*, pp. 32–53.

[22] Roland Barthes, 'The Discourse of History', reprinted in his *The Rustle of Language* (New York, 1986), p. 138.

Lawrence Stone can claim (yet). It is then no imaginary windmill I have in my sights, but a realist discourse that Maitland helped construct and which has ever since dominated the English historiographical tradition.

Maitland's fantasy was then that, if used properly, the archive could speak for itself. The irony was that in order to gain greater authority Maitland had to lose his authorial self, to project himself as a ventriloquist dummy speaking on behalf of History which wrote herself. There are few signs of Maitland (and Pollock) the author(s) outside of the Preface in which they fleetingly acknowledge their presence in a brief discussion of authorial intent, as for instance when they define the way 'we are to speak in this book ... we ought perhaps to say here that in our opinion ...' (p. xxviii). Yet, increasingly, the subjective pronouns 'we' and 'our' seem to merge the authors with their objects, the reading audience and English medieval law. We, the audience, are continually invited to trace our own history in such habitually repeated phrases as 'as we shall see' (p. xvii), 'our English medieval law' (p. xxix), 'our laws' (p. xxx), 'our record' (p. xxxi) and so on. Later, I make much of this merging of the figure of the historian with his reading public, but for the time being I want to pay particular attention to the way Maitland sacrificed his authorial ego on the altar of his other object – the archive as the source of 'the real'.

Few historians have identified themselves so closely with their sources. At times he appears to lose any sense of the alterity of the past, praising those sources which most resemble his own *History*. FitzNeal's 'Dialogue' is commended because, like Maitland, 'He will not deal in generalities, he will condescend to minute details' (p. 161), just as Glanvill's *Tractatus de Legibus* is praised because 'He writes not as a statesmen, but as a lawyer ... he is not ashamed to confess that he raises more questions than he can answer' (p. 164). In letting the sources speak for themselves Maitland also (con)fused himself with the characters he portrayed. As Henry II receives nothing but praise it is not long before one suspects Maitland wants to be Henry, or for Henry to be Maitland, especially when the strength of his rule owed much to the fact that he 'was at heart a lawyer, quite competent to criticize minutely the wording of a charter, to frame a new clause and give his vice-chancellor a lesson in conveyancing; quite willing on the other hand to confess that there were problems that he could not solve' (p. 159). Behold the lawyer-cum-historian as king! No wonder then that, like Maitland's discourse of 'the real', the 'system created by Henry II was so strong that it would do its work though the king was an absentee' (p. 169).

The authority gained by losing himself in the object of his History, was accentuated by his repeatedly modest claim that mastery escaped him; that, like Glanvill and Henry II, there were questions he could not answer, problems he could not solve. Elsewhere the text is anxious to resolve itself in a masterful closure. Even in the Introduction we are given sinister warnings of the consequences of failing to achieve closure, that 'confusion is natural and may be dangerous' and 'certainty is of more importance than perfection' (pp. xxv and xxvi). And then we are bombarded with the resolute language of certainty: there is 'no doubt' about the 'actual result of facts of human nature and history' (p. xxiii), 'effects' can 'hardly be disputed', they are 'evident', 'clear', 'certain'. If Maitland doubted his ability to master the past there are no signs of it in the text which radiates a cool confidence in its ability to reach an unproblematic closure, one superior to the falsity of previous attempts at closure. Throughout the text he shadow-boxes with other (frequently nameless) historians, assuming that his audience will have prior knowledge. This is professional history written for professional historians. And there is something very English about the way Maitland avoids putting names to discredited arguments and kicking colleagues when they're down. But it is his dogged desire to have the last word, to account for every argument, to master the past through the discipline of archival research, that makes him most English. For the discourse of 'the real' entailed a denial of desire, a denial of ambiguity and doubt, a denial of the self and a denial of the pleasures of the past and its alterity.[23]

The genealogy of much of this can be found in Stubbs' *Constitutional History*. Remorselessly the chapters follow their chronological logic: each with its own introduction, a middle of progressively numbered sections in which each proposition is carefully demonstrated by archival sources, and a conclusion – the book itself ending with mathematical precision at section 500. Stubbs appears happier than Maitland to acknowledge his desire for closure, which he felt 'must be familiar to all who have approached the study of history with a real desire to understand it, but which are apt to strike the writer more forcibly at the end than at the beginning of his work' (p. 665). He believed his 'end will have been gained if he has succeeded in helping to train the judgement of his readers to discern the balance of truth and reality, and ... to rest content with nothing less than the attainable maximum of truth' (p. 668). Like Maitland he dealt in the certainty of 'the real', the belief that history 'is evident' (p. 319), 'clear' (p. 9), with a 'logical result' (p. 4),

---

[23] A point taken from Easthope 'Post-Modernism and the Historians'. See also his *British Post-Structuralism: Since 1968* (London, 1988), pp. 199–206.

so that 'It is impossible to avoid the conclusion' (p. 302) that 'no truth is more certain than this' (p. 667) and so on *ad infinitum*. The discourse of 'the real' was by no means Maitland's invention. Stubbs' belief in the 'recorded fact of history' (p. 2) was no less trenchant; facts were real, they were the 'evidence' (p. 284), 'the chain of proof' (p. 12) which wrote History for herself. Hence the recurring fear that 'we have very little information' (p. 283), 'equally scanty evidence' and a 'lack of documentary materials of proof' (p. 284).

As with Maitland, it was crucial for Stubbs that his authorial self did not come between the sources and his text and so he invented a narrator which he then referred to in the third person as 'the writer' (p. 665) and 'the author' (p. 668). This narrator then merges with the audience, invoking the shared project of 'our task' (p. 1), 'our subject', 'our Constitutional History' (p. 665); they become we, so that 'we have seen' (p. 304), 'we are told' (p. 305), 'We are not without a few good illustrations' (p. 315). In this progressive denial the authorial I is repressed behind the narrator who in turn suppresses himself on behalf of the object – the English reading public(s). As we shall see later, it was a denial born of a fantasy to make this object real, to embody the pure racial essence of Englishness.

Macaulay's desires ran no less deep despite his more troubled relationship with the discourse of 'the real'. There is none of the authoritative confidence displayed by Maitland and Stubbs in the *History of England*. Although he seems to believe in the reality of the past, promising in chapter 1 to 'recount' (p. 1), 'trace' (pp. 1, 3), 'relate' (pp. 1, 2, 3), and 'faithfully to record' it, providing nothing less than a 'true picture' (p. 3), the very notion of a picture raises the troubling spectre of representation, as do his other promises 'to write' (p. 1), to 'describe', 'portray' and 'sketch' that past (p. 3). With such a tension between 'the real' and the represented, Macaulay is left timidly pondering 'unless I greatly deceive myself, the general effect of this chequered narrative ...' (p. 2). In this context the presence of the authorial self could hardly be more significant. Unlike Maitland and Stubbs, Macaulay freely acknowledges his authorial presence, his very first four sentences beginning 'I purpose to write ... I shall recount ... I shall trace ... I shall relate'; although later on Macaulay also fuses his authorial self with the object of its narrative – the English people. It is this continual tension between 'the real' and the represented, the subject and the object, which is at the centre of Macaulay's *History*. The whole text is a rhetorical struggle to make the *History* real.

Such a reading helps explain the centrality of metaphors of visibility in the text. These metaphors seem to suggest that sight is a more reliable form of representation than language, that meaning is transparent and clear, that 'the real' is visible. Wandering through Wapping a scrivener, recognised, despite his disguise, the fleeing Judge Jeffries who had once so terrified him: 'he saw a well known face looking out of the window ... he could not be deceived ... there was no mistaking the savage eye' (p. 564). Sight could reveal all, it was dependable and real. It followed then that, like Judge Jeffreys, those fleeing from reality were disguised, hidden, 'blind to the obvious truth' (p. 633) like the 'blindness of a nation deluded' (p. 596). As the possibility of disguise suggested the duplicity of sight, that appearances could be deceptive, the convention of unveiling became crucial to reassert the visibility of 'the real'. Perth, James' Scottish Catholic Chancellor, may have escaped disguised as a woman but he is recognised and 'stripped' on his capture (p. 611). Priests who had hidden themselves 'in vaults and cocklofts ... came forth from their lurking places' (p. 579). The general revulsion at the 'girlish delight' displayed by Mary on her 'first appearance' back in London after the fall of her father, is revealed as 'a part' William had asked her to play, one that because it was 'uncongenial to her feelings, she had overacted' (p. 660). All is restored to normal, 'the real' is once more made visible and by unveiling it in this way it became more real.

Just as visibility had to be revealed as deceptive before it was made real, so for Macaulay language was a double bind, both real and imaginary, transparent and opaque. It was transparent and real when it entailed a sense of conviction, purpose and action, when words became deeds. So 'a few words of menace from William's lips generally meant something' (p. 578), just as when 'the nation, speaking through its representatives, demanded' (p. 657), or he who protested 'dared to raise his voice against the government' (p. 663). Typically, it was not until William and Mary were proclaimed 'in a loud voice' that they actually became king and queen. But alas words became opaque when they were 'preached' and 'harangued' in 'wild talk' (p. 572), they could be put into people's mouths (p. 661–2n.), and could become 'inexact and confused' (p. 631).

Despite the unreliability of language, Macaulay recognised that it was the source of power. The language of the constitution was then 'a question not merely verbal, but of grave practical importance' (p. 652) and because the 'constitution had begun to exist in times when statesmen were not much accustomed to frame exact definitions' (p. 655) its language was dangerously ambiguous. For Macaulay, the *History* represented an attempt 'to assert the rights of the people in such language as should terminate all controversy' (p. 665), 'to clear the fundamental laws of the realm from ambiguity' (p. 666).

Macaulay's double bind was that his *History* could only resolve the historic political conflict over the meaning of the constitution through language. His attempt to escape this conundrum, to get out of language, was to consider the language of the constitution, like his own text, 'not as words, but as deeds' (p. 631). In trying to escape the ambiguities of language as representation, Macaulay acknowledged the problematic nature of his conception of language as practice, and the tensions it created within his text between 'the real' and the represented, fact and fiction, history and literature. It is a text of two stories, each struggling against the other. In trying to enable the constitution, like his own text, escape the prison house of language and become real as a political act, he remained dependent on it. And ironically, it was precisely Macaulay's genius with language which made his *History* so real to its reading public and yet so fictional to subsequent historians.

III

In the rest of this essay I want to suggest that the politics of constructing historical knowledge upon the discourse of 'the real' was intricately linked to anxieties about constitutional reform in late Victorian England. For the discourse of 'the real' could not simply be legitimated by its own rhetorical strategies, it had to make sense and be meaningful to the audience it had itself constructed, it had to endow both author and reading public with a sense of agency and purpose. The difficulty was that different audiences were being constructed and appealed to. On the one hand, Stubbs and Maitland sought to create and empower an audience of professional historians, while simultaneously, like Macaulay, invoking the imaginary and slippery category of 'the people' to legitimate their definitions of the constitution and its History.

What I am trying to suggest here, is that to understand the fantasies of these texts to secure and fix the meaning of the constitution and History we must look beyond them to their institutional and political contexts, as if anyone had ever denied it. Who better to make this point than Jacques Derrida, wearily insisting in *Limited Inc.* that

the concept of text or of context which guides me embraces and does not exclude the world, reality, history. Once again (and this probably makes a thousand times I have had to repeat this, but when will it finally be heard, and why this resistance?): as I understand it ... the text is not the book, it is not confined in a volume itself confined to the library. It does not suspend reference – to history, to the world, to reality, to being.[24]

In what follows I draw upon this radically different formulation of the relationship between text and context, acknowledging how contexts are themselves textualised instead of the usual insistence that texts are always in the last instance determined by their contexts.

We have already seen how Maitland and Stubbs used the discourse of 'the real' to exorcise the epistemological doubts raised by the spectre of History as a literary form of representation. Equally important was the way in which the discourse of 'the real' enabled them to distance the discipline they sought to define from the study of law, especially the voguish practice of legal science. Although Stubbs was the first to be appointed Regius Professor of Modern History at Oxford in 1866, he spent six years in the joint School of Law and History under the shadow of the long-established discipline of the Law. Published in 1873, a year after the creation of an independent School of History at Oxford, and two years before the same event at Cambridge, the first volume of Stubbs' *Constitutional History* reads very much like a declaration of intellectual and professional independence.[25] It is difficult to convey the vehemence of the text's tirade against lawyers and their use of ahistoric, universal principles be it 'the absolutist tendencies' of Roman law or Benthamite constitutional systems, from both of which English history had mercifully been 'spared from the curse' (pp. 11 and 6). And yet, Bishop Stubbs, the self-appointed high priest of History, was not adverse to appropriating the language of the Law to reinforce the authority of History's use of discourse of 'the real'. He liked to imagine the historian as lawyer, one committed to 'a judicial examination of [history's] evidences, a fair and equitable estimate of the rights and wrongs of policy, dynasty, and party' that assures that 'the truth, the whole truth and nothing but the truth, is what history would extract from her witnesses: the truth which leaves no pitfalls for unwary advocates, and which is the fairest measure of equity to all' (p. 666). It was a canny discursive move, turning the authority of the law back upon itself.

True to form though it was not long before the legal profession contested such claims. David Sugarman has suggested that A. V. Dicey's invention of legal science in the snappily titled *Introduction to the Study of the Law of the Constitution* (1885), must be understood in part as a

[24] Jacques Derrida, *Limited Inc.* (Evanston, IL, 1988), p. 137.
[25] Burrows, *A Liberal Descent*, pp. 133 ff.

response to Stubbs, a refusal to let History take the intellectual and institutional initiative.[26] It too was the manifesto of a man only recently awarded the Vinerian Chair in Law at Oxford in 1882. Distrusting History's new-found discourse of 'the real' with its fetishism for facts and antiquarian obsession with medieval history, Dicey wanted to modernise English constitutional law by creating a system of constitutional principles based on logic rather than historical accident. Viewed from this angle '*The Law of the Constitution* [represented] an attempt to reduce Britain's unwritten constitution to a partially written code', to enshrine the meaning of the constitution in a set of legal principles that only lawyers could dispute.[27]

It was a project which merely reaffirmed the worst fears of historians. Maitland, picking up the baton from Stubbs, began *The History of English Law* by railing against the abstract theories of 'the dogmatic science of law'. 'The matter of legal science is not an ideal result of ethical or political analysis; it is the actual result of the facts of human nature and history' (p. xxiii). Events not ideas, 'the real' not the abstract, the particular not the universal, change not continuity, these were a few of historians' favourite things. Worse still, Maitland, the Downing Professor of the Laws of England at Cambridge from 1888, the lawyer-turned-historian (he was offered the Regius chair of history on Acton's death in 1902), mocked Dicey's legal science for its self-congratulatory Whiggish celebration of legal professionalism. Whereas legal science was elitist and addressed lawyers alone, his history of the law was concerned with the 'whole body of citizens' (p. xxvii). In this contest History, if not the constitution itself, was the people's own – although, as we shall see, this raises the question as to who Maitland considered to be 'the people' or the 'whole body of citizens'.

It is a question that can only be answered by reading these texts as attempts to provide definitive definitions of the constitution and its history, to reinvent society's systems of authority in a rapidly changing world. A world which for many teetered on the edge of a democratic abyss following the revolutionary scares of 1848, the electoral reforms of 1867 and 1884, the gathering storm-clouds in Ireland, and the declara-

[26] David Sugarman, 'The Legal Boundaries of Liberty: Dicey, Liberalism and Legal Science', *The Modern Law Review*, 46 (January 1983), pp. 102–11. See also Richard A. Cosgrove, *The Rule of Law: Albert Venn Dicey, Victorian Jurist* (London, 1980).

[27] Sugarman, 'The Legal Boudaries of Liberty', p. 110. The crisis of Dicey's 'rule of law' in the early twentieth century is well contextualised by Ian Christopher Fletcher, '"This Zeal for Lawlessness": A. V. Dicey, *The Law of the Constitution*, and the Challenge of Popular Politics, 1885–1915' *Parliamentary History* (forthcoming).

tion of a sex war by militant suffragettes.[28] It was not just that constitutional historians like Maitland had to make sense of a constitution which, because it was unwritten and constantly changed by reform, appeared increasingly fragile, but that, in doing so, they defined who belonged to the political nation and what their rights and duties as citizens were. The intriguing thing is how Macaulay, Stubbs and Maitland all appealed to the very category of 'the people' they had themselves constructed to legitimate not only their interpretation of the constitution but History itself. As Linda Orr has noted of French romantic historiography, the category of 'the people' works as both metaphor and social referent, it

circulates in and out of social class, professional and political groups, in and out of official or unofficial power, both the innermost self and common whole. It gives justification and identity to all of the above, without shape or name. But everything in which it circulates, contradictory and warring, gives it back the effect of a most physical shape, something thick and consistent, with adamant desires and a will.[29]

IV

In the revolutionary aftermath of 1848, the fantasy of Macaulay's *History of England* was to preserve England's unique political and social stability by reinventing the agency and authority of Whig politics:

It is because we had a preserving revolution in the seventeenth century that we have not had a destroying revolution in the nineteenth. It is because we had freedom in the midst of servitude that we have order in the midst of anarchy. For the authority of law, for the security of property, for the peace of our streets, for the happiness of our homes, our gratitude is due under Him who raises and pulls down nations at his pleasure, to the Long Parliament, to the Convention and to William of Orange.   (p. 671)

This desire for freedom, order, authority, security, peace, happiness and divine guidance oozes out of every paragraph urging us to be vigilant, to do our duty and protect England's utopian Protestant liberty from sliding into the hell of continental anarchy. For although some people are like William of Orange – reasonable, ordered, Protestant and a lover of liberty – others are like the Stuart King James

---

[28] For some interesting parallels see C. Harvie, *The Lights of Liberalism: University Liberals and the Challenge of Democracy 1860–1886* (London, 1976); C. Kent, *Brains and Numbers: Elitism, Comtism and Democracy in Mid-Victorian England* (London, 1978).

[29] Orr, *Headless History*, p. 16.

– passionate, undisciplined, Catholic and tyrannical. The whole text is consumed by the continual tension between these oppositions.

Ironically, to preserve order and liberty the text evokes images of bondage and force, and it is only when these are released that the destructive and passionate forces of tyranny threaten. (This inversion in which bondage secures liberty, and liberty ensures tyranny is also echoed in the struggle between 'the real' and the imaginary; there bondage secures 'the real' and release unshackles the imaginary.) Metaphors of bondage and release dominate the opening pages where things are 'secured' and 'bound', there are 'encroachments', 'abuses', 'interference', 'dependencies' and 'ties' are broken by 'domination', 'strength' and 'greatness' which in turn allow the freedom of release when all is done 'faithfully', 'justly' and 'effectually'. The danger of such abandon is immediately apparent as it gives way to 'disaster', 'crimes and follies', 'evils' and 'just retribution'. To restrain the destructive forces of such undisciplined passion and freedom one needed a 'system' (p. 608), the 'machine of government' (p. 598, p. 657), which holds together 'the whole vast fabric of society' (p. 664) and secures 'the very foundations of our polity' (p. 641). This mechanical system had to be 'strictly obeyed' (p. 555) so that the 'restraints of discipline' (p. 555) could 'preserve order' or 'restore order and security' (p. 568), 'reassembling' society and 'bringing it into order' (p. 569).

In the shadow of 1848, Macaulay's fantasy was to be William of Orange who, during the revolutionary crisis of 1688, on finding the 'whole machine of government was disordered', quickly 'addressed himself with vigour to the work of restoring order' (p. 598) and the 'general sense of security' (p. 599). How quickly consensus returned in William's England: all of a sudden there were 'scarcely any contests' (p. 608), 'little difference of opinion' (p. 612). Where discord appeared it was the fault of a 'hateful' and 'very small faction' of 'bigots' with 'extreme opinions' who, bearing an uncanny resemblance to the Chartists, 'were generally held in abhorrence' by the 'great majority of the nation' (p. 613). In parliament resolutions were passed without 'one dissentient voice', 'adopted with scarcely any debate, and without a division' (p. 640), for they recognised that 'any government [was] better than no government' (p. 653), unlike the French who were always 'impatient to demolish and unable to construct' (p. 663). Both in 1688 and 1848, it was English discipline and restraint which had prevented the nation having 'risen up in some moment of wild excitement against our masters' (p. 666) and rushed 'wildly from extreme to extreme' as so much of revolutionary Europe had in 1848. There was nothing wild about the English, they had been disciplined enough to recognise that it was 'necessary to sacrifice even liberty in order to save civilisation' and that by maintaining 'the regular course of government ... we never lost what others are wildly and blindly seeking to regain' (p. 670).

Who then were 'the people' Macaulay credited with having maintained English order and liberty in 1688, and on whose shoulders should the constitution rest after 1848? One thing was for sure, they were men. The manliness of James and his supporters was repeatedly questioned, they were too emotional with their 'womanish tremors and childish fancies' (p. 593). Perth was even captured trying to escape dressed as a woman and was metaphorically raped for his pains, being 'stripped, hustled and plundered. Bayonets were held to his breast. Begging for life with unmanly cries' (p. 611). In contrast the forces of order 'joined like one man to resist the dictation of the mob of the capital' (p. 646), led as they were by William, a man's man, who would 'not submit to be tied to the apron strings even of the best of wives' (p. 650). These real men were also Londoners. All roads in *The History* lead to London. William's triumphal journey from Torbay to the centre of power in London is mirrored by James' flight from the centre to the periphery. London, we are assured, was the 'stronghold of Protestantism and Whiggism' (p. 580), the centre of the 'public mind' (p. 613).

Masculine and metropolitan, the political nation consisted of English statesmen and those Whig 'politicians' who manned London's 'coffee-houses ... presses ... pamphlets ... [and] ... parties' (p. 613). These 'enlightened statesmen' are the heroes of Macaulay's text, they sat in the House of Commons 'as orators and as munificent patrons of genius and learning' (p. 625), using their qualities of 'descent, fortune, knowledge, experience, eloquence' (p. 626). Only occasionally were publics beyond Westminster included in this 'folklore of the governing classes',[30] and only then when the requisite qualities of restraint and order were demonstrated. So that

It is honourable to the English character that, notwithstanding the aversion with which the Roman Catholic religion and the Irish race were then regarded, notwithstanding the anarchy which was the effect of the flight of James, notwithstanding the artful machinations which were employed to scare the multitude into cruelty, no atrocious crime was perpetrated at this conjuncture ... The mob showed no inclination to blood, except in the case of Jeffreys; and the hatred which that bad man inspired had more affinity with humanity than with cruelty. (pp. 567–8)

[30] Burrows, *A Liberal Descent*, p. 90.

Nonetheless, it is typical that even those in pursuit of the legitimate target that was Jeffreys were characterised as 'the mob'. Macaulay was terrified by how quickly the 'great multitude' (p. 567) or 'the common people' (578) could lose their self-discipline and become the 'rabble' or 'mob of the capital' holding their 'unlawful assemblies' 'without the walls of Parliament' (p. 645). Just as in 1688, it was the rabble that was the enemy within for Macaulay, that Other England of 'drunkards', 'prostitutes', 'housebreakers and highwaymen, cutpurses and ringdrop-pers', 'idle apprentices' (p. 560), 'plunderers', 'marauders' (p. 561) – the 'lawless part of the population', the dangerous fluid excess of demos.

In struggling to accommodate 'the Other' in his *History* Macaulay sought to calm the fears of propertied middle-England by revitalising the agency of Whig politics, claiming that only disinterested aristocratic government could prevent revolution in England.[31] It was not just the narrative forms of the text which created this sense of agency – the moralisation of the world into a struggle between corrupt and tyrannical Catholic aristocrats and virtuous, Protestant, freeborn, middle-Eng-lishmen – but the very act of its writing, the sense of an unfolding, self-justifying telos in which 'the people' complete the Whig project. As Burrows recognised, the

History, as we have it, chronicles only the beginning of better things. The original plan, to take it up to the eve of the Reform Act, was more ambitious and optimistic. Yet there is a sense in which the Reform Act would not have been the end, because the consummation of Macaulay's *History*, like that of Hegel's philosophy of history ... is its own conception; the final act of the projected History is the *History* itself.[32]

Given that historians are now tracing not only the continued saliency and resonance of an aristocratic Whig politics into the late Victorian period, but also the critical role of Macaulay's *History* in creating a 'middle-class' identity and history, it becomes increasingly difficult to distinguish the boundaries between text and context.[33]

Twenty years later, years full of the kind of consensus Macaulay had

[31] Gossman, 'History as Decipherment: Romantic Historiography and the Discovery of "the Other"', in his *Between History and Literature* (Cambridge, MA, 1990), pp. 257–84.
[32] Burrows, *A Liberal Descent*, pp. 79–80.
[33] On the persistence of the Whig political project see Peter Mandler, *Aristocratic Government in the Age of Reform: Whigs and Liberals, 1830–1850* (Oxford, 1990); Richard Bellamy (ed.), *Victorian Liberalism: Nineteenth Century Political Thought and Practice* (London, 1990); Jonathan Parry, *The Rise and Fall of Liberal Government in Victorian Britain* (London, 1993); Peter Mandler and Susan Pedersen (eds.), *After the Victorians: Private Conscience and Public Duty in Modern Britain* (London, 1994). On Macaulay's invention of 'the middle class' see Dror

craved for, with the Second Reform Act of 1867 safely through parliament and 'the people' returning Conservative governments, Stubbs' *Constitutional History of England* could well afford a more radical tone. Informed by the lengthy debates about the nature of representative government during the 1850s and 1860s, the text sought to privilege the peoples' spontaneity, not discipline it as Macaulay's had. In doing so it provided plenty of intellectual ammunition for those radicals who evoked ancient constitutional standards in the long battle against the pernicious, oligarchic and centralising Benthamite reforms of the Poor Law, the police, and local government. Stubbs' critique of the tyranny of a centralised, unaccountable state and his belief in local self-government as a means of educating a virtuous citizenry, had long been, and continued to remain, standard radical fayre.[34] Yet Anglican bishops and Oxford professors are not renowned for their radicalism, and as Stubbs was both it is perhaps unsurprising that he is better remembered for his criticism of nostalgic radical notions of the proto-democratic virtues of the ancient Anglo-Saxon constitution's before the imposition of the 'Norman Yoke'.[35] For his *Constitutional History* constructed 1066 as a confirmation, even a strengthening of the English libertarian constitution, not as in radical readings a calamitous rupture and break. By marrying an efficient centralised and autocratic Norman administrative system with the somewhat chaotic localised and democratic Anglo-Saxon representative system, he argued the Norman Conquest gave England the best of both worlds.

It is this tension between the desire for the spontaneous pleasures of the people's local self-government and the desire for a disciplining centralised authority that is played out in Stubbs' text. The former is evoked with natural images of the body, the latter (as with Macaulay) with mechanical metaphors. Stubbs' fantasy was that both these were compatible, even complementary, so that the Normans' 'importation of

Wahrman, *Imagining the Middle Class: The Political Representation of Class in Britain, c.1780–1840* (Cambridge, 1995).

34 On these debates see, for example, Bryan Keith Lucas, *English Local Government Franchise* (Oxford, 1952); John Davis, *Reforming London: The London Government Problem, 1855–1900* (Oxford, 1988); John Prest, *Liberty and Locality: Parliament, Permissive Legislation and Ratepayers' Democracies in the Nineteenth Century* (Oxford, 1990); Vernon, *Politics and the People*; Floyd Parsons, 'Thomas Hare and the Victorian Proportional Representation Reform Movement, 1857–1888' (Ph.D, Cambridge University, 1990).

35 Christopher Hill, 'The Norman Yoke', in his *Puritanism and Revolution* (London, 1955); Anne Pallister, *Magna Carta: The Heritage of Liberty* (Oxford, 1977); J. G. A. Pocock, *The Ancient Constitution and the Feudal Law: A Study of English Historical Thought in the Seventeenth Century. A Re-Issue with Retrospect* (Cambridge, 1987); R. J. Smith, *The Gothic Bequest: Medieval Institutions in British Political Thought, 1688–1863* (Cambridge, 1987); Vernon, *Politics and the People*.

new systems of administration ... furnished a disciplinary and formative machinery' (p. 283) which 'invigorated ... stimulated ... [and] ... roused the dormant spirit' (p. 282) and 'latent energies of the English ... forc[ing] out the new growth of life' (p. 283).

The principle of amalgamating the two laws and nationalities by superimposing the better consolidated Norman superstructure on the better consolidated English substructure, runs through the whole policy. The English system was strong in the cohesion of its lower organisms, the association of individuals in the township, in the hundred and in the shire; the Norman system was strong in its higher ranges, in the close relation to the crown of the tenants in chief whom the king had enriched ... The strongest elements of both were brought together.   (p. 314)

The natural base, the organism, of English liberty found its salvation in the mechanical Norman superstructure. The difficult thing was maintaining the balance between the state and the people, the public and the private, the oligarchic and the anarchic, the mechanical and the natural, discipline and pleasure, the English and the Norman, so as to avoid the 'explosion which is called revolution' (p. 4). During the 1860s and 1870s this type of discursive balancing act was common within the myriad languages of Liberalism, as older anti-statist discourses were challenged by newer interventionist 'social' discourses about public health, sanitation, poverty, the economy and the empire.[36] Stubbs was by no means alone in searching for this middle ground, the point at which the liberty of the freeborn Englishmen should remain sacred, free from the encroachments of an increasingly powerful state.

If Stubbs' text found it difficult to locate the endpoint of English liberty, it found the search for its origins much easier. The influence of German ethnography on Stubbs' quest for the ancestral freedom of the English folk has received much attention elsewhere.[37] It was, as Robert Colls has remarked, the distinguishing feature of the *Constitutional History*:

From village moot and forest clearing to national parliament was essentially a 'Whig' story, but the origins of the English species were now in the race, language, and custom of a Teutonic people rather than in the metropolitan deeds of elite-Whigs. Stubbs ... shifted the ground of Englishness from being something less about constitutional precedents to being something more about white skins, English tongues, and feelings about being free.[38]

---

[36] Denise Riley, *'Am I That Name?' Feminism and the Category of 'Women' in History* (London, 1988); Jose Harris, *Private Lives, Public Spirit: Britain 1870–1914* (Oxford, 1993).

[37] Burrows, *A Liberal Descent*, pp. 109–12; Blaas, *Continuity and Anachronism*, pp. 170–4.

[38] Robert Colls, 'Englishness and Political Culture', in R. Colls and P. Dodd (eds.), *Englishness: Politics and Culture, 1880–1920* (London, 1986), pp. 44–5.

Read in this way, the natural organic images of liberty become still more significant as the text continually pits its English 'purity and unmolested integrity' (2) against the corruption and 'admixture' of alien 'Others'.

Questions of ethnicity and 'race' are then at the centre of Stubbs' *Constitutional History*, they are 'the most important, and perhaps the only necessary ones, for all minor matters may be comprehended under them' (p. 2). By claiming that the English were embodied in the physical presence of 'the race' and endowed with a Teutonic ancestry, 'a people of German descent in the main constituents of blood, character and language' (p. 2), Stubbs could construct an ethnically cleansed empire of Teutonic Protestantism to help explain the collapse of previous un-Protestant empires. Much of the text reads like an extended paternity case, assuring us that 'the German element is the paternal element ... [and that] ... the chain of proof is to be found in the progressive persistent development of English constitutional history from the primeval polity of the common fatherland' (p. 12). Of course, it is not only significant that the past of the 'nation-race' is conceived in masculine terms through the male ancestral line, but that it is also always defined against a corrupting imperial Roman 'Other'. The Anglo-Saxon 'tongue' remains 'pure' because it was never 'penetrated' by the Romans, like medieval Germany it remained 'unadulterated' (p. 8), just as the 'purely indigenous' English 'genius of government' had been 'spared from the curse of the imperial system' (p. 6). The corrupting influence of the Roman empire is contrasted to the purity of the English polity, 'the purest product of their primitive instinct' (p. 11).

The attention to ethnicity obviously created a much broader definition of 'the people' than was evident in Macaulay's *History of England*, one that invited all 'those [men] who could possibly claim to have the right skins, show the right tongues and be identified with the right feelings' to join the Whig celebration of English constitutional liberty.[39] And yet, however much broader Stubbs' definition of the constitution was, its privileging of English men was no less predicated upon the exclusion of others. Read in the aftermath of 'colonial' disturbances such as the Indian Mutiny (1857), the Morant Bay Rebellion (1865), and inescapably informed by continuing concerns about Irish nationalism and Fenian 'outrages', Stubbs' account of the constitution helped re-establish the boundaries between England and its empire, excluding all those not privy to England's glorious constitutional history from its

---

[39] Colls, 'Englishness and Political Culture', p. 45.

standards of civility, liberty and, of course, citizenship.[40] It was a
distinction tied to a wider intellectual and scientific history of the
forward march of English civilisation, to the politics and development of
evolution, the origins and superiority of the species.[41] Stubbs' fantasy
was then that English constitutional history secured the borders of
England's 'island race', insulating its Protestant constitution from the
claims of colonial 'savages' and English women.

Ironically, Maitland's *The History of English Law*, the most epistemologically conservative text, had the most politically radical implications.
Of course, Maitland himself was always at pains to stress, in Burrows'
phrase, 'the political chastity of his historical writing' and as we have
seen his work has often been dutifully received in this way as a model of
the new scientific objectivity.[42] And, indeed, much of the text can be
read as a denial of fantasy, an iconoclastic *tour de force*, disparaging the
highly charged and 'hasty talk about national character' (p. xxxvi),
stressing the unparliamentary origins of parliament, and the vague
idealism of notions of 'the village community'. Yet published in 1895,
The History of English Law encouraged a sense of the possibilities of
progressive change that had informed not only Gladstone's last and
most radical government between 1892 and 1895, but also the campaigns
of the suffragettes and the independent labour movement.[43]

Maitland's public were both the object of his text and its collective
author. He spoke on behalf of and to the 'community at large', the
'general body of citizens' about the way in which the law represented
the public will and its 'common rules of morals and manners', binding
them together as a 'civilized Commonwealth'. It was by observing this
'rule of law' that one became a citizen, just as by breaking it one became
a subject and expected the coercive powers of the state to restore 'public
justice' on behalf of the 'community' (p. xxiv). 'Such are for the citizen,
the lawyer, and the historian, the practical elements of law' (p. xxv).

[40] See Catharine Hall, 'Rethinking Imperial Histories: The Reform Act of 1867', *New Left Review* (December 1994), pp. 3–29.

[41] John Burrows, *Evolution and Society: A Study in Victorian Social Theory* (London, 1966); George Stocking, *Victorian Anthropology* (London, 1987); Nancy Stepan, *The Idea of Race in Science: Great Britain, 1800–1960* (London, 1982); James Urry, *Before Social Anthropology: Essays on the History of British Anthropology* (Reading, 1993); Robert Young, *Colonial Desire: Hybridity in Theory, Culture and Race* (London, 1995).

[42] Burrows, ' "The Village Community" and the Uses of History in Late Nineteenth Century England', in N. McKendrick (ed.), *Historical Perspectives: Studies in English Thought and Society in Honour of J. H. Plumb* (London, 1974), p. 276.

[43] For a good flavour of these troubled times see Elaine Showalter, *Sexual Anarchy: Gender and Culture at the Fin de Siècle* (London, 1992); Riley, *'Am I That Name?'*; Harris, *Private Lives, Public Spirit*; S. Ledger and S. McCracken (eds.), *Cultural Politics at the Fin de Siècle* (Cambridge, 1995).

Indeed, in Maitland's fantasy the figures of the citizen, lawyer and historian are as one. The mark of 'a high state of civilization' was then the degree to which 'uncontrolled private force' was 'regulated by legislation, and controlled by courts of justice' on the 'public authority' of the citizenry. This primitive sociology of the law, in which the law is legitimated by a popular referent, gave *The History of English Law* its radical twist. The text exhibits a faith in the law as a system capable of modernisation; there is no sense of the citizen being trapped in the history of the 'common law mind'; indeed, the duty of the historian is to free the citizenry from the tyranny of a continuous organic past. Constitutional law had to be continually reinvented, it could not be based upon the search for 'anachronistic survivals' from the 'accumulated rubbish of the ages'.[44] Maitland invited his reading public to reflect on the merits and mortality of the ancient laws which still propped up England's late-nineteenth-century ancien régime – an invitation very much in tune with the Gladstonian Liberal project. Above all, for Maitland, it was the distinction between real and personal property which needed radical reform, for it was they that lay at the heart of those laws of inheritance and primogeniture so long identified as being critical to the survival of aristocratic 'Old Corruption'.[45] Clearly not content with the failed promises of Gladstone's final ministry to tax land values, ground rent and royalties, despite Harcourt's famous death duties budget of 1894, Maitland lamented that 'even now, after all our reforms, our courts are still from time to time compelled to construe statutes of Edward I's day, and, were Parliament to repeal some of those statutes and provide no substitute, the whole edifice of our land law would fall down with a crash' (p. xxxiv). It was a suitably apocalyptic tone for a *fin de siècle* England in which the old appeals to constitutional certainties and the rule of law seemed to be unravelling with a rising tide of militancy among suffragettes, socialists, Irish nationalists and the dark savages of English cities and imperial outposts.

And yet, it is as if Maitland, having looked over the precipice, drew back from the democratic logic of his argument. He may have constructed his *History of the English Law* as the peoples' but they were almost entirely absent from the text as acting subjects. For in privileging a

---

[44] Blaas, *Continuity and Anachronism*, p. 244.
[45] See Maitland's article 'The Law of Real Property' first published in the *Westminster Review* in 1879 and reprinted in *The Collected Papers of Frederick William Maitland. Vol. I* (Cambridge, 1911), pp. 162–201. See also Blaas, *Continuity and Anachronism*, pp. 242 ff. On the radical critique of primogeniture see W. D. Rubinstein, 'The End of "Old Corruption" in Britain 1780–1860', *Past and Present*, 101 (1984), pp. 55–86.

history of the social and administrative uses of the law over the political debates about its language and meaning, Maitland suggested that constitutional rights only existed in so far as they had been 'asserted in an action' (p. 148). It is not that the possibility of reform and resistance was denied, but that those capable of such action were ultimately lawyers and historians, politicians and administrators. His *History* may have spoken to 'the people' as its referent, but few were listening as it provided them with no sense of agency. If history was this full of irony why bother?

V

As I draw this essay towards closure let us be clear what I have not been saying. I have not argued that all history is fiction, that the past did not happen or that 'the real' does not exist. Rather I have examined some of the rhetorical techniques and political contexts which led to the invention of a discourse of 'the real' by nineteenth-century constitutional historians, a discourse central to the construction of a canon of English History. I hope that by exploring this process I have helped to problematise and historicise this canon and its essentialist categories of 'the real'. My reading of the foundational texts of Macaulay, Stubbs and Maitland has attempted to turn the canon back upon itself, to show how 'the real' was privileged over the represented in the literary struggle to suppress epistemological doubt and assert the authority of History as a discipline. Deconstructing this discourse does not mean dispensing with it, just that by understanding the conditions and techniques of its historical construction we can use it more critically and avoid the essentialist categories of its masculine and imperial politics.

I am, of course, painfully aware of the limitations of this attempt to historicise the discourse of 'the real'. My current work on the imagination of a Cornish national identity has reminded me how many areas of social life were shaped by such discourses from the mid nineteenth century – not least of all in the emerging social sciences of political economy, folklore and anthropology, statistics, and the social surveys of journalists, philanthropists and governments.[46] The history of 'the

---

[46] See, for example, Kent, *Brains and Numbers*; Stefan Collini, *Public Moralists: Political Thought and Intellectual Life in Britain 1850–1930* (Oxford, 1991); Lawrence Goldman, 'A Peculiarity of the English? The Social Science Association and the Absence of Sociology in Nineteenth Century Britain', *Past and Present*, 114 (1981), pp. 133–71; Mary Poovey, 'Figures of Arithmetic, Figures of Speech: The Discourse of Statistics in the 1830s' *Critical Inquiry*, 19 (1993), pp. 256–76.

social' is in large measure the history of the ways in which the discourse of 'the real' was mobilised to legitimate different techniques of rule and government, but that is another essay and I need to end this one.[47]

I have then tried to understand the uses of the discourse of 'the real' by Macaulay, Stubbs and Maitland as part of a broader set of political and institutional contexts. That is not to say that these contexts determined the meaning of their texts, but rather that the texts helped frame and constitute the contexts within which they operated. In a very real sense, the fantasies of Macaulay, Stubbs and Maitland came true. Their invention of a realist historiography helped establish a professional methodology which legitimated the creation of History as an independent academic discipline within the academy. Their narratives of the constitutional past became part of the histories they wrote, their definitions of the constitution merged within public political discourse, redirecting and reshaping it as they provided new resonances to those hoping to make sense of English political life and their role within it. They were fantasies about how to discipline and control, with their consent, those struggling to become democratic subjects. It is this understanding of how the real and the fantastical, context and text, history and literature, always work in relation with each other that I want to close with. Through it we have a glimpse of a different type of historical knowledge and a different type of constitutional history.

[47] Historians have begun to write this history of 'the social', largely from a Foucauldian perspective. See, for example, Riley, 'Am I That Name?'; Patrick Joyce, *Democratic Subjects: The Self and the Social in Nineteenth Century England* (Cambridge, 1994). See also the very important post-colonial contributions of Dipesh Chakrabarty, 'Postcoloniality and the Artifice of History: Who Speaks for "Indian" Pasts?', *Representations*, 37 (1992), pp. 1–26; Gyan Prakash, 'Science as a Sign of Modernity in Colonial India' (paper presented to History and Language conference at Warwick University, April 1994).

9

☙

Gender, class, and the nation: franchise reform in England, 1832–1928

ANNA CLARK

Mr Ayrton. 'He never entertained for a moment the idea that it was expedient to admit every person to the enjoyment of the franchise because he happened to be a man.' (Debate on extending franchise to urban male householders, 1867).[1]

Mr E. A. Leatham. 'It is not because men pay rates or taxes, or own or occupy property, that they have the vote, but because they are men...independent and free.' (Debate on extending franchise to female householders, 1884).[2]

Until 1918, masculinity was the fundamental basis for citizenship in Britain. While this may be obvious, what is rarely recognised is that persistently male definitions of suffrage drastically retarded the extension of the vote not only to women, but to all men as well. The manhood of citizenship always had to be earned, rather than claimed as an inherent human right based on reason. From the era of the French Revolution to the First World War, working men were consistently told that they had not yet attained the full masculine status of the citizen, the requirements for which shifted from propertyholding, to marrying and leading a household, to defending the empire with violence. In response, working men retorted that they, too, were men, and demanded their own political manhood. But by failing to support vigorously women's suffrage, the working-class movement accepted the linkage of masculinity and citizenship in a way which allowed inequality to endure.

To be sure, historians of women's suffrage have explored the failure

I would like to thank Lynda Whitehead, James Vernon and Susan Thorne for their helpful references and critiques of this essay. I would also like to thank the University of North Carolina at Charlotte for funding the research on which it is based.
[1] *Hansard's Parliamentary Debates*, 3rd series, vol. 186, 2 May 1867, col. 1883.
[2] *Ibid.*, 289, 12 June 1884, col. 103.

of the labour movement and feminists to cooperate.[3] Other historians of high politics explained the limited nature of the Reform Acts in the context of parliamentary manoeuvring.[4] While these approaches are important and necessary, this essay concentrates on tracing the evolution of gendered notions of the suffrage in constitutionalist debate. The masculinity of the vote, and the constitution itself, changed under pressures of industrialisation, class conflict, shifting marital ideologies, imperialism and war.[5]

In fact, the principles of the British constitution were never entirely clear or fixed.[6] Generally, electors were supposed to be property-holders, since the function of parliament was seen to be the protection of property.[7] But eighteenth-century politicians, trying to explain the tattered, irrational patchwork of the electorate in which some uninhabited hamlets elected two Members of Parliament while many large manufacturing towns had none, resorted to two main arguments.[8] First, they argued, Members of Parliament 'virtually represented' all English inhabitants, with or without a vote, because they used their wisdom to debate disinterestedly issues of national concern in parliament, rather than slavishly following constituent wishes.[9] For instance, Mackintosh

---

[3] Jill Liddington and Jill Norris, *One Hand Tied Behind Us: The Rise of the Woman's Suffrage Movement* (London, 1978); Sandra Stanley Holton, *Feminism and Democracy: Women's Suffrage and Reform Politics in Britain, 1900–1918* (Cambridge, 1986); Ray Strachey, *The Cause: A Short History of the Women's Movement in Great Britain* (1928; London, 1978); Constance Rover, *Women's Suffrage and Party Politics in Britain, 1866–1914* (London, 1867); Andrew Rosen, *Rise Up, Women! The Militant Campaign of the Women's Social and Political Union, 1903–1914* (London, 1914); David Rubinstein, *A Different World for Women: The Life of Millicent Garrett Fawcett* (Columbus, 1991).

[4] See F. B. Smith, *The Making of the Second Reform Bill* (Cambridge, 1966); Maurice Cowling, *1867: Disraeli, Gladstone and Revolution: The Passing of the Second Reform Bill* (Cambridge, 1967); Frances Gillespie, *Labour and Politics in England, 1850–1867* (Durham, NC, 1927); Royden Harrison, *Before the Socialists: Studies in Labour and Politics, 1861–1881* (London, 1981).

[5] For American considerations of this issue, where the framers of the American constitution still considered the franchise a right only available to propertied white men; see Linda K. Kerber, 'The Paradox of Women's Citizenship in the Early Republic: The Case of *Martin vs. Massachusetts*, 1805', *American Historical Review* (April 1992), pp. 349–78; Carroll Smith-Rosenberg, 'Discovering the Subject of the "Great Constitutional Discussion", 1786–1789', *The Journal of American History* (December 1992), pp. 841–73. For the debate in the American women's movement over whether to support first the franchise for black men or to demand full universal suffrage after the Civil War, debates which echo English debates over class and gender, see Ellen Carol Dubois, *Feminism and Suffrage* (Ithaca, 1978).

[6] J. A. W. Gunn, *Beyond Liberty and Property: The Process of Self-Recognition in Eighteenth Century Political Thought* (Kingston and Montreal, 1983), p. 189.

[7] D. C. Moore, *The Politics of Deference* (Brighton, 1976); Frank O'Gorman, *Voters, Patrons and Parties: The Unreformed Electoral System of Hanoverian England 1734–1832* (Oxford, 1989) for the actual workings of the system, which was much more dynamic than the theory.

[8] A. H. Birch, *Representative and Responsible Government: An Essay on the British Constitution* (Toronto, 1964), p. 24.

[9] Henry Jephson, *The Platform: Its Rise and Progress* (London, 1892), vol. 1, p. 80.

idealised the 'old' form of government as a 'sort of patriarchal chieftain-ship' in which 'settled heads of leaders' of villages and parishes influenced their neighbours.[10] Second, they upheld the British constitu-tion as representing a balance of interests. Landed property controlled most seats, but since a few working men and more than a few merchants could vote, in places such as Preston and Bristol, their representatives gave them a voice in parliament. As Mackintosh believed, the vote of token 'peasants' 'teaches them to feel that *they* also are men'.[11]

From the Levellers in the seventeenth century onwards, reformers insisted that franchise reform was needed to extend this sense of 'manly independence' more deeply through the population.[12] They differed from Mackintosh's paternalism, however, in focusing on the individual rather than the community as the unit of representation. Yet whether they based their demands on radical Puritanism, Lockean natural rights, civic humanism, the ancient constitution or utilitarianism, they tended to retain a patriarchal notion of the masculine head of household as the proper elector.

Locke, for instance, repudiated the paternalist notion of society as a hierarchy, and asserted the natural right of individual men to represen-tation to protect their property and personal liberty. However, he accepted sexual subordination as natural.[13] For Locke, the individual man was a head of household, not male servants, or wives and daughters. In fact, as Carole Pateman argues, it was the husband's ability to dominate subordinates in private which gave him the right to participate as an equal in the public sphere.[14]

Almost all eighteenth-century thinkers shared this assumption that the citizen was a male head of household, but their different philosophies of representation also inflected their notions of masculinity.[15] Civic huma-nists, harkening back to ancient Greece, believed only economically independent men should vote, comparing wage-earners to disenfran-

[10] [Sir James Mackintosh], 'Parliamentary Reform,' *Edinburgh Review*, 14, 28 (1809), pp. 285–6, quoted in Moore, *The Politics of Deference*, p. 195.
[11] Sir James Mackintosh, *Edinburgh Review*, 31 (1818), pp. 174–80, excerpted in H. J. Hanham (ed.), *The Nineteenth Century Constitution: Documents and Commentary* (Cambridge, 1969), p. 10.
[12] For the Levellers and the franchise, see C. B. Macpherson, *The Political Theory of Possessive Individualism* (Oxford, 1962), pp. 107–59.
[13] John Locke, *Two Treatises on Government*, ed. Peter Laslett, 2nd edn (Cambridge, 1967), vol. II, pp. 339, 350). For the feminist critique of this tradition, see Anne Phillips, *Engendering Democracy* (Pennsylvania, PA, 1991) pp. 23–60.
[14] Carole Pateman, *The Disorder of Women: Democratic Feminism and Political Theory* (Palo Alto, 1989) pp. 6, 53.
[15] For the debate on the importance of Locke versus the republican tradition, see Isaac Kramnick, *Republicanism and Bourgeois Radicalism: Political Ideology in Late Eighteenth-Century England and America* (Ithaca and London, 1990), pp. 2–7, 163–95.

chised slaves as lacking the proper independence.[16] Later eighteenth-century reformers modified this theory to stress the religious and cultural refinement of the middle-class men instead of the rough, rural, military virtues of the landed gentry.[17] In contrast, Major John Cartwright justified suffrage extension with the 'ancient constitution', alleging that in England's distant past all male householders deserved the vote because they bore arms in defence of their country.[18] Only Thomas Paine abandoned the notion that the citizen had to be a head of household, instead founding his theory of representation on inherent human reason; yet even he assumed the citizen would be male.[19]

In the era of the French Revolution, however, notions of 'natural rights' seemed far too dangerous and even parliamentary reformers shuddered at the idea of universal manhood suffrage.[20] By defining the proper elector as the male head of household, parliamentary reformers tried to avoid accusations that they espoused notions of universal suffrage as a natural right; instead of introducing the foreign, French notions of equality and fraternity, they stressed the respectability of fathers as potential electors. For instance, in 1790 Henry Flood moved to enfranchise householders, 'being masters, or fathers of families, they must be sufficiently responsible to be entitled to the franchise'.[21] When the notion of householder suffrage was revived in 1797, it is significant that reformers now emphasised the domestic affections of fathers, rather than the responsibilities of masters, perhaps responding to the French Revolution's perceived challenges to conventional morality. They declared that each father has 'some member of a little circle around his

[16] J. Pocock, *Virtue, Commerce, and History* (Cambridge, 1985), p. 260; Caroline Robbins, *The Eighteenth Century Commonwealthman* (Cambridge MA, 1959), p. 35.

[17] For earlier versions of warlike masculinity, see Hanna Pitkin, *Fortune was a Woman: Gender in the Political Thought of Nicolo Machiavelli* (Berkeley, California, 1984), p. 25; for the eighteenth-century middle class, see Leonore Davidoff and Catherine Hall, *Family Fortunes: Men and Women of the English Middle Class* (London, 1987), p. 110; and John Dwyer, *Virtuous Discourses: Sensibility and Community in late 18th Century Scotland* (Edinburgh, 1987), pp. 107, 96, 104.

[18] H. T. Dickinson, *Liberty and Property: Political Ideology in Eighteenth-Century Britain* (New York, 1977), p. 229. For the ancient constitution theory, see Christopher Hill, 'The Norman Yoke', in his *Puritanism and Revolution* (London, 1962), pp. 50–122; J. G. A. Pocock, *The Ancient Constitution and the Feudal Law* (New York, 1967), pp. 125–7; James A. Epstein, 'The Constitutional Idiom: Radical Reasoning, Rhetoric and Action in Early Nineteenth Century England', *Journal of Social History*, 23, 3 (1990), p. 562; James Vernon, *Politics and the People: a Study in English Political Culture, c. 1815–1867* (Cambridge, 1993), pp. 297–305.

[19] For a further discussion of why the gender-neutral potential of Painite ideas were not taken up, see Anna Clark, *The Struggle for the Breeches: Gender and the Making of the British Working Class* (Berkeley, California, 1996), chapter 8.

[20] For debates between Lockean and ancient constitution notions of the suffrage among late eighteenth-century middle-class reformers, see S. MacCoby, *The Radical Tradition, 1763–1914* (New York, 1957,) pp. 37–40; Gunn, *Beyond Liberty and Property*, p. 258.

[21] *The Parliamentary History of England* (London, 1818), vol. XXVIII, p. 459.

fireside' who gives him a 'stake in the public fate' or a 'hostage to society'.[22] At the same time, Fox reassured parliament that they were not espousing universal suffrage by using the idea of women voting to ridicule the notion of enfranchising the 'lowest classes' such as soldiers and servants.[23]

In the debates leading up to the 1832 Reform Act, most parliamentary reformers saw even household suffrage as much too radical. While James Mill used Bentham's utilitarian argument for universal manhood suffrage, he assumed that it would be sufficient to enfranchise all men over forty, who could represent the interests of their sons and women-folk.[24] Macaulay, however, again used women's enfranchisement to point out the contradictions of Mill's notion of universal suffrage; the propertied classes can 'kindly protect' the poor just like men protect women, therefore neither needed the vote.[25] Yet Mill's assumption that older men would represent younger men reflected an outdated patri-archalism; as Hawkins noted, 'The elector of the present day repre-sented, at most, his wife and children, frequently not even his sons.'[26]

The framers of the 1832 Reform Act hoped to preserve the constitu-tion by incorporating respectable middle-class 'public opinion' into the electorate and enfranchising large commercial and industrial towns.[27] By rationalising the definition of an elector, the act also narrowed possibilities for citizenship. The relative uniformity of the ten pound franchise (given to those owning, or in boroughs, occupying premises worth ten pounds a year) did away with anomalies which had allowed some working men to vote. It decreased, though not eliminated, the electoral power of the nascent working class.[28] And as James Vernon notes, for the first time, the vote was also defined as male.[29]

While Members of Parliament assumed voters would be propertied male heads of household, they did not debate the new electorate's specific qualities of masculinity or their domestic virtues.[30] Soon after

[22] The *Oxford English Dictionary*'s first citation for children as hostages to society or fortune is from Bacon, in 1607.

[23] *The Parliamentary History of England* (London, 1818), vol. XXXIII, pp. 650, 661, 726; for Fox's ambivalent relationship wit radicalism, see L. G. Mitchell, *Charles James Fox* (Oxford, 1992), p. 151.

[24] James Mill, 'Essay on Government', in Jack Lively and John Rees (eds.), *Utilitarian Logic and Politics* (Oxford, 1978), p. 79.

[25] Macauley, in *Edinburgh Review*, 1829, reprinted in Lively and Rees, *Utilitarian Logic*, p. 116.

[26] *Hansard*, 3rd series, 7, 19 September 1831, col. 206.

[27] Norman Gash, *Politics in the Age of Peel* (London, Longmans, 1953), p. 18.

[28] Frank O'Gorman, *Voters, Patrons and Parties: The Unreformed Electoral System of Hanoverian England, 1734–1832* (Oxford, 1989) p. 217.

[29] Vernon, *Politics and the People*, p. 15.

[30] Dror Wahrman, '"Middle-Class" Domesticity Goes Public: Gender, Class and Politics

the passage of the Reform Act, family issues, however, moved to the forefront of politics. The reformed parliament immediately refused to protect factory women and children with effective regulation, and then passed the draconian, Malthusian-tinged New Poor Law which aimed to deter the poor from reproducing. When the working-class Chartists demanded the vote to remedy these ills, conservatives justified granting suffrage to middle-class men because of their domestic virtues, while attacking working men as bad husbands. For instance, *Blackwood's Edinburgh Magazine* contrasted the middle-class man's 'self-denial' in supporting his family with the 'sensual indulgence' of 'excessive drinking, bastardy, and wife desertion by working men.'[31]

In response, the Chartists asserted the right of 'manhood suffrage', that citizenship was a 'universal political right of every human being' rather than a privilege of property.[32] However, most Chartists were reluctant to carry this principle to its logical conclusion: truly universal suffrage which included women as well as men. And their opponents used the spectre of a female franchise, as had Fox and Macaulay, to ridicule the philosophy of universal suffrage. Instead, the Chartists tried to redeploy the constitutionalist and Lockean arguments to their own ends by asserting that working men's property was inherent in their skill.[33] However, the fact that Chartists, with a few exceptions, disapproved of women's waged work reveals that property in labour was as much property in masculinity as property in craft.[34]

Middle-class reformers who wished for a further extension of the suffrage but feared Chartist democracy presented household suffrage as

from Queen Caroline to Queen Victoria', *Journal of British Studies*, 32 (October, 1993), p. 417.

[31] 'The Chartists and Universal Suffrage', *Blackwood's Edinburgh Magazine*, 187, 46 (1839), pp. 296-7.

[32] 'Petition Adopted at the Crown and Anchor Meeting', 1838, in *The Early Chartists*, ed. Dorothy Thompson (Columbia, SC: 1971), p. 62; James Epstein, 'The Constitutionalist Idiom in Radical Reasoning, Rhetoric, and Action in Early 19th Century England', *Journal of Social History*, 23, 3 (1990), p. 565.

[33] For this tradition, see Epstein, 'Constitutionalist Idiom', p. 565; Clive Behagg, *Politics and Production in the Early Nineteenth Century* (London, 1990), p. 233. For Chartist notions of property of labour and gender, see Joan Scott, *Gender and the Politics of History* (New York, 1988), p. 54; For further development of the argument on Chartism and gender, see Anna Clark, 'The Rhetoric of Chartist Domesticity: Gender, Language and Class in the 1830s and 1840s', *Journal of British Studies*, 31 (1992), pp. 79-82.

[34] Bronterre O'Brien, editorial in the *Northern Star*, 8 September 1838 was an exception who addressed women as workers. For masculinity and skill, see also Sally Alexander, 'Women, Class and Sexual Difference: Some Reflections on the Writing of a Feminist History', *History Workshop Journal*, 17 (1984), p. 138; and for the second half of the nineteenth century, Sonya Rose, *Limited Livelihoods: Gender and Class in the Nineteenth Century* (Berkeley and Los Angeles, California, 1992), p. 15, and Sonya Rose, 'Gender Antagonism and Class Conflict', *Social History*, 13, 2 (1988), pp. 191-208.

an alternative to the universal franchise. Under this scheme, established male heads of household would qualify for the vote. If working men attained the breadwinner wage and properly took care of their families, they would share a notion of masculinity with the middle classes, presumably guaranteeing their political stability. The Chartists, however, long opposed the notion of 'household suffrage': *Northern Star* editorials denounced it because conservative fathers' votes would subsume radical sons' beliefs, but they did not see the contradiction in excluding wives from the vote in order to 'preserve harmony' in the family.[35]

When household suffrage was finally debated in parliament in 1848, Cobden argued for household suffrage on the basis that representation should be linked with taxation, not that it was a natural right. He asked his colleagues, 'what danger can there be in giving the franchise to householders? They are the fathers of families – the persons who fill your churches and your workshops – in fact, the people of the country.'[36] However, the relationship between fatherhood and political status was still problematic. For Feargus O'Connor, the Chartist leader, who eventually dropped his insistence on manhood suffrage, the want of a vote prevented artisans from maintaining their families and attaining the status of householder.[37] For opponents of extended suffrage, however, Malthusian logic forbade giving the vote to men who could not support their families. Serjeant Talfourd termed 'fallacious and absurd' the notion that 'every man who was the father of children he could not maintain' should vote.[38] Henry Drummond countered advocates of household suffrage by reiterating the classical republican notion that in Rome only freemen were citizens, not slaves; like slaves, even 'intelligent operatives' who could not support their families would be prone to follow demagogues in their misery.[39]

During the next two decades, opponents of a wider franchise continued to portray working-class men as violent trade unionists and bad husbands. They often attacked working men as brutal wifebeaters who didn't know how to rule with love at home. The conservative religious journal *The British Workman*, dedicated to turning working men away from radical action, told them: 'Gentlemen, there are two ways of governing a family: the first is by force, the other is by mild and vigilant

---

[35] *Northern Star* 19 September 1840, 2 January 1841.
[36] *Hansard*, 3rd series, 100, 6 July 1848, col. 185.
[37] *Ibid.*, col. 208; for O'Connor's shifts in opinion, see Frances Elma Gillespie, *Labor and Politics in England 1850–1867* (Durham, NC, 1927), pp. 30, 90, 264.
[38] *Hansard*, 3rd series, 100, 6 July 1848, col. 176.   [39] *Ibid.*, col. 907.

authority...A husband deserves to lose his empire altogether, by making an attempt to force it with violence.'[40]

Yet organised working men themselves turned the ideology of domesticity towards their own ends. By accepting the notion of the breadwinner wage and the gender division of labour, employers made concessions to their workers and ensured labour peace around a shared patriarchal, paternalist conception of family and community in many northern textile towns.[41] One by one, Liberals became more aware of the need to modify political economy to allow for social reforms as they contemplated the wreckage of working-class families.[42] Issues around international liberty also provided common ground between Liberals and working men, as in the General Heynau affair when working men portrayed themselves as chivalrous defenders of abused Hungarian women.[43] As labour unions grew more moderate and disciplined, concentrating on the exclusive interests of skilled working men and cooperating with Liberals on issues such as municipal reform, the prospects for franchise extension improved.[44]

While the organised skilled working class was more disciplined and non-violent, the harsh economic conditions of the mid-1860s, as Freda Harcourt points out, raised fears of riots in London by unskilled working men. Furthermore, Britain's imperial ventures were facing a turning point when Governor Eyre in Jamaica brutally suppressed an uprising of former slaves, and Fenians threatened terrorism at home.[45] These conditions made the question of reform both more urgent and more controversial. Was the solution harsh repression of both the British working class and colonised subjects? Or could working men be incorporated into the nation? Disagreements about these issues came to centre around different notions of masculinity and political authority.[46]

---

[40] *British Workman*, 1 October 1855.
[41] Patrick Joyce, *Work, Society and Politics* (Brighton, 1980); Rose, *Limited Livelihoods*, pp. 33–45.
[42] Margot Finn, *After Chartism: Class and Nation in English Radical Politics 1848–1874* (New York and Cambridge, 1993), pp. 198, 189.
[43] For Heynau, see A. James Hammerton, 'The Targets of Rough Music: Respectability and Domestic Violence in Victorian England', *Gender and History*, 3, 1 (spring, 1991), pp. 31–5; for international liberty and other areas in common, see Finn, *After Chartism*, p. 189.
[44] Vernon, *Politics and the People*, p. 321.
[45] Freda Harcourt, 'Disraeli's Imperialism, 1866–1868: A Question of Timing', *Historical Journal*, 23, 1 (1980), p. 89; Thomas Holt, *The Problem of Freedom: Race, Labor and Politics in Jamaica and Britain* (Baltimore, 1992), p. 280.
[46] For general discussions of mid-century notions of masculinity, see Catherine Hall, 'Competing Masculinities: Thomas Carlyle, John Stuart Mill and the Case of Governor Eyre', in her *White, Male and Middle-class: Explorations in Feminism and History* (Cambridge, 1992), p. 285; Norman Vance, *The Sinews of the Spirit: the Ideal of Christian Manliness in Victorian Literature and Religious Thought* (Cambridge, 1985), p. 14.

Three main strands of thought can be identified in these debates: first, opponents of a wider suffrage who believed the violence of the working classes made it necessary to rule them by force; second, those liberals who believed working men deserved the vote as fathers of families, and third, liberals who believed that intellect was more important than household status as a qualification for citizenship.

Conservative opponents of reform were unconvinced by the new working-class discipline and persisted in regarding them as violent inferiors. These conservatives espoused a notion of rugged masculinity, most vividly articulated by Carlyle, based on strong rule over subordinates – whether Jamaican, Irish or working-class.[47] Sir Thomas Bateson declared that the 1866 Reform Bill would lead to 'emasculation of the aristocracy'.[48] When J. S. Mill extolled the virtues of working men, Butler-Johnstone satirically portrayed him 'fall[ing] in love' and 'shed[ding] tears' over the working classes.[49]

Opponents even compared the working class to colonial natives, both requiring firm, unflinching, unsentimental, control.[50] In fact, they often seemed to perceive working men as a race apart, characterising them as passionate, violent and impulsive; evoking stereotypes of black slaves in the United States.[51] Robert Lowe ridiculed the notion of the absolute right to the franchise by claiming this would give the same right to the 'Australian savage and Hottentot of the Cape as [to] the educated and refined Englishman'.[52] One pamphlet on earlier reform efforts referred to the 'ignorance and passions of the masses' and asked why should the Irish who were improvident and married young be able to outvote hardworking Scots who married late.[53] Earl Russell argued that the Reform Bill of 1866 went against 'natural order' by 'seeking to make the Governed Governors' instead of 'independent, thoughtful voters', who can combat 'cholera, cattle pest, the Nigger Pest – white murder by blacks – and Fenians.'[54] Increasingly, the vote was defined in national, imperialist as well as gender terms.

Not surprisingly, in response, working men and their allies felt they were excluded from the nation. John Bright told working men at a reform meeting, 'You are to have no vote – no share in the government – the country you live in is not to be your country. You are to be like the

---

[47] Hall, 'Competing Masculinities', p. 270; Holt, *The Problem of Freedom*, p. 280.
[48] *Hansard* 3rd series, 183, 4 June 1866, c. 1856.   [49] *Ibid.*, 27 April 1866, col. 32.
[50] Hall, 'Competing Masculinities', p. 285.
[51] *Weekly Dispatch*, 17 February 1867, letter by Publicola.
[52] Lowe, *Speeches and Letters on Reform* (London, 1867), pp. 48, 36.
[53] *Reform: Or Look before You Leap* (London, 1859), p. 20.
[54] Earl Russell, KG, *The Final Reform Bill* (London, 1866), pp. 7–8.

coolies or Chinese, imported into the West Indies or California.'[55] Imlack complained that upper-class legislators 'often treat us as a distinct race of beings from themselves – giving and keeping as they see fit'.[56]

Gladstone and his Liberal supporters therefore formulated a moral vision of the nation and masculinity which could unite working men and the middle classes into 'the people', instead of what he perceived as the Conservatives' adherence to a class-divided society.[57] He introduced his Reform Bill extending the franchise to urban male working-class house-holders by arguing that they were 'the fathers of families' and 'our own flesh and blood'.[58] Gladstone hoped to bring the working classes 'within the pale of the constitution' a phrase which as Ramsden notes referred to Ireland where the Pale represented the zone of English settlement and 'evoked images of the electorate as civilized settlers surrounded by savages without'.[59] By portraying working men as fathers of families, Gladstone pointed out their commonalities with middle-class men, part of his effort to prove they were 'our flesh and blood' rather than an alien race.

Gladstone and Bright stressed the domestic virtues of working men in part because fatherhood – in a loving yet very patriarchal version – was so important to them on a personal and religious level.[60] Proponents of working men's votes portrayed them as sharing the manly virtues of the middle class: they were 'men of piety, intelligence and good conduct' as demonstrated by saving and temperance.[61] Even for Christian socialists,

[55] *Beehive*, 1 September 1866.
[56] *National Reformer*, 11 November 1866. In fact, as Susan Thorne argues, Evangelicals had regarded the working classes as a race apart in the 1830s and 1840s: 'The Conversion of England and the Conversion of the World Inseparable: Missionary Imperialism and the Language of Class in Early Industrial England' (unpublished paper), 1994, p. 16.
[57] For Gladstone's view of deferential working class; in 1866 debate he said that working men should have the vote because they have done their duty to their superiors. *Hansard*, 3rd series, 182, 12 March 1866, cols. 56–60; also H. C. G. Matthew, *Gladstone 1809–1874* (Oxford, 1986), p. 140. For Gladstone's moral vision, see Boyd Hilton, 'Gladstone's Theological Politics', in Michael Bentley and John Stevenson (eds.), *High and Low Politics in Modern Britain* (Oxford, 1983), p. 30. For class conflict versus the notion of 'the people', see Patrick Joyce, *Visions of the People: Industrial England and the Question of Class 1848–1914* (Cambridge, 1991), p. 49; Keith McClelland, 'Masculinity and the Representative Artisan in Britain, 1850–1900', in Michael Roper and John Tosh (eds.), *Manful Assertions: Masculinity in Britain Since 1800* (London, 1991), p. 84.
[58] *Hansard*, 3rd series, 183, 31 May 1866, col. 1642.
[59] Glyn Williams and John Ramsden, *Ruling Britannia: A Political History of Britain 1688–1988* (London and New York, 1990), p. 254.
[60] H. C. G. Matthew, *Gladstone 1809–1874* (Oxford, 1986), p. 98; John Vincent, *The Formation of the Liberal Party* (London, 1966), p. 209.
[61] *Hansard* 3rd series,183, 27 April 1866, col. 58.

such as Kingsley, having a family was a very important part of a vigorous 'muscular Christianity' which could reconcile the classes.[62]

While working men's reform associations occasionally endorsed household suffrage, they usually did so only as a compromise to get middle-class support, and much preferred 'residential manhood suffrage'.[63] They argued that they deserved the vote because of their property in skill, but to many parliamentarians this notion implied they needed representation for their class interest. Instead of class, these Liberals wished to focus on character.[64] Whereas the debates around the 1832 Reform Act focused on property as a guarantor of independence, clearly delineating class divisions, fatherhood was an element in a man's character shared by working men and middle-class men alike. Liberal advocates of reform could therefore claim that working men deserved the vote as fathers, rather than needing the vote to represent their distinct class interests. W. E. Forster advocated household suffrage because 'it gave a man a share in the Government, not on the ground that he possessed any particular property, but because he was the head of a family; household suffrage had well been called 'hearthstone suffrage'.[65] For Gladstone and many of his supporters, the status of fatherhood guaranteed the stability of working men, for their wives and children represented a stake in the country which would deter them from revolutionary agitation. Echoing the 1797 debate, the radical MP for Sheffield, Roebuck, argued that 'if a man has a settled home, in which he has lived with his family for a number of years, you have a man who has given hostages to the state, and you have in these circumstances a guarantee for that man's virtue'.[66] A 'Devonshire Man' even proposed that every third child should earn its father an additional vote.[67] For Bagehot, enfranchising working men as a class would ignite dangerous 'democratic passions', whereas granting the vote to them as individual heads of household, he hoped, would make them more deferential to aristocratic influence.[68]

The focus on working men as fathers of families was also a way of separating out the skilled working men, who could pay taxes and keep

---

[62] Vance, *Sinews of the Spirit*, p. 115.

[63] Frances Elma Gillespie, *Labor and Politics in England 1850–1867* (Durham, NC, 1927) pp. 30, 90, 264. Tony Dickson (ed.) *Scottish Capitalism* (London, 1980), p. 228.

[64] Stefan Collini, 'The Idea of "Character" in Victorian Political Thought', *Transactions of the Royal Historical Society*, 5th series, 35 (1985), p. 31; Moore, *Politics of Deference*, p. 433.

[65] Hansard, 3rd series, 186, 12 April 1867. col. 1609.

[66] *Ibid.*, col. 1602. See also Eugenio Biagini, *Liberty, Retrenchment and Reform* (Cambridge; Cambridge, 1992), p. 310.

[67] A Devonshire Man, *Rough Sketches of a New Reform Bill* (Exeter, 1866), p. 25.

[68] Walter Bagehot, *The English Constitution* (1872; New York and London, 1978), p. xxx.

up a household, from the 'residuum' of the working class perceived as undisciplined, unskilled and disorderly. Roebuck described factory operatives as swearing at their wives, beating their children, and getting drunk every night at the alehouse.[69] Some Liberal opponents of reform doubted that working men were virtuous enough heads of households. The Liberal Robert Lowe, most known for objecting to giving the vote to working men he described as corrupt and drunken, also suggested that if working men wanted the vote, they could simply take a house worth ten pounds a year, which would have the side benefit of preventing 'the most frightful impurities' (probably incest) he alleged were rife in overcrowded working-class homes.[70]

The opposition to household suffrage also reveals the influence of Malthusian political economy on constitutional thought. Even J. S. Mill argued that neither middle-class nor working men should marry until they could support a family.[71] In the pages of the *Working Man* and the *National Reformer*, some correspondents would deny the vote to men who married in their teens, and called for labourers to be 'educated in the crime of indulging their instincts to have more children than they can provide for'. In response, letter-writers signing themselves 'Working men' declared that large families were evidence of their virtue, for they 'struggled manfully' to support them.[72]

Many middle-class intellectuals believed that education rather than fatherhood qualified a man for the vote.[73] They feared that ignorant working men with large families would be rewarded with the franchise whereas highly educated professional men who happened to be bachelor lodgers would be deprived of it. Henry Rich argued that taxpaying bachelor lodgers should have the vote 'although they may not have

---

[69] Quoted in *National Reformer*, 11 November 1866, p. 316.

[70] Robert Lowe, *Speeches and Letters on Reform* (London, 1867), p. 48; interestingly enough, this point echoes a comment by Governor Eyre that the Jamaicans should have separate sleeping quarters for their families, presumably in the interests of morality (Holt, *Problem of Freedom*, p. 273) and Carlyle's obsessive fear of black sexuality; Hall, 'Competing Masculinities', p. 273.

[71] J. S. Mill, 'Principles of Political Economy', in J. M. Robson (ed.), *Collected Works of J.S. Mill* (Toronto, 1972), vol. II p. 358; reiterated in the Westminster campaign, 'Speech at Westminster,' 1865 in *Collected Works*, vol. XXVIII, p. 31. A Liberal, *A Review of Mr J. S. Mill's Essay on Liberty* (London, 1867), p. 45, opposes Mill's view that it is legitimate for the state to prohibit a poor man from marrying unless he can show he can support a family.' Mill, he said, was deficient in sympathy for the poor man who has 'just as much right to be married as a rich man'.

[72] *Working Man*, 7 April 1866; 28 April 1866, p. 270; *National Reformer*, 10 June 1866; 14 October 1866; 18 November 1866.

[73] For a discussion of the intellectual and personal milieu of some of these men, some of whom were required to remain unmarried as university dons, see Peter Allen, *The Cambridge Apostles: The Early Years* (Cambridge, 1978), p. 198.

given hostages to their country, are not the less men of active business habits, and enquiring minds, and moreover, much frequently less straightened in their means, and more independent in their habits, than the struggling family man'. Men such as scientists, university men and clerks deserved the vote because their bachelor status meant they had exerted the moral control necessary to postpone or forgo marriage.[74] Instead of the muscular manliness of the Victorian patriarch, some intellectuals celebrated the disinterested civic virtue of the unmarried scholar.[75]

However, Gladstone initially opposed enfranchising lodgers because he saw them as an 'immature' element without a settled stake in society.[76] Bright denounced the idea of giving the franchise to bachelors 'who can speak two dead languages' while depriving heads of household of the vote.[77] While intellectual bachelors defined themselves as self-controlled because they gave up marriage, men like Gladstone perhaps believed that bachelors did not have the self-discipline to sacrifice their own desires within marriage, as he himself tried to do.[78] Although the fear that bachelors would be homosexual was never hinted at in these debates (unlike in earlier radical debates), some may have feared the libidinal freedom and putative political irresponsibility of the unmarried man.[79] For instance, Edward Cox preferred married householders as voters because they were safe, unlike the 'intelligent, unsettled lodgers, who dislike an order of things in which their merits are not sufficiently recognized', and who might be prone to revolutionary ideas.[80]

Of course, the Reform Act was eventually manoeuvred through parliament by Disraeli rather than Gladstone. In the end, the final bill gave the vote to practically all urban rate-paying male householders in boroughs, but as a compromise, also to lodgers renting rooms worth ten

---

[74] Henry Rich, MP, *Parliamentary Reform: What and Where*, 2nd edn (London, 1848). See also *Reform Bill* 1859 in British Library pamphlet collection 8139.ff.39 (2); H. R. Symythe, *Parliamentary Reform Considered* (London,1854), p. 48.

[75] Linda Dowling, *Hellenism and Homosexuality in Victorian Oxford* (Ithaca and London, 1994), p. 58.

[76] *Hansard*, 183, 30 May 1866, col. 1482.   [77] *Ibid.*, col. 1516.

[78] Matthew, *Gladstone*, p. 237.

[79] For earlier radical debates, see Anna Clark, *The Struggle for the Breeches*, chapter 8. For bachelors' libidinal freedom and fear of fraternal politics, see Juliet Flower MacCannell, *The Regime of the Brother: After the Patriarchy* (New York and London, 1991), p. 55. As Eve Kosovsky Sedgewick argues, Victorian culture was pervaded by an implicit fear of homosexual bonds between men, often projected onto women or men of another class or culture. *Between Men: English Literature and Male Homosocial Desire* (New York, 1985), p. 198. And as Linda Dowling points out, hellenic scholars were developing a new version of classical republicanism which celebrated love between men (*Hellenism and Homosexuality*, p. 72).

[80] Edward W. Cox, *Representative Reform* 3rd edn (London, 1867), p. 3.

pounds a year.[81] While working men sometimes used their families as a justification for obtaining the vote, their reform organisations also insisted on a lodger franchise, because many were single lodgers, or family men who could not afford to keep a house and shared lodgings with other families.[82] By setting the franchise at ten pounds for lodgers, the government hoped to keep out the potentially revolutionary poor lodger and retain the professional bachelor, as well as making a concession to well-paid artisans in the big cities.

Disraeli realised that by incorporating working men into the constitution, he could conceivably turn their 'muscle and might' as evidenced in the Hyde Park demonstrations away from a threat to the established order into a masculine defence of the empire in which all classes could be united. Immediately after the passage of the Reform Act, he embarked on highly symbolic imperialist adventures which aroused popular fervour for the government and patriotic frenzy.[83] As a result of the 1866–7 Reform Act debates, therefore, politicians hoped to incorporate working-class masculinity into the Nation and defuse class conflict.[84] However, different versions of masculinity co-existed. For instance, Liberal middle-class and working men alike espoused the virtues of temperance and self-denial, and a moral vision of international politics. On the other, a Tory imperialist masculinity tried to co-opt working-class 'sinew and muscle' into a belligerent celebration of heavy drinking and jingoist adventures.[85]

I

Despite this focus on masculinity, the debates over franchise reform also stimulated agitation for women's suffrage, which J. S. Mill unsuccessfully tried to add to the 1867 Reform Bill. The vote for unmarried female householders in municipal politics was attained in 1869, but the parliamentary franchise was delayed for decades.[86] In the next fifty

---

[81] Representation of the People Act, 1867, in H. J. Hanham (ed.), *The Nineteenth Century Constitution, 1815–1914: Documents and Commentary* (Cambridge, 1969), p. 273; Harrison, *Before the Socialists*, p. 99; but see John Davis, 'Slums and the Vote, 1867–90', *Historical Research*, 64, 155 (October 1991), p. 387.

[82] *Beehive*, 9 March 1867.   [83] Harcourt, 'Disraeli's Imperialism', p. 98.

[84] Whether they succeeded is the subject of much historiographical debate. See Geoff Eley, 'Social Imperialism – the use and abuse of an idea', *Social History*, 3 (October 1976), pp. 265–90. Thanks to Susan Thorne for a fruitful discussion on this point.

[85] For different versions of masculinity, see Michael Roper and John Tosh, *Manful Assertions: Masculinity in Britain since 1800* (London, 1991).

[86] Hobhouse's Vestries Act of 1831 had given women ratepayers the right to vote at parish elections. Vernon, *Politics and the People*, pp. 19–20.

years, the challenge of women's suffrage foregrounded important philosophical principles about citizenship. How much was the right to a vote dependent on qualities such as property-owning and being a head of household, and how much on masculinity? How much did this masculinity depend on women's subordination?

The 1867 Reform Act did establish several important potentially gender-neutral principles: first, that the vote was based on the status of taxpaying head of household; second, that the vote could be extended to those who proved their moral virtues; and third, that virtual representation was no longer valid, for citizens deserved to choose their own representatives. Advocates for the women's vote, with a few exceptions, tried to turn these principles to fit women, rather than taking the more radical stance of the natural human right to representation. For instance, Helen Taylor accepted the notion that rights were attached to property rather than persons, but argued that women property-holders should therefore be represented.[87] Suffragists often proposed that women should simply get the vote on the same basis as men; that is, as unmarried or widowed ratepaying heads of households.[88] They portrayed female householders as most deserving of the vote, being law-abiding and highly educated; temperate, frugal, and self-denying, as opposed to the 'residuum' which conservatives believed the 1867 act had enfranchised.[89] Conversely, advocates also believed that women needed representation, just as working men; for instance, in the 1871 parliamentary debate, Jacob Bright argued that those households without the benefit of the support of a man should still be represented in parliament, portraying them as pitiful spinsters deprived of the privilege of the domestic sphere and virtual representation by husband or father.[90]

But women suffrage advocates faced the problem that spinster householders were widely seen as an unfortunate anomaly, while most married women had little or no rights over their property. Indeed, by stressing the paternal virtues of the male householder who cared for his dependents, the reformers of 1867 linked property and masculinity even more closely. When suffragists campaigned for married women's prop-

[87] Helen Taylor, in the *Westminster Review* 1867, reprinted in Jane Lewis (ed.), *Before the Vote was Won: Arguments for and against Women's Suffrage* (New York and London, 1987), p. 24.
[88] Philippa Levine, *Victorian Feminism* (Tallahasee, 1987), p. 60.
[89] Arabella Shore, 'The Present Aspect of Women's Suffrage Considered', *Englishwoman's Review*, 14 May 1877, in Lewis, *Before the Vote was Won*, p. 284; for other advocacy of women's suffrage for householders, see *ibid.*, p. 397, quoting Isabella M. S. Todd; also Louisa Bigg, 1879; Helen Blackburn, p. 318.
[90] Lewis, *Before the Vote was Won*, p. 54.

erty rights, conservatives opposed them because they feared married women could therefore claim political rights as well. Conversely, the failure of parliament to pass effective married women's property protection in 1870 fuelled the flames of women's suffrage efforts. Women's rights advocates pointed out that parliament could not claim to 'virtually represent' women when it refused them rights to property. Even the more effective Married Women's Property Act of 1882 left many issues unresolved, such as child custody.[91]

Not only women suffragists, but many men remained discontent with the limitations of the 1867 Reform Act. By 1884, agricultural labourers, miners and many urban workers left out of the Second Reform Act insisted on further extension of the franchise. When parliament yielded to their demands by enfranchising county as well as borough householders, it could be seen to have ceded the principle that numbers should be represented, not 'property or interest'.[92] But the debate over an amendment adding women's suffrage also reveals that this issue was a touchstone for philosophical differences around the possibility of further franchise extension to more men, let alone women. By arguing for the vote for women on the constitutionalist grounds that electors represented their property, suffragists therefore called upon a rationale that was fast fading even for the vote for men.[93] Some advocates for women's suffrage therefore lost radical support by claiming that female householders would aid the interests of property against newly enfranchised working men and Irish.[94] Arthur Arnold asked why a woman is not fit to vote when 'the most drunken and ignorant and sordid clown may' if he met the householder qualification.[95]

Some conservatives, however, feared that granting suffrage to female householders would be just another step on the way to universal suffrage. While some trade unionists such as George Howell welcomed women's suffrage on the same grounds, they rarely focused on this issue

91 Levine, *Victorian Feminism, 1850–1900*, p. 139; Lee Holcombe, *Wives and Property: Reform of the Married Women's Property Law in Nineteenth Century England* (Toronto and Buffalo, 1983), p. 202.
92 Charles Seymour, *Electoral Reform in England and Wales* (New Haven, 1915), p. 468; Glyn Williams and John Ramsden, *Ruling Britannia: A Political History of Britain, 1688–1988* (New York and London, 1990), p. 286.
93 As Davis points out various legal decisions extended the right to vote to poorer lodgers in slums, despite the intentions of the framers of the 1867 act; Davis, 'Slums and the Vote', p. 381.
94 *Hansard*, 3rd series, 289,12 June, 1884, col. 111.
95 National Social Science Congress, *Sessional Proceedings* (London, 1871–2), p. 117. Similar arguments made in a *Report of a Meeting of the London National Society for Women's Suffrage* (London, 1870) p. 14 by Mrs Grote and Mr Jacob Bright, MP, pp. 14, 27; see also Frances Power Cobbe, *Why Women Desire the Franchise* (London, 1872).

in parliament.[96] Instead, radicals justified voting against enfranchising propertied single women because it went against the principle of universal suffrage.[97] Yet their failure to insist on true universal suffrage meant that for radicals, 'manhood suffrage' meant manhood, *not* human beings including men and women.

While politicians as varied as Gladstone, John Bright and Joseph Chamberlain denounced the notion that employers could paternalistically 'virtually represent' agricultural labourers, they hypocritically continued to insist that men 'virtually represented women.'[98] In fact, when women demanded the vote, even if it were only for unmarried females, they implicitly challenged the very basis for the vote for men – the notion that citizens were rightfully male heads of households who virtually represented their women's interests. The independence of the male voter therefore required the dependence of women. For Gladstone, female suffrage violated the notion of separate spheres, the feminine delicacy which he believed the polling booth would contaminate. It is clear that for him his sacramental notion of the vote as a privilege of a male head of household, a fatherly status which extended across the classes, depended on the father's ability to protect his adoring, pure females at home.[99] Similarly, as Vincent notes, John Bright firmly opposed women's suffrage, for 'his household suffrage amounted to a confederacy of absolute despots', he did not even allow his female relatives to speak on politics, and desired them to be absolutely dependent.[100]

Some women's suffrage advocates tried to avoid the accusation that the female suffrage would undermine the family by claiming that married women did not need the vote, only single women, although the movement split over this issue in the 1890s.[101] Emily Pfeiffer argued that

---

[96] Jill Liddington and Jill Norris, *One Hand Tied Behind Us: The Rise of the Women's Suffrage Movement* (London, Virago, 1978), p. 150. The most notable exception before 1900 was George Howell, a trade unionist who worked as a paid agent for the women's suffrage cause; but when he became an MP, he focused on manhood suffrage. F. M. Leventhal, *Respectable Radical. George Howell and Victorian Working-Class Politics* (London, 1971), pp. 195, 207. See also Howell Collection, Bishopsgate Library, London.

[97] Andrew Jones, *The Politics of Reform 1884* (Cambridge, 1972), p. 129.

[98] *Pall Mall Gazette*, 7 July 1883. Similarly, the Bishop of Carlisle on Women's Suffrage, 9 August 1884, both in *Women's Suffrage: Opinions of the Press 1883* (London, 1883); and Millicent Garret Fawcett, 'Women's Suffrage and the Franchise Bill', in Jane Lewis, *Before the Vote was Won: Arguments for and against Women's Suffrage* (New York and London, 1987), p. 393.

[99] Lewis, *Before the Vote was Won*, pp. 68–9, quoting Gladstone in 1871 debate over women's suffrage.

[100] Vincent, *Formation of the Liberal Party*, p. 209.

[101] Lucy Bland, 'The Married Woman, the "New Woman" and the Feminist: Sexual Politics

unmarried women voters would protect the interests of marriage, while 'marriage's high duties would compensate for married women not having the vote'.[102] But Pfeiffer also implied that men could not protect the interests of marriage. In fact, by demanding the vote, suffragists *were* attacking the foundation of the Victorian family. They refused to accept the notion that only men needed political rights, because they could chivalrously protect women in the home. Instead, they revealed this notion of citizenship as a sexual contract in which women exchanged subordination for 'protection', while men enjoyed public rights.[103] They began to attack the injustices of conventional marriage by raising the issue of wifebeating.[104] For instance, Mrs Shearer declared that the 'daily brutal outrages' of domestic violence proved men could not represent women.[105]

The more militant activists in the women's movement also pointed out the hypocrisy of the double standard by attacking the exploitation of women in prostitution. The campaigns against the Contagious Diseases Acts in the 1870s and the White Slavery scandal of the 1880s undercut Victorian men's claims that they wished to keep women in the domestic sphere to protect their purity. Eventually, militant suffragettes increasingly attacked men for failing to uphold these virtues, demanding 'Votes for Women and Chastity for Men'. The women's movement, therefore, did not just demand constitutional change, but a wider social transformation.[106]

Alarmed by these developments, opponents of women's suffrage feared that the vote would give women an alternative to marriage.[107] Indeed, by the 1870s and 1880s, increasing numbers of women were able to make their own living at new female occupations such as teaching, nursing and clerical work. Lydia Becker forthrightly pointed out that many women chose not to marry because of the disabilities of marriage.[108] In response, opponents of women's suffrage turned the feminist concern with prostitution on its head; they claimed that most

---

of the 1890s', in Jane Rendall (ed.), *Equal or Different: Women's Politics 1800–1914* (Oxford, 1987), p. 143.

[102] Emily Pfeiffer, *Woman's Claim*, repr. from *Contemporary Review* February 1881, pp. 6, 11.

[103] Carole Pateman, *The Sexual Contract* (Stanford, 1988) pp. 162–64.

[104] *Report of a meeting of the London National Society for Women's Suffrage* (London, 1870), p. 7.

[105] *Report of the Fourth Annual Meeting of the Edinburgh National Society for Women's Suffrage* (Edinburgh, 1882), p. 11.

[106] Susan Kingsley Kent, *Sex and Suffrage in Britain, 1860–1914* (Princeton, 1987), for a general discussion of sexuality and suffrage; see also Bland, 'The Married Woman', p. 147.

[107] Grantham R. Dodd, *The Rights or Claims of Women* (London, 1881), p. 4

[108] Martha Vicinus, *Independent Women: Work and Community for Single Women* (Chicago, 1985), p. 27.

unmarried women were immoral social failures who should not be rewarded with the vote. Samuel Smith, MP, feared that if women were enfranchised, young women living in lodgings, such as barmaids and shop girls would get the vote – including 'appalling numbers of fallen women'.[109] Opponents of women's suffrage viciously reiterated these sentiments in the 1884 debate, claiming 'odious' bad women would be able to vote.[110] As Brian Harrison points out, ironically many of those who opposed women's suffrage were bachelors themselves, or preferred to spend time at their men's clubs rather than with their families.[111] But such sentiments were not confined to men. Mrs Humphrey Ward even argued that 'If votes be given to unmarried women on the same terms as they are given to men, large numbers of women leading immoral lives will be enfranchised.'[112]

The women's suffrage debate therefore fuelled a sense of crisis about masculinity and femininity endemic in the last two decades of the nineteenth century and into the twentieth.[113] For instance, the debates about marriage printed in the *Daily Telegraph*, in which men and women bitterly complained about each other, exposed long-festering sores in British sexual relations.[114] Challenged by critiques of the hypocrisy of chivalry, male opponents of women's suffrage began to degenerate into blatant misogyny. Mr Leatham argued that if women vote, a 'feminine alloy will penetrate into your policy... a feminine flutter [will be] in your courage at the moment when you require to be the most manly and robust'. The threat of women's suffrage forced him to admit that men are qualified to vote not because of property 'but because they are men'.[115] Labouchere straightforwardly asserted that giving women householders the vote would lead to 'petticoat government' and 'deprive men of the vote'.[116] In 1892, S. Smith depicted a frightening vision of enfranchised women as so unfeminine young men would be *even* more reluctant to marry.[117]

---

[109] Samuel Smith, 'Women's Suffrage' (1891) in Lewis, *Before the Vote was Won*, pp. 426–7.

[110] *Hansard*, 3rd series, 289, 12 June, 1884, col. 134.

[111] Brian Harrison, *Separate Spheres: the Opposition to Women's Suffrage in Britain* (New York, 1978), pp. 51, 69, 97.

[112] Lewis, *Before the Vote was Won*, p. 409. Mrs Humphey Ward et al against female suffrage 1889.

[113] Elaine Showalter, *Sexual Anarchy. Gender and Culture at the Fin de Siècle* (New York, 1990), p. 79. For more on the suffragists and the gender debate, see Susan Kingsley Kent, *Sex and Suffrage*.

[114] Judith Walkowitz, *City of Dangerous Delight: Narratives of Sexual Danger in Late Victorian London* (Chicago, 1992), p. 167; Bland, 'Sexual Politics of the 1890s', p. 146.

[115] *Hansard*, 3rd series 289, 12 June 1884, col. 103.   [116] *Ibid.*, cols. 173–74.

[117] *Ibid.*, 4th series 3, 27 April 1892, col. 1483.

Opponents of women's suffrage gained ammunition from the philosophy of Liberal but authoritarian jurist James Fitzjames Stephens, who linked force in government to a rigid patriarchy in the home. For Stephens and his followers, manhood rested on physical virility: 'strength, in all its forms, is life and manhood. To be less strong is to be less of a man.' For Stephens, marriage was parallel to the government in its ultimate dependence on force. He argued that since men were stronger, they should have authority, while wives should submit: 'submission and protection are correlative, withdraw the one and the other is lost, and force will assert itself a hundred times more harshly'.[118] By these statements, he implicitly defended as acceptable what feminists had pointed out as the flaw in the theory of chivalry and virtual representation: wifebeating.

Stephens' experience trying to impose a consolidated code of law on India led him to a view of government based on the ability to uphold laws through physical power, rather than democracy.[119] For instance, he compared women to natives who could not enforce their will.[120] His opinions therefore influenced the later transition in notions of manliness from the earlier Victorian 'moral earnestness' with its gentle religious fervour and home-centredness to the later 'respect for muscle and might' linked with imperialism.[121] As British imperialism faced growing challenges from the Boers and competition from Germany, opponents of women's suffrage asserted that the defense of the empire required virile men and submissive, fertile women.[122] Whereas working men had been attacked in 1867 for having too large families, early-twentieth-century anti-reformers lambasted suffragettes for concentrating on politics instead of childbearing for the empire.[123] While Mr Woodall, in moving for women's household suffrage in 1884, claimed that women were 'our flesh and blood',[124] as Gladstone had described working men in 1867, opponents often compared giving the vote to women to giving the vote to blacks or natives in the empire.[125] F. E. Smith even declared in parliament that 'An adult white woman differs far more from a white man than a negress or pigmy woman from her

[118] James Fitzjames Stephens, *Liberty, Equality, Fraternity*, 2nd edn (London, 1874), p. 284.
[119] Harrison, *Separate Spheres*, p. 73.   [120] Stephens, *Liberty*, p. 237.
[121] Roper and Tosh, *Manful Assertions*, p. 1–14; Patrick Dunnae, 'Boys' Literature and the Idea of Empire, 1870–1914', *Victorian Studies* 24, 1 (autumn 1980), pp. 105–21.
[122] For instance, Albert V. Dicey, *Letters to a Friend on Votes for Women*, (London, 1909), p. 55.
[123] J. A. Mangan, 'The Grit of Our Forefathers: Invented Traditions, Propanda, and Imperialism', in John M. Mackenzie (ed.), *Imperialism and Popular Culture* (Manchester, 1986), p. 129; Walter Heape, *Sex Antagonism* (London, 1913), pp. 206–14.
[124] *Hansard*, 3rd series, 288, 10 June, 1884, col. 1954.   [125] Kent, *Sex and Suffrage*, p. 30

equivalent male.'[126] Natives did not deserve the vote because they were not adequately sexually differentiated; white working men were sufficiently 'masculine' and dominant over women to deserve it. Sir Almroth E. Wright even declared, 'a virile and imperial race will not brook any attempt at forcible control by women'.[127] In 1909, Mr Bertram opposed adult suffrage and women's suffrage because 'it is of vast importance that our [imperial] policy should be directed in the same masculine, virile way'.[128] As late as 1917, Sir F. Banbury proclaimed that if Britain gave the vote to women the Orientals of the empire would never trust a female-influenced government.[129] Of course, the suffragettes themselves were not beyond inverting these racial arguments to claim that middle-class women deserved the vote more than the degenerate 'residuum' in order to protect the empire.[130]

This notion of the vote may also reflect the breakdown in a consensus about masculinity and the body politic apparent in the years after the Boer War. While Conservatives and Liberal Unionists had tried to incorporate working men into popular imperialism, by the twentieth century they increasingly feared that working men would turn this belligerent masculinity to hooliganism or class conflict.[131] While Gladstone's vision of the suffrage had been based on an expectation that working men shared moral values with middle-class men, but would be deferential to them, the increasing influence of labour and socialist groups made this consensus quite fragile. Violence threatened to erupt on both sides of labour conflicts, the Irish question and the suffrage controversy.[132]

Not surprisingly, this sense of crisis strengthened the linkage of physical force with the vote. Implying the possibility of civil war,

---

[126] Quoted in Constance Rover, *Women's Suffrage and Party Politics in Britain, 1866–1914* (London, 1867), p. 43.

[127] Sir Almroth E. Wright, *The Unexpurgated Case against Women's Suffrage* (London, 1913), pp. 11, 32, p. 73.

[128] *Hansard*, new series, 2, 19 March 1909, col. 1391.

[129] *Ibid.*, new series, 94, 28 March 1917, col. 1645, also Mr Burdett-Coutts, 1667.

[130] For racism in the women's movement, see Antoinette Burton, 'The Feminist Quest for Identity: British Imperial Suffragism and "Global Sisterhood" 1900–1915', *Journal of Women's History* 3, 2 (1991) pp. 46–81.

[131] Seth Koven, 'From Rough Lads to Hooligans: Boy Life, National Culture and Social Reform', in Andrew Parker *et al.*, (eds.), *Nationalisms and Sexualities* (New York and London, 1992), p. 366; Wilfried Fest, 'Jingoism and Xenophobia in Strategies of British Ruling Elites before 1914', in Paul Kennedy and Anthony Nicholls (ed.), *Nationalist and Racialist Movements in Britain and Germany before 1914* (London, 1986) p. 285; for discussions of whether the working class adopted popular imperialism, see John M. Mackenzie, *Imperialism and Popular Culture* (Manchester, 1986); Richard Price, *An Imperial War and the British Working Class* (London, 1972).

[132] Vicinus, *Independent Women*, p. 254.

Mackine declared that the majority must have the physical power to resist the minority, for 'A vote is a cheque or draft on power, and ultimately, on physical power.'[133] Therefore, he – and many others – declared that women should not be able to vote because they did not have the physical force to defend their opinions – presumably in brawls on the way to the polling station. Ironically, however, opponents also used the suffragettes' own violence to deny them the vote, portraying them as extremist and out of control, despite the fact that male workers had resorted to the threat of force in 1867.[134]

Yet despite the fear of social explosion, most trade unionists and Labour party activists simply wanted representation in government based on a shared notion of the male citizen as the stable, skilled adult male householder. Eager to conciliate Labour voters, Liberals granted welfare benefits such as unemployment and sickness insurance for male breadwinners, not women workers.[135] Labour was only lukewarm in its efforts to press for full adult suffrage, even though in the early 1900s only 59 per cent of the male population were qualified to vote.[136] The men who still lacked the franchise were sons living with their fathers – assumed to be virtually represented by them; paupers; or those who moved so frequently they could not qualify for residence – assumed not likely to vote Labour.[137] At the same time, many Liberal and Labour MPs opposed bills granting the vote to women on the same basis as men, i.e. to ratepaying householders, on the grounds that this would enfranchise propertied women while leaving working men out in the cold. Yet these very rational arguments for adult suffrage often concealed private misogyny, as Sandra Stanley Holton points out.[138] Eventually, however, Labour and Liberal-oriented suffragists, using women's volunteer time and money, pressured more and more Members of Parliament to make the female franchise a priority.[139]

Yet all men – and most women – only won the vote when the First World War exploded conventional notions of masculinity. As the war dragged on, suffrage again became an issue, as it had been in 1867, of uniting working men and women into the nation. The old Victorian

[133] Hansard, new series, 25, 5 May 1911, col. 762.
[134] Mary E. Gawthorpe, Votes for Men, How They Were Won (London, 1909?).
[135] Koven, 'Rough Lads', p. 382.
[136] Neal Blewett, 'The Franchise in the United Kingdom 1885–1918', Past and Present, 32 (1965) p. 31.
[137] Davis, 'Slums and the Vote', p. 387; Martin Pugh, Electoral Reform in War and Peace 1906–1918 (London, 1978), p. 30.
[138] Sandra Stanley Holton, Feminism and Democracy: Women's Suffrage and Reform Politics in Britain, 1900–1918 (Cambridge, 1986), p. 54.
[139] Holton, Feminism and Democracy, p. 124.

notion that only the respectable head of household, firmly established in his community, deserved the vote, lost its legitimacy as men of all ages were torn from homes and streets to fight and die in the trenches.[140] How could men be expected to fight if they were denied the vote because they were away from home and could not establish a household or residency?[141] Even the disenfranchised 'residuum' of the 'outcast poor' now became heroic soldiers and sailors who deserved the vote.[142] By late 1917, fears of the Russian Revolution inspired some, especially in the Lords, to advocate abandoning old notions of 'fitness' for the vote and instead grant universal enfranchisement as the only alternative to rebellion.[143] For others, the horrors of the war undermined the masculinist notion that physical force should underly the vote, as J. Simon observed in the parliamentary debate over suffrage in 1917.[144] As Susan Kingsley Kent points out, politicians wanted to avoid a recurrence of the 'sex war' which had wracked Britain before 1914.[145] Instead, they cited women's service in the war, labouring hard, and sometimes even dying, in munitions factories and ambulance corps, as a reason for changing their minds about women's suffrage.[146] To be sure, they may have been quite hypocritical; since they excluded women under thirty from the franchise, the young women war workers had to wait for their reward.[147] Although parliament basically abandoned the notion of fitness for the vote in favour of a universal franchise for men, they, ironically, returned to the notion of household status as a requisite for the vote by only enfranchising women householders over thirty or wives of male householders.[148]

II

True universal suffrage took so long to attain in Britain because gendered notions of citizenship as head of household hindered the

---

[140] For the crisis in masculinity, see Sandra M. Gilbert and Susan Gubar, *No Man's Land: The Place of the Woman Writer in the Twentieth Century* vol. II *Sexchanges* (New Haven and London, 1989), p. 262.

[141] Pugh, *Electoral Reform*, p. 178.

[142] For the disappearance of the term 'residuum' during the First World War, see Gareth Stedman Jones quoted by Rosalind Coward, 'Whipping Boys', *The Guardian* 3 September 1994, p. 35.

[143] Susan Kingsley Kent, *Making Peace: The Reconstruction of Gender in Interwar Britain* (Princeton, 1993), p. 85.

[144] *Hansard*, 4th series, 94, 1917, col. 1676, 1917.

[145] Kent, *Making Peace*, pp. 89–91.

[146] Holton, *Feminism and Democracy*, p. 145; *Hansard*, 4th series, 92, 28 March 1917, Asquith, col. 469; Lloyd George, col. 493, P. Magnus, col. 541; 94, 1917, col. 1662, Lord H. Cecil.

[147] Martin Pugh, *Women and the Women's Movement in Britain, 1914–1959* (London, 1992), p. 38.

[148] Kent, *Making Peace*, p. 91.

extension of the franchise both to working men and to women in general. But these masculine notions of citizenship changed significantly over this period. The earlier assumption of a master who represented not only his wife and sons but also servants faded by 1832, when the voter was assumed to be the middle-class, propertied, patriarch. By 1867, Gladstone and Disraeli sought to replace a class-specific notion of manhood as a privilege of propertied men and slowly extend the vote to all men who lived up to their patriarchal duties.

Women suffragists tried to exploit the ambiguities of the British constitutional tradition by asserting that the vote should be based on property and taxation, rather than masculinity. But by claiming political rights for themselves, they exposed the fact that male citizenship was based on the subordination of women in marriage. As women demanded property rights for wives and denounced prostitution and wifebeating, they tore away the veil of chivalry which had sanctified the denial of women's suffrage. By the beginning of the twentieth century, this open sexual antagonism, along with imperial pressures and potential class conflict, revealed a vision of masculine citizenship starkly based on force. While the First World War fractured this militaristic masculinity, the universal suffrage which resulted soon became enmeshed in a notion of social citizenship whose gender and racial implications need to be explored.[149]

---

[149] For a beginning, see Susan Pedersen, 'Gender, Welfare and Citizenship in Britain during the Great War', *American Historical Review* 95, 4 (1990), pp. 985–99; for race and empire, E. J. B. Rose *et al.*, *Colour and Citizenship* (London, 1969).

INDEX